American Machiavelli

Alexander Hamilton rose from his humble beginnings as an illegitimate West Indian orphan and emigrant to become the premier state builder and strategic thinker of the American Founding generation. This book is the first detailed narrative study of his foreign policy role and ideas to appear in more than thirty years. It focuses on Hamilton's controversial activities as a key member of President George Washington's cabinet and as an aspiring military leader in the 1790s, a decade of profound division over the shape and powers of the federal government and U.S. policy toward the warring powers of Europe. Drawing parallels between Hamilton and the Florentine diplomatist and thinker Niccolò Machiavelli, prize-winning historian John Lamberton Harper offers an insightful and accessible account of the origins of Hamilton's outlook, his bitter personal rivalries with Thomas Jefferson and John Adams, and his indispensable part in designing and implementing a foreign policy able to ensure the survival of the infant United States.

John Lamberton Harper is Professor of American Foreign Policy and European Studies at the Bologna Center of The Johns Hopkins University Paul H. Nitze School of Advanced International Studies. He is the author of *America and the Reconstruction of Italy, 1945–1948* (winner of the 1987 Marraro Prize from the Society for Italian Historical Studies), and *American Visions of Europe: Franklin D. Roosevelt, George F. Kennan, and Dean G. Acheson* (winner of the 1995 Robert H. Ferrell Book Prize from the Society for Historians of American Foreign Relations). His articles and reviews have appeared in *The American Historical Review*, *The Journal of American History*, *The Times Literary Supplement*, *Foreign Affairs*, *The National Interest*, *Survival*, *World Policy Journal*, *SAIS Review*, and other publications.

American Machiavelli

Alexander Hamilton and the Origins of U.S. Foreign Policy

JOHN LAMBERTON HARPER

The Bologna Center of The Johns Hopkins University

CAMBRIDGE
UNIVERSITY PRESS

PUBLISHED BY THE PRESS SYNDICATE OF THE UNIVERSITY OF CAMBRIDGE
The Pitt Building, Trumpington Street, Cambridge, United Kingdom

CAMBRIDGE UNIVERSITY PRESS
The Edinburgh Building, Cambridge CB2 2RU, UK
40 West 20th Street, New York, NY 10011-4211, USA
477 Williamstown Road, Port Melbourne, VIC 3207, Australia
Ruiz de Alarcón 13, 28014 Madrid, Spain
Dock House, The Waterfront, Cape Town 8001, South Africa

http://www.cambridge.org

First published 2004

Printed in the United States of America

Typeface Sabon 10/12 pt.   *System* LATEX 2$_\varepsilon$ [TB]

A catalog record for this book is available from the British Library.

Library of Congress Cataloging in Publication Data
Harper, John Lamberton.
American Machiavelli : Alexander Hamilton and the origins of U.S. foreign policy /
John Lamberton Harper.
p.   cm.
Includes bibliographical references and index.
ISBN 0-521-83485-6
1. Hamilton, Alexander, 1757–1804. 2. Hamilton, Alexander, 1757–1804 – Views on
international relations. 3. Statesmen – United States – Biography.
4. United States – Foreign relations – 1775–1783. 5. United States – Foreign
relations – 1783–1815. 6. United States – Foreign relations – Philosophy.
7. Machiavelli, Niccolò, 1469–1527. I. Title.
E302.6.H2H37   2004
327.73′0092 – dc22   2003055907
[B]

ISBN 0 521 83485 6 hardback

To Maria Antonia and Sara
and to the memory of
Rinda and Giovanni

Contents

Illustrations

Illustrations appear following page 188.

Acknowledgments

Several years ago, having dedicated time to the study of U.S. foreign relations in the early post–World War II period, I felt the urge to delve deeper into the roots of the subject, namely foreign policy during the era of the Founding Fathers. This led to a somewhat impulsive decision to "parachute" into the late eighteenth century (followed by an unplanned visit to the late fifteenth). I was carrying, in a scholarly sense, the equivalent of the clothes on my back, and I arrived uninvited and unannounced. Taking my bearings in new surroundings was a rather lonely experience, but I took heart from the thought that I was carrying forward the enterprise of old teachers and friends at The Johns Hopkins University School of Advanced International Studies. They include the late Robert E. Osgood; Simon Serfaty, who taught me American Foreign Policy at the SAIS Bologna Center; and my dissertation supervisor, David P. Calleo. Robert W. Tucker, in particular, has been an inspiration during the writing of this book. Hacking my way through the historiographical undergrowth, I was lucky to be able to turn at one point to a leading authority on eighteenth-century America, Jack N. Rakove of Stanford University. He bears no responsibility for the book's content, and I doubt if he approves of interlopers in his century, but (perhaps out of sympathy for a fellow graduate of Haverford College) he provided useful criticism and advice. I would also like to thank my editor at Cambridge, Frank Smith, for his confidence and encouragement, Frank's assistant Eric Crahan for his help on the project, as well as the anonymous readers who read the manuscript for the Press.

Those who remember will forgive me if, as in the acknowledgments of a previous book, I again paraphrase Henry Adams on the subject of writing history. After calculating what it had cost him to finish his *History of the United States of America During the Administrations of Jefferson and Madison*, he concluded that history is the most aristocratic of the academic disciplines. To do it properly requires practically unlimited means and leisure time. Most of us depend instead on the generosity of others. In my case, it was the Parachini Family Fund, dedicated to the support of Bologna

Center faculty, which allowed me to finish a first draft during a sabbatical and leave of absence in 2002. In this connection I thank John V. Parachini and the former director of the Bologna Center, Robert H. Evans. I also thank two research assistants, Jason E. Bruder and Alexandra Jaeckh, in particular, for their help, as well as Cole Frates, Aaron Brady, Ben Canavan, Kate Joseph, Matt Lieber, Deanna Gentry, Jennifer Sweitzer, Jeremy Levine, Mike Crowley, Mary Beth Wilson, and Euan Roddin.

Words of appreciation are due, as ever, to Gail Martin, John Williams, and the staff of the Bologna Center Library. Finally, I would like to acknowledge Harold C. Syrett, Jacob E. Cooke, and the other editors of the definitive edition of Alexander Hamilton's papers. Without that remarkable set of volumes, and the meticulously prepared papers of other eighteenth-century American statesmen, many of them ongoing projects, it would have been impossible for me to write this book.

Bologna
July 25, 2003

American Machiavelli

Introduction

The twentieth century belonged to Thomas Jefferson. One of Washington, D.C.'s most prominent monuments is consecrated to the Sage of Monticello. As for his historic rival, Alexander Hamilton, there is no Palladian temple, only a run-of-the mill statue on the south side of the Treasury Department.[1] If the point were to commemorate their respective contributions to the building of the country, Hamilton, arguably, would have the monument and Jefferson a mere statue. He was as responsible as anyone for the establishment of the American union: the consolidation and funding of the national debt, the tax system, the customs service, and the first Bank of the United States. Jefferson, his ally James Madison, and their followers did all they could to sabotage Hamilton's program of developing these sinews of national strength.

The key to Jefferson's popularity perhaps lies less in what he accomplished than in what he so eloquently spoke for: liberty and equality. There has also been a great deal of deliberate promotion. It was Franklin Roosevelt, after all, who put Jefferson's face on the five-cent piece and built the memorial. FDR wrapped himself in Jefferson's mantle, and helped to make him the patron saint of the New Deal and modern liberalism. Even as they adopted Hamiltonian methods with gusto during the Great Depression and after World War II, Democrats cast the elitist and "economic royalist" Hamilton as the villain of the piece. The tenders of the Jefferson flame included a group of prominent historians, Claude Bowers, Dumas Malone, Julian Boyd, Merrill Peterson, and Adrienne Koch, whose semihagiographical treatment of Jefferson and sometimes-lurid portrayal of Hamilton was for many years the mainstream view.[2]

Hamilton became a Republican Party icon after the triumph of the Union in the Civil War and the darling of Theodore Roosevelt, Henry Cabot Lodge, and other proponents of an assertive, martial foreign policy at the turn of the century. The Hamilton statue was erected by a conservative Republican president, Warren G. Harding, and his multimillionaire treasury secretary, Andrew Mellon, in 1923. Since World War II, Hamilton has not been without able conservative champions, for example, Clinton Rossiter and Forrest McDonald.[3] But the Republican Party dropped Hamilton as a symbol after the 1930s. Postwar American conservatism, by and large, has been either libertarian (in reaction to New Deal liberalism) or hostile to a secularized industrial society. Hamilton was neither of those things. Along with the animosity of Jeffersonians and the abandonment of Republicans, another burden on Hamilton's reputation has been the contempt of "Adamsites." In the 1950s, Russell Kirk, an admirer of John Adams, dismissed Hamilton as a pseudoconservative. Following in the footsteps of Adams, his grandson Charles Francis Adams, and his great-grandson Henry Adams, a postwar school of historians, including Manning J. Dauer, Stephen G. Kurtz, John Ferling, and David McCullough, have kept alive the view of Hamilton as a manipulator and a cad.[4]

If the twentieth century was not particularly kind to Hamilton, what are the prospects for the twenty-first? In recent years Jefferson's stock has fallen, for reasons that have little to do with Hamilton but have tended to buoy his reputation. One commentator has asked, for example, whether someone who favored transporting African Americans back to Africa is an appropriate hero for a multicultural society. Subtler revisionists have had a field day with Jefferson's many contradictions and hypocrisies.[5] If Jeffersonian liberalism is one of the sources of a foreign policy promoting economic globalization and the universalization of democracy, it is natural that skeptics of such an approach, favoring a less grandiose and ideological U.S. strategy, have turned to Hamilton for inspiration. By the same token, it is not surprising that those hoping to base U.S. predominance on unchallenged military power should look to a statesman who took a serious interest in military questions and foresaw the rise of the United States. The 1990s witnessed a renewed and sympathetic attention to Hamilton on the part of conservative scholars and commentators, in particular.[6] If the number of recent publications dealing with him is any indication, a kind of Hamilton revival is underway.[7]

It is reassuring but slightly unnerving for a historian to discover that he is in tune with the *Zeitgeist*: interest in Hamilton and the other Founding Fathers has grown in the context of post–Cold War uncertainty, but are there new insights to be gleaned? The answer is that the new literature, like the old, is mostly hostile or partisan. Relatively little recent attention has been paid, moreover, to Hamilton's foreign policy role and ideas.[8] The time is ripe for a balanced study of that subject, one that does not minimize the foreign policy differences between Jefferson and Hamilton,[9] that takes seriously the arguments that Hamilton was emotionally tied to Britain and a driven, manipulative character, and that sees his prescriptions as clearly superior to those of his opponents, but with troubling implications over time. Regardless of the attention he has received, Hamilton remains a paradoxical and elusive personality. His early life is poorly documented. He produced prodigious amounts of letters and public documents, but no personal memoirs or diary. And there is the persistent feeling of life imitating art.

The student of Hamilton is sooner or later bound to ask whether his subject is not the stuff of a Stendahl or a Dickens. The breathtaking, semitropical setting of his early years recalls the novels of Robert Louis Stevenson and Defoe. His is the story of a gifted boy, born in precarious circumstances on the tiny British leeward island of Nevis on January 11, 1757 (according to some, 1755).[10] None-too-robust, auburn-haired, with eyes the deep blue of the surrounding Caribbean, he is determined to realize the great destiny he imagines for himself beyond the horizon. Thanks to native genius, benefaction, and good luck he overcomes seemingly insuperable odds to success.

Hamilton's life-cum-tour-de-force inevitably invites comparisons with the story of another wisp of a boy born twelve (or fourteen) years later on the island of Corsica, whose meteoric course intersected Hamilton's own in the late 1790s. Both Hamilton and Napoleon had petty noble connections through their fathers, mothers known for their beauty, and an early penchant for the artillery, the most intellectually demanding branch of the army. In the lives of both there was a fundamental connection between the marginality of their places of birth and the grandness of their dreams. It is no coincidence that Jefferson, Adams, and their disciples saw Hamilton as "our Buonaparte," an interloper, military adventurer, and menace to the values of the American Revolution.[11]

Studying Hamilton I have come to a different conclusion: a more compelling and revealing parallel is with an Italian born exactly three centuries before Napoleon: Niccolò Machiavelli. Naturally, this begs the question "Which Machiavelli?" Much ink has been spilled over the contradictions between the writer of *The Prince*, a manual for rising authoritarian rulers, and that of the *Discourses on the First Ten Books of Livy*, an exhaustive guide for republicans.[12] Thirty years ago Isaiah Berlin identified more than a score of arguments concerning Machiavelli. These included the theories that *The Prince* was in reality a satire, that its author was a humanist anguished by the need to divorce politics from ethics, a cold and morally neutral scientist, a passionate patriot, a conscientious Christian, or else a man inspired by the Devil. This last was the view of Elizabethan dramatists and scholars and, more recently, Professor Leo Strauss.[13] Since Berlin's essay still more interpretations have appeared, including one that sees Machiavelli and other Renaissance thinkers as embodying the ancient ideal of civic humanism. In reply, followers of Strauss have portrayed him as the self-conscious prophet of "modernity," a fundamentally pernicious figure who broke with both Christianity and the Greek view of politics as the arena for the development of man's nobler faculties rather than (as in the modern case) the containment of his animal nature and the satisfaction of his material needs.[14]

This book's Machiavelli is closer to Berlin's own, more sympathetic, view. Machiavelli's implicit point was that there is not a single, intelligible system of morality, but (at least) two distinct and incompatible moral worlds; let us call them the Christian and the Roman republican. In choosing the latter, Machiavelli was driven by the vision of a "strong, united, effective, morally regenerated, splendid, and victorious *patria*."[15] My view is that Machiavelli's radical ideas and purposes must be understood first and foremost in the context of his times, including the corruption and decay of the Catholic church, the debilitating rivalries and internal weakness of the Italian states, and the political–military catastrophe that befell the peninsula after 1494. If he was a prophet, his basic message was regeneration. As with all prophets, his call was directed in the first instance to the people of his day.

There are a number of views, moreover, of Machiavelli's connection, or lack of it, to the Anglo-American political tradition. The most famous of these is that the Machiavelli who influenced the American founding was not the prophet of a dynamic and powerful *patria*, but the vigilant citizen who feared the destruction of the republic by corruption and saw civic virtue (corruption's antidote) as dependent on a land-based economy and a robust civilian militia. According to J. G. A. Pocock, Machiavelli (as reformulated by the English republican writer James Harrington) inspired the so-called "Old Whig" and "Country Party" opposition to the late-seventeenth- and early-eighteenth-century British state, with its standing armies, funded public debt, and systematic corruption of parliament by the crown. Jefferson, Madison, Adams, and the American Whigs drew on the same "Machiavellian vocabulary" to explain and oppose British rule in America and then Hamilton's attempt to build a British-style power state.[16]

A complementary argument is that there is a distinctive Anglo-American tradition in foreign policy arising out of conditions of insularity and relative security: "This [the Anglo-American] was a philosophy of choice ... which was bound to be ethical, over against a [continental] philosophy of necessity, in which forces beyond moral control were believed to prevail." According to another commentator, "Americans have never accepted the principles of Europe's old order, never embraced the Machiavellian perspective." For an authoritative voice, when all is said and done, American thinking about foreign affairs bears the stamp of the British liberal and evangelical tradition, with its belief in progress, human rights, and the eventual brotherhood of man. The same tradition (Woodrow Wilson was its great American exponent) informs the belief in the possibility of "the end of history," that major conflict will subside once the entire world has been integrated into a liberal world economy and adopted democracy as its creed.[17]

A recent, thought-provoking analysis makes a sharp distinction between "continental realism" and the American or Hamiltonian variety of realism: "when the Hamiltonians came to consider the foreign policy interests of the United States, they came up with a radically different list of interests than those drawn up in most of the chancelleries of Europe. European powers were surrounded by jealous and powerful rivals, and their relations alternated between war and armed truce. European states were forced to understand their interests primarily in military terms." Inspired by the British example, Hamiltonians put freedom of the seas, access to markets, protection of U.S. industry, sound finance, and a "special relationship" with the United Kingdom on their list of interests. Hamiltonians were (and are) prone to the "intoxicating vision of a win–win world order" based on expanding trade and international law.[18]

This book has a different thesis. The outlooks of Hamilton and the Hamiltonians, on the one hand, and of the "continental realists," on the other, overlap to a greater degree than the conventional wisdom would have it. Hamilton and his followers were concerned with land power and the European balance; they believed in the inevitability of interstate conflict and the necessity of heroic leadership – the hallmarks of "continental realism." (By the same token, a continental power like France was preoccupied during much of its modern history with supposedly "Anglo-American" concerns like internal economic development, naval power, and empire overseas.[19])

In short, Hamilton and Machiavelli, the father of continental realism, inhabited the same moral and intellectual world, one where emerging states had to adapt themselves to the law of the jungle and to look to successful models to survive. Hamilton's view of human nature, politics, and statecraft was strikingly similar to Machiavelli's, but the affinity runs deeper than ideas to the level of character. They shared a set of visceral likes and dislikes; in particular, they deplored the "middle path." Despite their reputations, neither had the temperament of a cold-blooded realist. Hamilton remarked, "my heart has always been the Master of my Judgment." Of Machiavelli it has been said: "He could be emotional, and the storms of passion could throw all caution to the wind."[20] At another level, Hamilton personifies Machiavelli's famous model of leadership, the parvenu "new prince." At times it seems as though Hamilton were acting a series of roles scripted for him by Machiavelli: soldier, adviser to the executive, aspiring prince in his own right.

This begs another question: how did the American Founder come to resemble the notorious Florentine? No person is an intellectual carbon copy of another, especially when they are separated by centuries, cultures, and continents. Hamilton did not identify himself with Machiavelli and would probably take umbrage at the notion that he was a conduit for his ideas. The "teacher of evil" (in Leo Strauss's words) and presumed atheist was not much revered in the eighteenth century, the heyday of deism and of belief in natural rights. In Hamilton's America, "God's ultimate authority over both the universe and the affairs of men was questioned, if at all, only by a very few." Of the Revolutionary generation, it appears that only the frank and feisty Adams admitted to having learned from Machiavelli.[21]

And yet, as a discerning scholar observes, "It is unlikely that anyone as well read as Hamilton would *not* have read Machiavelli," though equally unlikely that he would have admitted any debts. What is certain is that Hamilton and Machiavelli steeped themselves in classical and contemporary history and drew often-identical conclusions about human nature and politics. It is probable, moreover, that Hamilton absorbed Machiavelli through the words and deeds of contemporaries who had studied him carefully. An historian notes the following:

Debts acquired at second hand remain debts whether we are witting or not; and despite his well-earned reputation as a teacher of evil, Machiavelli exercised a species of intellectual hegemony over republican thought in the eighteenth century exceeded by none but John Locke.

The Scottish philosopher David Hume and King Frederick the Great of Prussia, though hardly republicans, were pupils of Machiavelli. Hamilton studied both.[22]

There is a second, though until now entirely overlooked, reason for the uncanny resemblance: their similar life experiences. Both were diplomatic-military advisers in the aftermath of upheavals that gave rise to popular governments. Both struggled with the problem of designing and safeguarding their fledgling republics in the context of internal divisions over the use of force, of controversial alliances, and of constant external peril. Both towered above most of their contemporaries intellectually, but were unable, partly because of their suspect origins, to attain the highest offices. Despite, or rather because of, their extraordinary abilities they suffered the slings and arrows of vindictive enemies and the myopia of ordinary mortals. Each was driven by a vision of national greatness, but destined for personal disenchantment and defeat. As the reader will see, Hamilton did not mechanically imitate Machiavelli. Not every situation Hamilton faced had a precedent in Machiavelli's career or had been analyzed in Machiavelli's writings. Nonetheless, Hamilton was an "American Machiavelli" both in the sense that his ideas were similar to those of Machiavelli and that he resembled Machiavelli, the flesh-and-blood human being.

The author's intellectual home is at the intersection of biography, diplomatic history, and the history of ideas. Thus, this book is intended to be not a complete but rather a "partial biography" of Hamilton. It focuses on his foreign policy outlook and role in the 1790s, a dangerous decade in which Americans split into bitterly divided camps over a pair of recurrent questions: What is the proper relationship of the United States to the world of European power politics, and is it destined to be a great power in the traditional meaning of the term? Hamilton's career during those years suggests that American foreign policy has been more "continental," more guided by a "philosophy of necessity," more geared to self-aggrandizement, than Americans, with their short memories and deep belief in their own exceptionalism, prefer to believe.

This should give us pause. It should prompt us to ask whether Hamilton is our true guide for the early twenty-first century. But it is not meant as a negative judgment. Had it been otherwise in the 1790s, the history of the United States as an independent nation might well have ended soon after it began. The argument *is* intended as a plea to Americans to transcend their characteristic solipsism, their inability to appreciate the world beyond their own borders or to see themselves as others see them. One of Hamilton's Machiavellian gifts was his ability to acknowledge the selfish, power-seeking elements in his country's behavior and to take into account the impact of American behavior on others and thence on ourselves. Perhaps not since the 1790s has such a capacity been as important to our security and well-being as it is today.

For nations as well as individuals seeking to gain insight into their futures, rarely has there been better advice than the words inscribed above the entrance to the temple of Apollo at Delphi: γνωθι σεαυτον (*gnothi seauton*). Know thyself.

PART I

THE COMING OF NECESSITY

I

From Providence into Fortune, 1757 (?)–1781

Introduction

In September 1494, King Charles VIII of France invaded Italy with an army of 18,000 men and a horse-drawn siege train of at least forty pieces of artillery. Charles's aim was to enforce his claim to the throne of the Kingdom of Naples by ousting its Aragonese holder. At the height of their artistic splendor but tragically divided, the Italian states became the objects of a struggle between France and Spain lasting more than thirty years. Unable to ensure the safety and dignity of Florence, the Medici family regime, which had ruled the city for sixty years, collapsed in November 1494. In its place, the Florentines refounded their republic. Its cumbersome institutions included the Great Council, newly enfranchising about 3,000 citizens (of a total of some 60,000), the Major Council, composed of about 1,000 citizens, ages twenty-nine or older, the Council of Eighty, limited to men over forty, the *signoria*, or rotating ten-man executive headed by a *gonfaloniere*, or standard-bearer, plus a number of specialized commissions.[1]

In May 1498, twenty-nine-year-old Niccolò Machiavelli was appointed secretary and head of the Second Chancery, a bureau dealing with the city's outlying dominions (they included most of the present-day Region of Tuscany, except for the provinces of Lucca, Siena, and Grosseto). He was also made secretary of "The Ten of Liberty and Peace," a commission overseeing military and diplomatic affairs. On behalf of "The Ten," Machiavelli would mount his horse innumerable times, gallop along the rough roads of Renaissance Europe, and parley with the mighty of his day. But despite his energy and brilliance, Machiavelli faced a built-in ceiling to his career. He sprang from a none-too-prosperous and (according to rumor) illegitimate branch of a distinguished family. His father, Bernardo, owed a debt of back taxes to the city government and thus Machiavelli was excluded from high political office. This was something that the city's haughty patriciate (the so-called *ottimati*, who looked with suspicion on the republic's policies) did not let him forget.[2]

Machiavelli did not devise a philosophical system. His political notions were the trenchantly stated lessons of his personal experience, and reinforced by the study of history, rather than precisely defined concepts. "Things human being in constant motion," an idea traceable to the Greek philosopher Heraclitus, lay at the heart of his worldview. So did the assumption that human nature itself is unchangeable over time. After a revolt against Florentine rule in Arezzo and the surrounding Valdichiana (south of Florence) in 1502, he reminded his superiors that men "have always had the same passions; there were always those who serve and those who command, and those who serve against their will, and those who serve willingly." History was a treasure house of such insights for those who bothered to look for them. He would make the same point about passions in his *Discourses*, written largely after the republic's collapse and his own forced retirement in 1512.[3]

What were those inescapable driving passions? Fundamentally, they were to possess what belonged to others in a world of finite resources and constant flux. History and everyday life demonstrated that "the nature of men is ambitious and suspicious." Human beings were restless, perpetually dissatisfied creatures whose desires outstripped their powers of acquisition. Enmities developed, wars erupted, and states rose and fell, because some men always wanted more than they had, whereas others feared losing what they had acquired.[4]

Machiavelli grasped from an early age that human affairs were constantly subject to unreason, chance, and contingency. The nonrational, unexplainable forces at work in the world he and his contemporaries often referred to as *fortuna* or fortune. He did not operate on (and did not pay hypocritical lip service to) the assumption that God ruled the world, with the implication that people must passively accept their destinies. Although early Christian theology had attempted to consign the old Roman Goddess of Fortune to oblivion, replacing her with Divine Providence, Machiavelli and fellow Italian humanists reversed the transformation by reviving the ancient goddess. As he famously put it, "fortune is a woman," and as such she is susceptible to being possessed and controlled. On another occasion he compared fortune to "one of those ruinous rivers" that, when flooded, might destroy everything in its path. In quieter times men must build barriers to channel the torrent and contain its destructive potential. Human beings, by playing their cards well and by possessing *virtù*, might make their own luck to a degree.[5]

Together with *fortuna*, *virtù* was a basic notion in Machiavelli's outlook. The term is not to be confused with "virtue" in the classical or Christian sense of moral goodness or moderation. It is the Italian version of the Latin *virtus*, which in turn derives from *vir* or *man*. *Virtù* is something that can be found and systematically developed in both states and individuals. That much Machiavelli scholars agree on, though little else. For one, it is "the fundamental quality of man which enables him to achieve great works and deeds." For another, it is something baser and purely utilitarian, that which enables self-aggrandizement, which, for Machiavelli, was the one measure of success.[6] *Virtù* is best understood as encompassing both the vital energy and the manly qualities necessary for success in war and politics, including discipline, courage, guile, and skill at arms. It is both the will to power and the means by which to acquire and maintain it. As embodied in a polity, *virtù* is dedication to the collective good as opposed to the interests of some faction or private individual. A precondition and generator of *virtù* is *necessità* or necessity. Machiavelli writes at one point, "necessity makes *virtù*." But necessity does not guarantee effective action. A city "never agrees to a new law concerning a new order ... unless it is shown by necessity that it must be done; and since this necessity cannot come without danger, the republic may easily be ruined before it is led to perfect its laws."[7]

In the final analysis, *virtù* has something in common with other elusive concepts: It is hard to define exactly, but one usually knows it when one sees it. Alexander Hamilton is a case in point.

Nevis, St. Croix, and New York

The details are sketchy and the evidence is open to interpretation, but the Hamilton family story is without doubt an exemplary tale of the West Indies: its central themes are the weakness of the flesh and sudden death. The islands of Alexander's boyhood were an exotic paradise for a planter elite fabled for its hedonism and extravagance. They were also a volatile and vulnerable world, subject to practically every known calamity: war, epidemic, drought, deadly storms, volcanic eruptions, slave revolts, and economic boom and bust. During the War of the Austrian Succession in the 1740s, and fifteen years later during the Seven Year's War, the leeward (including Nevis) and windward islands were major prizes in the ongoing struggle between France and Britain. In 1759, a British expedition seized the rich sugar-, coffee-, cocoa-, and cotton-producing islands of Guadaloupe and Marie-Galante. In 1762, the British added Martinique, St. Lucia, St. Vincent, and Grenada to their list of acquisitions.[8]

Hamilton's maternal grandparents, the physician and planter John Faucett and his wife, lost five of seven children to disease, after which their marriage fell apart. Their daughter Rachel Faucett, Hamilton's mother, married at sixteen, abandoned her indebted husband and young son, and bore two children out of wedlock – Alexander and an older brother – by James Hamilton, a lackadaisical merchant with whom she cohabited for ten years. In February 1768, three years after separating from the elder Hamilton, she died of a tropical fever at age thirty-two.

The family of Rachel Faucett's half-sister, Ann Lytton, and her husband, James Lytton, a successful planter, also disintegrated. One daughter's husband died in poverty, and the daughter and a second husband soon followed suit. Another daughter's husband went bankrupt, while one of the sons ran off with slaves belonging to his first wife's estate. Ann Lytton died in 1767, a year before Rachel. James Lytton died in 1769. Their son, Peter, legal guardian of the orphans Alexander and James Hamilton, committed suicide after his investments went bad, also in 1769. James Lytton's surviving children litigated for years over his estate.[9]

The mid-eighteenth-century West Indies may not invite comparisons to early sixteenth-century Italy, but it is easy to see why Hamilton's grasp of the notion of *fortuna*, the force of circumstance, was more or less innate. His belief, as he later put it, that human beings were "ambitious, vindictive, and rapacious" was practically in his blood. Here was a powerful antidote in his makeup to the Enlightenment belief in the triumph of Reason over man's lower drives.[10]

According to one historian, what everyday life and the study of history taught Hamilton about human nature his family's Calvinism reinforced: all men were equal in the eyes of God and equally marked by sin. When a devastating hurricane struck the leeward islands in August 1772, Hamilton wrote, "Our distressed, helpless condition taught us humility and contempt of ourselves...But see the Lord relents. He hears our prayer." At the time, Hamilton was under the influence of Hugh Knox, a local Presbyterian minister and scholar who had taken an interest in his welfare. But except during his adolescence, and after tragedy struck him late in life, Hamilton showed few signs of religious piety. His parents did not have him baptized, and he did not see fit to do so on his own. Like Machiavelli, he would become a devout believer in the political utility of religion. But in 1787, when Benjamin Franklin suggested that sessions of the Constitutional Convention pause for prayer, Hamilton is said to have remarked that "he did not see the necessity of calling in foreign aid."[11]

Hamilton's life suggests that he put his faith mainly in himself and a few like-minded companions. It suggests that he shared something close to the view that "the *vir*, the man of true manliness," could shape fortune.[12] Along with a deep-seated pessimism and fatalism, the West Indian setting fostered a powerful drive in Hamilton to dominate adverse circumstances and to create order, as well as an abhorrence of potential gone to waste. It also suggests that he was an enormously gifted but somehow vulnerable individual; in those close to him he could evoke feelings of protectiveness as well as awe.

Rachel Faucett's role in forming her son's character is a matter of dispute. For a time at least, she seems to have been a footloose as well as physically attractive woman. Her estranged husband, one Johann Michael Lavien, had her jailed and cited her for "whoring with everyone" in his petition for divorce. According to James Thomas Flexner's influential biography, the home she kept was a "shambles," and her "betrayal" of the young Hamilton left him emotionally crippled and with a lifelong fear of dependency. In fact, he later wrote that he wished to keep himself "free from particular attachments," and his "happiness independent on [sic] the caprice of others."

But this picture is overdrawn. By betrayal, Flexner means that Rachel dropped the surname Hamilton in later life, something that her sons must have taken as "a repudiation of themselves." But it strains credulity to think that she would not have explained to them that she was not entitled by law to use the name. It is at least equally plausible to assume that she was an affectionate mother and encouraged Alex (as he was called) to be self-reliant – a lesson driven brutally home by her death. It is true that Hamilton rarely mentioned his mother in later life, but this does not mean, as some suggest, that he harbored deeply hostile feelings toward her. In a letter written in 1800, he referred to her as "a handsome young woman having a *snug* fortune" who had entered into an unhappy marriage with the "fortune-hunter" Lavien "against her own inclination."[13]

Rachel Faucett and James Hamilton may well have led a relatively stable, if marginal, life on the island of St. Kitts, near Nevis. After her separation, she ran a small store with Alex's help in Christiansted, the capital of the Danish island of St. Croix. She may have encouraged her son to follow in the footsteps of his maternal grandfather – Hamilton's initial course of study in college was medicine. Of Huguenot origin, she helped him to acquire his good French and stimulated his ambition and escapism through literature, including Alexander Pope's poetry and Plutarch's *Lives*. Her collection of some thirty books is said to have included a French translation of *The Prince*.[14]

The reason for the end of his parents' relationship is also a matter of controversy. Hamilton's observation in 1774 that "the law ruins many a good honest family" suggests what may have been his own interpretation. Years later, he told a correspondent that a marriage had actually taken place between his parents, but on moving from St. Kitts to St. Croix in 1765, they found that, under Danish law, Rachel was forbidden to remarry after being divorced by Lavien in 1759. It may have been this discovery, or perhaps other legal problems, that precipitated the breakup of the family and James Hamilton's return alone to St. Kitts.[15]

Hamilton naturally wished to minimize a central fact: his illegitimacy. But he knew that there was little solid ground for doing so. John Adams's reference to him as "the bastard Bratt [sic] of a Scotch Pedlar" expressed, albeit crudely, a basic truth. In this existential sense, Hamilton resembled not only Machiavelli himself, but the upstart figure who was the focus of the Florentine's famous study. The basic problem Machiavelli analyzed in *The Prince* was how "to make a new prince appear to be an established one." Hamilton's life story, in essence, is that of a would-be prince who uses exceptional intelligence, daring, and cunning – in a word, *virtù* – in search of legitimacy and lasting fame.[16]

A Gentleman and a Whig

In reality, Machiavelli's father, Bernardo, had not been a miserable deadbeat, but a cultivated gentleman. By the same token, Hamilton's father, James, was not exactly the lowly peddler of Adams family lore. He was the fourth son of Alexander Hamilton, Laird of the Grange, Ayrshire, in southwestern Scotland, and of his wife, Elizabeth, the daughter of a baronet. He was remembered as a dreamer, drifter, and heavy drinker, but also a generous (when he had money) and charming character. Hamilton never saw his father again after the latter left St. Croix in 1765. His feelings toward him were a mixture of shame, loyalty, and compassion. In 1785, he wrote, "My heart bleeds at the recollection of his misfortunes and embarrassments." On another occasion he recalled, "It was his fault to have had too much pride and too large a portion of indolence – but his character was otherwise without reproach and his manners those of a Gentleman." The elder Hamilton was an ever-present negative example, both fortune's victim and someone who had failed to capitalize on his opportunities. A basic source of Hamilton's phenomenal energy and competitiveness was the desire to avoid his father's fate, as well as the wish to vindicate him and realize his frustrated hopes for success.[17]

If the Machiavelli family's social position is the key to Niccolò's visceral preference for broad-based politics in his native city, Hamilton's feelings toward his father help to explain his early political orientation. In 1773, with generous financial help from his New York-based cousin, Ann Lytton Mitchell, and local St. Croix supporters, Hamilton left the West Indies to study in North America. He was never to return. Once there, he developed sympathy for the Whig cause against the British crown. This was natural enough insofar as the people who had recognized his promise and arranged his departure – Hugh Knox and the merchant Nicholas Cruger, who had employed the precocious youth in his St. Croix office – were solid Whigs. Knox's prominent New Jersey friends, William Livingston and Elias Boudinot, who looked after Hamilton in 1773, and his tutor, Francis Barber, were also Whigs. Hamilton later wrote his Scottish uncle, William Hamilton: "my principles led me to take part" in the revolution, and presumably he meant the Whig principles drummed into him by Knox. As Hamilton proclaimed in a 1774 political pamphlet, "no laws have any validity, or binding force, without the consent and approbation of the *people*."[18]

Principle was not the whole story. According to an eyewitness, during the buildup to the revolution, people lived "a joy unutterable and an exhultation [sic] never felt before." Even at a staid institution like King's College (later Columbia), where Hamilton matriculated in 1774, the mood was insurrectionary. Moreover, "[b]eneath all the specific constitutional grievances against British authority lay a more elusive social and political rancor that lent passion to the Revolutionary movement." According to George

Clinton, the future Governor of New York, the Whig spirit was a "Spirit of Resentment." The resentment was aimed at an "unmerited aristocracy" of colonial officeholders who owed their positions to royal patronage and family connections. Hamilton, too, felt a sense of injustice toward a system that humiliated its subjects and failed to recognize merit, like the one that had conferred all of the family privileges on the eldest son (James Hamilton's brother William) and had cast his father to the winds.[19]

But there was another, contradictory, emotion connected to his family background: the envy and ambition of a déclassé British gentleman, the feeling that what was wrong was not the winner-take-all system itself, but where he stood on the social ladder. Hamilton and his college roommate, Robert Troup, recalled that in some political discussions in 1773–74, he had taken the British side. Contrary to the conventional account, it is probable that Hamilton preferred Anglican King's College to the Whig and Presbyterian College of New Jersey (Princeton). Hamilton and Troup helped to save the Loyalist president of King's from a Whig lynch mob in May 1775.[20] Despite, or rather because of, his family's modest circumstances and his illegitimacy, it was impressed on Hamilton early on that *he* was a gentleman. He must have known that he had been named for his grandfather, the laird, and always referred to his own father as a "Gentleman." At age fourteen, toiling as a clerk in Cruger's counting house, he referred in a letter to his "character." "Character" in the eighteenth century signified a gentleman's reputation. The boy was trapped not only on an island but in a social position where he did not belong. Evidently, he saw no possible middle way between rotting there and going for broke.[21]

The role of gentleman came naturally to Hamilton, even if his West Indian élan would rub some American-born aristocrats the wrong way. Despite what his enemies would later insist (and following his father's example), Hamilton was never interested in the bourgeois pursuit of accumulating money. He was to be known for his gallantry, extreme touchiness on questions of honor, and sophisticated tastes. When his illegitimacy was bruited about in the late 1790s, he wrote a friend that he had "better pretensions than most of those who in this Country plume themselves on Ancestry."[22]

The same juvenile letter to his friend Edward Stevens revealed what was perhaps the most visceral reason why Hamilton threw himself into the American revolution: "to confess my weakness, Ned, my Ambition is prevalent that I contemn the grov'ling and condition of a Clerk or the like, to which my Fortune &c. condemns me and would willingly risk my life tho' not my Character to exalt my Station...I wish there was a War." Machiavelli's advice to the new prince had been to "have no other objective nor other thought, nor take anything as his art, except war and its ways and discipline; because that is the only art that belongs to one who commands; and is of such *virtù* that it not only maintains in power those who are born princes, but often times raises men of private fortune to that station."[23]

Schools for Statesmen

The historian Felix Gilbert observed that Machiavelli "was deeply involved in the political world, yet he also looked upon it from a distance." The sense of distance had several, mutually reinforcing sources: his social position, a developing historical perspective on contemporary events, and the opportunity and the ability to see his country through foreign eyes.[24]

In 1500, his political masters dispatched Machiavelli to the French court at Lyon. France and Florence had been nominal allies for many years, and France was the republic's ostensible protector. But it was also an emerging unitary state ruled by a strong king (after 1498, Louis XII), whereas Florence was a mere city with some outlying dominions. Crossing the Alps on the first of four missions to France, Machiavelli found "that to anyone schooled in the ways of modern kingship, Florence's governmental machinery appeared absurdly vacillating and weak.... Even more humiliatingly Machiavelli discovered that his native city's sense of its own importance seemed to the French to be ludicrously out of line with the realities of its military position and its wealth." As a mere civil servant lacking ambassadorial powers, Machiavelli spent six months following the itinerant court while Florence debated whether to send an envoy to renegotiate its existing alliance. He informed the *signoria* that the French "call you Mr. Nothing."[25]

In fact, Florence's dealings with France recall the adage, "With friends like these, who needs enemies?" The flight of the Medicis and refounding of the republic in 1494 had been brought about by popular outrage over Piero de' Medici's abject cession to France of Florence's western strong points and seaports, including Sarzana, Pietrasanta, Pisa, and Livorno. When Charles VIII had encamped in Florence for eleven days in November 1494, en route to conquer the Kingdom of Naples, his army and the local citizenry had come close to a bloody confrontation. The French had promised to return what they had taken at the end of the war, but instead had sold Sarzana to Genoa and given Pietrasanta to Lucca. In the case of Pisa (near the mouth of the Arno River and controlling Florence's access to the Mediterranean), the French commander had sold the local fortress to the Pisans and pocketed the proceeds.

Lacking their own military forces, the Florentines were obliged to hire a famous Roman *condottiere*, Paolo Vitelli, and later 1,500 Swiss and Gascon soldiers under French command, to try to recapture Pisa. Both campaigns ended in ignominious, hugely expensive failures. The Florentines beheaded Vitelli, and it was after the latter debacle that they dispatched Machiavelli to France. The King demanded that Florence settle an unpaid bill of thirty-eight thousand gold florins, even though the Swiss and Gascons had mutinied before the walls of Pisa. Although they eventually reined him in, the French backed the bold and ruthless Cesare Borgia, son of Pope Alexander VI. Borgia's lightening conquests in the Romagna and the Marches, and support for the return of the Medicis to Florence, threatened the republic's survival in 1499–1502. Last but not least, it was France's withdrawal from Italy after its costly victory over the "Holy League" (the papacy, Spain, Venice) at the battle of Ravenna that paved the way for the republic's overthrow at the hands of Pope Julius II and Spanish troops in 1512.[26]

It is no wonder that Machiavelli wrote that the French character was marked by "greed and lack of good faith." Nor is it surprising that he developed a revulsion for the temporizing and half-measures that typified Florentine foreign policy. "Weak states," he wrote, "are always ambiguous in taking a decision and slow deliberations are always harmful." Another lesson learned the hard way was that states must rely on their own efforts rather than those of marauding and double-dealing mercenaries. Fortunately, history furnished examples of excellent statecraft and military organization. One in particular was to become Machiavelli's model and *ideé fixe*.[27]

* * *

Hamilton, like Machiavelli, was a person who managed to be deeply immersed in the political world while retaining the perspective of the historian and outsider. His resentment of the British colonial system and his burning ambition tied him to the Whig cause from the moment he landed in America. But his exposure to the prerevolutionary climate was superficial. Other instinctive feelings tended to separate him from his adopted country. With Hamilton, there is always the sense that, although America was the stage on which he was acting, the part he was playing originated somewhere else.

The constructive force of American nationalism grew out of "continentalism," the perspective of those who spent the war years (1775–83) in the army, on the war committees of the Continental Congress, or on diplomatic missions in Europe. Those who sacrificed, while the majority sat by or feathered their own nests, came to see themselves as a kind of virtuous elite. Speaking of the melting-pot effect of the war on officers from different sections of the country, George Washington wrote: "A century in the ordinary intercourse, would not have accomplished what the Seven years association in Arms did." Hamilton was an instinctive continentalist. The intensity of national feeling he brought to the war effort was connected to his recent arrival and lack of provincial roots. The army reinforced this feeling and gave him a sense of the gulf dividing him from the majority of Americans who put state and local loyalties above national ties.[28]

Hamilton's native *virtù* was on display from the beginning of the war. A self-taught artilleryman, he was appointed captain of a New York provincial company and took part in the unsuccessful defense of the city against Sir William Howe's invading army in the fall of 1776. He met and impressed General Nathanael Greene and the commander of artillery, General Henry Knox. It was perhaps their recommendation, as well as his competence during the Continental Army's retreat across New Jersey, that brought him to the Commander-in-Chief's attention in early 1777.

Joining Washington's small personal staff, or "family" as it was known, marked his "early, sudden, and protracted introduction to public life." In November 1777, Washington sent his 20-year-old aide on a solitary ride from Philadelphia to the upper Hudson River valley to negotiate the dispatch of reinforcements from his rival general, Horatio Gates, after Gates's victory over the British at the battle of Saratoga. As a trusted draftsman and adviser, Lieutenant Colonel Hamilton assisted Washington in conducting complex and demanding negotiations with the Continental Congress and, after early 1778, the French.[29]

Hamilton developed a revulsion for what he considered the politicians' dithering and parochially minded conduct. From Washington's winter encampment at Valley Forge in early 1778, he wrote, "Folly, caprice, a want of foresight, comprehension and dignity, characterise [sic] the general tenor of their actions." How, he asked, "can we hope for success in our European negociations [sic], if the nations of Europe have no confidence in the wisdom and vigor, of the great Continental Government?" "Without a speedy change," he wrote in 1780, "the army must dissolve. It is now a mob rather than an army, without clothing, without pay, without provision, without morals, without discipline." Several years later he would ask, "Is respectability in the eyes of foreign powers a safeguard against foreign encroachments?" Unfortunately, "[t]he imbecility of our Government even forbids them to treat with us: Our ambassadors abroad are the mere pageants of mimic sovereignty."[30]

In his (one is tempted to call them Machiavellian) moments of pessimism and alienation, Hamilton at times fantasized about a glorious martyrdom.[31] He wrote his closest wartime friend, Lieutenant Colonel John Laurens, in January 1780, "I am disgusted with everything in this world but yourself and very *few* more honest fellows and I have no other wish than as soon as possible to make a brilliant exit. 'Tis a weakness; but I feel I am not fit for this terrestreal [sic] country." This was not simply idle talk. He was frequently under fire during the campaign leading to the British occupation of Philadelphia in September–October 1777 and during the battle of Monmouth, New Jersey, in June 1778. In early 1781, he quit Washington's staff and eventually joined a New York infantry regiment. During the decisive battle of Yorktown (October 1781), he led his bayonet-wielding battalion up the side of a British redoubt, forcing its abrupt surrender. Colonel Laurens, a cultivated, rashly brave South Carolinian, knew what Hamilton was talking about. In August 1782, with the war for all intents and purposes over, he was killed leading skirmishers against an enemy force several times larger than his own.[32]

The pathetic weakness of "rule by committee" and the American government's incapacity to mobilize the resources of the country, even to feed and clothe its own army, helped to crystallize Hamilton's political thinking. His wartime reading of Plutarch on the lives of ancient Greek and Roman luminaries reinforced the view that human nature was static and that it was vain to put great faith in human rationality. One biographer speaks as well of his "new-found Humean perspective." Even before the war, Hamilton had cited the Scottish philosopher to the effect "that in contriving any system of government... *every man* ought to be supposed a *knave*; and to have no other end in all his actions, but *private interest*. By this interest we must govern him, and by means of it, *make him co-operate to public good.*" Hamilton did not believe that all men *were* knavish. (He later wrote: "The supposition of universal venality in human nature is little less an error in political reasoning than the supposition of universal rectitude.") But experience taught that the "ruling passion" of many was the love of wealth or power. It also taught that a noble handful were ruled by a higher passion, the love of fame of the sort achieved by carrying out "extensive and arduous enterprises" for the public good.[33] Hume's maxim was taken nearly verbatim from Machiavelli: "it is necessary to those who set up a republic and order its laws to presuppose that all men are delinquents." Machiavelli had also written that "never or rarely does it happen that a republic or kingdom is well ordered from the beginning, or completely renewed, if it is not done by a single man." At the top of his hierarchy of greatness were the founders and lawgivers like Moses, Cyrus, and Romulus: "And truly the heavens cannot give men a greater chance for glory, nor can men desire greater glory" than that to be gained by reordering a corrupt state.[34]

Models to Live by

At the end of the day, what history and contemporary events taught Machiavelli was that "It is impossible for a republic to manage to stand still and enjoy its liberty and limited confines: because if it won't molest its neighbor, it will be molested by him; and being molested gives rise to the desire and the necessity to acquire [territory]." Given the imperative to acquire or be acquired, moreover, he professed that republics, allowing popular participation, were more energetic and successful at the business than autocracies. Accommodating the plebians' demand for power through the institution of the tribunate, arming its own citizens, and giving them a stake in the conquest of adjacent areas helped to explain the miracle by which a tiny, hemmed-in city had become the mistress of Italy and eventually the entire Mediterranean. Though he was not consistent on the point (and one senses a certain wishful thinking), Machiavelli wrote: "One sees by experience that cities have never increased in dominion or wealth until they became free."[35]

If Machiavelli developed a feeling of kinship with the Roman republic and looked to its experience for guidance, Hamilton was emotionally and intellectually attached to his own model. He knew Roman history, referred to it in his writings, and as pseudonyms usually chose Roman republican characters. But his real inspiration was contemporary Britain. The Roman and British models were far from identical, but they did have much in common. The constitutions of both had been works in progress whose mixture of democratic (tribunate and commons), aristocratic (senate and lords), and autocratic (consulate and crown) elements had emerged from bitter civil strife. Both were dynamic, self-aggrandizing states who saw expansion as essential to security and prosperity. Starting from small bases, both had hit upon enormously successful formulas for generating wealth and power. At least for a time, they had managed to combine liberty at home and foreign empire. Both were inclined to prefer glory to longevity, and to republican purity, if that became the choice.

Paradoxical though it may seem, the war served to strengthen Hamilton's attachment to the British model while reinforcing a fundamentally Machiavellian view of France. In a political pamphlet he wrote in early 1775, several months before the first shots of the war were fired at Lexington and Concord, Hamilton had argued that the American colonies were bound to the monarchy – "the great connecting principle" – but should enjoy complete legislative autonomy. "Prudence and sound policy" on Britain's part strongly recommended that it accept a federative arrangement:

In fifty or sixty years, America will be in no need of protection from Great-Britain. She will then be able to protect herself both at home and abroad.... She will indeed owe a debt of gratitude to the parent state, for past services; but the scale will then begin to turn in her favour, and the obligation for future services, will be on the side of Great-Britain.

The British would do well to retain the colonists' loyalty by "affectionate and parental conduct" because someday it would be Britain who needed America.[36] The idea of a federative system, with the parts linked to the king rather than parliament and in which London continued to regulate the vast, mutually profitable trade of the empire, had been developed by the Virginian Richard Bland and the Pennsylvanian Benjamin Franklin, among others. It was the position of conservatives at the Continental Congress for a time, the resolution on independence coming only in June 1776. Hamilton was never to abandon the idea of Anglo-American cooperation based on common interests. He did not believe, like John Adams, that war between America and Britain must end in "an incurable animosity" between the two.[37]

Hamilton's weighing of the odds in case of war had been prescient, if overly optimistic. For the British to use force would be nothing less than "*the grossest infatuation, madness itself.*" They could never win if the colonists adopted a temporizing, Fabian strategy (as was to be the case). What the colonies lacked in war supplies, France, Spain, and Holland would provide. France may have promised not to interfere in the dispute, but "the promises of princes and statesmen are of little weight.... If we consult the known character of the French, we shall be disposed to conclude, that their present, seemingly pacific and friendly disposition is merely a piece of *finesse.*" Concluding, Hamilton attested: "I earnestly lament the unnatural quarrel, between the parent state and the colonies; and most ardently wish for a speedy reconciliation, a perpetual and *mutually* beneficial union, that I am a warm advocate for limited monarchy, and an unfeigned well-wisher to the present Royal Family." The best way to secure a "permanent and happy union" was to permit the colonies "to be as free, as they desire."[38]

Hamilton was anything but an uncritical admirer of British statecraft. In 1783, after seven years of war, he wrote, "The situation of Great Britain puts her under a necessity at all events of fulfilling her engagements and cultivating the good will of this country. This is no doubt her true policy." But recent history had proved that "passion makes us depart from the dictates of reason... [W]e have seen that passion has had so much influence in the conduct of the British councils in the whole course of the war." Hamilton reacted in disgust whenever spite or anger led the British to pursue what was basically an "unnatural quarrel."[39]

When Henry Cabot Lodge in the 1880s, and Clinton Rossiter in the 1960s, argued that Hamilton's "thoughts were fixed on the United States unbiased by a sentiment for or against any other nation," they were denying the obvious. Samuel Flagg Bemis, one of the first historians to analyze Hamilton's foreign policy role, was closer to the truth: "The sympathies of Hamilton were wholly with Great Britain but for no sentimental or even philosophical reason." But it is not, *pace* Bemis, a case of either/or. Rather, to paraphrase Hamilton himself, "calculations and passions conspired." This does not mean that the national interest was at odds with Hamilton's personal bias, and certainly he rarely if ever saw a contradiction between the two.[40] In his attitude toward Britain one senses the feeling "I have something to prove to you, and the effort is worth little if it does not receive your approbation." His outlook was infused with a feeling of kinship, a psychic need to measure up, and a desire for respect and recognition. It is little wonder that he clashed with those contemporaries who never ceased to look on Britain as an evil empire and a whore.[41]

During the war, Hamilton moved toward the position he took at the Constitutional Convention in 1787. The British constitution was "the best in the world: and... he doubted much whether anything short of it would do in America." He also embraced the British financial revolution launched in the 1690s. According to J. G. A. Pocock:

The institutions of the new finance, of which the Bank of England and the National Debt came to be the most important, were essentially a series of devices for encouraging the large or small investor to lend capital to the state, investing in its future political stability and strengthening this by the act of investment itself, while deriving a guaranteed income from the return on the sum invested. With the aid of the invested capital, the state was able to maintain larger and more permanent armies and bureaucracies – incidentally increasing the resources at the disposal of political patronage – and as long as its affairs visibly prospered, it was able to attract further investments and conduct larger and longer wars. The era of the *condottiere* – the short-term military contractor – ended, his place being taken by the military administrator as one arm of the bureaucratic state.

With its high land taxes, large military establishment, and cohorts of crown officials, stock jobbers, and speculators, the system had been the favorite target of the opposition to Sir Robert Walpole's rule in the early to mideighteenth century. "Old Whig" and "Country party" spokesmen adopted the conspiracy theory according to which the court was using the system to corrupt parliament and destroy English liberties. American patriots embraced the same theory in the 1760s, because it provided a plausible and psychologically satisfying explanation of royal policy toward themselves in the wake of the Seven Year's War.[42]

For Hamilton to advocate a national bank and funded debt was thus like waving a red flag in the face of the average Whig. He was well aware that the system was subject to abuse, witness the crushing debt accumulated by the British government. But other concerns were paramount. Nathanael Greene, commanding American troops in the South, wrote Hamilton in January 1781:

The army is in such a wretched condition that I hardly know what to do with it. The officers have got such a habit of negligence [sic], and the soldiers so loose and disorderly that it is next to impossible to give it a military complexion. Without clothing I am sure I shall never do it.

With the soldiers defending the Whig cause forced to fight barefoot, Hamilton naturally looked with favor on a mechanism that had allowed Britain to mobilize wealth on an unprecedented scale to wage war. Together with the system of regulated overseas trade, it had made Britain the most powerful country in the world. In 1781, Hamilton wrote Robert Morris, the Pennsylvania merchant who had played a key role in financing the war effort: "A national debt if it is not excessive will be to us a national blessing; it will be a powerful cement of our union."[43]

Hamilton's view of France, meanwhile, contained several layers. The most basic was an instinctive suspicion and dislike of dependency, connected to his family background: the typical Huguenot was raised on stories of French intolerance and cruelty during the reign of Louis XIV. It is probably no coincidence that three of his closest friends had French Huguenot backgrounds: John Laurens, Gouverneur Morris, and John Jay. At another level, Hamilton admired France's mastery of power politics, a game, he believed, that America would have to equip itself to play. This is what Charles Maurice de Talleyrand-Périgord, no mean judge of the matter (and who knew Hamilton during his American sojourn, 1794–96), meant when he said of Hamilton that *"il avait deviné l'Europe."* The youthful author of the 1775 pamphlet had in fact divined France's policy of revenge for its defeat by Britain in the Seven Year's War, which was being planned even as Hamilton wrote by the French foreign minister, Charles Gravier, the comte de Vergennes. Pierre Caron de Beaumarchais, better known as the author of *The Barber of Seville*, would shortly begin his career as gunrunner to the American rebels on behalf of Louis XVI.[44]

As a French-speaking aide-de-camp, Hamilton was thrown into close contact with the French officer corps. He became fast friends with several Frenchmen, including his endearing brother-in-arms, eight months his junior, the Marquis de Lafayette. But by and large, the wave of aristocratic volunteers seeking plum positions in the American army proved to be an annoyance and an embarrassment. As the war dragged on longer than he had predicted, Hamilton knew better than anyone, as he put it to Laurens, that "the friendship of France is our *unum necessarium.*" But the fact that French money and regular forces might "save us in spite of ourselves" was not exactly reassuring. When it finally arrived, the French army was smaller than expected, and its high command dismissed Washington's appeal for a frontal assault on New York. When Laurens was to be sent as envoy to Paris, Hamilton worried that his friend might be too honest and warm-tempered to be effective at the French court: "A politician My Dear Friend must be at all times supple – he must often dissemble." Hamilton would follow his own advice as a member of Washington's court after 1789.[45]

As the war wound down (after Yorktown, there was no major fighting in North America), he favored the continuation of close Franco-American friendship, including privileged commercial relations. When a new British administration under the Earl of Shelburne offered generous terms to America in late 1782, Hamilton wrote Washington that he suspected British "insincerity and duplicity." Those words betray not just distrust, but anxiety that news of a definitive peace would destroy efforts by nationalists in Congress to create a stronger central government. And they were written before he had learned what he might have suspected: the French had been prepared to end the war *without* securing American independence and had opposed the American bid (granted by the British) to establish the United States's western boundary on the Mississippi River.[46]

Years later, Hamilton recalled that during his service in Congress as a New York delegate in the early 1780s, he had been "struck with disgust at the appearance, in the very cradle of our Republic, of a party actuated by an undue complaisance to foreign power" – namely France – and had "resolved at once to resist this bias in our affairs." By the mid-1780s Hamilton believed – by and large correctly – that France did not want a strong America, that its help could not be counted on a day longer than selfish interests dictated, and that the alliance signed in 1778 was a marriage of convenience. The foundations of a longer term community of interests – trade, finance, language, religion, a shared political culture – simply did not exist.[47]

2

Prepared To Be Not Good, 1781–1788

Back to the Books

At the end of December 1780, Hamilton took leave from Washington's staff for one of the most important appointments of his life: his marriage to Elizabeth "Eliza" Schuyler in Albany, New York. It was a choice in which romantic attachment went hand in hand with social and political opportunism. One of Hamilton's fellow officers described the bride, about Hamilton's age, as "A brunette with the most good-natured, lively dark eyes that I ever saw which threw a beam of good temper and benevolence over her whole countenance."[1] She was also the second of four daughters of the upstate New York landholder, and future Hamilton supporter, General Philip Schuyler. After Yorktown, Hamilton left the army, ensconced himself in the Schuyler family's orange brick mansion overlooking the Hudson River at Albany, and prepared for the bar. He was admitted an attorney qualified to practice before the New York Supreme Court the following July and as counsel (equivalent of the English barrister) in October 1782.[2]

Among the authors who left an impression on Hamilton during his legal studies was the leading eighteenth-century authority on the law of nations, the Swiss Emmerich de Vattel. From seventeenth century, post-Machiavellian writers like Thomas Hobbes and John Locke, Vattel had inherited the notion of a "state of nature" (existing before the formation of polities) in which all human beings possessed "natural rights," that is, to life, liberty, and property. According to Vattel, what was true of individuals in the state of nature was also true of nations: they were endowed with equal rights. "Power or weakness does not in this respect produce any difference. A dwarf is as much a man as a giant; a small kingdom is no less a sovereign state than the most powerful kingdom."[3] Along with rights came obligations: "Since the universal society of the human race is an institution of nature . . . all men of whatever condition are bound to advance its interests and to fulfil [sic] its duties." When people formed states those obligations did not end: it devolved upon "the state, and its rulers, to fulfil [sic] the duties of humanity towards strangers... and it is the state more particularly that is to perform those duties towards other states."[4]

Out of a mixture of youthful conviction and deference to contemporary political correctness, Hamilton endorsed this scheme of natural rights. In his early 1775 pamphlet *The Farmer Refuted*, he had written that, prior to the formation of governments, no one had "any *moral* power to deprive another of his life, limbs, property or liberty; nor the least authority to command, or exact obedience from him." Man was a being whose "sacred rights" were written, "as with a sun beam, in the whole *volume* of human nature, by the hand of the divinity itself." Men contracted to form governments in order to secure those rights.[5]

As a practical matter, however, Hamilton assumed that "society naturally divided itself into two political divisions – the *few* and the *many*." Likewise, international society, operating in the state of nature, divided itself into the strong and the weak. Vattel was no Machiavelli, but neither was he a pro-genitor of the idea that the "international community" should intervene in the internal affairs of sovereign states. Vattel's 1759 treatise, which provided the framework for much late-eighteenth-century discussion of international politics, maintained that in practice many obligations among states could be interpreted as nonbinding. It was up to the individual state to decide "whether she can perform any office for another nation without neglecting the duty which she owes to herself." Vattel's vision was of a system which enhanced sovereignty, and counteracted the evil that had beset Europe since the Franco-Spanish struggle over Italy in the sixteenth century: the drive for hegemony by a single state.[6]

For Vattel a state's honor and reputation were not questions of vanity but of self-preservation: "A nation whose reputation is well established – especially one whose glory is illustrious – is courted by all sovereigns; they desire its friendship, and are afraid of offending it. Its friends, and those who wish to become so, favour its enterprises; and those who envy its prosperity are afraid to shew their ill-will." Running through Vattel was another thread that appealed to Hamilton, Britain as model state:

That illustrious nation distinguishes itself in a glorious manner by its application to every thing that can render the state more flourishing. An admirable constitution there places every citizen in a situation that enables him to contribute to this great end and every where diffuses that spirit of genuine patriotism which zealously exerts itself for the public welfare.

And Vattel praised England's essential role in preserving the European balance of power: "a system of policy which is in itself highly just and wise...."[7]

In his classic account of the origins of Washington's "Farewell Address," Felix Gilbert suggests that Hamilton also studied the seventeenth- and eighteenth-century "school of the interests of states." The exponents of that school had tried to distill the "true interests" of the great powers and to express them as permanent maxims. If Hamilton was indeed familiar with these authors, it would constitute another example of debts acquired secondhand: the writers in question were steeped in Machiavelli. Unfortunately, Gilbert does not provide much evidence for Hamilton's knowledge of the school.[8] A stronger case can be made that Hamilton studied Frederick the Great of Prussia: his library contained the *Oeuvres Posthumes de Fréderic, Roi de Prusse*. As a young man Frederick had written an essay attacking Machiavelli, yet went on to become one of his aptest pupils. The reality of international politics, combined with his personal will to power, led him to the view that "one must blindly follow the interests of the state." Frederick's base of operations was a rising but still relatively weak and unconsolidated kingdom. For such a state, Frederick wrote, "Reputation is a thing of incomparable value, and is worth more than power." Hamilton would probably have agreed. A sense of present precariousness and great deeds to be performed in the future lay at the heart of their respective views.[9]

Saving States from Themselves

The feature of Machiavelli's writings that had scandalized young Frederick and countless other readers was, of course, the attack on Christian morality. The Florentine's dislike of Christianity arose from a number of considerations. On one hand, the moral turpitude and corruption of the Italian church hierarchy had undermined *genuine* religious devotion and discipline of the kind which had been the backbone of the Roman state. On the other, Machiavelli had witnessed the rise and fall of Girolamo Savonarola, the austere Dominican friar who had helped to reestablish the Florentine republic, but whose charisma and religious fervor had not saved him from being burned at the stake in 1498. As Machiavelli put it in *The Prince*, "all the armed prophets [e.g., Moses] were successful and the unarmed ones [e.g., Savonarola] were ruined."

The fundamental problem with Christian doctrine was that it taught men to turn the other cheek and their backs on the worldly necessity that generates *virtù* – a sure recipe for the loss of political liberty. As he put it in *The Prince*, it was "more useful to go straight to the effectual truth of the thing than to the imagination of it," namely that so-called good behavior could lose one a state, whereas so-called vice was often necessary to save it. In a world of evil and domineering people it was "necessary for a prince, wanting to maintain himself, to learn to be able to be not good, and to use this or not use it, according to necessity." In plain English, this meant not only that nice rulers finished last but also that others paid a price for their pusillanimity or naiveté. The example foremost in Machiavelli's mind was that of his patron, Piero Soderini, *gonfaloniere* of the Florentine Republic. Soderini was a worthy character, but his timidity and bungling had contributed to the republic's downfall and the Medici restoration in 1512. Machiavelli quipped that when Soderini arrived at the gates of Hell, Pluto had ordered him to "Limbo with the infants."[10]

What he lacked in conventional religious belief, Machiavelli more than made up for in his faith in humanity's capacity for terrestrial achievement. Indeed, his hostility toward Christianity and his belief in the possibility of finding "new modes and orders" were two sides of the same coin. With the help of good leaders, constitutional arrangements, and habits, human beings could shape their own destinies to a degree. For example, in a state whose apparently secure geographical situation inevitably gave rise to an insidious idleness, laws could counteract the bad effects of location by requiring military exercise and hard work.[11]

The often-remarked differences between *The Prince* and the *Discourses* should not be minimized, but are explicable in terms of the author's life experience. For one thing, he wrote *The Prince* in 1513, a moment of understandable disillusionment with republicanism. He was eager to make himself useful to the Medicis and probably felt greater hostility toward the notables (*ottimati*) who had opposed his prized projects than toward the new powers-that-be. Basically, he believed that moments of crisis and renewal required the strong, skillful hand of an exceptional leader, while the people were steadier and more prudent in ordinary times.[12] His ideal was a system where one could have one's cake and eat it; where the decisiveness and *virtù* of the individual ruler was combined with the popular participation and adaptability of the republic. This, he believed, is what the Roman republic had achieved. When necessity dictated, for example, the Romans had resorted to the use of a temporary dictator. Machiavelli quoted with approval their maxim: "in the conduct of important business, it is a most useful rule that the high command be vested in a single individual." But the Roman system was flexible enough to be able to change leaders according to circumstances. Rather than immediately try to dominate their neighbors, the Romans formed leagues and alliances with them, accreting their own strength and facilitating territorial expansion. Machiavelli saw no nexus between republicanism and peaceful international behavior – rather, he saw the opposite. Given the unavoidable choice of states to dominate or be dominated, the proof of the superiority of republics lay precisely in their capacity to mobilize power and to expand.[13]

In the last chapter of *The Prince*, Machiavelli provided a dramatic description of Italy's plight after 1494: "leaderless, without order, beaten, despoiled, torn apart, overrun." Some commentators dispute the view that he favored Italian unity as the solution to this humiliating situation, even as they acknowledge his admiration for the emerging states of France and (especially) Spain. But given his knowledge of the weakness of the Italian statelets and his fixation on Rome's achievement, it is difficult to believe that Machiavelli would have called – as he did in the same chapter – for a prince to expel the "barbarians" from Italy without having some form of political unity in mind. In the *Discourses*, he observed: "The Church, not having been strong enough to be able to occupy Italy, nor having allowed someone else to occupy it, has been a reason why it [Italy] has not come under a single chief; but has been under several princes and lords, from which such disunion and such weakness has been born that it has become prey not only to the powerful barbarians, but to anyone who assaults it." In 1513, the year Machiavelli made his call, the Medici clan had suddenly acquired control not only of Florence and its dominions, but of the adjacent Papal States (the Romagna, Umbria, the Marches, Lazio) – no mean base from which to begin to unify the peninsula. What is beyond question is that in Machiavelli a kind of romantic faith in Italy's regeneration, and in the vindication of Italian honor, was a fundamental driving force.[14]

* * *

The United States of America under the "Articles of Confederation and perpetual Union," agreed to by the Continental Congress on November 15, 1777, and in force as of March 1, 1781, was essentially a defensive league designed to win and maintain the independence of the individual states. Article II of the "Articles" stated: "Each state retains its sovereignty, freedom, and independence, and every power, jurisdiction, and right, which is not by this Confederation expressly delegated to the United States, in Congress assembled." Delegates to Congress were chosen and paid by the states. Each state, regardless of size, possessed a single vote. According to Article III, the states were bound together in a collective security pact against outside attack, and (as per Article VI) no state could engage in war unless attacked, or negotiate agreements with foreign powers, without permission of Congress. According to Article IX, "The United States in Congress assembled" had the sole power to determine peace and war, to send and receive ambassadors, and to make treaties and alliances.

In reality, however, even in those few areas, Congress shared power with, or was subject to veto by, the states. Congress was forbidden from making treaties that restrained the individual states "from imposing such imposts and duties on foreigners, as their own people are subjected to, or from prohibiting the exportation or importation of any species of goods or commodities whatsoever" (Article IX). To exercise its powers, and to borrow and appropriate money, Congress required a majority of nine of thirteen states. It had no independent source of revenue and relied on requisitions from the states. Adoption of the Articles, as well as amendments vesting *new* powers in the confederation, required ratification by the legislatures of all thirteen states. There was no central bank or national currency. Though the "central government" had tiny departments of foreign affairs, war, and finance, it had no chief executive charged with taking "care that the laws be faithfully executed" (as per Article II, Section 3 of the U.S. Constitution) – indeed, none was needed because the bulk of legislation affecting individuals and economic operators was in the hands of the states.[15]

Along with the war, the period of weak and – literally – bankrupt central authority running from the adoption of the Articles until the ratification of the new constitution was a key chapter in Hamilton's political education. His budding legal career was interrupted by service in a series of offices: collector of Continental taxes for the state of New York (May–October 1782), delegate to the Confederation Congress (November 1782–August 1783), New York State Assemblyman and delegate to the Annapolis convention (1786–87), delegate to the Philadelphia convention (May–September 1787), and delegate to the New York State ratifying convention (June–July 1788).

One of the advantages of a moderate national debt, Hamilton wrote (April 1781) Robert Morris, the Confederation's newly appointed Superintendent of Finance, was that it would

create a necessity for keeping up taxation to a degree which without being oppressive, will be a spur to industry; remote as we are from Europe and shall be from danger, it were otherwise to be feared our popular maxims would incline to too great parsimony and indulgence. We labour less now than any civilized nation of Europe, and a habit of labour in the people is as essential to the health and vigor of their minds and bodies as it is conducive to the welfare of the State. We ought not to suffer our self-love to deceive us in a comparrison [sic] on these points.[16]

America should exploit the advantages of distance from the Old World but avoid the trap of thinking that its location was synonymous with either superiority or safety. "A little time hence," he had written in 1780, "some of the states [e.g., New York] will be powerful empires, and we are so remote from other nations that we shall have all the leisure and opportunity we can wish to cut each others throats." History taught that states in close proximity would either unite under one government or else fight each other: "This is in human nature; and we have no reason to think ourselves wiser, or better, than other men." He later asked, "Have we not already seen enough of the fallacy and extravagance of those idle theories which have amused us with promises of an exemption from the imperfections, weaknesses and evils incident to society in every shape?"[17]

One such theory, associated with the French political philosopher the baron de Montesquieu, held that commerce softened the warlike habits of sovereigns by fostering economic interdependence and prosperity. Thanks to commerce, Montesquieu wrote, "We begin to be cured of Machiavellianism." A related notion, advanced by the English radical Thomas Paine as well as Montesquieu, was that wars were caused by the ambitions and caprices of princes, and therefore republicanism was the foundation of international peace. As Paine put it, "In the early ages of the world there were no kings, the consequence of which was there were no wars."[18]

Hamilton instinctively dismissed this set of ideas. As he would later write in defense of the Constitution of 1787, "Is it not time to awake from the deceitful dream of a golden age, and to adopt as a practical maxim... that we, as well as the other inhabitants of the globe, are yet remote from the happy empire of perfect wisdom and perfect virtue?" Citing the aggressive behavior of Athens, Carthage, Venice, Holland, and Britain (whose constitution had marked republican features), he asked, "Have republics in practice been less addicted to war than monarchies?" According to Hamilton, there had been "almost as many popular as royal wars." The American states were themselves a set of ambitious commercial republics who would inevitably quarrel over trade and control of the west. Despite – or partly because of – their democratic politics, they were destined to collide.[19]

In the end, the assumption of a natural harmony among the American states arising from their republicanism, and of a natural security arising from remoteness from Europe, would lead to the opposite result: the American states would become "the foot ball of European politics." Contending coalitions would ally with competing European powers and "be gradually entangled in all the pernicious labyrinths of European politics and wars...." Just as internecine conflict within the ancient Greek confederations had prompted Macedonian and Roman interventions, the American states "would be likely to become prey to the artifices and machinations of powers equally the enemies of them all. *Divide et impera* must be the motto of every nation that either hates, or fears us." America was not yet in the position of Italy in the early sixteenth century, where the local elites had lost control of their destinies to foreigners, but Hamilton feared a comparable situation unless "impending anarchy" were staved off. "We may," he wrote in 1788, "indeed with propriety be said to have reached almost the last stage of national humiliation."[20]

The Newburgh Conspiracy

As a delegate to the Convention Congress, Hamilton fought for the kind of government required to avoid that result. A potentially explosive crisis had developed in early 1783. The legislature of tiny Rhode Island refused to ratify an amendment to the Articles of Confederation giving the central government a modest source of independent income in the form of a five percent impost on imported goods, and Virginia repealed its earlier approval. Faced with the prospect that Congress would not pay the pensions (half-pay for life as in the British service) it had promised them, embittered Continental Army officers (numbering some five hundred fifty, in command of about nine thousand enlisted men) in winter quarters at Newburgh, New York, seemed prepared to take matters into their own hands.

Hamilton's advice to Washington (February 13, 1783) was that "The claims of the army urged with moderation, but with firmness, may operate on those weak minds which are influenced by their apprehensions more than their judgements." Rather than disapprove of the army's efforts to gain redress, Washington should "*take the direction of them.* This however must not appear: it is of moment to the public tranquility that Your Excellency should preserve the confidence of the army without losing that of the people. This will enable you in case of extremity to guide the torrent, and bring order perhaps even good, out of confusion." The end Hamilton had in mind was "the establishment of general [central government] funds, which alone can do justice to the Creditors of the United States (of whom the army forms the most meritorious class), restore public credit and supply the future wants of government." In effect, Hamilton's advice to Washington was that the interests of the state required him "to be not good."[21]

It appears, at least, that Hamilton himself was ready to follow such a course. The so-called Newburgh conspiracy remains shrouded in mystery. But the most detailed modern account argues that Superintendent of Finance Robert Morris, his assistant Gouverneur Morris, and Hamilton, in their eagerness to secure independent central government revenues before a definitive peace brought the dispersal of the army and ended the sense of emergency, were prepared to play with fire. In early March 1783 (though the evidence connecting Hamilton is not direct), they apparently encouraged extremist officers associated with General Horatio Gates to threaten a mutiny at Newburgh, not because they hoped or believed it would succeed, but for its demonstrative effect on a recalcitrant Congress in Philadelphia.[22]

Fearing what he called the "fatal tendency" of using the army as a political tool, Washington rejected Hamilton's February 13 advice and later warned him, "the Army ... is a dangerous instrument to play with." On the Ides of March, 1783, Washington made a dramatic appeal to a meeting of his officers at Newburgh. Moved by his words, they rejected a call circulated in camp by the Gates faction for an ultimatum to Congress. The officers were furloughed soon after the news (March 24, 1783) of the definitive peace with Britain. Hamilton knew full well that the actual resort to violence would have led to the army's ruin. But such was his passion (and pessimism) on the subject, he confessed to Washington, that "could force avail I should almost wish to see it employed. I have an indifferent opinion of the honesty of this country, and ill-forebodings as to its future system." In another letter around the same time, he told Washington, "Necessity alone can work a reform. But how [to] apply it and how [to] keep it within salutary bounds?"[23]

The shock of the near-mutiny at Newburgh did serve to persuade Congress to approve a bill providing the officers five years' full pay (in lieu of pensions), as well as an amendment for a new impost. But not only would the amendment have to be ratified by all the states, it also "contained such a jumble of compromises, [and] so many concessions to sectional jealousy and state sovereignty" that Hamilton (while knowing Congress would pass it) cast a symbolic dissenting vote. With the definitive peace at hand, necessity would have to wait.[24]

Necessity at Last

Necessity of the kind Hamilton had invoked to Washington began to rear its head later in the decade. By the mid-1780s, the Confederation found itself in the throes of a threefold crisis, threatening to compromise its republican character and destroy its fragile unity. The crisis arose from simultaneous developments within the states, in their relations with each other, and with the outside world. It was a situation similar in some ways to the one facing the European Union states in the 1990s and early twenty-first century, except that the prospects for the EU to preserve and strengthen itself looked more promising than those of the "United States." Nationalist reformers, though they disagreed on the shape and extent of change, sought to create a higher authority capable of providing external discipline and correcting abuses *within* the states, of averting conflicts *between* them, and of permitting the union to act effectively *as a whole* toward the world of the great powers. The vast majority of Americans, however, considered their state to be their "country." Though not content with the status quo, they opposed creating a new central government able to tax and to regulate commerce. Getting rid of such a government had been a basic objective of the war.

The context of the "internal" political crisis was a postwar economic depression. With independence, American exporters of food and other primary products no longer enjoyed privileged access to Britain and British colonial markets. The American merchant marine was excluded from the lucrative carrying trade to the West Indies and Canada. A shortage of specie aggravated the downturn. In these conditions, state legislatures dominated by small farmers and other debtor interests issued paper currencies, postponed taxes, and passed "stay laws" imposing moratoria on the collection of private debts. These measures, in turn, raised the spectre of a "tyranny of the majority" and a backlash by property owners against the very idea of popular government. Among Hamilton's earliest clients were British subjects and former Loyalists whose property rights were violated by punitive New York state laws like the Trespass Act of 1783. In the case of *Rutgers v. Waddington* (1784), he argued that the states were bound by the peace treaty between the United States and Britain, which had reciprocally cancelled the claims of U.S. and British citizens growing out of the war. In an early assertion of the power of "judicial review," Hamilton argued that the courts had the right to invalidate statutes like the Trespass Act.

Simultaneously, the confederation was subject to growing divisions between the states. A Massachusetts conservative lamented, "We look with indifference, often with hatred, fear and aversion to the other states."[25] Basically, there were three orders of intrastate and sectional conflict. Small states feared domination by their larger brethren – an issue that would nearly paralyze the Constitutional Convention – hence their insistence on one vote per state in Congress. States whose colonial charters had delimited their borders clashed with states with large claims on land west of the Appalachian Mountains. The "landless" states had insisted that western lands be put under Congress's jurisdiction, and one of them – Maryland – had held up ratification of the Articles until New York and Virginia ceded their vast claims to the confederation. Even as the Constitutional Convention met in Philadelphia in mid-1787, the Confederation Congress in New York addressed this issue by creating the Northwest Territory (north and west of the Ohio River), under congressional control. But without a strong central government able to secure navigation of the Mississippi, and to guarantee the entry of new states into the union on the basis of equality, future conflict looked inevitable. This might take the form of clashes among the existing states over western lands, between the United States and a breakaway western confederation (or confederations), or between the United States and various European powers over control of the west.

The most serious fault line was between the slave-holding and exclusively agricultural states of the south and the non-slave-holding and mercantile (as well as agricultural) states of the northeast. The two sections clashed over the basis on which to assess state requisitions to the confederation. New Englanders, assuming that land values in their section were higher than in the south, favored population as the basis. Southerners, with large numbers of slaves to be (partially) counted in the bargain, favored land values and initially managed to outvote New England. A more serious controversy came to a head in 1786. Though weak militarily, Spain claimed extensive territories in the Old Southwest (the lands south of the Ohio River between the Appalachian Mountains and the Mississippi) and encouraged its Indian allies there to prey on American pioneers. Through its control of both banks of the lower Mississippi, Spain could influence the destiny of the entire region. To market their furs, tobacco, wheat, hemp, lumber, and naval stores, American settlers needed the river and a port of deposit near New Orleans. In an attempt to enhance its leverage over the settlers, Spain declared the river closed to American shipping in 1784.

Secretary for Foreign Affairs John Jay of New York and a Spanish envoy, Don Diego de Gardoqui, attempted to settle the question. The debonair Gardoqui charmed Jay's beautiful wife, advanced five thousand dollars to a member of Congress, and presented a Spanish breeding donkey to George Washington. More interested in Spanish markets than in the Mississippi, a bloc of seven northern states (from Pennsylvania to Massachusetts) voted in Congress in 1786 to instruct Jay to "forbear" the U.S. right to navigate the river for twenty-five or thirty years, in return for partial access to Spanish ports. Southerners and western settlers were outraged by the vote. Accepting closure of the river would only facilitate Spanish plans to woo westerners away from the union in return for free use of the river. It would also lower land values in the southwest and slow the settlement and incorporation of an area which the southern states considered vital to their future weight in the confederation. Though the advice to Jay was later overturned, there was talk of secession south of the Mason–Dixon line.

Like Europeans today, Americans were – and would remain – divided and ambivalent on the fundamental question of whether the confederation should aspire to become a great power in the traditional meaning of the term. Still, there was broad agreement that the third dimension of the crisis – the confederation's inability to deal effectively with the outside world – must be urgently addressed. Not only did Spain threaten from the rear, but Britain (using the pretext of the U.S. failure to fulfill peace treaty pledges) continued to hold strategic posts south of the border between the United States and Canada. Lacking internal cohesion and a central government monopoly over commercial policy, the confederation was unable to bargain as a bloc to break down foreign barriers to American exports and shipping. This served, in turn, to prolong the economic plight of the states. And as the bankrupt states failed to deliver their requisitions, the central government found itself unable to pay its domestic or foreign creditors or even to supply a handful of soldiers on the western border. Meanwhile, the imminent entry of *new* states into the union, starting with Vermont and Kentucky, promised to make unanimous approval of additional powers for the central government practically impossible to obtain.[26]

In September 1786, Hamilton, his former fellow delegate to Congress, James Madison, and others attended a convention at Annapolis, Maryland, to discuss a uniform commercial policy for the confederation. Hamilton made the suggestion, adopted by the delegates, that a convention be called the following year to consider across-the-board reform. Around the same time, bands of overtaxed and debt-ridden Massachusetts farmers led by former Continental Army lieutenant Daniel Shays threatened to seize the armory at Springfield and perhaps join forces with insurgents from other states. Because Congress had neither soldiers nor money at its disposal, Massachusetts militiamen were called out to suppress "Shays's rebellion." A few months later, in early 1787, the New York Assembly dealt a death blow to the impost amendment. On this news Congress embraced the proposal of a constitutional convention. Necessity was at hand.[27]

Hamilton as Publius

Hamilton, in the end, did not play a prominent part in the secret proceedings at Philadelphia (May–September 1787). Since the New York delegation consisted of himself and a pair of chaperones opposed to more than tinkering with the Articles of Confederation, and since each state was allotted a single vote, he carried little weight. More importantly, his radical views and Machiavellian inclination to reject the "middle way" separated him from influential reformers like Madison and James Wilson of Pennsylvania.

Madison deplored the assaults on property rights at the state level and feared an antirepublican reaction. Just as a multiplicity of sects helped to guarantee religious freedom, he reasoned, the plurality of interest groups present in a geographically extensive republic would make it hard for tyrannical majorities to come together to oppress minorities. And though Virginia was the largest and most populous state, Madison feared that it would be vulnerable to attack, and therefore obliged to adopt liberty-threatening taxes and military forces, should the confederation split into hostile blocs. His initial proposal (the "Virginia Plan") called for a central government veto over state laws and a house and senate elected according to proportional representation. (At the convention, he fought the proposal for a senate in which the states had equal representation because he feared, in light of the Jay–Gardoqui vote, that it would become a tool for Northern domination.) But Madison favored a *compound* rather than a consolidated system in which the central government would be fully sovereign over the states only in a carefully enumerated set of areas, such as commercial policy. Madison, revealingly, had not supported the tactics or the objectives of Hamilton and the two Morris's in 1782–83.[28]

By contrast, and as he set out in his one major speech to the convention (on June 18, 1787, lasting more than five hours), Hamilton's ideal was a *consolidated* system in which the capacity of the states to rival the new central government would disappear. The central government would appoint the state governors and would have an absolute veto over state laws. Hamilton's was a republican system: Its executive and legislative branches were elected (the lower house directly by the people), and there was no suggestion of a hereditary aristocracy. But it contained strong British elements, including a senate, whose members served "during good behavior" (in effect, for life). Crowning the system was a "governor" endowed with an absolute veto and able to furnish energy, continuity, and direction, especially in foreign and military policy. Also serving for life (like Venice's *doge* and, after 1502, Florence's *gonfaloniere*), the chief magistrate would have the scope to display *virtù*, but no incentive to grab additional powers, or occasion to sell himself to intriguing foreigners. Hamilton, like Machiavelli, wanted to have his cake and eat it: he "proposed to take the best of both worlds – monarchism and republicanism – and to combine them into a single system of government."[29]

Hamilton, in short, was not a federalist and viewed the results of the convention with considerable skepticism. That the central government would have to be strengthened, he had little doubt. (In one of his "Machiavellian moments" he would call the Constitution "a frail and worthless fabric.")

But if the Constitution was not accepted by the states, he wrote, "it is probable the discussion of the question will beget such struggles animosities and heats in the community that this circumstance conspiring with the *real necessity* of an essential change in our present situation will produce civil war." In a feat of advocacy and statesmanship, he undertook to fight for the draft constitution as the best alternative during the close-run battle for ratification in New York.[30]

Writing in the New York press, Hamilton took the name "Publius Valerius" (shortened to "Publius"), the Roman leader who had helped to establish the republic after the revolt against the Tarquin kings in 509 B.C. Hamilton as Publius (John Jay and Madison wrote under the same name) sometimes disguised his real views. For example, he emphasized the checks and controls operating on the U.S. president compared with the British monarch. But the essays, which became known as the *The Federalist*, contain much vintage Hamilton. If "safety from external danger is the most powerful director of national conduct," this meant a strong executive. "Of all the cares or concerns of government, the direction of war most peculiarly demands those qualities which distinguish the exercise of power by a single hand." In contrast to the constitution's opponents (now branded "Antifederalists") who seemed to prefer government by committee, Hamilton believed that "the sense of responsibility is always strongest, in proportion as it is undivided." In arguing for a vigorous, unified executive he invoked, perhaps incautiously, the Roman example:

Every man the least conversant in Roman story [sic] knows how often that republic was obliged to take refuge in the absolute power of a single man, under the formidable title of dictator, as well against the intrigues of ambitious individuals, who aspired to the tyranny, and the seditions of whole classes of the community, whose conduct threatened the existence of all government, as against the invasions of external enemies, who menaced the conquest and destruction of Rome.[31]

For Hamilton, the federal government had to be "cloathed with all the powers requisite to the complete execution of its trust." Among the most important were the interrelated powers to tax and to borrow:

In the modern system of war, nations the most wealthy are obliged to have recourse to large loans. A country so little opulent as ours, must feel this necessity in a much stronger degree. But who would lend to a government that prefaced its overtures for borrowing, by an act which demonstrated that no reliance could be placed on the steadiness of its measure for paying?

Equally essential was the power to conduct a single tariff policy. This would enable the central government to monopolize the collection of import duties and maximize its leverage in commercial relations with Europe. Hamilton also called for a federal navy, to whose upkeep each part of the country would have something to contribute, and professional military forces. War, as some

Americans had discovered, was "a science to be acquired and perfected by diligence, by perseverance, by time, and by practice."[32]

Once the creation of a strong union had obviated the risk that the country would become the "foot ball" of Europe, the United States could capitalize on its physical situation in order to grow strong. In the previous century, the British had been forced to resolve grave internal problems. In the eighteenth century, after internal peace and unity (including union with Scotland) had been established, "An insular situation, and a powerful marine, guarding it [Britain] in a great measure against the possibility of foreign invasion, supercede[d] the necessity of a numerous army within the kingdom." If they secured their own internal unity, the United States could "enjoy an advantage similar to that of an insulated situation."[33]

But an "insulated situation" did not mean self-sufficiency or isolation – a state of affairs encouraging negative habits. It meant, literally, having the characteristics of an island. As American power increased, Hamilton said in "The Federalist No. 11":

A price would be set not only upon our friendship, but upon our neutrality.... [W]e may hope ere long to become the Arbiter of Europe in America; and to be able to incline the ballance [sic] of European competitions in this part of the world [in the West Indies, for example] as our interests may dictate.

For Hamilton, "our situation invites, and our interests prompt us, to aim at an ascendant in the system of American affairs. The world may politically, as well as geographically, be divided into four parts, each having a distinct set of interests." He concluded, "Let Americans disdain to be the instruments of European greatness!" Let us create "one great American system, superior to the controul [sic] of all trans-atlantic force or influence, and able to dictate the terms of the connection between the old and the new world!"[34]

The thrust of the message was as follows: let us prove that we will not be bested in the game of power politics. Like Britain in its relations with the continent, America would eventually be able to operate from a secure base and to dictate to others, rather than the reverse. In speaking of the four parts of the world, Hamilton did not mean that America would be unaffected by developments in Europe or vice versa. On the contrary, his analysis followed, consciously or not, the lines of a well-known 1780 pamphlet by the former royal governor of Massachusetts, Thomas Pownall. For Pownall, "North America is become a new primary planet in the system of the world, which while it takes its own course, in its own orbit, must have effect on the orbit of every other planet, and shift the common center of gravity of the whole system of the European world." America, Pownall had predicted, would "become the Arbitress of the commercial [world] and perhaps the Mediatrix of peace, and of the political business of the world."[35]

Hamilton's contributions to *The Federalist* leave the impression that he saw Europe and America growing not less but more entangled over time.

Commerce would only increase, and Hamilton was sensitive to technological improvements: "Though a wide ocean separates the United States from Europe; yet there are various considerations that warn us against an excess of confidence or security . . . The improvements in the art of navigation have, as to the facility of communication, rendered distant nations in a great measure neighbors." One of Hamilton's chief themes was the possibility of a conflict involving the United States during its period of consolidation. The creation of a strong union obviated internecine conflict, but not foreign war.[36]

His most revealing and prescient statement on future relations with Europe can be found in "The Federalist No. 34." Hamilton refuted those who wanted to limit the capacity of the federal government to tax, based on misleading estimates of future danger:

Observations confined to the mere prospects of internal attacks, can deserve no weight, though even these will admit of no satisfactory calculation: But if we mean to be a commercial people, it must form a part of our policy, to be able one day to defend that commerce. The support of a navy, and of naval wars must baffle all the efforts of political arithmetic admitting that we ought to try the novel and absurd experiment in politics, of tying up the hands of Government from offensive war, founded upon reasons of state. Yet, certainly we ought not to disable it from guarding the community against the enmity or ambition of other Nations.

In other words, even if the United States were rash enough to rule out taking the initiative in war, it would still have its hands full with the problems of defense.

"The Federalist No. 34" continued:

A cloud has been for sometime hanging over the European world. If it should break forth into a storm, who can insure us, that in its progress, a part of its fury would not be spent on us? . . . Let us recollect, that peace or war, will not always be left to our option; and that however moderate or unambitious we may be, we cannot count upon the moderation, or hope to extinguish the ambitions of others.[37]

What was true of a moderate, unambitious America, moreover, was doubly true of the America Hamilton envisioned: a great power in the traditional meaning of the term. Hamilton wrote these words in January 1788. The cloud would burst five years later. In early 1793, after a hiatus of ten years, France and Britain were once again at war.

PART II

BATTLE LINES ARE DRAWN

3

At Washington's Side Again, 1789

Introduction

Hundreds of years before eighteenth-century Britain, medieval Italian communes like Venice and Florence had experimented with the system of a funded debt, whereby receipts from indirect taxes were dedicated to the repayment of loans received (or forced) from the citizenry.[1] Machiavelli's pungent observations to the effect that money was not "the nerve of war," and that "gold is not sufficient to find good soldiers, but good soldiers are more than sufficient to find gold," have lent themselves to the view that he was indifferent to questions of finance. In reality, such statements were part of his polemic against reliance on mercenary forces. One of his most incisive pieces of writing as a young Second Chancery official was *"Parole da dirle sopra la provisione del danaio"* ("Words to pronounce on the provision of money"), a speech intended for delivery by the *gonfaloniere* in April 1503.

The previous year Florence had been forced to deal with the revolt in the Valdichiana and found itself practically defenseless in the face of Cesare Borgia's depredations. The emergency underlined the urgent need to strengthen the republic's institutions – for fear of tyranny, the chief magistrate and members of the *signoria* were changed every two months. In September 1502, after much hand-wringing and debate, it was decided to create a *gonfaloniere a vita* (for life). Soderini, elected to the office, wrote Machiavelli that Florence's financial situation was in a very disordered state. In February–March 1503, he presented seven proposals for the raising of new taxes. All were rejected, prompting him to turn to Machiavelli for a persuasive argument.

Machiavelli did not enter into the technical details of how to design the city's taxes. Instead he made a brutal appeal to the Florentines to face the link between raising the money to pay for war and survival: "without force cities don't maintain themselves but come to their end. The end is either desolation or servitude; this year you've come close to both." As for Florence's immediate Tuscan neighborhood: "You find yourself amidst two or three cities who desire your death more than their own lives." It was better to spend money to fight the Venetians, he argued, than to pay them off with a large sum that would then be used to injure Florence. And to those who thought they could rely on the French ally for protection, he warned that there was never a wise lord or republic who wanted to keep the state "at the discretion of others or, keeping it so, thought it was secure." Only by arming and relying mainly on itself could Florence command the respect and consideration of both enemies and allies.[2]

* * *

On September 13, 1789, Hamilton called at the 39–41 Broadway house of Eleanor François Elie, Comte de Moustier, France's minister plenipotentiary to the United States since late 1787. The count was known for his bizarre manners (at Hamilton's house he had once refused a meal and called on his own chef to cook one on the spot) and believed to be the lover of his live-in sister-in-law, Madame de Bréhan. Thanks to quiet diplomacy on both sides of the Atlantic, the notorious couple was soon to depart for home. Perhaps a smile crossed Hamilton's lips as he approached the count's doorstep. But he had weightier matters on his mind.

The new federal Congress had been in session in New York for six months, meeting at Federal Hall in lower Manhattan, near Hamilton's house at 57 Wall Street and the Treasury office on Broadway. After his unanimous election as president, Washington had journeyed north in triumph from his Mount Vernon home to take the oath of office at the end of April. He had appointed Hamilton secretary of the treasury near the end of the congressional session, on September 11, 1789.

The main business of Congress had been to organize the executive departments of the federal government and secure the revenues necessary to sustain it. Signs of a future political tempest had appeared in early summer, when Madison, now a member of the House of Representatives from Virginia, had tried to impose higher tonnage duties on British merchantmen entering U.S. ports than on those of countries with whom the United States had commercial treaties. The United States and France had been joined by a commercial treaty and political alliance since 1778. Britain had rejected U.S. terms for a treaty, including the key demand that American ships share in the carrying trade with the British West Indies and Canada, as they had before the war.[3]

As Hamilton knew when he met de Moustier, the United States had borrowed over $10,000,000 in Europe to finance the war, most of it in Paris and Amsterdam. This included a loan of $1,089,000 (6,000,000 *livres*) from the French royal treasury, contracted in February 1783. Hamilton had not yet prepared his "Report on the Public Credit" (presented to Congress on January 9, 1790), but he had some notion of the figures it would contain:

$1,651,127 in "arrearages of interest" on the European loans, and nearly $1,400,000 on payments of principal. The annual cost of servicing the European debt was over $1,000,000, a figure equal to the total revenues derived from taxing foreign imports, as provided for by Congress's Tariff Act of July 4, 1789.[4]

The foreign debt was only the tip of the iceberg. About forty-one million dollars in several kinds of Continental obligations circulated in 1789. Used to pay soldiers and suppliers of the Continental Army, the certificates had collapsed in value during the 1780s, and the bulk had been sold by their original holders to speculators at a fraction of face value. The individual states had issued twenty-five million dollars in paper debt during and after the war. There was also the tangled question of intergovernmental debts and credits. State governments had contributed varying amounts, known as "common charges," to the war effort on the presumption that the total (over one hundred million dollars) would eventually be apportioned on the basis of a fair standard of capacity to pay, such as state land values or population. States that had contributed more than their fair share awaited compensation, whereas those in the opposite situation were expected to pay up.[5]

In an Independence Day, 1789, eulogy for General Nathanael Greene, Hamilton had spoken of the coming task as "rearing the superstructure of American greatness." His indispensable contribution lay in reforming the public finances of the United States. Through "funding," or refinancing, the old Continental paper debt at its original value, Hamilton aimed to transform the national debt into a "national blessing." Funding rewarded the mercantile and financial elite in whose hands the debt was concentrated by 1789. It also gave them a stake in the survival of the new federal government while enlarging the economy's monetary base (and hence the capacity for productive investment) in the form of privately held federal debt. At the same time, through federal government "assumption" of (or commitment to pay off) the state debts, which he astutely linked to the settlement of the Revolutionary War accounts (the "common charges"), Hamilton tied state creditors to the federal cause and further widened the national credit base. By tying specific revenues to the payment of interest on this consolidated debt, he was able to put the credit of the federal government on a solid foundation and to reduce immediate servicing costs from six to around four percent.[6]

All this lay in the future, even if the system's outline was already in his mind, when Hamilton met with the French minister on September 13, 1789. Their main topic of conversation was the U.S. debt to France. The visit's timing, a Sunday afternoon forty-eight hours after his appointment, suggests that relations with France ranked high on Hamilton's list of priorities. He told de Moustier that the arrears owed France would be paid by borrowing additional money in The Netherlands. (This was not a new idea. A Dutch loan arranged by John Adams and Thomas Jefferson had allowed the

United States to avoid default on its earlier French loan. Betting on the new government's prospects, the "avaricious & indefatigable" firm of Wilhem and Jan Willink, and Nicholaas and Jacob Van Staphorst, and Nicholas Hubbard would shortly launch a loan of three million florins – one million two hundred thousand dollars – for the United States without official authorization from New York.) Indeed, after asking Lafayette's help in arranging a temporary suspension of principal payments, Hamilton worked through the U.S. chargé d'affaires and Treasury agent in Paris, William Short, over the next several years to try to pay off the debt to France.

De Moustier, revealingly, saw no particular advantage to France in a quick liquidation of the debt. His government did not favor a strong American union, no longer dependent on France and able to oppose French efforts to reestablish a North American empire. Anticipating French policy in the 1790s, de Moustier had written a dispatch on the benefits of reacquiring New Orleans and the vast Louisiana territory west of the Mississippi (ceded by France to Spain in 1763). In addition to the wealth of Louisiana, France's control of a vital artery like the Mississippi would give it considerable political leverage over the United States. In light of these considerations, de Moustier sized up the new treasury secretary as a problem: "He was born English and I do not believe very well disposed toward France; he would ask nothing better than to disengage entirely this Republic and place it in more intimate relations with the Estates General of the Netherlands, present Allies of England." Neither Madison nor Thomas Jefferson, the American minister to France (nominated secretary of state on September 25, 1789), had come to this conclusion at the time.[7]

Few would question Hamilton's "Englishness" if this means that he favored British constitutional and financial methods. Most agree that the Hamiltonian system, including a "sinking fund" for retiring the public debt and a national bank (he launched the Bank of the United States in December 1791), was based on British precedents. Hamilton called British commercial and manufacturing success "a wonderful spectacle" to behold. William Pitt the younger, a mere twenty-four when he became chancellor of the Exchequer and first lord of the Treasury in December 1783 and inheriting a national debt that had nearly doubled during the war, had used devices like the sinking fund to restore national strength. A pair of historians have suggested: "It may well be that Pitt's example was so pervasive an influence [on Hamilton] that it operated . . . as the model of a career."[8] Hamilton also desired harmonious trade relations with Britain, and staunchly opposed Madison's tonnage bill. The reasoning was simple: His funding system depended on a steady flow of federal revenues; the most reliable source was the duty on imported goods, of which ninety percent were British. Another salient fact was that British investors held a significant share of the consolidated debt (and later of Bank of the United States stock). A commercial war of the kind Madison's bill would unleash, or worse, a real war, would devastate Hamilton's financial handiwork and the credit of the federal government.

Elkins and McKitrick sketch out Hamilton's broader vision of "an immensely expanded and far-flung Anglo-American economy" as American settlers poured west. An essential precondition was the end of hostilities with the Indians in the Northwest Territory. Another was British withdrawal from the seven strategically positioned forts and trading posts on U.S. territory, held in violation of Article 2 of the Peace Treaty. (They were located at Dutchman's Point and Pointe au Fer at the north end of Lake Champlain; Oswegatchie on the St. Lawrence River; Oswego on Lake Ontario; Niagara, between Lakes Ontario and Erie; Detroit, between Lakes Erie and Huron; and Michilimackinac, controlling the passages connecting Lakes Huron, Michigan, and Superior.) Hamilton imagined that

The British, perceiving a vast new market to be supplied by way of the St. Lawrence and the Great Lakes, and the prospects for cheap food for the West Indies shipped down the Mississippi and across the Gulf, would find it entirely in their interest to assist us in getting the Mississippi opened, and to help protect our trade once it had been established there.... It was wholly to their advantage to foster American trade, American growth, and even American territorial expansion: it all added up to ever-greater markets for British goods.

It was "[a] dazzling vision" though, as Elkins and McKitrick describe it, of an essentially economic kind.[9]

In assessing Hamilton's program, it is also useful to remember that the West Indian emigrant was now established socially and politically in New York. As treasury secretary he became spokesman for the interests that made up the nascent Federalist party, and his success depended on their support. In New York, this meant most of the large Hudson Valley land owners (like his father-in-law Schuyler, elected a U.S. senator in 1789) and the overlapping bloc of bond holders who stood to gain from funding. The creditor bloc was composed of old New York City money like Nicholas Low and Issac Roosevelt (FDR's ancestor), Hamilton's treasury assistant and fellow West Indian William Duer, and nouveau riche Irishmen like William Constable, Alexander Macomb, and William Edgar, who had made a killing as army contractors and speculators. Madison's poet-editor friend Philip Freneau was referring to the latter element when he wrote:

On coaches now, gay coats of arms are wore
By *some* who hardly wore a coat before...

Another essential component of the Federalist alliance were the former Loyalists. Ex-Loyalists joined other conservatives in supporting ratification of the U.S. Constitution because they wanted a strong central government able to defend their civil and property rights against a vindictive state legislature. As Hamilton's friend Robert Troup later put it, "Soon after we regained possession of New York, we permitted the Tories to enlist under our banners; and they have since manfully fought by our side in every important battle."[10]

Last but not least came the New York merchant and ship-owning community, including a specific "British interest": Anglo-American firms, agents of British merchants, and American exporters dependent on British markets and on the unmatchable credit terms available from British banks. Britain and its empire were far and away America's most important market in 1789 and destined to grow in importance in the 1790s. Even without a commercial treaty, the British (strictly in their own interests) granted preferential treatment to imported American naval stores, furs, and tobacco. Though banned from the carrying trade with Canada and the West Indies, the United States continued to export huge amounts of flour, grain, and fish there in British bottoms, and American captains carried on a flourishing illegal trade with the connivance of local British authorities. American ships calling at British home ports paid the same tonnage duties as British ships. Fearing the end of these privileges, New York merchants, together with Boston, Philadelphia, Baltimore, and Charleston colleagues, vigorously opposed Madison when he tried to open economic hostilities with Britain in 1789.[11]

Hamilton's position on Britain was thus based on a series of practical considerations: the imperative of financial stability and hence of a steady flow of British imports, the reliance of American merchants on British credit and markets, and the prospect of deepening Anglo-American interdependence in the West. But he also thought in terms of an entente that harkened back to the federative schemes advanced as alternatives to complete independence before 1776.[12] Hamilton's policy, as it unfolded after 1789, had at least three political ends in mind. First, he wished to resolve the thorny disputes connected with nonfulfillment by both sides of the peace treaty and to prevent a disastrous war. Second, he looked favorably on joint action with the British to end Spanish control over the Floridas and New Orleans. Third, Hamilton would eventually favor a stance helpful to Britain in the war against France and to the effort to preserve the European balance of power. Although Hamilton was always on guard against British highhandedness and would grow hypersensitive to the charge of Anglophilia, there was a purely personal factor driving these policies: the search for reconciliation and respect.

A shrewd observer like the Comte de Moustier saw this. Since many Americans had been "born English," he was suggesting that in Hamilton's case, "Englishness" was an animating factor. De Moustier's intuition also told him that, although Hamilton was not in charge of foreign policy, he would play a role in that domain. The Frenchman was wrong on some of the details: the United States did not try to transfer its indebtedness from Paris to Amsterdam. With the value of French revolutionary assignats (paper certificates) depreciating against the Dutch florin, Hamilton later preferred to pay France by borrowing in The Netherlands rather than trying to have the entire debt converted into florins. (To keep the Dutch honest, the United States also borrowed money in Antwerp.) But on an essential point, de Moustier's report to the foreign ministry was accurate. Hamilton aimed to steer the United States out of France's orbit and toward a closer connection with the former parent state.[13]

Opening a Back Channel

Another lower Manhattan meeting, occurring not long after the one just discussed, bore out the de Moustier thesis. In October 1789, Hamilton spoke for the first time with George Beckwith, a British army major and aide to Lord Dorchester, the governor general of British North America. The main purpose of Beckwith's trip to New York was to deliver Home Secretary William Grenville's warning that London would terminate preferential treatment of U.S. shipping in British home ports if a discriminatory bill such as Madison's were to become law. Beckwith made the point to Philip Schuyler, among others. When Schuyler asked if he could report their exchange to his son-in-law, the major replied "by all means." Beckwith must have been delighted when "Colonel Hamilton," as he was known, a former soldier about his own age and a top administration official, arranged a tête-à-tête.[14]

Hamilton told the Briton that it was "safe for any Nation to Enter into Treaties with us, Either Commercial or Political, which has not hitherto been the Case; I have always preferred a connexion with you, to that of any other Country, *We think in English*, and have a similarity of prejudices, and of predilections." He wanted the British to see the advantages of a close relationship. "We wish to form a Commercial treaty with you to Every Extent, to which you may think it for Your interest to go." Hamilton did not think the plan "upon a very broad scale" once favored by the Marquis of Landsdowne was "now Attainable." Still, "we are, and shall be, great Consumers" of British goods. A treaty allowing access for U.S. ships of limited size to the West Indies was much preferable to the trade war that current British policy might provoke (a reference to Madison's bill) and that had been encouraged by France in the recent congressional session.[15]

Landsdowne, then the Earl of Shelburne, had been head of the ministry that had negotiated the preliminary peace in 1782. His American Intercourse Bill, supported by West Indian planters heavily reliant on North American provisions, would have allowed American ships to carry goods to and from the islands as they had before the war. By exporting freely to the West Indies, Shelburne reasoned, the Americans would earn the money to buy more English manufactures. But Shelburne's resignation in early 1783 had doomed the bill. The order-in-council of July 2, 1783 (ratified by the government's Committee for Trade on May 31, 1784), reaffirmed the traditional policy of excluding foreign shipping from the colonies. John Adams's mission to London in the mid-1780s, aiming to secure access to the West Indies, had run into a brick wall. Thomas Jefferson, who briefly joined Adams in London in 1786, had concluded, "That nation hates us, the ministers hate us, and their king more than any other man." For their part, the British had concluded that not only was the traditional policy in their best interest, but that it was impossible to conclude a treaty as long as the U.S. government was unable to enforce its obligations on the states.[16]

In his conversation with Beckwith, Hamilton also raised the crucial question of the navigation of the Mississippi. America's western territories "*must have that outlet, without it they will be lost to us.*" He coupled this with the point that the United States had no interest in expanding northward: "our Country is Already sufficiently large, more so perhaps than prudence might wish." He appealed to Britain's political as well as economic interests. By making limited concessions, the British would avoid an outcome favorable to Paris. If the United States were "under the necessity" of a French alliance, "such a connexion...may become important to your West India possessions. On the other hand, connected with you, by strong ties of Commercial, perhaps of political, friendships, our naval Exertions, in future wars, may in your scale be greatly important; And decisive." Because, according to the 1778 Treaty of Alliance (Articles 11 and 12), the United States was pledged to guarantee French possessions in the West Indies in case of war, Hamilton was suggesting a possible reversal of alliances. He added: "These are my opinions, they are the sentiments, which I have long Entertained, on which I have acted, and I think them suited to the future welfare of both countries." Although admitting that he was not "sufficiently Authorized to say so," Hamilton volunteered that a diplomatic representative would soon be on his way to London. Beckwith pointed out that a bias on the part of such a person toward some other power "might Altogether frustrate the objects of his mission." Hamilton replied that if the emissary Washington had in mind had any bias, "it is decidedly to You." This was a reference to Gouverneur Morris, living in Paris at the time.[17]

Overall, the conversation suggested a sense of urgency. Hamilton told Beckwith that he had been "anxious" to talk to him. He made it clear that there was an opportunity to negotiate a treaty, but "If the present favourable occasion shall pass away," the forces advocating higher duties on British shipping had in mind a "*much stronger measure.*" Beckwith took this to mean a ban on British ships carrying goods from U.S. ports to the West Indies or Canada.[18] Along with the insight it provides into Hamilton's views, the meeting illustrates his modus operandi as a member of the cabinet. Hamilton told Beckwith that his sentiments were those of "the most Enlightened men in this country, they are those of General Washington, I can Confidently assure You."[19] But there is no evidence that Washington had authorized Hamilton to speak to Beckwith or that he ever knew that the meeting had taken place.

Hamilton and His Chief

In one sense it was perfectly natural for Hamilton to presume to speak for the president. He had acquired the habit of putting words into Washington's mouth during the three and a half years when he wore the green sash of an aide-de-camp. Hamilton had the quicker, sharper mind, and Washington had grown dependent on his drafting and administrative skills. The younger man had good reason to take Washington's confidence in him for granted at the time of his conversation with Beckwith. The president had conspicuously confirmed it by appointing him to the cabinet several weeks before. Both men were strong nationalists and centralizers, devoted to a policy of peace through strength for the infant United States, and strength through peace. Washington shared Hamilton's reservations about the French, observing of them that "it is a maxim founded on the universal experience of mankind, that no nation is to be trusted farther than it is bound by its interest."[20]

The Washington–Hamilton personal relationship defies easy deciphering. It is hard not to be struck by its stiffness, even for an age of fussy, punctilious manners like the late eighteenth century. (Among close friends letters never began with first names and rarely surnames but rather with "My Dear Sir." During the war his officers addressed Washington as "Your Excellency.") In February 1781, Hamilton had abruptly quit Washington's staff after a seemingly banal incident at headquarters in New Windsor, New York, during which Washington had rebuked him for (allegedly) being late to respond to a summons. One view is that the incident was the logical consequence of the chemistry that developed after Hamilton joined Washington's staff in 1777: "Despite what has been written ten thousand times, there can be no doubt that Hamilton did not now become – he was never to become – a particular object of Washington's affections." In other words, although the younger man's services were invaluable to him, Washington remained cold, demanding, and at least outwardly unappreciative. Hamilton may have temporarily found a "new father" and a "new family" but eventually he rebelled.[21]

Hamilton's own account (Washington, characteristically, did not leave one) suggests a rather different dynamic: the run-in may have occurred because Washington was piqued by Hamilton's failure to pay attention to him more generally. According to Hamilton

The truth is our own dispositions are the opposites of each other & the pride of my temper would not suffer me to profess what I did not feel. Indeed when advances of this kind have been made to me on his [Washington's] part, they were received in a manner that showed at least I had no inclination to court them, and that I wished to stand rather upon a footing of military confidence rather than of private attachment.[22]

Washington was a fundamentally shy character. He stood on ceremony and cultivated a dignified aloofness from his subordinates. Standing nearly six feet, four inches tall, or superbly seated on horseback, he literally towered over them. But he may well have made the sporadic "advances" of

friendship that Hamilton referred to. Initially, Hamilton may have recip-
rocated, though at a certain point have begun to hold the older man at a
distance. Shortly after joining his staff, Hamilton praised Washington as a
"Cautious and enterprising General." After the battle of Monmouth (June
1778), where Washington had halted the flight of the army, Hamilton wrote,
"I never saw the General to so much advantage. His coolness and firmness
were admirable." Living with him day in/day out in a series of cramped
headquarters, however, Hamilton had to cope with Washington's irritating
slowness in making decisions and his volcanic temper. The vivacious, brilliant younger man, one can practically infer from his words, came to see
Washington as a tyrant and a bore.[23]

The context of the early 1781 incident sheds further light on Hamilton's
behavior. Several months earlier, Washington had rejected the request of
Hamilton and fellow officers that the condemned spy Major John André,
adjutant-general of Sir Henry Clinton, be shot by a firing squad rather than
suffer the ignominy of hanging. Hamilton had been much taken, in his words,
by the Englishman's "peculiar elegance of mind and manners." Hamilton
was also tired, frustrated, and desperate to escape a deadening routine for
combat duty. On at least two occasions, Washington had turned down his
requests to be able to join a fighting unit. It has oddly escaped biographers,
moreover, that the famous incident occurred shortly after his wedding and
return to headquarters with Elizabeth. In his own eyes, at least, Hamilton
was now a man and no longer dependent on Washington's patronage. As
for his fatigue, he hinted to a brother officer that he was as ardent in his
"matrimonial occupations" as in everything else he did. (The couple's first
child, Philip, was born in January 1782.)[24]

Be that as it may, the rigid self-control exercised on both sides of the
Washington–Hamilton relationship prompts one to look for a repressed, hid-
den dimension. James Thomas Flexner wrote (in a different context), "Without accusing anyone of homosexuality it must be said – how ridiculous to
deny that normal males are physically attracted or repelled by other males! –
that Washington exerted an almost hypnotic charm particularly on men."
But this looks like a case where Washington, though hesitant and awkward
in showing it, was smitten by someone else's verve and charm. It seems likely
that he kept Hamilton chained to a desk not only to exploit his talents, but
because of a paternal concern that the headstrong, somehow fragile, young
man might be killed. (After the run-in, he tried to persuade Hamilton to stay,
though he eventually relented and granted his request to leave.) For his part,
perhaps Hamilton simply did not feel Washington's magnetism. Or perhaps
he felt it but was determined to control his feelings and instinctively drew
back.[25]

What is clear is that Hamilton retained a deep, lifelong sense of loyalty
to Washington and a desire to serve – one is tempted to say "to please" –
the older man. Those sentiments went hand in hand with his awareness of

Washington's unique stature and value to the national cause. He wrote his father-in-law just after his resignation,

The General is a very honest man. His competitors [e.g., Horatio Gates] have slender abilities and less integrity. His popularity has often been essential to the safety of America, and is still of great importance to it. These considerations have influenced my past conduct respecting him, and will influence my future. I think it is necessary he should be supported.

Hamilton never deviated from this view. As adviser and amanuensis, he would demonstrate extraordinary energy and skill in helping Washington to play the role of indispensable symbol and rallying point. In effect, he helped to put into practice Machiavelli's maxim that to retain popularity and prestige the prince must take care to say nothing not full of piety, faith, integrity, humanity, and religion.[26]

Machiavelli's own influence had ultimately depended on the friendship and patronage of Soderini and ended abruptly with the latter's fall. The ultimate reason for Hamilton's impulsive resignation in 1781 was probably that he chaffed at a similar kind of dependency. Neither then nor later did he want to be treated, or to be seen, as Washington's fair-haired boy. But the "break" did not really change things in this respect. If, as seems reasonable to suggest, Hamilton was a kind of surrogate son for Washington, the latter was Hamilton's substitute father, at least in the political sense of the term. Remarkably, and unlike scores of lesser courtiers, Hamilton never visited Washington at Mount Vernon. But notwithstanding the carefully maintained distance, the former aide-de-camp was to remain reliant on the protection – and the affection – of his general for as long as the latter was alive.[27]

A Mission to London

If Hamilton occupied a special place in the cabinet, he by no means enjoyed a monopoly of influence. Washington had sometimes rejected his advice (during the Newburgh episode, for example), and Hamilton knew that the president's view of Britain did not exactly coincide with his own. At heart, Washington did want good relations with London and was particularly concerned about the occupation of the forts. But he had an understandable, highly personal, touchiness on the subject of the British, dating from the Seven Year's War, when the British Army had thwarted his consuming ambition to be commissioned as a regular officer. Hamilton also knew that as president, Washington would want to cultivate a reputation for sage and high-minded impartiality and that by habit and temperament he would seek advice from a variety of points of view. The nomination of Jefferson as secretary of state showed this, if any proof were required. In short, Hamilton was engaged in a contest in which a degree of cunning would be essential. Thus he did not scruple about maintaining a back channel to the British government. Through it Hamilton hoped to provide each side with *his* interpretation of the other's intentions, to keep relations moving in what he believed to be the right direction and on an even keel. When Beckwith asked permission to pass his views on to Quebec, Hamilton replied, "Yes, And by Lord Dorchester to Your Ministry [in London] . . . but I should not chuse [sic] to have this go any further in America."[28]

Hamilton had at least one concrete reason to be confident of his ability to persuade the president: the Morris mission to London. Madison had advised Washington to delay it until Jefferson, en route from France, could have his say. According to Washington's diary, Madison and John Jay thought Morris "a man of superior talents," but that "his imagination sometimes runs ahead of his judgment – that his Manners before he is known – and where known are oftentimes disgusting – and from that, and immoral & loose expressions had created opinions of himself that were not favourable to him and which he did not merit." This kind of scuttlebutt about Morris probably amused Washington because the two were longtime friends. During the recess of the Constitutional Convention in mid-1787, they had gone fishing together at Valley Forge. When the president asked Hamilton's opinion, the treasury secretary called Morris "well qualified." Washington agreed.

On October 13, 1789, the president sent Morris a letter of credence and instructions to ascertain British willingness to fulfill the peace treaty and conclude a treaty of commerce. He also entrusted him with the delicate task of selecting and shipping mirrored serving trays and wine coolers for the presidential table. Hamilton knew, in other words, when he told Beckwith that he was sure of the president's mind, that Washington had followed his advice on two points: to proceed with the mission to London *without* waiting for Jefferson and to entrust it to their redoubtable New York friend.[29]

4

Hamilton versus the Virginians, 1789–1791

Introduction

Major George Beckwith was a well-connected and seasoned observer of American politics. He had been an intelligence officer under Lord Dorchester (then Sir Guy Carleton) in New York toward the end of the war and had visited the city in 1787 and 1788. During their October 1789 meeting, he nonetheless admitted his puzzlement to Hamilton on one point. He had been "much surprized [sic] to find among those Gentlemen so decidedly hostile" to Britain, "a person, from whose Character for good sense, and other qualifications, [he] should have been led to Expect a very different conduct." Hamilton immediately understood and admitted that he too had been "rather surprised." Said Hamilton, "The truth is, that although this gentleman is a clever man, he is very little Acquainted with the world. That he is Uncorrupted And incorruptible I have not a doubt; he has the same End in view that I have, And so have those gentlemen, who Act with him, but their mode of attaining it is very different." A year later Hamilton offered a different analysis: "You know we have two parties with us; there are gentlemen, who think we ought to be connected with France in the most intimate terms...there are others who are at least as numerous, and influential, who decidedly prefer an English connexion." By 1790–91, Hamilton was no longer in a position to say that he and the gentleman had "the same End in view."[1]

Hamilton and Madison

The gentleman was James Madison. Hamilton was unprepared for the depth, thoroughness, and implacability of Madison's opposition to his policies and found it difficult to explain. If by "very little acquainted with the world," he was suggesting that Madison had been indelibly marked by his Virginia background, Hamilton had put his finger on an essential factor. Madison was born in 1751 at Montpelier, a plantation near the Rapidan River in the Virginia piedmont. His father, Colonel James Madison, was the largest landowner in Orange County. Diminutive and reserved, Madison had a mind whose powers matched Hamilton's, and he was equally competitive and strong-willed. Though an Anglican, Madison had studied at the Presbyterian College of New Jersey (Princeton), where a republican spirit dominated in the 1760s and 1770s. Early in the war he attended the provincial constitutional convention and served on the Virginia Council of State. It was there that he became the lieutenant and friend of Governor Thomas Jefferson. Madison's senior by eight years, Jefferson was also the son of a militia colonel and large landowner in the piedmont region. Madison had fully subscribed to the radical Whig view according to which a vicious ministry, and with George III's arrival on the scene, a malevolent monarch, had been determined to destroy English liberties. For a Virginian of his social class, moreover, the province's position in the imperial economy had been an inescapable fact of life and source of rancor. British (mainly Scottish) middlemen had monopolized the purchase of Virginia tobacco and resold it at a handsome profit. When prices fell, the Virginia planters ran up large debts to merchants in London and Glasgow. The often extravagant lifestyles of the same planters meant that debts were frequently passed from father to son or, as in Jefferson's case, from father-in-law to son-in-law. In the 1770s Virginia owed more money than any other colony to British creditors. It was only natural that British "exploitation," as well as – or instead of – Virginia's propensity to live beyond its means, should take the blame. In 1774–75, Jefferson and the Virginia delegation to the Continental Congress meeting in Philadelphia had quickly allied themselves with the Massachusetts radicals John and Samuel Adams in support of total independence.[2]

To add insult to injury, the British had invaded Virginia late in the war. Marauding soldiers had destroyed crops and livestock, including Jefferson's own, torched the state capital at Richmond, and carried off hundreds of slaves to be set free. Virginia's Anglophobia, and view of itself as the innocent victim, deepened. After the war, it was only natural for Virginians to use the loss of the slaves as an excuse not to pay their prewar British debts, totaling £2.3 million in 1790. What made Virginia distinctive, however, was that although it had suffered much, it had contributed relatively little in blood and treasure to the national cause, or even to its own defense. Virginians like Henry "Light Horse Harry" Lee (the father of Robert E. Lee), and John Marshall (the future chief justice), not to mention Washington, served with distinction in the Continental Army and became leading Federalists. But the efforts of Governor Jefferson to organize resistance at home had been notably ineffectual, provoking calls for an investigation into his conduct.

A discerning European visitor, seeking to explain the Anglophilia of Federalists like Hamilton in the mid-1790s, observed that "resentments do not subsist when you have won. Satisfied pride reserves no desire for revenge."

Whether or not Talleyrand realized it, the same psychological principle applied in reverse to Virginia. There people did *not* have such a clear-cut sense of having won. The struggle for independence from the economic coils of the Mother Country continued after 1783. Nor could one really say that Virginia's pride had been satisfied or its honor vindicated by its wartime performance. Hence the chip on the shoulder that Virginians carried vis-à-vis the British – let us call it the "Virginia syndrome" – and their recurrent urge to strike another blow.[3]

Although the two kept up a steady correspondence, Jefferson's influence on Madison waxed and waned depending on their physical proximity. After spending the war in Virginia, and a brief postwar stint in Congress, Jefferson left the United States to join the commission charged with negotiating commercial treaties in Europe. In 1785, he succeeded Benjamin Franklin as U.S. minister to France. Madison was a delegate to Congress between early 1780 and late 1783. He distinguished himself for his energy and political acumen and met Hamilton when the New Yorker took his seat in 1782. For most of the decade, their political differences were overshadowed by a shared conviction that the confederation, rent by sectional conflicts and at the mercy of populist state politicians, must be replaced by a strong central government and nationally minded leadership. Their collaboration culminated in the writing of *The Federalist* in New York in late 1787–early 1788.

Once the new government had been established it was only natural, even if something of a surprise to Hamilton, that Madison's Virginia Anglophobia should reemerge. For Madison, "There was a kind of self-evidence in the assumption that freeing America's commercial life from the arbitrary pleasure of Great Britain had been one of the objects of the Revolution and that keeping it so should be the constant care of the new federal government." Indeed, one of the basic purposes of creating that government, in Madison's mind, had been to be able to attack mercantilist restrictions on American exports and shipping. Nor did he fear confrontation: on offering his anti-British commercial bill in 1789, he boldly stated, "Her [Britain's] interests can be wounded almost mortally, while ours are invulnerable." British manufacturers, shippers, and West Indian importers relied on the United States and were highly susceptible to retaliation. If the British did not give in to U.S. pressure, *they* would pay the price.[4]

It was less predictable, and understandably dismaying to Hamilton, that someone who had previously favored the assumption of state debts and opposed discrimination in favor of the original bond holders when funding the continental debt should reverse his stand and fight the treasury secretary tooth and nail on both questions. It was also less predictable that the author of "The Federalist No. 44," who had set out the doctrine of "implied powers," would seemingly eat his words and argue for a strict interpretation of the Constitution in opposing Hamilton's national bank. It was deeply disturbing to Hamilton that an exponent of executive power would assert the treaty-making prerogatives of the House of Representatives in opposing the Jay Treaty in 1795. Few would have dreamed, finally, that a man known for his abhorrence of factions, and who had favored a federal veto over state laws at the Constitutional Convention, would help to organize a political party that championed states rights.[5]

The motives behind Madison's reversal, if that is what it was, have always been something of a mystery. One plausible explanation focuses on the twist in Madison's career in 1788–89. Antifederalist heavyweights Patrick Henry and George Mason argued that the new constitution would be used to oppress Virginia and vigorously opposed it during the state ratifying convention. The Antifederalists then denied Madison a seat in the U.S. Senate, and he ended instead in the House of Representatives. Having engineered a narrow victory in the state convention by presenting the constitution as a limited instrument, Madison felt honor-bound to defend a strict interpretation. The episode also reminded him of where his political bread was buttered, and his positions henceforth closely reflected Virginia's interests and sentiments. His support for the Bill of Rights, and opposition to assumption until the state had received a generous payoff in the form of placing the capital city on the Potomac and in the settlement of the revolutionary financial accounts, are obvious examples. Madison's opposition to funding without discrimination in favor of the original holders (the veterans, widows, and orphans who had sold their securities to speculators) was a matter of elementary fairness, but also reflected a Virginia horror of faceless financial operators. Madison's opposition to a national bank likewise reflected Old Dominion views. A lesser known example is his deft role in shaping a resolution in early 1790 that prohibited the federal Congress from ever concerning itself with the emancipation or treatment of slaves.[6]

Recent scholarship stresses that Madison's opposition to Hamilton arose from consistently held Whig and republican principles. Madison did not reverse course in the 1790s; rather, he reacted to what he saw as Hamilton's assault on the values of the revolution. Hamilton favored a consolidated system. Madison had always taken the "middle ground" between the Antifederalists and the radical centralizers. Hamilton wanted a British-style system able to hold its own in the arena of power politics. Madison had always abhorred the British system and foresaw a republic dominated by agricultural producers who would reject a European-style foreign policy:

No more than [Patrick] Henry...did Madison approve the vision of a splendid, mighty future; and whatever was the case with other Federalists, *his* fear of the majority had always been accompanied by a continuing awareness of the dangers posed by unresponsive rulers or excessive central power.[7]

This view is convincing to a point, but glosses over a pair of considerations. First, it was not simply that Hamilton looked to a "splendid, mighty future" and Madison did not. During the debate at Philadelphia (in response to a statement by Charles Pinckney of South Carolina), Hamilton had observed:

It had been said that respectability in the eyes of foreign Nations was not the object at which we aimed; that the proper object of republican Government was domestic tranquility & happiness. This was an ideal distinction. No Governmt. [sic] could give us tranquility & happiness at home, which did not possess sufficient stability and strength to make us respectable abroad.

It was well and good for Madison to renounce glory, while at the same time declaring that Britain would be the loser in the coming showdown. But if he believed that geography or Providence, in the absence of the traditional accoutrements of power, would protect the United States, then he was, as Hamilton remarked, little acquainted with the world.[8]

Second, there was a more visceral element in Madison's reaction to Hamilton's program. Thomas Sully's portrait of Madison shows him standing in elegant black, looking into the eyes of the viewer, with the fingertips of his left hand poised on a copy of the Constitution. He seems to be saying: "This is my handiwork." Few would have disputed the fact that he was the main architect of the new ship of state or that he was appalled for reasons of principle by the course Hamilton was charting. But he was also disturbed to see someone other than himself at the captain's side, with a hand on the helm. At the height of his prestige following the adoption of the Constitution, Madison had authored Washington's first inaugural address and acted as his closest adviser during the period between ratification and the launching of the new executive departments. It is difficult to believe that there was not an element of personal rivalry, and bitter jealousy, in Madison's across-the-board opposition to Hamilton. The more laurels the younger man accumulated, the more intransigent he became.[9]

Hamilton and Jefferson

Madison was a dogged, as well as an intellectually gifted leader, ready to challenge his opponents face to face. His friend, the new secretary of state, was a rather different animal, both physically and temperamentally. Tall, donnish, a brilliant literary craftsman and inspirational party leader, Jefferson was thin-skinned and inclined to shun confrontation. If his obsession with Hamilton's program, and eventually the man himself, ran even deeper than Madison's, one reason is that it was nurtured in the privacy of the writing cabinet and rarely found release in the thrust and parry of debate. Thomas Jefferson was born in 1743, at Shadwell, the family home in what would become Albemarle County, near the western edge of Virginia. Through his mother, Jane Randolph, he was related to one of the grandest families of the Tidewater region and spent six of his first nine years at Tuckahoe, the

eastern estate of his uncle, William Randolph. His father, Peter Jefferson, was
a more rough-hewn squire, known for his enterprising spirit and physical
vigor. Jefferson revered his father – according to family tradition of Welsh
stock – who died when Jefferson was an adolescent, while endeavoring to
establish his independence from his controlling, English-born mother. Those
relationships seem to prefigure his later political orientation, even if little is
known of Jefferson's early years. What is clear is that he acquired a kind of
fundamentalist attachment to the agrarian-frontier values of liberty, equality, and self-reliance represented by his father, along with a typical Virginia
loathing of the monied economy and the modern British state.

Jefferson swallowed the radical Whig critique of Britain hook, line, and
sinker and incorporated it into his political philosophy. In *A Summary View
of the Rights of British America* (1774), Jefferson wrote that "Single acts of
tyranny may be ascribed to the accidental opinion of the day; but a series of
oppressions, begun at a distinguished period, and pursued unalterably thro'
every change of minister, too plainly prove a deliberate, systematical plan of
reducing us to slavery." As if economic exploitation were not enough, Virginia had also been the object of an ongoing political conspiracy. Jefferson's
Anglophobia was literally the stuff of fable. Throughout his life, he held the
belief that the Saxons had lived in freedom and harmony in England before
the imposition of feudalism by cruel Norman overlords. According to the
equally fabulous theory of "expatriation," which Jefferson unsuccessfully
tried to write into the text of the Declaration of Independence, America's
original settlers had expatriated themselves "unassisted by the wealth or the
strength of Great Britain" in order to recover the values of the Saxon Golden
Age.[10]

Jefferson, needless to say, played no part in the Philadelphia Convention.
Though he became convinced of the Constitution's utility in the realm of
foreign and commercial policy, he remained ambivalent toward the idea of a
strong central government. Many point to early 1791, as the moment when
open hostilities began with Hamilton. In February 1791, Washington decided to back Hamilton against Madison and Jefferson on the controversial
national bank issue, and the treasury secretary's prestige was at its height.
The Virginians were horrified by the frenzy of speculation that followed the
issuing of bank stock later in the year. In May–June 1791, Jefferson and
Madison took a much-noticed "vacation" in New York state, where, along
with bird-watching and sight-seeing, they talked national opposition strategy with Chancellor Robert R. Livingston, Jr. Passed over for high office, the
disgruntled former secretary for foreign affairs had recently turned against
his friends Jay and Hamilton and helped to replace Philip Schuyler in the
U.S. Senate with the New York lawyer and former Continental officer Aaron
Burr.

The last straw for Jefferson (if one can rely upon his "Anas") was an April
1791 dinner he hosted for Hamilton and Vice President John Adams. Over

port, the conversation turned to the British constitution. Adams, an expert on the subject, noted, "Purge that constitution of its corruption, and give to its popular branch equality of representation, and it would be the most perfect constitution ever devised by the wit of man." Hamilton commented, "Purge it of its corruption, and give to its popular branch equality of representation and it would become an *impracticable* government: as it stands at present, with all its supposed defects, it is the most perfect government which ever existed." Not for the first time, Hamilton was making Hume's point that the functioning of the British system depended on crown patronage to gain support for its policies in the House of Commons. But with his radical Whig baggage, and in the context of the bank battle, Jefferson took Hamilton's remark as proof that another "deliberate, systematical plan" to subvert liberty was underway.[11]

If Hamilton sought reconciliation and respect, the secretary of state's political–psychological "agenda" with regard to the Mother Country was differentiation and defiance. Jefferson's official task as a negotiator in the 1780s had been to work with Adams to foster a "general system of commerce by treaties with other nations." The treaties were to be based on principles that Adams and a Congressional committee had laid down in what was known as the Plan of 1776 and which Jefferson revised. The principles included reciprocal most-favored-nation status, American access to foreign colonial markets, and freedom of the seas. Freedom of the seas was ambitiously defined as "free [neutral] ships make free goods." As a practical matter, this meant that during a war between France and Britain, noncontraband French property shipped in American vessels should be immune from seizure by the British navy. Freedom of the seas also meant a narrow definition of contraband, those items that could legally be taken from a neutral ship. For example, the list should include weapons, but not flour or naval stores (e.g., tar, timber, and cordage). The Americans touted their principles as a modern, liberal conception of international commerce. But as Adams's grandson later put it, "their philanthrophy was not wholly free from the suspicion of incidental benefit to ensue to themselves." In fact, it was a conception tailored to the needs of a major exporter of agricultural products, but which lacked a navy to protect itself.[12]

In theory, Britain was supposed to be co-opted into the community of nations embracing these enlightened rules. A major obstacle, however, was the British belief that keeping aggressive American shippers out of British colonial markets was necessary to maintain a healthy merchant marine and to train the pool of seamen – the Royal Navy faced a chronic shortage – necessary in war. Moreover, asking Britain to allow neutrals to carry food and naval stores to its enemies in wartime was asking it to fight with one hand tied behind its back. The restrictions that Adams, Jefferson, and Madison saw as proof of British hatred of America had a compelling national security as well as an economic rationale. For the British, it was adding insult to injury that under a "free ships make free goods" regime, neutral powers would line their pockets while the belligerents fought it out.

Jefferson welcomed the prospect, as he once put it, that the New World might "fatten on the follies of the old." A more fundamental point of his 1780s policy (prefiguring Madison's commercial legislation) was to force Britain either to abandon its haughty mercantile and naval pretensions or else be hemmed in and contained by a coalition adhering to the principles of the United States.[13] (A precedent for joint action on the basis of such principles was the League of Armed Neutrality – Russia, Denmark-Norway, Sweden, and Prussia – formed in 1780 to resist British interference with neutral shipping. On June 12, 1783, with advantageous peace terms in hand from London, Congress had voted against adherence to the "Armed Neutrality." According to the resolution, the United States "should be as little as possible entangled in the politics and controversies of European nations." It is possible to see that decision as the beginning of an historic consensus with respect to a policy of nonentanglement. But for Hamilton, at least, nonentanglement was not an end in itself, but the means to preserve peace and avoid a collision with Britain. The Armed Neutrality, after all, was an anti-British front.[14])

According to Henry Adams, the "essence and genius" of Jefferson's statecraft was peace. The Virginian hated war and the means required to conduct it: an invasive executive, standing armies and navies, high taxes, and a funded debt. Jefferson sought to rely instead on a popular militia and on what he called "peaceable means of coercion" – commercial sanctions and embargoes – to reap the fruits of battle without having to resort to force. Historians have generally accepted Adams's argument. Bemis, for example, observes: "Jefferson never desired war with any nation under any circumstances." But to suggest that Jefferson did not want war, and the proof is that he did not prepare for it, is like saying that the gambler with an empty bank account does not want to lose. Jefferson's policy of containment of Britain (like post-1945 U.S. policy toward the Soviet Union) was often ambiguous on a basic point: whether it aimed through sustained pressure to convert the adversary to U.S. principles or simply to deter it from encroaching on one's own sphere. But tough, confrontational policies were required in either case.[15]

For Jefferson, the secret to containing Britain was the Franco-American connection launched in 1778. Jefferson never forgot that, acting together, France and the United States (with limited help from Spain) had managed to put Britain's back against the wall. Along with their Treaty of Alliance, the two countries had signed a Treaty of Amity and Commerce that followed Plan of 1776 lines. After 1785, installed in his luxurious, three-story mansion on the Champs-Elysées, Jefferson dedicated himself to strengthening U.S. political and economic ties to France. The French, he believed, held the solution to the basic weakness of his strategy: America's continuing dependence on British manufactures, capital, and markets. With foreign ministry support, Jefferson succeeded in having French duties on American whale oil lifted. He also helped to break Robert Morris's monopoly on U.S. tobacco exports to France, maintained through the Philadelphian's connections with the Farmer's-General, a financial syndicate that controlled the local trade.

Overall, however, Jefferson's efforts were a failure. His friends of the so-called Physiocrat school advocated free trade, but the ancien régime economy was a byzantine maze of regulations. French bankers, exporters, and shippers lacked the knowledge and long-standing connections of their British competitors in the United States. France simply did not make the staple goods that American consumers wanted. After a London shopping spree, Jefferson plaintively told Lafayette that he had bought the plated harness and oil lamps he had sought there not because he loved England, but because the items were not available in Paris. But neither the frustration of his diplomacy nor the suspicion that France desired a dependent America caused Jefferson to deviate from his basic course. He wrote Madison on January 30, 1787, "nothing should be spared, on our part, to attach this country to us. It is the only one on which we can rely for support, under every event. Its inhabitants love us more, I think, than they do any other nation on earth."[16]

Jefferson was a sympathetic witness to the events leading to the outbreak of the French Revolution. He numbered among his friends some of the liberal nobles active in its early stages and was prodigal with his advice. Like many Americans, he believed France was following in America's footsteps, that the two experiments constituted the wave of the future, and that their fates were intertwined. In January 1793, after the Revolution had taken a disturbingly violent turn, he wrote William Short (who had had the temerity to call the French National Assembly, "mad, wicked and atrocious"):

The liberty of the whole earth was depending on the issue of the contest, and was ever such a prize won with so little innocent blood? My own affections have been deeply wounded by some of the martyrs to this cause, but rather than it should have failed, I would have seen half the earth desolated. Were there but an Adam and Eve, left in every country, and left free, it would be better than it now is. I have expressed to you my sentiments, because they are really those of 99 in a hundred of our citizens.

On the two Revolutions' broader implications, Jefferson wrote, "This ball of liberty, I believe most piously, is now so well in motion that it will roll around the globe." In other words (and to pursue the analogy with twentieth-century U.S. foreign policy), he believed that French events enhanced the odds for a successful "roll back" of tyranny around the world.[17]

Hamilton's view of the same events, as he wrote Lafayette several months after the storming of the Bastille, was "a mixture of Pleasure and apprehension." He rejoiced at French efforts to establish liberty, but feared "for the danger in case the success of innovations greater than will consist with the real felicity of your Nation," in other words, that the Revolution might get out of hand. Along with the "vehement character of your people" and the "interested refractoriness of your nobles," he dreaded "the reveries of your Philosophic politicians" – an unwitting reference to Jefferson's salon friends.[18]

These statements suggest a striking difference of perspective and one destined to grow wider and bitterer as the French situation evolved. But although it severely aggravated matters, it is clear that the French Revolution was not the *cause* of the contemporaneous battle royale in the United States. The cause lay in the basically different conceptions of the nation's destiny, including relations with Britain and (pre-Revolutionary) France, which divided Hamilton and his supporters from the Virginians. If the old régime in France had managed to limp along for another decade, Hamilton and the secretary of state-designate would still have been on a collision course when Jefferson, together with his daughters Patsy and Polly, his slaves James and Sally Hemmings, and their copious baggage, boarded the vessel *Clermont* and sailed for home in late 1789. Indeed, a near-collision occurred in mid-1790, during the first foreign policy crisis to confront the Washington administration. The reaction of Hamilton and Jefferson to the prospect of a European war, and to a possible British request to cross U.S. territory to attack the Spanish, provided a kind of dress rehearsal for the cabinet drama that began in 1793.[19]

5

The Nootka Sound Crisis, Part One:
The Morris Mission

Introduction

The United States in 1790 was not the first young, geopolitically vulnerable republic to face the possibility that its security and honor might be seriously at risk in a situation that it was practically powerless to affect. Flush from his subjugation of the Romagna around 1500, Cesare Borgia sent a message to Florence requesting that his forces be allowed to cross the republic's territory unhindered on their way to Rome. Machiavelli used this incident to illustrate the thesis of a chapter of the *Discourses* called "Weak republics are irresolute and don't know how to decide."

He first recounted an episode in which the Romans, unable because of a plague to come to the defense of a unarmed, dependent city against an attacking enemy, and faced with the certainty that the city would arm itself even if Rome disapproved, had made the gesture of consenting. In so doing, argued Machiavelli, the Romans had preserved a modicum of reputation and honor under circumstances of *necessità*. Similarly pressed by necessity, no one in Florence recommended that formal consent be given to Borgia to do something that he was certain to do regardless of Florentine approval or disapproval. Unfortunately, in other words, "the Roman way wasn't followed: because with the Duke [Borgia] heavily armed and the Florentines unequipped to prevent his passage, it was much more to their honor, that he appear to pass with their consent than by force." When he subsequently marched without permission, Borgia not only humiliated Florence; in his anger he also inflicted physical destruction that he probably otherwise would have avoided. The Florentines' indecisiveness and lack of realism had cost them once again.[1]

At the same time, according to Machiavelli, there were circumstances where the weaker party was well advised to resist in order to salvage something of its honor and reputation. In a case where a state was unable to make a concession appear to be of its own free will, it was almost always better

that the object in question "be taken by force rather than the fear of force."
In trying to avoid war in such a case you would probably fail, "because the
person to whom with open cowardice you have made the concession will
not be satisfied but will want to take other things of yours." Though Machiavelli did not say so explicitly, Borgia's marching *without* having bothered
to ask Florence's permission (and thus not giving it the opportunity to save
face) would logically have been a case where the weaker party was obliged
to fight.[2]

Background to the Nootka Sound Crisis

Britain's official position in 1789 was that it continued to occupy the seven
strategic posts on U.S. territory because the United States had failed to fulfill
key provisions of the 1783 peace treaty (namely Article 4, stating that there
should be no lawful impediment to the recovery of prewar debts owed to
British creditors, and Article 5, stating that Congress should recommend
to the states the restitution of estates confiscated from Loyalists). American
nonfulfillment was a useful pretext, but Britain had more compelling reasons.
British officials on the spot had persuaded London that the frontier posts
were essential to the fur trade controlled by Montreal merchants (valued
at two hundred thousand pounds per year) and to protect Canada against
"pushful and procreative American pioneers." The posts played an essential
role in maintaining Britain's contacts with its only allies in the recent war: the
Indians of the Northwest Territory, who now found themselves sandwiched
between Canada and the United States. Despite the promulgation of the
Constitution, some London officials continued to see the United States as
weak and subject to British pressure. Plans circulated for an independent
Indian state northwest of the Ohio, which would undo the cession of the
area to America in 1783. Spain, meanwhile, refused to accept a U.S.–Spanish
border on the Mississippi and the 31st parallel and continued to deny free
navigation of the river to the United States.[3]

   An incident raising the possibility of a major war occurred at Nootka
Sound, a remote inlet on the Pacific side of what is today Vancouver Island. Inspired by the publication of Captain James Cook's account of his
voyage along the northwest coast of North America, and the prospect of
a fur trade between North America and the Orient, an Englishman named
John Meares bought land from the local Indian chief and opened a trading
depot there in 1788. On July 5, 1789, responding to the claim of a British
captain that he was taking possession of the area in the name of George III,
Don Estaban José Martinez, commanding a Spanish frigate, arrested Captain
James Colnett and his crew and escorted the three British ships present at
Nootka Sound to a base in California. Though Spain had not occupied land
north of San Francisco, Martinez asserted that the entire Pacific coast from

Cape Horn to the 60th parallel (southern Alaska) belonged to the Spanish crown.

Sketchy news of the incident reached London in January 1790. The British government asked for the return of one ship reportedly seized and for compensation, but neither side sought a confrontation. This changed when Meares arrived in London and told the story of the prior British purchase and claim, the Union Jack lowered at gunpoint, and seamen rotting in a Spanish jail. On April 20, 1790, Spain promised to release the men, but with no mention of compensation, and reasserted its exclusive claim. On April 30, Pitt and the cabinet decided to demand satisfaction and to assemble a fleet of forty ships of the line.

The British made plans for a sea-borne assault on New Orleans, to be followed by a possible ground campaign against Mexico. Pitt and his cousin, Home Secretary Grenville (responsible for colonial affairs), met with the Venezuelan soldier Francisco de Miranda to discuss support for a revolution in the Spanish colonies. The British were also in secret contact with Americans in Vermont (not yet part of the union) and in Kentucky (still part of Virginia), with a view to deterring a U.S attack on the posts or taking joint action against Spanish territory. Because the French and Spanish Bourbons were united by a Family Compact dating from 1761, an Anglo-Spanish war might also involve France. On May 22, 1790, the French National Assembly declared that the king could not decide on war without the Assembly's approval, making war with Britain appear less likely. On August 26, however, the same body authorized the king to negotiate a "national treaty" of alliance with Spain and to arm a fleet of forty-five ships of the line.[4]

Hamilton's role during the first phase of the crisis consisted of his contacts with Major George Beckwith (who was ordered to proceed posthaste from Quebec to New York with the news of the confrontation). After arriving at Monticello and taking his time to decide whether to accept Washington's offer, Jefferson had assumed his duties as secretary of state only in March, 1790. For the time being, the main American "protagonist" was the U.S. envoy to Britain, Gouverneur Morris. Washington had not authorized Morris to negotiate but rather to ascertain British "sentiments and intentions" concerning fulfillment of the peace treaty. He was also to sound them out on a commercial treaty, a provision of which must be access for American vessels to the West Indies. Given its timing, Morris's mission was inevitably caught up in the question of Nootka Sound.[5]

Washington's Man in London

Gouverneur Morris was born in 1752 on the family estate in Westchester County, known by a royal patent as the Lordship or Manor of Morrisania. He belonged, in the words of a famous biographer, to the "proud, polished, and powerful aristocracy" of New York. There are striking parallels in the lives of Morris and Hamilton: a West Indian connection (Morris's ancestor Colonel Lewis Morris came to New York via Barbados), a Huguenot mother (Morris's was Sarah Gouverneur), and a fatherless adolescence (Morris's father Lewis died in 1764). Both learned French at an early age, studied at King's College, and adopted a Continentalist position in the war. Both were lawyers with a gift for financial questions. After his collaboration with Robert Morris, Gouverneur had been a Pennsylvania delegate to the 1787 Convention and served as the main draftsman of the Constitution. He had then become involved in a myriad of European-based business schemes, including trying to save Morris's French tobacco business, selling American land to French aristocrats, and buying up the American debt to France.[6]

Morris's motto in dealing with his fellow human beings might have been the following entry from his diary: "Those who have nothing to hide and those who wish to hide nothing say what comes uppermost." He had once told prissy John Jay that "luxury is not so bad a thing as it is often supposed to be." Along with luxury, he loved life "in the fastlane" and was hardly slowed by the loss of a leg below the knee after being thrown from his speeding phaeton. Though a religious diarist and correspondent, he was apt to postpone business to hop from salon to salon, drink madeira until dawn with convivial strangers, or pursue the possibilities suggested by the glance of an enticing female. After meeting a Lady Tancred on his first full day in London, he wrote (typically) in his diary, "A very goodlooking Woman, and as she desires very politely to see me I think I shall become a Visitant, for if I am to stay here any Time some Resource or other will certainly be wanting." After Morris's accident, Jay confessed to Robert Morris, "I am almost tempted to wish he had lost something else."[7]

According to Theodore Roosevelt, Morris was "alike free from truckling subserviency to European opinion ... and from the uneasy self-assertion that springs partly from sensitive vanity, and partly from a smothered doubt as to one's true position." In reality, the chemistry of Morris's connection to Europe was a bit more complicated. In obvious ways he was the most British of the leading Americans (as Hamilton had implied to Beckwith). He had been among the last of the New York Whigs to be converted to independence. His older half-brother and godfather, Staats Morris, was a general in the British army and had been married to the Duchess dowager of Gordon. His sister, Euphemia, who also lived in London, was married to a New York Loyalist.

But this did not incline him to defer to those he considered his brothers and equals. He later said, "I respect the English nation highly ... and love many individuals among them, but I do not love their manners." He was on constant guard against British coldness and favored a preemptive, reverse-snob approach. Rather than emollient smoothness, he later wrote Robert Morris:

If you mean to make a good treaty with Britain, support your pretentions with spirit *and they will respect you for it.* You must give them *visible reasons* because they will *have to justify their conduct*; and it will not do to say to a House of Commons, *the American Minister was such a charming fellow that we could not resist him.*

He undoubtedly had a point. But his own attitude suggested a doubt or two as to his true position or perhaps a need to compensate for his earlier views and ties. Even an admirer like TR admitted that Morris could "not altogether be freed of the charge of having clung too long to the hope of reconciliation and to a policy of half measures" before the war.[8]

Morris's feelings toward France were equally complicated. As a good Huguenot, he instinctively distrusted Catholicism and the French character. In April 1789, after two months' residence in Paris, he wrote to Washington of "the extreme rottenness" of French society. On such a foundation, the "great Edifice of Freedom" to be erected might well "fall and crush the builders." On a May morning Morris made an outing to see the Seine Valley from atop the Aqueduct of Marly:

The View is exquisite.... At a Distance the Domes of Paris on one Side, the Palace of St Germains very near on the other, a vast Forest behind and the Palace of Marli [sic] in the Front of it, but embowered in a deep shade. The Bells from a thousand Steeples at different Distances murmuring thro the Air. The Fragrance of the Morning. The vernal Freshness of the Air. Ah how delicious! I stand at this Moment on a vast Monument of human Pride and behold every Gradation from Wretchedness to Magnificence in the Scale of human Existence. Oh! my Country, how infinitely preferable that equal Partition of Fortune's Gifts which you enjoy! Where none are Vassals, none are Lords, but all are Men.

Morris was alternately attracted, awed, amused, and appalled by fin-de-régime France, and always aware of the unbridgeable differentness between it and himself.[9]

But as it turned out (and as Hamilton only belatedly realized), it was a mistake to assume that Morris would approach his mission with a bias against the French. By the time he arrived in London in March 1790, his emotional involvement with France had grown intense. For one thing, the mission interrupted his passionately physical and time-consuming relationship with Adelaide Marie Emilie, Comtesse de Flahaut. Morris was obliged to share Adèle's attentions with the father of her child, and his fellow cripple, Talleyrand. The two sometimes bumped into each other on the narrow stairway of Adèle's Louvre apartment, leading to impromptu dinners and political strategy sessions. Each attempted to dodge her husband, the count (whose fate, like countless contemporaries, was to endure both the insult of cuckoldry and the injury of the guillotine).[10]

Like Jefferson, Morris was a prodigal advice giver, for example, to Lafayette, whom he came to see as well-intentioned, but fundamentally vain and out of his depth. Unlike Jefferson, Morris did not develop an enthusiasm for radical bourgeois France and felt premonitions of terror and disorder. As events precipitated, he became increasingly entangled in the threatened lives of the friends he frequented at the noble Club Valois. The Revolution served to deepen his sense of solidarity with the old ruling class, corrupt and feckless though they may have been, who had actually helped America to win its independence. He was on friendly terms with the American minister himself, though he found him something of a snob in his personal judgments, although "in many respects too democratical in his Ideas." Adèle, whose discernment Morris admired as much as he did her body, called Jefferson "*faux et emporté*" (false and carried away).[11]

Morris on the Job

Morris made a forthright presentation of the issues, including British non-fulfillment of the peace treaty and failure to send a minister to America, to Foreign Secretary Lord Leeds on March 29, 1790. He then settled into a Covent Garden hotel, began his social and business rounds in a rented carriage, and waited for a reply. It did not come for a month, and when it did was curtly negative on the treaty and noncommittal on commercial negotiations. How much Morris himself was to blame for the British attitude has generated a lively argument. According to one view, Morris behaved badly, missed opportunities, and was more or less *persona non grata* when he finally returned to France. Another view is that Morris behaved well enough, but the question is basically irrelevant. The problem was that the British were simply not interested in changing the status quo. A variation on the latter interpretation is that Morris's presence hardly registered on the British. They had bigger fish to fry.[12]

The least that can be said is that Morris's judgment left much to be desired. In January 1790, shortly after receiving Washington's request to go to London, Morris communicated the purpose of his mission to the French foreign minister Montmorin. While the main goal of a commercial treaty with Britain would be access to the West Indies, Morris told Montmorin, "I prefer much a close Connection with France." On Sunday, March 28, the morning after his arrival in London, Morris went to the house of the French ambassador, the Marquis de La Luzerne, told him that he was in London to seek a performance of the treaty, and asked him to keep the information secret. "I think it prudent," he told his diary, "to be in a Situation to say always to the French Court that every Step taken by us has been with their Privity." But because the French had no interest in an Anglo-American rapprochement, it is not improbable that the foreign minister or the ambassador let the British government know that France was privy to Morris's mission in order to undermine its credibility in British eyes. (The irony is that in 1781, Morris had deplored the Continental Congress's instructions – requested by the same La Luzerne – to the American peace negotiators in

Paris, Franklin, Adams, and Jay, to put themselves under French supervision. Foreign minister Vergennes had been prepared to end the war on terms highly unsatisfactory to the United States. Suspecting French treachery, the American negotiators had decided to ignore their instructions.)[13]

The British government, in any event, could draw its own conclusions about Morris. Between March and September 1790, the American envoy visited La Luzerne at least thirty times. Though he later denied it, he was also a frequent guest at the Sackville Street, Picadilly, house of Mr. and Mrs. John Barker Church. Church had been commissary-general to the French troops in America during the war and was now an opposition member of Parliament. The Churches arranged for Morris to dine with the leader of the opposition, Charles James Fox. (The irony here is that Church was Hamilton's brother-in-law. In 1777 he had eloped with Elizabeth Schuyler's older sister, Angelica.)

Bemis asserts that Morris went out of his way to avoid meeting anyone connected to the Court. Morris's diary tends to confirm this, also that he found the wine adulterated, the restaurants overpriced, and the local habit of after dinner card playing a tremendous bore. His studied standoffishness did not prevent him from feeling irritated when he received little high-level attention. When finally presented to the Duchess of Gordon, he was eager to see more of her and to accept her offer of a dinner with William Pitt. This does not mean that Morris was wrong to conclude, as he wrote Washington on May 1, 1790, that the British were unwilling or unready to improve relations. It does mean that his conduct furnished an additional argument to someone like Lord Hawkesbury, head of the Committee on Trade, for turning a cold shoulder to America and little to help those who were open to change like Grenville and Pitt himself. Beckwith, after all, must have had a reason when he warned Hamilton that the views of the American envoy would carry weight.[14]

The second phase of Morris's mission began with the breaking of the Nootka Sound crisis. Morris quickly concluded that his success now depended on war, or the serious prospect of it, involving Britain, Spain, and France. As he put it: "I incline on the whole to the Opinion that if France should put thirty Ships of the Line into Commission we may settle a Treaty with this Country upon such Terms as we may think proper. But if the present Clouds break away they will become again intractable." This analysis may or may not have been accurate, but it prompted an action that modern accounts of the mission strangely overlook. Morris's move was typical of the kind of amateurish strategizing and wishful thinking that marked his (as will be seen, not only his) approach to Nootka Sound.[15] On May 7, the day the British challenge to Spain became public, Morris wrote Lafayette, urging a French preemptive strike on Britain's ally, The Netherlands, with the aim of tying down British troops on the continent. He also recommended the capture (and refusal to exchange) of British seamen as the means to "ruin both their Marine and Finance." As for France's troubled finances, "I think that they may be restored during War better than in Peace. You want also Something to turn Men's Attention from their present Discontents." To William Carmichael, U.S. chargé d'affaires in Madrid, Morris proffered advice for the Spanish government on how to deliver to the British "dreadful blows" by sea.[16]

Morris had a sudden opening on May 21. On the 20th he had visited Leeds to protest the impressment of American seamen in London. Leeds told Morris to come back the next day, and when he did, he found not only the foreign secretary, but Pitt himself. Pitt's surprise appearance was obviously due to the Nootka Sound crisis, but it did not mean that the British were seeking a deal at any price. Morris, however, convinced himself that the British were preparing to climb down from their high horse. The two sides rehashed the issues of the abducted slaves, the strategic posts, the commercial treaty, and the British failure to send an accredited minister to the United States. Morris said that his country did not want war over the posts, but that "we reserved our Rights and would certainly make Use of them when Time & Circumstances should suit." Pitt seemed to want to move beyond the impasse, but then learned that Morris was not authorized to negotiate. He assured him that, contrary to the American's impression, the British government was "disposed to cultivate a [formal] Connection." If so, replied Morris, it would have to put it in writing for transmission to the United States.[17]

As it happened, a message (dated April 7, 1790) from Beckwith arrived in London several days after the Pitt–Morris conversation. Beckwith reported an official American desire "to cultivate a connection" with Britain, but also that military operations were in preparation against the Indians. Such operations, London inferred, might endanger the posts in the case of war with Spain. Bemis seems right to argue that Beckwith's report, coming soon after Morris's thinly veiled threat, "could not but have been disturbing" to the British. Nevertheless, they conducted no further business with Morris. What to do with the United States in case of war would remain undecided for now and would be handled through channels other than the American envoy.[18]

Morris's mission entered another waiting phase. He remained sure that war would come even after Spain folded under British pressure on July 24, and agreed to pay reparations for the seizures at Nootka Sound. The British proceeded to raise the ante by challenging Spain's exclusive claim to the unoccupied areas of the Pacific Northwest. Morris was convinced that Pitt had overreached himself. Spain could not yield the point without opening its domains to the fatal penetration of British fishermen and traders.[19]

The decisive phase of the Nootka Sound crisis began in late August 1790. Morris's patience had worn thin, his health was poor, and he had begun to despair of French backing of Madrid. Then, unexpectedly, the French

National Assembly authorized the king to arm a fleet and negotiate a new alliance with Spain. On September 8, the British ambassador at Madrid presented London's demands for commercial access to northwestern North America. Morris seized the opportunity to prod the British into revealing their intentions toward the United States. On September 10, he wrote Leeds that he must soon depart and expressed disappointment that the "friendly Connection" he had been led to believe might take place had failed to materialize. To some degree, of course, Morris had been led to believe this by himself.

Leeds's reply was noncommittal, indicating that the cabinet had not yet adopted a policy. And the letter was a personal one, confirming that the British intended to have no further official dealings with Morris. The American nonetheless took up Leed's invitation to make a farewell call on September 15, 1790. Leeds said that he hoped to decide soon on a minister for the United States and that he was "earnestly desirous of a real *bona fide* Connection, not meerly by the Words of a Treaty but in Reality." On the treaty stumbling blocks, however, Leeds had nothing new to say. A vexed Morris warned how badly this might be taken and how the United States could injure British trade and its West Indies colonies in the event of war. He had tarried in London because he had "supposed they [the British] would naturally square their Conduct toward us by their Position in Respect to other Nations." Since the British had decided to face down Madrid, Morris had "thought it probable that they were prepared to speak definitively" to the United States. Morris waited for an answer, but Leeds tried to change the subject. With this last statement, Morris had finally put his cards on the table. Unbeknownst to him, the game had ended some time before, as far as his own part in it was concerned.[20]

6

Nootka Sound, Part Two: The View from New York

Introduction

Angered by his discovery of Hamilton's role at the outset of the Washington administration, Julian Boyd, the historian and long-time editor of Thomas Jefferson's papers, prepared a dramatic exposé, *Number 7: Alexander Hamilton's Secret Attempts to Control American Foreign Policy*. According to Boyd, George Beckwith was a "secret agent" ("7" being his code name for Hamilton, his mole inside the U.S. government), and Hamilton's relationship with him constituted a story of intrigue and deceit. Hamilton either concealed his contacts with Beckwith or reported them in a way designed to advance aims in conflict with official policy. His disclosure to Beckwith of the purpose of military operations planned for the fall of 1790 – they were directed at the Shawnee and Miami tribes in the Maumee River Valley of Ohio, not the British-held post at Detroit – contributed to the embarrassing losses suffered by Brigadier General Josiah Harmar's force of fifteen hundred men. With Hamilton's "act of deception there opened a decade of divisiveness in the highest councils of the state."[1]

Boyd's obsession with Hamilton (mirroring Jefferson's own) makes it difficult to take him seriously. If Beckwith was a spy, he was a careless one for an officer whom Boyd portrays as experienced and competent. In fact, Beckwith's connection to Lord Dorchester was common knowledge, and Boyd himself shows that he was authorized to deliver messages from the British government. He also points out that General Arthur St. Clair, Governor of the Northwest Territory, was authorized to tell the British that they were not the target of Harmar's operation. Incompetence and poor equipment were the chief causes of his failure. This was more dramatically the case a year later on November 4, 1791, when Miami, Shawnee, and Delaware warriors surprised a larger expedition under the command of the unlucky St. Clair himself in east-central Ohio, leaving over nine hundred American dead on the field. Gilbert Lycan, among others, dismisses Boyd's "concerted attack" on Hamilton. Although their methods differed, he argues, Hamilton and Jefferson actually had similar objectives. "Both were convinced that an Anglo-Spanish conflict would present a splendid opportunity for obtaining redress of grievances from each belligerent, but both believed any such gains were to be sought primarily through negotiations." Both "looked with equanimity on a course of action that would lead logically to the termination of the United States's alliance with France." Other historians call Boyd "overwrought" and contend that Hamilton and Jefferson "worked in relative accord on most objects of American interest."[2]

Despite its flaws, Boyd's pamphlet has the merit of emphasizing that Hamilton did have his own foreign policy agenda and little compunction about operating behind the backs of his cabinet colleagues. It also usefully reminds us that Hamilton and Jefferson did *not* agree during the Nootka Sound affair. Where Boyd seriously misleads is in saying that Jefferson, unlike Hamilton, followed a policy of neutrality "consistently and out of profound conviction." In reality, neither pursued neutrality out of deep conviction. In his zeal to expose Hamilton's disingenuousness, moreover, Boyd overlooked the transparent deviousness of Jefferson's approach. The Nootka Sound crisis shows that both men could be "Machiavellian" in the quotidian (pejorative) meaning of the term. The basic difference between them is that Hamilton had absorbed Machiavelli's foreign policy realism, while Jefferson had not.

Hamilton and Beckwith Reunited

As Morris cooled his heels in London, the Washington administration began to formulate an approach of its own to Nootka Sound. What was said and done initially was mainly on the basis of Morris's reports. To this was added an alternative source of information in early July with Beckwith's arrival. On May 6, Home Secretary Grenville had written Dorchester, warning him of possible American demands on the posts and Spanish inducements to the United States in case of war. He sent copies of an exchange of letters between Leeds and Morris, noting that, while it had been necessary "to hold a language of firmness...it will certainly be our object to establish, if possible, a greater degree of interest than we have hitherto had in that country." Dorchester should send someone to America "to forward this object" and to report any hostile activity. Grenville believed that "it would by no means be impossible to turn the tide of the opinion and wishes of America in our favour" in case of war. The carrot Britain might hold out was the opening of the Mississippi. This was "at least as important as the possession of the Forts, and perhaps it would not be difficult to shew, that the former is much more easily attainable with the assistance of Great Britain against Spain, than the latter is by their joining Spain." The minister added, "I throw out these ideas to your Lordship fully persuaded that you will omit no opportunity of improving them as far as circumstances will admit."[3]

Dorchester's envoy carried two sets of instructions, one to be divulged to the Americans and one secret (both dated June 27, 1790). In the open instructions, Dorchester told Beckwith to express his hope that

neither the appearance of a War with Spain nor its actually taking place, will make any alteration in the good disposition of the United States to establish a firm friendship and Alliance with Great Britain to the Mutual advantage of both Countries; I am persuaded it can make none on the part of Great Britain, whose liberal treatment of the United States in point of Commerce sufficiently evinces her friendly disposition, notwithstanding the non execution of the treaty on their part, which, and various misrepresentations, I have always attributed to an unsettled state of their government, and of the minds of the multitude, influenced perhaps by a power not very cordial even to the United States.

The rights asserted by Spain in the Pacific Northwest "being to the exclusion of all the world...I think the interests of the United States in case of a War, may be more effectively served by a junction with Great Britain, than otherwise." His secret orders required Beckwith to collect intelligence on the disposition of the United States to join Spain, military preparations, and American intentions toward the Indians. "Should you find them disposed to be more friendly, you will endeavor to discover what might induce them to unite with us in the event of a war." Dorchester advised caution, but concluded, "In general you may assert it as your own opinion that in case of a War with Spain you see no reason why we should not assist in forwarding whatever their interests may require."[4]

Reaching New York, Beckwith went immediately to see Hamilton. Around noon the same day, July 8, 1790, the treasury secretary called on Washington and Jefferson (the president was still convalescing from a near-fatal case of pneumonia) at the four-story Broadway mansion, with a panoramic rear view of the Hudson, where Washington had moved earlier in the year. According to Hamilton, Dorchester wished the administration to know that if Morris had received an impression of "backwardness," this would not "be well-founded." His lordship believed that the cabinet "entertained a disposition not only towards a friendly intercourse but towards an alliance with the United States." He also wished to say that he deplored, and had tried to prevent, Indian raids in the Northwest territory. Beckwith had showed Hamilton a copy of the open instructions. They "contained ideas similar to those" that Beckwith had expressed orally, "though in more guarded terms and without any allusion to instructions from the British Cabinet." When Hamilton had noted to Beckwith that the instructions seemed to reflect Dorchester's thinking alone, the Englishman had assured him that Dorchester was well aware of the consequences of misrepresenting the views of his superiors.[5]

This episode was grist for the mill of Boyd's indictment of Hamilton as a liar and manipulator. According to Boyd, because Dorchester was not in a position to know of problems with the Morris negotiation, Hamilton must have invented the reference to Morris in his report to Washington and Jefferson to lower Anglo-American tensions. In fact, however, Dorchester had read the Morris–Leeds correspondence, and Grenville had told him that it had been necessary to adopt a language of "firmness." The British could easily imagine the tenor of Morris's reports and wished to offset the bad impression they had given. In fact, Washington had received a discouraging report from Morris around July 1. Hamilton was undoubtedly aware of Morris's reception and would have attempted to put a positive "spin" on Beckwith's message. But it was not necessary for him to dream up words and attribute them to Dorchester.[6]

More seriously, according to Boyd, Hamilton reshaped and concealed "the true meaning of Dorchester's message" regarding an alliance: the governor general had not intended to go beyond the approach taken by the British before May 1790 – as if Nootka Sound had had no impact on the British view of the United States. In his open instructions, Dorchester had simply expressed his hope that war, or the possibility of one, would not alter the "good disposition" of the United States "to establish a firm friendship and Alliance," and his conviction that it would not alter Britain's disposition to do the same. There may be a difference of emphasis but not, as Boyd claims, a "glaring discrepancy" between that statement and Hamilton's rendering of it to Washington and Jefferson: "he [Dorchester] had reason to believe that the Cabinet of Great Britain entertained a disposition not only towards a friendly intercourse but towards an alliance with the United States." Hamilton did not invent the fact that Dorchester, in line with Grenville's orders, wanted to know the U.S. reaction to the idea of military cooperation against the Spanish. Indeed, it seems probable that if Grenville, a cabinet heavyweight compared to Lord Leeds, and directly charged with the defense of Canada, had been handling Morris, and if the British had trusted the American envoy, the alliance question would have been taken up with him.[7]

If Hamilton hoped (as he undoubtedly did) that Dorchester's message would advance Anglo-American cooperation, he must have been disappointed by Washington's reaction. The president wrote in his diary:

The aspect of this business in the moment of its communication to me appeared simply, and no other than this; – We [the British] did not incline to give any satisfactory answer to Mr. Morris, who was *officially* commissioned to ascertain our intentions with respect to the evacuation of the Western posts within the territory of the United States and other matters into which he was empowered to enquire until by this [Beckwith's] unauthenticated mode we can discover whether you will enter into an alliance with us and make Common cause against Spain. In that case we will enter into a Commercial Treaty with you and *promise perhaps* to fulfil what they already stand engaged to perform.

Rather than jump to conclusions, however, Washington asked his cabinet to reflect on the question and to report back to him in a few days.[8]

Jefferson's answer (July 12, 1790) focused on the danger of a British conquest of the Floridas and Louisiana, in which case Britain would "encircle us compleatly [sic].... Instead of two neighbors balancing each other, we shall have one, with more than the strength of both." Beckwith should be told that the United States preferred "amicable" to "adversary" commercial relations with Britain, but that the latter were within American power. As to an alliance, "we can say nothing till it's [sic] object be shewn, and that it is not to be inconsistent with existing engagements," namely the 1778 pact with France. In the case of an Anglo-Spanish war, the United States was "disposed to be strictly neutral" but would view "with extreme uneasiness" any British attempt to seize Spanish territory bordering on the United States. Having more or less ruled out cooperation with the British, Jefferson recommended obtaining French help to pressure Spain to accept an independent Florida and Louisiana, guaranteed by the United States, as an outcome preferable to British conquest. If Britain tried and failed to take Louisiana and the Floridas, or took them and then lost them to Spain and France, so much the better. Otherwise, "we [the United States] should have to re-take them." In the meantime, "delay enables us to be better prepared: To obtain from the allies [Spain and France] a price for our assistance."[9]

Before deciding whether to endorse Jefferson's elaborate analysis, Washington directed Hamilton to meet again with Beckwith. He was to treat the major's communications "very civilly," but to "intimate, delicately" that he was not officially accredited, nor was the "precise object" of an alliance very clear. Instead of rejecting an alliance, however, Hamilton was to "extract as much as he could" from Beckwith without committing the United States.[10]

Hamilton did Washington's bidding on July 15, politely reminding Beckwith that his credentials were "neither formal nor authoritative." On the key question of an alliance, he said:

this opens a wide field. The thing is susceptible of a vast variety of forms. 'Tis not possible to judge what would be proper or what could be done unless points were brought into view. If you are in condition to mention particulars; it may afford better grounds of conversation.

Beckwith "replied that he could say nothing more particular than he had already done." Hamilton assured him that if the British came forward in a properly authorized way, he had no doubt that his government would be prepared "to converse freely upon it." He did not "mean either to raise or repress expectation." Beckwith admitted that, under the circumstances, nothing more explicit could be expected. When Beckwith asked whether there was any agreement between Spain and the United States, Hamilton assured him that there was "no particular connection." According to Hamilton's account (though not Beckwith's), they discussed the "probable course of military operations" in case of war. Beckwith supposed British action would be directed at South America. Hamilton hinted at the administration's dislike of an attack on New Orleans.[11]

Up to this point, Hamilton's report to Washington suggested that he had spoken to Beckwith from a script agreed to with the president. Hamilton wrote on the back of his copy of the report: "The views of the government were to discard suspicion that any engagements with Spain or intentions hostile to Great Britain existed – to leave the ground in other respects vague & open, so as that in case of rupture between GB & S–the U States might be in the best situation to turn it to account in reference to the disputes between them & GB on the one hand & Spain on the other." Beckwith's account reveals that Hamilton, in line with their back-channel relationship, made a pair of points which he did not report to Washington. The first was an allusion to Morris, namely that it would be "mutually advantageous" if Anglo-American negotiations "could be carried on at our seat of government, as it would produce dispatch and obviate misconception."[12]

Hamilton had seen by now that his New York friend was a diplomatic loose cannon. He later told Beckwith that Morris had been "too shy" in his answer to the question of whether the United States would send a minister if the British did. On another occasion, he confided to Beckwith that there had been something in Morris's conduct during his meeting with Pitt and Leeds of which he did not "altogether approve." In fact, Hamilton must have been appalled when he read Morris's report home after that key encounter. Observed Morris:

you will consider that the Characteristic of this [British] Nation is Pride; whence it follows that if they are brought to sacrifice a little of their Self Importance they will readily add some other Sacrifices. I kept therefore a little aloof and did not, as I might have done, obtain an Assurance that they would appoint a Minister if you would. On the contrary, it now stands on such Ground that they must write a letter making the first Advance.

One of the few concrete results of Morris's mission was to confirm Hamilton's determination to take the reins of policy toward Britain in his hands.[13]

Hamilton's second unauthorized statement was that if Anglo-American negotiations did take place in the United States, "in the turn of such affairs the most minute circumstances, mere trifles, give a favorable bias or otherwise to the whole." This was the basic lesson of the Morris mission: personalities, their quirks and attitudes, *did* matter, given the prickliness of both sides. Washington himself, Hamilton reassured Beckwith, was "perfectly dispassionate." (He knew perfectly well that Washington was touchy on the subject of the British.) As for Jefferson, however, although "a gentleman of honor" and zealous in pursuit of his duty, "from some opinions which he has given respecting Your government, and possible predilections elsewhere, there may be difficulties which may possibly frustrate the whole, and which might be readily explained away." Without divulging Jefferson's recent recommendations, Hamilton was telling the British that the secretary of state might try to sabotage Anglo-American negotiations and attempt to shift the blame. If problems arose, Hamilton requested that he be informed of them directly by the British, so that he could make sure they were "clearly understood [by Washington] and candidly examined."[14]

Jefferson's Nootka Sound Démarche

According to William Pitt's biographer, the British government "placed weight" on what it learned from Hamilton during the Nootka Sound crisis. What little he had to tell Washington, however, did not advance his ends. Because Beckwith had not been authorized to say anything specific about an alliance, Hamilton was not in a strong position to counter the complicated démarche that Jefferson now persuaded Washington to undertake.[15] Jefferson's plan called for Colonel David Humphreys, Washington's hand-picked envoy, to travel to London, Lisbon, and Madrid. In London, he was to forward letters from Washington to various French personalities including La Luzerne and Lafayette. To Carmichael in Madrid, he was to deliver instructions and a detailed "Outline of Policy" to guide the chargé's negotiations with the Spanish. By separate courier, Jefferson sent a copy of the documents destined for Carmichael to William Short in Paris, with instructions to show them to Lafayette in case of war, and to enlist French aid in achieving the aims of the "Outline." At the end of August, Jefferson also replied to Washington's request for advice on a contingency which greatly bothered the president. How should the United States react if Dorchester sent British forces south from Detroit across U.S. territory to the Mississippi to attack Spanish posts on the river, in conjunction with a British sea-borne assault on New Orleans? Washington observed, "The *Consequences* of having so formidable and enterprising a people as the British on both our flanks and rear, with their Navy in front, as they respect our Western settlements which may be seduced thereby, as they regard the security of the Union and its commerce with the West Indies, are too obvious to need enumeration."[16]

Washington's letter to Lafayette (drafted by Jefferson) referred to America's policy of "strict neutrality," but the phrase does not really capture the secretary of state's reasoning: "we shall be the gainers, whether the powers of the old world may be in peace or war, but more especially in the latter case." America would reap commercial gains and its friendship would be courted. The letter added, tellingly, "Our dispositions would not be indifferent to Britain or Spain. Why will not Spain be wise and liberal at once?" As Jefferson's communications to Carmichael made clear, Spain should cede navigation of the Mississippi and a port of deposit at New Orleans to the United States. Carmichael was to impress on the Spanish "the necessity of an early and even immediate settlement of this matter." Jefferson's "Outline of Policy" listed the arguments to be used. The United States was in a position to take what it wanted by force, acting alone or with the British. The Outline admitted that "such an alliance is not what we should wish," and Jefferson was not prepared to talk seriously to London. On the other hand, the threat of armed pressure by Western settlers might not be without effect on Madrid. If there were any doubt that Jefferson was bluffing in threatening Spain with Anglo-American action, it was removed by his instructions to Morris in London. If war broke out between Britain and Spain, Morris was to renew his threats to the British government. The United States would remain neutral *"if they will execute the treaty fairly,* and *attempt no conquests adjoining us."* And, Jefferson added, "in no case need they think of our accepting any equivalent for the posts."[17]

By threatening Madrid, Jefferson now hoped to drive a harder bargain than the one contemplated in his previous (July 12, 1790) memo to Washington: Spain would cede outright "to us all territory on our side of the Mississippi [e.g., the Floridas]: On condition that we guarantee all her possessions on the Western waters of that river: She agreeing further, to subsidize us, if the guarantee brings us into the war." Thus, "If we are forced into the war, it will be, *as we wish,* on the side of the H. of Bourbon." Carmichael should remind Madrid that it was "safer for Spain that we should be her neighbor, than England. Conquest not in our principles: inconsistent with our government. Not in our interest to cross the Mississippi for ages. And will never be our interest to remain united with those who do." Jefferson's letter to Short makes clear that he assumed that, in case of war, France would be involved, and (under U.S. pressure) it would see its interest in persuading Spain to accept further American demands, including the cession of New Orleans itself. The first assumption was reasonable; the latter seems dubious at best.[18]

What did Jefferson intend to do if the British, as seemed likely, not only failed to execute the peace treaty (including evacuation of the posts) in response to U.S. verbal threats but also asked to march across poorly defended U.S. territory to attack Spanish positions in case of war? The answer, contained in Jefferson's reply to Washington's request, is singular, among other reasons, for being the precise opposite of what Machiavelli would have advised under the circumstances. For Jefferson, saying yes to a British request in order to try to limit the damage and save face was evidently out of the question. But refusing to comply, in which case the British would march anyway, meant either immediate war or "an acknowledged insult in the face of the world." Jefferson therefore recommended what he called a "middle course," that is, to "avoid giving any answer." In effect, this was the same ostrichlike stance Florence had adopted toward Cesare Borgia's request to cross its territory. On the other hand, if the British moved *without* asking permission, in utter contempt of the U.S. government, Jefferson did not favor armed resistance to avoid disgrace and to deter further spoliations. Rather, the U.S. government should merely express its dissatisfaction, "keeping alive an altercation on the subject, till events should decide whether it is most expedient to accept their apologies, or profit of the aggression as a cause of war." How the United States might later find itself in the position to choose between accepting an apology, or profiting from British aggression in order to go to war, Jefferson did not – could not – explain.[19]

Hamilton's Alternative

Jefferson had answered Washington in a page and a half, and on the same day, August 27, 1790, as he received the request. Hamilton's answer occupies twenty pages in his published papers and was dated September 15, 1790. He attributed the delay to the press of business, the desire to reflect, and the wish to set out some *"comprehensive principles."* It is probable that he was also waiting for news from Europe, including a possible British offer of alliance. Hamilton wrote his wife on September 15, that he was the sole member of the administration left in New York and that "it might be very awkward" for him to go. Washington and Jefferson had left for Virginia and thence the new capital in Philadelphia. Beckwith would later move into the same Philadelphia boarding house as Madison (prompting Jefferson to invite his friend "to come and take a bed and plate" in his house, equipped with five servants and a French *maître d'hôtel*). But for the time being, the major was also in New York. Among the reasons for Hamilton's lingering there was probably that he considered it unsafe to communicate with Beckwith through the mails.[20] Hamilton's lengthy answer to Washington indicates, finally, that he wanted to take full advantage of an opportunity to regain the initiative from Jefferson. The result is a classic illustration of his technique of occupying the high ground of impartiality to appeal to Washington while advancing purposes that were other than even-handed.

Hamilton devoted most of his essay to the question of an explicit British request for passage. After a *de rigueur* but inconclusive discussion of the views of Puffendorf, Barbeyrac, Grotius, and Vattel, he laid out arguments against and for (in that order) the "propriety of a refusal." The former included the lack of any formal connection with Spain and the appearance of bias against Britain. Refusal, on the other hand, could be justified on the grounds (here he echoed Washington's language) that "it is safer for us, to have two powerful, but *rival* nations, bordering upon our two extremities, than to have one powerful nation pressing us on both sides and in capacity, hereafter, by posts and settlements, to invelop [sic] our whole interior frontier."[21]

He then asked if the right to *consent* to a British request stood "upon ground equally unexceptionable." His answer was that it did. Indeed, Hamilton adduced "a general rule that a neutral state, unfettered by any stipulation, is not bound to expose itself to war, merely to shelter a neighbour from the approaches of its enemy." Did present circumstances suggest an exception to this rule? Did the United States have "obligations of gratitude" toward Spain and France? The answer was no, because

gratitude is a duty or sentiment which between nations can rarely have any solid foundation. Gratitude is only due to a kindness or service, the predominant object of which is the interest or benefit of the party to whom it is performed. Where the interest or benefit of the party performing is the predominant cause of it . . . there can be no room for the sentiment of gratitude.

France and Spain had supported American independence in order to diminish British power. True, France was entitled to American esteem and good will, but this was "*very distinct from a spirit of* romantic gratitude calling for sacrifices of our substantial interests." As for Spain, its obstruction of the Mississippi gave it "slender claims to peculiar good will from us." If war came "there can be no reasonable ground of doubt that we should be at liberty, if we thought it our interest, consistently with our present engagements with France, to join Britain against Spain." Hamilton concluded that there was a right either to refuse or consent to a British request, "as shall be judged for the Interest of the United States; though the right to consent is less questionable than that to refuse."[22]

Hamilton proceeded to examine the *consequences* of consent or refusal, beginning with the former. British control of the Mississippi would facilitate their undivided control of the Indian tribes along the borderlands. It might enable them to win over the Western settlers by giving them free navigation, which in turn would injure the exports of the Atlantic states. But this had to be weighed against the consequences of refusal: either a war with Britain for which the United States was not prepared or, in case it was decided to refuse consent but not to resist, "absolute disgrace." In line with Machiavelli, Hamilton argued that if the United States consented, "more [British] good humour may beget greater moderation" and possible concessions. "An explicit recognition of our right to navigate the Mississippi and to and from the Ocean with the possession of New Orleans, would greatly mitigate the causes of apprehension from the conquest of the Floridas by the British."[23]

Not only would refusal to consent fail to prevent the undesired consequences, it would present the United States with the choice between the humiliation of letting the British defy the American refusal with impunity and a war to uphold the national dignity. "For it is a *sound maxim*, that a state had better hazard any calamity than submit tamely to absolute disgrace." But the fact was that "a Government scarcely ever had stronger motives to avoid war than that of the United States, at the present juncture." The country was only now recovering from the effects of the previous war, and was vulnerable by land and sea. "Measures have been recently entered upon for the restoration of Credit, which a war could hardly fail to disconcert."

Hamilton proceeded to set out what amounted to a doctrine of "ostensible neutrality." Its purpose, if not to favor the British, was to avoid a collision with them if at all possible. As he put it, the considerations he had just set out were "additional admonitions to avoid as far as possible any step that may embroil us with Great Britain. It seems evidently our true policy to cultivate neutrality." For Hamilton the two aims always went hand in hand. He thus recommended a noncommittal policy for as long as possible, during which the United States might be able to negotiate the return of the posts and the opening of the Mississippi. On the face of it, a waiting game was also Jefferson's policy, except that Jefferson contemplated an eventual alliance with France and Spain.

Even if one assumed, Hamilton continued, that it *was* in America's "permanent interest" to cement "an intimate connection with France and Spain," this "ought not to hurry us into premature hazards." However, "the reality of such an interest is a thing about which the best and ablest men of this country are far from being agreed. There are of this number, who, if the United States were at perfect liberty, would prefer an intimate connection between them and Great Britain." This was Hamilton's own view, though he avoided saying so. Rather, anticipating the language of the 1796 Farewell Address, he took the kind of impartial position congenial to Washington, and which made Jefferson look like the narrow partisan:

the most general opinion is, that it is our true policy, to steer as clear as possible of all foreign connection, other than commercial.... An attentive consideration of the vicissitudes which have attended the friendships of nations, except in a very few instances, from very peculiar circumstances, gives little countenance to systems which proceed on the supposition of a permanent interest to prefer a particular connection. The position of the United States, detached as they are from Europe admonishes them to unusual circumspection on that point. The same position, as far as it has relation to the possessions of European powers in their Vicinity, strengthens the admonition.[24]

Hamilton's elaboration on this general rule suggests that he wanted to discredit some, but not all "particular connections." He could see no reasons "of justice or policy" for favoring Spain, including the basic issue of principle involved at Nootka Sound. And if Spain continued to bar the Mississippi, war was to be preferred to a detachment of the western settlements. "In an event of this sort we should naturally seek aid from Great Britain. This would probably involve France on the opposite side, and effect a revolution in the state of our foreign affairs." In summarizing the case for consenting to a request, Hamilton admitted Washington's point that British acquisition of Spanish territory would be "dangerous to us." Yet "evil is seldom as great, in the reality, as in the prospect." The British might make concessions on the Mississippi in return for U.S. neutrality. War with Spain would add to Britain's debt and give it further motives "for not provoking our resentment." Having argued that Spanish possession of the river meant probable war or loss of the west, he did not see either of those things necessarily following from a British conquest.[25]

Toward the end of his argument, Hamilton directly attacked Jefferson's recommendation (with which he was evidently familiar). Such "an evasive conduct" was "never dignified, seldom politic." The British would probably consider it a refusal, and the rest of the world would see it as an "indication of timidity." Unlike Jefferson, moreover, Hamilton had considered the logistics of a British move. The map indicated they would descend the Wabash on their way to the Mississippi and necessarily encounter the U.S. post situated on the former river. Unless consent were given to the British to pass unmolested, armed conflict would be inevitable. Jefferson's policy of silence, "with less dignity, would produce the same ill consequence, as refusal," namely war.[26]

Up to this point, Hamilton's reasoning was close to Machiavelli's on the subject of unwelcome requests for passage, notably in its dismissal of a "middle course."[27] The same was true at the end of his paper when he addressed a second contingency – one he said was actually more likely to materialize. This was that the British would cross U.S. territory *without* asking permission. If, he argued, British forces moved through uninhabited country, resulting in no contact with U.S. citizens or posts, it would be enough to remonstrate, without committing the United States to war. "But, if as it is to be feared will necessarily be the case, our post on the Wabash should be *forced* ... there seems to be no alternative but to go to war with them; unwelcome as it may be. It seems to be this, or absolute and unqualified humiliation: Which as has already been noticed, is in almost every situation a greater evil than war." If events unfolded in this manner, Congress should be convened immediately and the most vigorous preparations undertaken. Hesitation and half-measures would not do.[28]

Conclusion

An intriguing, though unanswerable, question is whether Hamilton really believed that the British would wish to cross U.S. territory in case of war. For whatever it is worth, Beckwith and Hamilton apparently did not discuss the kind of operation that Washington had in mind. Hamilton did, however, put the British on notice again concerning the Mississippi. In late September, he told Beckwith, "*We look forward to procuring the means of export for our western country, and we must have it* ... undoubtedly we look forward to the possession of New Orleans."[29]

At the same time, Hamilton continued to press the issue of a commercial and political understanding:

foreign nations in commerce are guided solely by their respective interests ... between you and us there are other circumstances; originally one people, we have a similiarity of tastes, of language and general manners .... You have considerable American and West Indian possessions, our friendship or enmity may soon become important with respect to their security, and I cannot foresee any solid grounds of national difference between us.

In describing the U.S. political spectrum to Beckwith, Hamilton referred not to three (as he had to Washington), but two basic positions: a pro-British and a pro-French party, with current Anglo-American relations favoring the latter. "[T]he present therefore is the moment to take up the matter seriously and dispassionately, and I wish it done without loss of time." Hamilton added that the United States was "perfectly at liberty to act with respect to Spain in any way most conducive to our interests, even to the going to war with that power, if we shall think it advisable to join you."[30]

On October 16, 1790, the British mail packet arrived in New York, carrying reports of the French National Assembly's decision in August to support Madrid. In mentioning this to Beckwith the next day, Hamilton urged an Anglo-American deal: "the friendship of this country is not unimportant to you even at present, and will become infinitely more so." It might be advantageous to open the West Indies to U.S. trade on a limited basis if war began. In reply to Beckwith's question about how French participation in the war would affect matters, Hamilton answered that the United States would still be inclined to resolve the New Orleans–Mississippi question with Spain and would see itself "perfectly free with respect to France, *even if she should go to war as a principal.*" In this final conversation with Beckwith before the resolution of the crisis, Hamilton reiterated a view he had held since writing "The Farmer Refuted" fifteen years before: Britain should recognize America's growing strength and draw the logical conclusions. Already "we are capable of making considerable exertions, even maritime ones, if from circumstances it became a measure of government to encourage them ... [L]ooking forward, particularly to what may be the expected condition of this country, in a few years, it would be an act of wisdom in the Ministry of Great Britain to attach and connect the [United] States upon political as well as commercial considerations."[31]

In late October, a bitterly divided Spanish government surrendered to British demands for commercial access to the Northwest Pacific coast. The Anglo-Spanish-French war, which Morris, Jefferson, and Hamilton, each for his own reasons would have welcomed, was not to be. There is no evidence that Washington was converted by Hamilton's September 15, 1790, advice and would have followed it in preference to his secretary of state's recommendations. When Hamilton questioned Morris's performance (attributing mainly to Beckwith his own doubts), the president dismissed the criticisms out of hand. Indeed, Washington transmitted Morris's correspondence with Leeds, and other documents, to Congress in February 1791. Morris's negative reports, laced with his personal resentment, provided useful ammunition for Madison and Jefferson in their continuing campaign to pass discriminatory legislation against British trade.[32]

At the same time, Washington, on reflection, presumably realized that Jefferson's combination of trying to blackmail Spain into ceding the Floridas, threatening Britain in the absence of U.S. military preparations, and vacillating in the case of a British request to cross U.S. territory did not add up to a coherent policy. It is probably fortunate that Morris had left London by the time David Humphreys arrived there with Jefferson's instructions and that the crisis ended without war. Jefferson's démarche, if circumstances had allowed its execution, might have led to a renewal of the 1778–1783 conflict, with Britain pitted against France, Spain, and the United States. At some level of his consciousness, this prospect was probably a welcome one to Jefferson, but such a war would not necessarily have ended brilliantly. Alternatively, Madrid might have defied Jefferson's attempt to take New Orleans and the Floridas on the cheap, possibly leading to war with Spain, but without British help.

In the end, the war that did not take place confirmed Boyd's point that Hamilton was a determined and disingenuous poacher in the realm of foreign policy. But *pace* Boyd, Hamilton's approach was grounded in the realities of the situation, that of a rising but vulnerable country, still liable to have its career as a great power nipped in the bud. Jefferson's diplomatic behavior – mirroring in a way the insouciant management of his domestic affairs – once again resembled that of a gambler with an empty bank account.

7

Liaisons Dangereuses, 1791–1792

Introduction

Machiavelli devoted Chapter 6 of *The Prince* to the subject of parvenus who acquire the state thanks to their own arms and *virtù*. In it, he warned "that there is nothing more difficult to execute, nor more doubtful of success, nor more dangerous to manage, than to introduce new orders; because the innovator has as enemies all those who benefit from the old orders, and has only lukewarm support from those who would do well from the new orders."[1] The establishment of the Bank of the United States in early 1791 was Hamilton's crowning victory in the domestic arena. He was now the virtual prime minister of Washington's government and the toast of Philadelphia high society. But as Machiavelli might have predicted, his ambitious program was simultaneously undermined by the passionate opposition of the partisans of a more traditional order and the shortsighted behavior of those he had considered his natural collaborators.

The latter included investors like William Duer, former assistant secretary of the Treasury, whom Hamilton had counted on to spearhead the development of the American economy. Instead they borrowed large sums and generated a speculative frenzy in Bank stock and government securities. When the bubble burst in August 1791, the Treasury was forced to buy government paper to support the price. Hamilton warned Duer, "If the infatuation had continued progressive & any extensive mischiefs had ensued you would certainly have had a large portion of the blame." Around the same time, another New York friend, Robert Troup, wrote that there had been "every appearance of a passionate courtship between the Chancellor [Robert R. Livingston], Burr, Jefferson & Madison when the latter two were in Town." Troup warned Hamilton, "Delenda est Carthago [Carthage must be destroyed] I suppose is the Maxim adopted with respect to you."[2]

Worried by this, or chastened by the Bank scrip panic, Hamilton made a small fence-mending effort. In the preface to the recently published American edition of Thomas Paine's *The Rights of Man*, Jefferson had attacked "the political heresies which have sprung up among us." This was a reference to John Adams's *Discourses on Davila*, a series of articles attacking the French Revolution and making the case for social titles and distinctions. In an August 13, 1791, conversation with Jefferson, Hamilton averred that he disagreed with Adams. "[T]hat mind must be truly depraved which would not prefer the equality of political rights which is the foundation of pure republicanism, if it can be obtained consistently with order." Jefferson thought Hamilton's words were "intended to qualify some less guarded expressions," meaning his praise of "corruption" the previous April. But Hamilton's gesture was too little, too late for Jefferson and his friends.[3]

In the course of their subsequent efforts to drive Hamilton from office, a group of Republicans (as the Jeffersonians now styled themselves – in contrast to the Hamiltonian "monarchists") found that the secretary had been incautious in ways they had not expected to uncover. Unlike Hamilton's friendship with Duer, his relationship with Maria Reynolds, wife of a small-time speculator in war veterans claims, James Reynolds, did not cost him politically at the time. When, in December 1792, Hamilton convinced Congressman Abraham Venable (Virginia), Speaker of the House Frederick Muhlenberg (Pennsylvania), and Senator James Monroe (Virginia) that money he had paid Mr. Reynolds (one thousand dollars initially, followed by lesser "loans") was blackmail and not, as Reynolds charged, part of a scheme to speculate in Treasury securities, the three decided to let the matter rest. They were on the scent of financial rather than sexual misconduct. But the incident did cost Hamilton when he later felt compelled to publish the facts, and it has raised questions about his character ever since.[4]

Hamilton's instincts cannot be described as strongly monogamous. His flirtatious correspondence with his sister-in-law, Angelica Church, suggests both that she nursed sexual fantasies about him and that he may at times have been more attracted to her than to his less cultivated (and less ostentatious) wife. Full of youthful charm and animation, he was admired by the opposite sex; ardent, and not devoid of vanity, he could be smitten in return. But despite the rumors surrounding his behavior, Hamilton could not fairly be compared to inveterate womanizers like Gouverneur Morris or Aaron Burr. Though far from prudish, he was usually too self-controlled and shy of the risks to his reputation and family to take the plunge.[5]

When it came, the plunge was head-over-heels. The lady in question was an innocent – or so it seemed – fetching, dark-haired twenty-three-year-old from a respectable Dutchess County, New York, family. One sultry summer day in 1791, she appeared on Hamilton's doorstep at 79 South Third Street in Philadelphia and recounted a tale of woe. When he went to her nearby lodgings the same evening to give her some money, she once again revealed her secrets, this time in the literal sense of the term. A passionate affair began on the spot and lasted more than a year. Maria Reynolds may well have been the brilliant con-artist that Hamilton eventually concluded she was, and biographers have generally accepted his version of events. It is also possible that she was more or less what she seemed to be when she first approached Hamilton: a distraught woman, estranged from her husband, in financial straits, and seeking help. If it was a simple "sting" operation, it seems strange that the chronically penurious Reynolds waited until the middle of December to tell Hamilton that he had discovered the affair and would be happy to be paid off. (True, sometime before December Hamilton had turned down his request for a job at the Treasury.) Maria divorced Reynolds in 1793. It is also possible that she was in love with Hamilton (as he for a time thought she was) *and* helping to swindle him or gain access to information useful to her husband's schemes.[6]

Coinciding more or less with the financial panic provoked by Duer and his associates, Hamilton's reckless, distracting affair with Maria became a major source of stress. There are signs of depression, and a trace of self-pity, in a November 1791 letter to Angelica: "Things are tending fast to a point, which will enable me honorably to retreat from a situation in which I make the greatest possible sacrifices to a little *empty praise*, or if you like the turn better, to a disposition to make others happy. But this disposition must have its limits."[7]

With Friends Like These...

Not the least of Hamilton's frustrations was the course of Anglo-American relations. He had told Beckwith early in the year that he was happy to hear London had finally decided to send an accredited minister to America. Through William Short in Paris, he had pursued a plan to float a loan for the first time on the London market. Through Beckwith (according to Julian Boyd) he made a private request to Dorchester to use his good offices to end hostilities between the United States and the Indians, which threatened to inflame Anglo-American relations. But since the end of the Nootka Sound crisis, his plan for a rapprochement with the British had gone nowhere.[8] In one of his frankest statements on the subject, Hamilton told Beckwith in February:

In the present state of things, nothing has happened between us and France, to give a tolerable pretence, for breaking off our treaty of Alliance with that Power and immediately forming one with you. A regard for National Decorum, puts such a decisive step as this, out of our reach, but I tell you candidly as an individual, that I think the formation of a [Anglo-American] treaty of commerce, would by degrees have led to this measure, which undoubtedly that Party with us, whose remaining animosities and French partialities influence their whole political conduct, regard with dissatisfaction.

Such a "decisive step" was apparently still his hope, but neither the party he referred to nor the British themselves facilitated matters.[9]

A British minister duly arrived in Philadelphia in October and presented his credentials to Washington on November 11, 1791. Though only twenty-eight, George Hammond had served in Paris, Vienna, Copenhagen, and Madrid. Personable (he was soon engaged to Margaret Allen, daughter of a former Loyalist) and conscientious, Hammond faced two serious and interrelated obstacles: the nature of his mandate and the attitude of his main interlocutor. Hammond carried instructions written by Lord Hawkesbury, president of the Board of Trade and author of a January 28, 1791, report on commerce with the United States. The report held tenaciously to the line that U.S. shipping must be kept out of the West Indies. For military and commercial reasons, moreover, Hawkesbury preferred to retain the posts, "If the Conduct of the United States should continue to justify this measure on the part of Great Britain."[10] The new foreign secretary, Lord Grenville, authorized Hammond to begin negotiation of a commercial treaty, but not to conclude one on his own. Access to the West Indies was also out of the question for Whitehall, as was "allowing the ships of the United States to protect the property of the enemies of Great Britain in time of war." Hammond's "leading object," was to seek U.S. fulfillment of Articles 4, 5, and 6 of the peace treaty and, in return (here Grenville was more flexible than Hawkesbury), to hold out the prospect of "some practicable and reasonable arrangement" on the strategic posts. But that might include an Indian buffer state, leaving neither Britain nor the United States in control of the forts.[11]

Though supposedly secret, Hawkesbury's report was common knowledge in Philadelphia long before Hammond's arrival, and its assumption that Britain could rely on a "growing English interest" there had irritated and embarrassed Hamilton's supporters. To complicate matters, the French National Assembly approved a decree on June 2, 1791, providing for the negotiation of a new commercial treaty with the United States. In August, Hamilton told Beckwith that Franco-American negotiations were in the offing. In early October, he wrote Washington, quoting a letter from John Church: "Lord Hawkesbury is lately admitted into the cabinet, & his prejudices are strong against you, & the enthusiasm for maintaining the navigation Act is such, that there is not a shadow of probability they will in any shape relax."[12] The following day he paid a lengthy visit to Jean Baptiste de Ternant, the new French minister to Philadelphia. According to Ternant's report, Hamilton indicated strong interest in a new commercial treaty with France and eagerness to learn the minister's instructions on the subject. He assured Ternant that the presumed British aim to negotiate both an alliance and commercial treaty would be rejected by the United States.[13]

Containing Jefferson's Containment: The "Report on the Subject of Manufactures"

Hamilton's approach to Ternant obviously reflected his frustration with the Hawkesbury line and was part of an effort to pressure the British into adopting a more flexible position. It is also possible that Hamilton had the ulterior purpose of complicating matters with the French. Ternant, at least, thought he smelled a rat when Hamilton "made the greatest of protestations" of attachment to France and went out of his way to say that the true interest of the United States excluded a political alliance with any other power. The minister suspected that Hamilton "had not come entirely of his own accord" and perhaps had been sent by the president. In reality, Hamilton was pursuing a private campaign against Jefferson in hopes that, at the end of the day, the president would be on his side.[14]

Indeed, Hamilton persuaded Washington to propose a draft commercial treaty to France on a take-it-or-leave-it basis. Jefferson immediately opposed this because, as he put it, "such a volunteer project would be binding on us, and not them; that it would enable them to find out how far we would go, and avail themselves of it." When the secretary of state dutifully drew up a treaty scheme, Hamilton objected that the proposed duties on France were too low. He also argued that, having discussed trade informally with Ternant, the same approach be taken with Hammond. Jefferson thought he saw a "trap." Hamilton was trying "to get us engaged first with Ternant, merely that he might have a pretext to engage us on the same ground with Hammond, taking care... to render it impossible we should come to any conclusion with Ternant." Jefferson countered by insisting on freezing discussions for the time being with both ministers.[15]

Jefferson's account seems basically accurate, though misleading, on several points. Hamilton probably assumed that negotiations with Ternant would reveal that France was an even more demanding interlocutor than Britain. Jefferson did resume discussions with Ternant, telling him a more liberal Franco-American treaty was urgently needed. And Jefferson's treatment of Hammond was not simply a reaction to Hamilton's maneuvering. The Hammond–Jefferson dialogue of the deaf was connected to the renewal of the secretary of state's old campaign to contain British power.[16]

In February 1791, Washington had submitted his report on the Gouverneur Morris mission to the Senate. Drafted by Jefferson, it had put the blame for Morris's failure entirely on the British and cast doubt on their intention to send a minister. Around the same time, Jefferson had submitted a major report on the New England cod and whale fisheries to Congress, attacking British restrictions on U.S. exports and shipping, and proposing retaliation: "Admitting their right to keep their market to themselves, ours cannot be denied of keeping our carrying trade to ourselves." Thus Jefferson had thrown down the gauntlet to the British even before news of

Hawkesbury's report reached the United States.[17] In a coordinated move, a House committee that included Madison reported a bill prohibiting the importation of goods not grown or produced by the country in whose vessels they were shipped to be applied against countries that prohibited the import of American goods in American vessels. Thus British-owned ships would no longer be allowed to carry Chinese, East Indian, French, or Dutch goods to U.S. ports. Fearing a trade war, Hamilton and his allies had managed to stop the bill from reaching the floor but not to kill it. With Congress about to recess until early October, the committee referred the bill to Jefferson with instructions that he prepare a comprehensive report on American commerce. It was the news of this bill, reaching London in May, that had prompted London to dispatch Hammond to Philadelphia.[18]

In anticipation of Congress's passage of the bill during its next session, Jefferson sought to use it in pursuit of a Franco-American-Spanish combination against Britain. In March, he sent a copy of the bill to William Short, suggesting that it be translated, printed, and circulated to the French National Assembly. If the U.S. minister agreed, he should "have it done at the public expense . . . concealing the quarter from whence it is distributed: or take any other method you think better to see whether that assembly will not pass a similar act," an apparent invitation to his former secretary to bribe the French government. In a similar letter to William Carmichael in Madrid, Jefferson wrote that the British either "must repeal their navigation act, in order to be let in to a share of foreign carriage, or the shipping they now employ in foreign carriage will be out of employ, and this act frustrated on which their naval power is built." The beauty of the policy was that the British merchant marine, the training school of the navy, would suffer whether the British yielded and let foreign ships take over part of their colonial trade, or whether they did not. As Jefferson wrote David Humphreys, newly appointed minister to Lisbon, if France, Spain, and Portugal joined the United States in adopting the navigation bill, "it would soon be fatally felt" by the Royal Navy. Jefferson's move was nothing less than "an extraordinary effort to redress the European balance of power by a concerted challenge to Great Britain's dominion of the seas."[19]

Unfortunately for Jefferson, Hammond's arrival challenged the argument that the British did not want an accommodation and complicated passage of the bill on which Jefferson's policy depended. Jefferson countered by informing Hammond that their communications would be only in writing and moved to sidetrack commercial discussions on the grounds that the minister had the power to begin, but not to conclude, negotiations. On December 15, Jefferson proposed that they engage in what soon became a sterile debate over who had first violated the peace treaty and was therefore to blame for the present impasse.[20]

In late 1791 and early 1792, Hamilton intensified his efforts to counter Jefferson's policies. Despite misgivings, he backed Washington's choice of

Morris to be minister to France. (Jefferson by now saw Morris as "a high-flying monarchy man" who had poisoned Washington's mind about the French Revolution and wanted to send him back to London as minister.) In his first serious conversation with Hammond, Hamilton indicated that he was preparing his own report on U.S. navigation and commerce, presumably to use against Jefferson's. At the end of December, Jefferson announced that he was ready to present his report recommending commercial retaliation against the British. Hamilton, according to Jefferson, "opposed it violently," arguing that a trade war would prompt the British to hold on even more tightly to the posts. Obtaining the posts alone "would free us from the expense of the Indian wars." Coming just after the shocking news of St. Clair's defeat by the Indians in Ohio (November 4, 1791) had reached Philadelphia, Hamilton's argument carried weight.[21]

Jefferson reluctantly agreed to delay his controversial report until receiving Hammond's answer to his December 15 message delineating British violations of the peace treaty. If Hammond offered "a glimmering hope" that the British meant to turn over the posts, he would delay his report until the next session of Congress. When Hammond did not answer until March 5, Jefferson assumed that Hamilton had encouraged him to procrastinate. In fact, Hamilton listened sympathetically when the young minister came to discuss his answer to Jefferson. But when Hammond asked about Jefferson's report, Hamilton said he believed that since the Briton's arrival, Jefferson had "abandoned his intention of making any such report."[22] This was not accurate, but neither did Hamilton tell Hammond to drag his feet. Presumably he figured he did not need to do so. Hammond's response to Jefferson would call forth its own answer. In fact, the Jefferson–Hammond exchange over treaty violations culminated in the secretary of state's May 29, 1792, memorandum rejecting British claims at every point. When Jefferson asked his colleagues for comments on a draft of the memo, Hamilton made a handful, but saw little use in trying to reason with someone intent not on expediting a settlement but rather extracting a *mea culpa* from the other side.

Hamilton spoke again to Hammond in late May, "briefly and coldly" dismissing Grenville's pet project for an Indian buffer state fixing the U.S. border on the Ohio River. Several days later, however, Hamilton lamented to Hammond the "intemperate violence" of Jefferson's May 29 memorandum, telling him that it "was far from meeting his approbation, or from containing a faithful exposition of the sentiments" of the administration. Pro-Jefferson historians indignantly – and accurately – argue that Hamilton was deliberately sabotaging Jefferson's "magnificent paper." It is also true that Jefferson, by allowing himself to become bogged down in the preparation of his broadside (with its exhaustively researched arguments and sixty appendices) had distracted himself from his more basic aim of passing retaliatory legislation and challenging British power.[23]

The most important card Hamilton attempted to play to contain Jeffersonian containment, however, was not his maneuvering with Ternant and Hammond. It was his celebrated "Report on the Subject of Manufactures," commissioned by Congress in January 1790 and issued on December 5, 1791. In it Hamilton wrote:

Not only the wealth; but the independence and security of a Country, appear to be materially connected with the prosperity of manufactures. Every nation, with a view to those great objects, ought to endeavour to possess within itself all the essentials of national supply. These comprise the means of *Subsistence habitation clothing* and *defence* .... The extreme embarassments of the United States during the late War, from an incapacity of supplying themselves, are still a matter of keen recollection: A future war might be expected again to exemplify the mischiefs and dangers of a situation, to which that incapacity is still in too great a degree applicable.[24]

Hamilton had long held these views. Washington fully shared them. The Nootka Sound war scare had underlined their validity: a considerable degree of self-sufficiency in goods related to national security was absolutely indispensable.

But there was also a clear message intended for Hawkesbury and the British. Hamilton had told Beckwith two years before that the increase in American manufacturing would doubtless be "proportioned to your Conduct." His report, calling for bounties to encourage domestic manufacturing, argued: "If the system of perfect liberty to industry and commerce were the prevailing system of nations – the arguments which dissuade a country in the predicament of the United States, from the zealous pursuits of manufactures would doubtless have great force." But this was not the case:

The United States are to a certain extent in the situation of a country precluded from foreign Commerce. They can indeed, without difficulty obtain from abroad the manufactured supplies, of which they are in want; but they experience numerous and very injurious impediments to the emission and vent of their own commodities .... In such a position of things, the United States cannot exchange with Europe on equal terms; and this want of reciprocity would render them the victim of a system, which should induce them to confine their views to Agriculture and refrain from Manufactures. A constant and encreasing necessity, on their part, for the commodities of Europe, and only a partial and occasional demand for their own, in return, could not but expose them to a state of impovrishment, compared with the opulence to which their political and natural advantages authorise them to aspire.[25]

Although Hamilton did not name names in the *Report's* final version, an earlier draft shows that he was referring to the British "Corn Laws" limiting American wheat exports and the exclusion of American bottoms from the West Indies. The same draft also spelled out French treatment of American flour, oils, and tobacco. Indeed, "ineligible as is the footing upon which our Trade with Britain is carried on it stands at this time upon a still less eligible footing in regard to France."[26]

Overall, the report suggests that, aside from national security considerations (and despite the reading later given it by Friedrich List and others),
Hamilton was not a doctrinaire, but a rather reluctant mercantilist and advocate of domestic manufacturing. Certainly, his zeal on the subject did not
approach that of his assistant, who authored the first draft of the *Report*, the
Pennsylvania economist Tench Coxe. The context, as well as the content, of
the *Report* clearly indicate that (with the important exception of arms and
munitions) the West Indian emigrant viewed encouraging U.S. manufactures
as a lever to push British policy in a more liberal direction, and to counter
Jefferson's confrontational strategy, as much as an end in itself. The beauty of
Hamilton's proposal was that it would bring pressure to bear on Britain gradually and indirectly, without unleashing the kind of devastating trade war
that would follow from the Madison–Jefferson approach. Not only that –
and the report was quite explicit on this point – the manufacturing areas
of the United States would themselves constitute an emerging market for
American food production. The agricultural South would find itself less dependent on foreign markets and less inclined to see its interests as being in
direct conflict with those of Britain than was presently the case.[27]

The Open Feud

Jefferson's "Anas" contains a detailed account of a conversation between the
president and the secretary of state that took place on the morning of February 29, 1792. Each man spoke of his desire to resign, Washington allowing
that "he really felt himself growing old, his bodily health less firm, his memory, always bad, becoming worse, and perhaps the other faculties of his mind
showing a decay to others of which he was insensible himself." The latter
possibility "particularly oppressed him." Jefferson was also "heartily tired,"
but Washington tried to dissuade him from quitting at the end of the presidential term: "symptoms of dissatisfaction had lately shown themselves"
far beyond what the president could have imagined. This was Jefferson's apparent cue to tell the president that the Treasury Department had instituted
an infernal system for "deluging the States with paper money," shifting the
people's attention from honest pursuits to "a species of gambling, destructive
of morality" and introducing "its poison into the government itself." Not
only had legislators "feathered their own nests with paper," the Constitution itself was being undermined. The real question, in fact, was "whether
we live under a limited or an unlimited government." When an incredulous
Washington asked for clarification, Jefferson pointed to the "Report on the
Subject of Manufactures" as the latest case in point.[28]

Even as they spoke, William Duer's ultimate plan to speculate in federal
securities was collapsing, with Duer himself headed for a New York prison
cell. (According to Dumas Malone, this was "really fortunate for him" because he was safe there from the wrath of those who had been ruined by

his scheme.) Hamilton was fortunate to be rid of an embarrassing associate, but the political fallout from the "Panic of 1792" was fatal to the *Report*. Around the time of Duer's arrest, Madison and his followers defeated a proposal in Congress for bounties to promote domestic industry on the pretext that they were "usurpations of power." Another casualty of the panic was the Society for the Establishment of Useful Manufactures (SEUM), a factory complex to be based near Paterson, New Jersey. Duer had been chief administrator of the SEUM.[29]

Duer's disgrace also coincided with the outbreak of the "Philadelphia newspaper war," pitting Philip Freneau's *National Gazette* against John Fenno's *Gazette of the United States*. Madison and Jefferson persuaded the arch-Anglophobe Freneau (Madison's Princeton classmate) to set up shop in Philadelphia, paying him a small salary as a translator at the State Department, where he would have access to inside information. In mid-March 1792, he became their journalistic attack dog against Hamilton's program, in his words, "a Pandora's box ... pregnant with every mischief." In the summer and fall, Hamilton himself entered the lists against Jefferson using a series of melodramatic pseudonyms, "an American," "Anti-Defamer," "Amicus," "Catullus," and "Metellus."[30]

The antagonists' views of each other emerge from a spate of letters written in mid-1792. Hamilton's to Edward Carrington, a prominent Virginia Federalist, was a pained though penetrating reconstruction of his relationship with Madison and Jefferson. Most of the letter dealt with domestic politics. On foreign policy, he observed:

the views of these Gentlemen are in my judgement equally unsound & dangerous. *They have a womanish attachment to France and a womanish resentment against Great Britain.* They would draw us into the closest embrace of the former & involve us in all the consequences of her politics, & they would risk the peace of the country in their endeavours to keep us at the greatest possible distance from the latter. This disposition goes to a length particularly in Mr. Jefferson of which, till, lately, I had no adequate Idea. Various circumstances prove to me that if these Gentlemen were left to pursue their own course there would be in less than six months *an open war between the U states & Great Britain.*

"Various circumstances" obviously referred to Jefferson's handling of Hammond and his proposals to contain British power.[31]

Hamilton's explanation of his enemies' motives, if overwrought, was not lacking in psychological insight. Since 1789, Madison and Jefferson had suffered a series of defeats, culminating in the national bank. In the process, they had persuaded themselves of "what they may have at first only sported to influence others – namely that there is some dreadful combination against State Government & republicanism." It is not clear if Hamilton realized that the current conspiracy theory was the direct descendant of the one they had entertained before 1776. But in the phrase "womanish resentment" he correctly pinpointed the role of Jefferson's wartime record, and of Virginia's chip on its shoulder vis-à-vis Britain, as a fundamental driving force.[32]

In a May 23 letter to the president, Jefferson spelled out what he had only hinted at in February: the "ultimate object" of Hamilton's "corrupt squadron" was "to prepare the way for a change from the present republican form of government to that of a monarchy." Sectional conflict loomed because the "monarchical federalists" and debt holders were concentrated in the North, whereas the treasury system's victims and antifederalist opponents of the Constitution were in the South. In February, Jefferson had not tried to dissuade Washington from retiring. Now he wrote, "North and South will hang together if they have you to hang on." Jefferson must have seen that Hamilton had been considerably weakened in the meantime by the financial panic, his defeat on the bounties, and Freneau's attacks. Jefferson's May appeal to Washington suggests that he may have realized that he had helped to let the genie of party strife out of the bottle. The monarchical plot, in any case, was now a fixation. It made no difference to Jefferson that Washington dismissed it in a July conversation while deploring Freneau's attacks.[33]

Washington forwarded a long paraphrase of Jefferson's charges to Hamilton, inviting him to reply. In a short private letter, Hamilton also urged Washington to run again, noting that the enmity of the opposition had been sharpened by the government's success and by "the resentments which flow from disappointed predictions and mortified vanity." In a second letter, Hamilton refuted Jefferson's charges point by point. It is doubtful that Washington gave the second letter careful study: It was extremely long and he did not take Jefferson's charges seriously to begin with. Even before reading it, he told Hamilton that he was persuaded it would give him "satisfaction and profit."[34]

Washington's deepest instinct was to preserve a political and sectional balance in his government, and he was disturbed by the increasingly public and personal nature of the quarrel. It was to be "regretted, exceedingly," he wrote Hamilton, "that subjects cannot be discussed . . . or decisions submitted to without having the motives which led to them, improperly implicated on the other." He hoped "there might be mutual forbearances and temporising yieldings *on all sides.*" Noting that he was sending the same message to "other Officers of the Government," it was his "earnest wish" that "balsam may be poured into *all* the wounds which have been given to prevent them from gangrening." Hamilton answered that "if any prospect shall open of healing or terminating the differences which exist, I shall most chearfully [sic] embrace it," but he considered himself "the deeply injured party."[35]

Jefferson's response to a similar appeal showed that he was no more ready to let bygones be bygones than Hamilton. The treasury secretary's derisive articles, and accurate claim that Jefferson was managing Freneau from behind the scenes, had rattled his precious composure. Jefferson's

September 9, 1792, letter to Washington was dripping with animosity. Hamilton was the corrupter of the legislature who gave out "treasury secrets among his friends . . . and who never slips an occasion of making friends with his means." Not only that, he was the leader of a monarchical party who considered the Constitution "a thing of nothing, which must be changed." Reluctant to conclude that Jefferson was either totally deluded or else deliberately lying to Washington, one biographer has evoked the secretary of state's attenuating "capacity to play hide-and-seek within himself." One part of his mind sincerely believed his false claim that he had not incited Freneau, or attempted to influence congressional action. It is doubtful that Washington believed Jefferson's denials on those counts, though no one could dispute his charge that Hamilton had intrigued against his foreign policy. Jefferson's letter rose to a crescendo of righteous indignation:

I will not suffer my retirement to be clouded by the slanders of a man whose history, from the moment at which history can stoop to notice him, is a tissue of machinations against the liberty of the country which has not only received and given him bread, but heaped its honors on his head.

Hamilton (as Jefferson later put it), "bewitched and perverted by the British example," was no ordinary enemy. He was as close as it came in politics to pure evil. Troup was right: "Cartago delenda est."[36]

PART III

SEIZING THE HELM

8

The Birth of American Neutrality,
February–May 1793

Introduction

One of Machiavelli's biographers describes Florence in the years 1510–12, as "caught like an earthen pot between two great vessels of bronze."[1] The republic found itself in the middle of renewed hostilities between its ally, France, and an opposing coalition, including Spain, England, the Holy Roman Emperor, and the pope, who condemned France's heretical conduct and sought to roll back its foreign acquisitions. Though Machiavelli never saw a clear alternative to the alliance, the danger inherent in Florence's traditional ties with France was a central theme of his career. The connection frequently entangled Florence in conflicts with France's enemies, with the French rarely prepared to provide concrete help.

During the third of his four missions to France (June–October 1510), Machiavelli urged Louis XII to avoid armed conflict and hoped Florence would be able to mediate the quarrel between the French king and the pope. Though he feared and opposed war, he concluded that "the hubris and the power" (*la superbia e la potenza*) of France would force Florence to become involved. Therefore the city should make virtue of necessity and try to extract a price from the French. On his return home, he attempted to strengthen the republic's capacity to resist incursions by any of the parties into its territory. But throughout the final crisis of the republic, Florence was crippled by serious internal divisions, for example, over the question of standing military forces. After France's withdrawal from Italy, and the sack of Prato by the Spanish, the republic quickly collapsed from within.[2]

Machiavelli reflected on the problem of weak states caught between two fires during his involuntary retirement. In his post-1512 writings, he generally advised states to eschew neutrality and take sides in their neighbors' conflicts. At the end of the war, a pusillanimous neutral was likely to be attacked by the victor, with little prospect of help from the loser whom he had failed to assist. Despite the outcome in 1512 – which he believed better military preparations might have avoided – he argued in *The Prince* that Florence had had no choice in the end but to take sides in the war between France and the Holy League. In the same breath, however, he warned that "a prince must never make an alliance with someone more powerful than himself in order to injure others, *unless necessity forces him*...because in victory he will remain his prisoner."[3]

* * *

Becoming France's prisoner was exactly what Hamilton had been trying to avoid since the end of the war in 1783. Moreover, and as Machiavelli would have recognized, he saw that distance afforded the United States a small degree of freedom from necessity and the luxury of remaining neutral in the wars of the big powers, something Florence had not enjoyed. Nonetheless, given the conflicting conceptions of the country's destiny in the 1790s, determining what American "neutrality" meant in practice would not be an easy task.

The European war that Hamilton had predicted in 1788 began with France's declaration of hostilities against Britain, the United Provinces (the modern Netherlands), and Spain on February 1, 1793. Shortly after the news reached the United States, the Washington administration issued a proclamation of neutrality, dated April 22, 1793. Writing of this period, one historian observes that Hamilton and Jefferson often "arrived at the same practical conclusion – for the simple reason that it was the most sensible one." For another, the principles of "steering clear of European conflicts at almost any cost and providing time and space" for economic development "remained a matter of consensus throughout the top reaches of the government." For other historians, "simply as a question of foreign policy, a division scarcely existed at all [in 1793]...." Jefferson's pro-French position, according to this latter view, was really domestic political posturing. The French cause was wildly popular, as evidenced by the parades and pyrotechnics lavished on the new French minister, Edmond Charles Genêt, from the minute he alighted from the frigate *Embuscade* at Charleston on April 8, 1793, and began a twenty-eight-day trip to Philadelphia. The point of stoking this "French frenzy" was not to help France, but to keep public opinion mobilized against the Hamiltonians. For Republican leaders, "the sentiment for France was a major means to this end, anything but an end in itself."[4]

The view that Jefferson was essentially a calculating party leader seems seriously misleading. One of the main reasons Jefferson favored American neutrality was that he considered it to be in the best interests of France, and he worked for a definition of neutrality that would provide maximum aid to France without involving his country in the war. (It is true that he believed that these policies would also advance the Republican cause at home.) Hamilton, for his part, now made a more open attempt to control foreign policy and to disentangle the United States from its permanent alliance. He operated in the knowledge (as Foreign Secretary Grenville put it to George Hammond) that U.S. neutrality was "necessary for the success" of British arms. The birth in 1793–94 of what became the "classic" American definition of neutrality was not the result of a basic consensus, but of a tug-of-war between contending midwives – one trying to help the French and other the British cause.[5]

Jefferson's "Polar Star"

With the rise of the Jacobins, the storming of the Tuileries Palace, and the imprisonment of the royal family in August 1792, the French Revolution entered a new and tumultuous phase. The National Assembly was disbanded, the Constitution of 1791 suspended, and a provisional government declared. The Paris Massacre in early September was followed by the convening of the National Convention and the declaration of a Republic on September 20, 1792. On the same day, a French army of over 50,000 repelled combined Austrian, Prussian, and French *émigré* forces at Valmy, in northeastern France. News of Valmy reached an exultant America in December. In his famous "Adam and Eve" letter (January 3, 1793), Jefferson rebuked William Short for daring to criticize the Revolution and strongly defended the decision to depose the king.[6]

The secretary of state's position on Franco-American relations emerges from a conversation with Washington in late December 1792. In October, Washington had rejected an explicit call by Hamilton for "a defensive treaty of alliance" with Britain in order to end Spanish support of the Indians, and to open the Mississippi to Anglo-American navigation. According to Jefferson's notes, the president had said that "the remedy would be worse than the disease."[7] By the end of the year, Washington was concerned about the possibility of a war between France and Britain, the latter allied with Spain. (Bourbon Spain would in fact go to war alongside Britain against the killers of Louis XVI.) Though this piece of news was not yet known, General Charles-François Dumouriez's army had gone on the offensive and conquered the Austrian Netherlands (modern Belgium) in November 1792, endangering Britain's ally, the United Provinces. Washington told Jefferson that "if we did not prepare in time some support [for France], in the event of a rupture with Spain and England, we might be charged with criminal negligence." According to Jefferson, Washington believed that "there was no nation on whom we could rely, at all times, but France." Jefferson wrote that he "was much pleased with the tone of these observations. It was the very doctrine which had been my polar star."[8]

By early 1793, Jefferson was also convinced of the link between the French cause and that of right-thinking people in the United States. He wrote his son-in-law that the tonic effect of recent French news on American opinion showed that "the form our own government was to take depended much more on the events of France than anybody had before imagined." Later in the year, worried about famine and a reversal of military fortunes, he wrote him, "I fear that if this summer should prove disastrous to the French, it will damp that energy of republicanism in our new Congress." Jefferson's fears for France were matched by hopes that the financial crisis provoked by the war, combined with the French example, would cause a revolution in Britain and a successful end to the war.[9]

Around this time, the Provisory Executive Council in Paris approved instructions, inspired by the Girondin faction leader Jacques Pierre Brissot de Warville, for the mission of "Citizen Genêt." In anticipation of war with Britain and Spain, the thirty-year-old fluent English speaker was empowered to negotiate a new treaty with the United States, to include a provision closing French and U.S. ports to British shipping, a reciprocal exemption of U.S. and French vessels from tonnage duties, and a renewal of the U.S. guarantee of France's Caribbean possessions. As a sweetener, he brought news of a decree opening French colonial ports to U.S. ships. In the meantime, Genêt was to insist on strict observance of the existing treaty, especially as it regarded privateering. Article 17 of the 1778 Treaty of Amity of Commerce permitted the privateers of the two countries to bring prizes into the ports of the other while denying that privilege to those at war with France or the United States. Article 22 prohibited the enemies of France or the United States from fitting out privateers in the ports of either country. France now interpreted this article as allowing (though it did not explicitly do so) its privateers to recruit and equip in U.S. ports, and Genêt carried stacks of blank letters of marque to be handed out in the United States. Indeed, anti-British privateers had begun to sail out of Charleston harbor even before he presented his credentials to Washington in May 1793. Genêt also carried a supply of blank military commissions to serve his most grandiose objective: the conquest of Canada, Louisiana, and the Floridas, using U.S. territory as a base. Genêt was to finance these operations, and secure arms, food, and provisions for the West Indies colonies and the metropole, by persuading the U.S. government to pay back its remaining debt to France (around $5.6 million) in advance. Indeed, it looked as though "the hubris and the power" of France might well involve its small and vulnerable client state in a war for which the latter was totally unprepared.[10]

In a February 20 conversation with Colonel William S. Smith – son-in-law of Vice President Adams and a paid agent of the Girondins – Jefferson learned that Genêt was on his way "with full powers to give us all the privileges we can desire" in the West Indies, that the French wanted the debt paid in the form of provisions, and that a major operation was planned to liberate South America, leaving East and West Florida to the United States. Smith also reported that Gouverneur Morris "cursed the French ministers, as a set of damned rascals" at his dinner table and was *persona non grata* in Paris. Jefferson's sly suggestion to Washington was that Morris be sent to London as minister, whereas Thomas Pinckney, a success as U.S. minister there, should be sent to France. Washington countered with the intriguing proposal that Jefferson himself replace Morris. Jefferson refused: "as to the opportunity of doing good, this was likely to be the scene of action, as Genêt was bringing powers to do the business here."[11]

Even if an off-hand suggestion, the president must have realized that Jefferson's departure would have significantly altered the local political landscape. Whether that was his purpose is not clear, but it may not have been a coincidence that a full-scale Republican campaign to expose the administration's alleged corruption was in full swing in the form of resolutions introduced by Virginia congressman William Branch Giles on January 23, 1793. Hamilton provided satisfactory answers to Giles's questions, but on February 27, with only three days left in the congressional session, Giles introduced a new set of resolutions of censure against the secretary of the treasury. Many suspected at the time what a historian proved two hundred years later: despite his assurance to Washington the previous September that it was not his habit to "intermeddle" with Congress, the resolutions were based on a draft written by Jefferson. Meanwhile, Freneau's newspaper ridiculed the pomp and ceremony of Washington's birthday celebration: "the monarchical farce of the birthday was as usual kept." Jefferson believed that Freneau's newspaper had "saved our constitution, which was galloping fast into monarchy," commenting that Washington, in judging the paper, had not displayed "his usual good sense and *sangue froid.*"[12]

On March 1, Hamilton's supporters in the House, led by William Loughton Smith of South Carolina and Fisher Ames of Massachusetts, completed the rout of William Giles. Only five congressmen, including James Madison and the hot-headed Giles himself, voted in favor of the resolutions. Even the partisan Dumas Malone chastises Jefferson at this point: "In dealing with a man whom he thought unscrupulous, perhaps he overbore his own scruples to some extent.... He and his fellow Virginians showed bad judgment, at all events. They overreached themselves."[13] In mid-March, rumors of King Louis XVI's decapitation (on January 21, 1793), arrived in the United States. The Jacobins, even in the view of some Republicans, had overreached themselves. This news was followed in early April by that of the European war. Jefferson, in an April 7 letter to Washington at Mount Vernon, recommended adopting "every justifiable measure for preserving our neutrality." At the same time, the United States must "provide those necessaries for war which must be brought across the Atlantic." Jefferson's challenge was to accomplish both of those things at the same time.[14]

The Battle of the Thirteen Questions

On one point at least, there was no room for disagreement: France had declared war on Britain, rather than the reverse. Hamilton was in a strong position as he contemplated his boldest move yet into Jefferson's bailiwick. In an April 9 letter to John Jay, he asked for advice on the question whether, in light of the king's death and the ongoing power struggle in France, it would not be preferable to refuse to receive Genêt or to do so with the qualification that the United States reserved the right to suspend the treaties, pending the outcome of events. In addition to various provisions of the Treaty of Amity and Commerce, the main point at issue was Article 11 of the Treaty of Alliance, by which the United States guaranteed the French West Indies. Hamilton admitted, "I doubt whether we could *bona fide* dispute the ultimate obligation of the Treaties." Their suspension would be the next best course.[15]

On April 12, just before leaving Mount Vernon for Philadelphia, Washington wrote Jefferson and Hamilton asking them to give serious thought to implementing a policy of "strict neutrality." On his first day back in the capital, April 18, he found that Jefferson had done nothing, while Hamilton had drawn up a list of thirteen questions for discussion. Washington copied (and perhaps paraphrased) the questions and sent them to the cabinet with orders to meet the next day. The most important questions were, number one, should a proclamation be issued and should it contain a declaration of neutrality? Two, should the French minister be received? Three, if received, should it be with qualifications? Four, might the United States renounce or suspend the treaties until a French government were established? Thirteen, should Congress be called into session to deal with the crisis?

The reasons for Jefferson's failure to act are a bit of a mystery. One pair of historians refer to other business and possible "nonchalance." For another, he was simply "too torn to draw up a plan." The most probable explanation is that he wanted to postpone a statement of policy, and thus Hamilton's move took him by surprise.[16]

Washington met with Jefferson, Hamilton, Secretary of War Henry Knox, and Attorney General Edmund Randolph at nine o'clock the next morning. Since the estrangement of Hamilton and Jefferson, Washington had begun to rely more on Randolph, a forty-year-old Williamsburg lawyer and former governor of Virginia of moderately pro-French sympathies. Accounts of the meeting vary widely. On the first question, one writer speaks of a "sharp debate"; for others, Jefferson "seems to have made no rebuttal" to Hamilton and agreed to the immediate issuance of a proclamation. Jefferson's own notes show that he correctly assumed the questions were Hamilton's and that they constituted a logical chain leading "to a declaration of the executive, that our treaty with France is void." But the same notes do not even mention the first question.[17]

Undoubtedly there *was* discussion of that key question, leaving each antagonist with the impression that he had made his point. Hamilton, supported by the president and secretary of war, favored a proclamation of neutrality without consulting Congress. Jefferson believed that "a declaration of neutrality was a declaration there should be no war to which the Executive was not competent." He also argued that "it would be better to hold back the declaration of neutrality, as a thing worth something to the powers at war, that they would bid for it, and we might reasonably ask a price, the *broadest privileges* of neutral nations." Those present readily understood that, by this, Jefferson meant respect for the principle of "free ships make free goods," in other words, that the U.S. flag protected noncontraband property belonging to the belligerents. He also meant a limited, so-called modern, definition of contraband, namely one excluding food.

Those present also grasped that for France, this was no price at all. The French depended on imported food carried by American merchantmen while "free ships make free goods" was already enshrined (Articles 14 and 23) in the Franco-American commercial treaty. The British, on the other hand, had never tolerated a rule that prevented them from cutting off supplies to their enemies and had insisted that food be considered contraband. What action did Jefferson intend to take if France agreed to his terms for American neutrality, but Britain – as was certain to be the case – refused? A March letter to Madison gives some indication: if Britain tried to prevent American provisions from reaching France, Congress (though it would be justified in doing so) should not declare a state of war. Rather, it should pass legislation to "instantly exclude" from U.S. ports "all the manufactures, produce, vessels and subjects of the nations committing this aggression, during the continuance of the aggression and till full satisfaction [was] made for it."[18]

For several reasons, Jefferson did not press his arguments during the April 19 meeting. He was outnumbered on question one, and it was hard to dispute the need for a prompt statement of U.S. policy. Furthermore, in return for accepting a proclamation, he obtained concessions: the document would not actually use the word "neutrality," Congress would not be bound by it, and it would contain language warning U.S. citizens against carrying "those articles deemed contraband by the modern usage of nations." To allow Jefferson to disassociate himself, the drafting of the proclamation was assigned to Randolph. In Jefferson's mind, despite the proclamation, the meaning of U.S. neutrality remained to be defined. He presumably hoped that insistence on "modern usage" would be a lever to make the British allow American food to reach France, or else face retaliation. "I proposed to insert the word *modern* in the proclamation," Jefferson recalled, in December 1793, "to open upon her [Britain] the idea that we should require the acquiescence in that principle as the condition of our remaining in peace." In late April and early May, he ordered minister Pinckney to urge the point on the British, as well as the principle that "free ships make free goods."[19]

Another reason, Jefferson explained to Madison (who called the proclamation "a most unfortunate error"), why it had not been "expedient to oppose it altogether" on April 19, was to be able to fight Hamilton on question two, "the boldest and greatest that ever was hazarded, and which would have called for extremities had it prevailed." This was the question of whether to receive Genêt. This time, it was Hamilton's turn to concede something that at least three of the others favored and to try to advance his purpose by attaching strings. Jefferson's "extremities" would no doubt have included an appeal to Congress and the country. In the event, Jefferson was prepared for the time being to agree with the others that Congress need not be called into emergency session.[20]

The most heated discussion turned out to be over question three (qualified reception of Genêt). Hamilton argued that because the treaties had been made when France was a monarchy, but might soon have a government rendering the alliance dangerous, the United States had the right to renounce or suspend the treaties. "Having the right of election now, if we receive their minister without any qualifications, it will amount to an act of election to continue the treaties." Moreover, choosing to continue them was equivalent to "making a new treaty at this time in the same form, that is to say with a clause of guarantee; but to make a treaty with a clause of guarantee, during a war, is a departure from neutrality, and would make us associates in the war." To renounce or suspend the treaties was therefore a necessary act of neutrality. Since Jefferson and Randolph favored Genêt's unqualified reception, Washington adjourned the meeting and asked for written opinions on question three.[21]

Hamilton's argument went beyond what he had told Jay, and it is doubtful that he expected to win an immediate renunciation of the treaties. He probably hoped to secure a more modest aim: receiving Genêt, but reserving the right to suspend or renounce the treaties. His written argument (May 2), addressing questions three and four together, appealed to Washington's indignation over the king's death and doubts about the longevity of the Paris regime. At its core was a citation from Vattel:

The ally *remains the ally of the State*, notwithstanding the change that has happened in it. *However* when this change renders the alliance *useless, dangerous*, or *disagreeable*, it may renounce it, for it may say upon a good foundation, that it would not have entered into an alliance with that nation, had it been under the present form of Government.

If there was a right to renounce the treaties under such circumstances, there must logically be a right to *suspend* them pending the outcome of events. Given the latter right, considerations of reputation and interest argued for suspension or, as Hamilton concluded, reserving the right to suspend. America's standing would suffer from connection with those "sullied by crimes and extravagancies." Hamilton repeated his somewhat tortured argument that not electing to suspend the treaties was tantamount to departing from neutrality.[22]

Not for the first time, Jefferson's answer (April 28) to a request from Washington was prompter and lacking the verbal overkill of Hamilton's. Jefferson considered "the people who constitute a society or nation as the source of all authority in that nation, as free to transact their common concerns by any agents they think proper." Thus, the treaties were not "between the US. & Louis Capet, but between the two nations... and the nations remaining in existence, tho' both of them have since changed their forms of government, the treaties are not annulled by these changes." To Hamilton's "scrap" of Vattel, Jefferson opposed his own exegesis. Based on the Swiss authority's arguments (including the one that the moral duties of individuals to each other in a state of nature accompanied them into a state of society), it was impossible to sustain the view that obligations could be annulled simply because they were considered "'dangerous, useless, or disagreeable.'" Rather, the "danger which absolves us must be great, inevitable & imminent." Was this truly the case now?

Does the Guarantee engage us to enter into the war in any event? Are we to enter into it before we are called on by our allies? Have we been called on by them? – shall we ever be called on by them? Is it their interest to call on us? .... Are we in a condition to go to war? .... If we cannot save them are we bound to go to war for a desperate object? .... Many, if not most of these questions offer grounds of doubt whether the clause of guarantee will draw us into war.

Jefferson denied that receiving Genêt without qualifications would have any implications for the treaties. He concluded that "not renouncing the treaties now is so far from being a breach of neutrality, that the doing it would be the breach, by giving just cause of war to France."[23]

The battle of the thirteen questions had ended in a draw. Washington himself did not doubt that the treaties were valid and planned (even before reading Jefferson's lucid paper) to receive Genêt without qualifications. But Hamilton had won the precedent-setting point that the executive would issue an immediate proclamation declaring neutrality in fact, if not in name. One suspects, moreover, that to refute Hamilton, Jefferson had allowed himself to be drawn onto ground he would have preferred to avoid. His April 28 paper argued, for example, that receiving Genêt did not imply a reaffirmation of the treaties and that the guarantee of the West Indies was a dead letter. This was all the more true if one believed, as Hamilton did, that the present war was "an *offensive war* on the part of France." In any case with the privateers *Sans Culottes* and *Citoyen Genêt* cruising the Atlantic, and Genêt's carriage clattering northward toward Philadelphia, the war over neutrality had only just begun.[24]

"Every Inch of Ground"

Hamilton's basic aim was now to impose his own interpretation of the new policy, in effect to nail Jefferson to the cross of the April 22 proclamation of neutrality and to hoist him on the petard of his April 28 paper. In early

May, Hammond informed Hamilton that provisions and grain shipped to France on U.S. vessels would be "liable to capture," the principle "free ships make free goods" would not be allowed, and no supplies of any kind could enter French ports blockaded or besieged by the British. According to Hammond's dispatch to Grenville, "In the justice of these principles Mr. Hamilton perfectly coincided, and assured me that he would be responsible for the concurrence of all the members of this administration in the admission of their propriety to the fullest extent."[25]

Jefferson found himself waging a defensive battle for what he termed "manly" as opposed to "mere English neutrality," that is, one that exploited every possible loophole in favor of the French. As he wrote James Monroe, "every inch of ground must be fought in our councils in desperation, in order to hold up the face of even a sneaking neutrality." By early June, he felt "worn down with labors from morning to night, and day by day; knowing them as fruitless to others as they are vexatious to myself, committed singly in desperate and eternal contest against a host who are systematically undermining the public liberty and prosperity." Among his other worries was that the "old spirit of 1776," rekindled by French military successes, might provoke a shooting war with Britain, something he knew would defeat his purpose of helping France.[26]

Cabinet battle lines formed again after the appropriately named *Embuscade* dropped anchor in Philadelphia harbor with two British merchantmen in tow. Philadelphians by the thousands crowded the Market Street wharf to cheer the French frigate and view her captures. The new showdown was precipitated by a flurry of complaints from the British minister (dated May 2 and May 8): one of the prizes, the *Grange*, had been taken while at anchor in Delaware Bay; a prize court set up by the French consul at Charleston had condemned two British brigantines captured by the *Embuscade* and presented them for public sale; two French privateers, with a number of American crewmen, had been equipped in Charleston; a large shipment of arms would soon leave New York for France. Hammond demanded that the British vessels captured by the privateers be restored. Washington called a cabinet meeting for May 15 to decide how to respond.[27]

Though he was determined to conduct himself even-handedly, Washington's private thoughts were running parallel to Hamilton's. On May 6, 1793, he wrote to the Governor of Virginia, Henry Lee, that the affairs of France seemed "to be in the highest paroxysm of disorder, not so much from the pressure of foreign enemies . . . but because those in whom the G[overnmen]t is entrusted are ready to tear each other to pieces and will more than probably prove the worst foes the Country has." He asked Lee to burn the letter as soon as he had read it. In a letter written two days later, Jefferson revealed his own thoughts to the Girondin leader (his old acquaintance), Brissot de Warville: "I continue eternally attached to the principles of your revolution. I hope it will end in the establishment of some firm government, friendly to liberty, & capable of maintaining it. If it does the world will become inevitably free."[28]

On May 15, the cabinet approved an answer to Hammond. The *Grange* had clearly been captured in U.S. territorial waters and should therefore be restored. The French consul's condemnation of a British vessel was a "judicial act" on U.S. soil unwarranted by either "the usage of nations" or Franco-American agreements and was therefore null and void. United States citizens, under the April 22 proclamation, were free to export arms and other contraband at their own risk. A more controversial point was the French right to fit out privateers on U.S. territory. Jefferson was probably tempted to uphold it under Article 22 of the Treaty of Amity and Commerce. In notes for the May cabinet meetings he wrote concerning France's right:

words of XXII. art. *shall not* be lawful for enemies of Fr. Fit out privateers. Implication [is] that it *shall* be lawful for French. So understood universally. by everyone here – by ourselves at Charleston – by Genêt. Still true that is not EXPRESSLY PERMITTED – may be forbidden. but till forbidden must be slight offense.

But Jefferson was now bound by what he had argued in his April 28 paper: the United States could refuse France the right, "there being no stipulation to the contrary, and we ought to refuse it on principles of fair neutrality." That position, taken in his eagerness to refute Hamilton's argument about the danger of the treaties, and apparently *before* he learned that the French were actually preparing privateers in Charleston, was affirmed as official U.S. policy on May 15. Hammond was assured that no "commissioning, equipping and manning" of privateers would be allowed in U.S. ports.[29]

Jefferson drew the line and fought bitterly for the French position on the last points at issue – whether prizes already taken by the Charleston privateers should be returned to their owners and whether those privateers would have to leave U.S. ports. His cabinet deadlocked, Washington once again adjourned the meeting and asked for written opinions. According to Jefferson's, Britain should have "a very moderate apology" but no returned prizes. The incidents had occurred early in the war, far from Philadelphia, and before official measures could be taken. Taking the prizes back at gunpoint could mean war with France. Provoking France to attack the United States, he thought, was just what Hamilton had in mind. Jefferson insisted, moreover, that the French privateers fitted out before the ban should be allowed to continue to operate out of U.S. ports.[30] Hamilton countered that France's activities in Charleston were a violation of U.S rights – "for which we have a *claim to reparation* and a right to make war if it be refused." Restitution of the property was thus "a species of reparation . . . and enabling us to do justice to the party, in injuring whom we have been made instrumental." Britain, in turn, would have "a right to consider our refusal to cause restitution to be made, as equivalent to our becoming an accomplice in the hostility – as a departure from neutrality – as an aggression upon her. Hence we furnish a cause of War." War with Britain, Hamilton suspected, was what Jefferson had in mind.[31]

The May 15 battle likewise ended in a draw. Washington, struggling to maintain an equilibrium in his government, adopted Randolph's compromise position that the prizes should not be returned to their British owners but nor should the French corsairs continue to enjoy the sanctuary of U.S. ports. An increasingly frustrated Washington reached this decision on May 19, 1793, three days after Genêt's arrival in Philadelphia. With the minister plenipotentiary of the French Republic finally on the scene, the struggle over neutrality entered its decisive phase.[32]

9

"A Most Distressing Dilemma," May–December 1793

Introduction

One thing that can be said of Edmond Genêt is that he did not adhere to Talleyrand's cynical motto, "*surtout pas trop de zèle*." This was partly because it was still too early in the saga of the French Revolution to have learned that particular lesson and partly because of his reception in the United States. A committee of thirty leading Republicans, pressed by a large crowd of ordinary citizens, greeted Genêt with a message of solidarity at his lodgings at the City Tavern on May 17. The next evening, after Genêt had presented his credentials to Washington, the French residents of the city hosted a sumptuous dinner, where guests sang the "Marseillaise" and Genêt showed off his own fine voice in a stirring patriotic solo. A line from his letter to the foreign minister in Paris the same day is indicative of his mood: "The true Americans are at the height of joy." Two weeks later he was still living in "the midst of perpetual fêtes." Nearly two hundred people, including Governor Thomas Mifflin and other state and federal officials, raised their glasses to Genêt and the French cause at Oeller's Hotel on June 1.[1]

The euphoria was catching. Jefferson wrote Madison two days after Genêt's arrival that "It is impossible for anything to be more affectionate, more magnanimous than the purport of his mission." He paraphrased Genêt's message thusly:

We know that under present circumstances we have a right to call upon you for the guarantee of our islands. Be we do not desire it. We wish you to do nothing but what is for your own good, and we will do all in our power to promote it. Cherish your own peace and prosperity. You have expressed a willingness to enter into a more liberal treaty of commerce with us; I bring full powers (and he produced them) to form such a treaty.... We see in you the only person on earth who can love us sincerely, and merit to be so loved.

In Jefferson's misleading characterization, Genêt "offers everything and asks nothing." He apparently had the sense to see that U.S. neutrality was the best way of helping France.[2]

But it was too good to be true. Jefferson soon found himself on the horns of what he called "the most distressing dilemma, between our regard for his nation, which is constant and sincere, and a regard for our laws." It was an excruciatingly personal dilemma and, though Jefferson would not have admitted it, partly of his own creation. He spontaneously took Genêt under his wing and confided that he was France's closest friend. He assured Genêt that the president, "out of respect to him & his country," would reconsider the question of the privateers. The sanguine and somewhat naive minister failed to grasp the ambiguity of Jefferson's position. It was perfectly reasonable for him to assume that the notorious "Veritas" essays, anonymously published in Freneau's paper starting June 1 and lambasting Washington for the neutrality policy, were the product of Jefferson's own pen. Egged on by the public, and Jefferson's seeming patronage, Genêt made demands that put Jefferson in a nearly untenable position as secretary of state.[3]

Genêt's first official letter (May 22) to Jefferson proposed that the United States liquidate its debt by shipping badly needed American supplies to France. Jefferson favored paying the current year's installments in advance, but realized that Genêt's plan was incompatible with U.S. law. A second letter (May 23) enclosed a copy of the decrees opening French colonial ports to U.S. ships and proposed negotiation of a "national compact" between the two republics. Jefferson was sympathetic but, as he rationalized to Madison, outnumbered four to one in the cabinet. It was better to delay the compact, Jefferson explained to Genêt, until the Senate returned in the fall.[4] In what he called a gesture of "deference and friendship" to the U.S. government, Genêt restored the *Grange* to its British owners, but was adamant that France had the right to fit out privateers, enroll American seamen, and operate consular courts on U.S. soil. Jefferson replied on June 5 that the president, on due reconsideration, believed it was the "*duty* of a neutral nation to prohibit such as would injure one of the warring powers." Genêt's answer (June 8) overflowed with indignation and disbelief. The United States ought to set the "example of a true neutrality, which does not consist in the cowardly abandonment of their friends in the moment when danger menaces them, but in adhering strictly, if they can do no better, to the obligations they have contracted with them." In a small concession, he had instructed French consuls to grant letters of marque only to those who swore to respect U.S. territory "and the political opinions of their President, until the representatives of the sovereign people shall have confirmed or rejected them." This last statement was in the spirit of Jefferson's own April reasoning: Congress would be free to overturn neutrality if it chose.[5]

On June 12, the cabinet decided that the captured British sloop *Polly*, being equipped as a French privateer in New York harbor, should be held and action taken by the U.S. attorney for the district of New York. The cabinet also requested that the governor of New York seize the British brigantine *Catherine*, taken in U.S. waters by the *Embuscade*, and that the U.S. attorney take steps to allow a U.S. court to rule in this and analogous cases. To the list of cases would soon be added the ships *William, Pilgrim, Fanny, Conyngham*, and *William Tell*. For Genêt, however, these actions were "in contempt of treaties." Coming just as he learned (from Jefferson's letter of June 11) that the U.S. government would not accommodate France on the debt question, the news confirmed his conviction that the executive was out of touch with the people and must be defied.[6] The cabinet approved Jefferson's answer to Genêt on June 17, pointing out that article 17 of the Treaty of Amity and Commerce allowed "the armed vessels of either party to enter the ports of the other, and to depart with their prizes freely." But the equipping, arming, and manning of armed vessels was another matter. Genêt dismissed Jefferson's arguments as old-fashioned legalisms and beneath the dignity of republican diplomacy. On June 24, shortly after Genêt's latest letter, Washington left Philadelphia for Mount Vernon. The cabinet's answer to Genêt would have to wait until his return.[7]

It is hard not to sympathize with Jefferson, counting the days until his retirement, but trapped in the meantime in an exhausting bureaucratic contest. Even worse, Genêt was playing into the hands of Jefferson's enemies by employing some of the secretary of state's earlier arguments. Jefferson wrote James Monroe in late June:

I am doing everything in my power to moderate the impetuosity of his movements, and to destroy the dangerous opinions [sic] which has been excited in him, that the people of the United States will disavow the acts of their government, and that he has an appeal from the Executive to Congress, and from both to the people.

Genêt, meanwhile, was coming to see Jefferson as a two-faced character, someone "endowed with good qualities, but weak enough to sign what he does not believe and to defend officially threats which he condemns in his conversations and anonymous writings."[8]

It was particularly galling for Jefferson to have to defend the U.S. government against Genêt's charge that it had failed to prevent British cruisers from taking French property off U.S. ships, in other words, to enforce the principle of "free ships make free goods." Jefferson had explained to Genêt that he was trying through Pinckney to get the British to agree to the principle, but that in the meantime, the United States did not have the legal right to make war to uphold it. Genêt, in turn, threatened that unless the United States took "effectual measures" against the British, French cruisers would begin to seize British property on U.S. ships. (In the meantime, Jefferson noted, the French were doing very well from the corollary to free ships make free goods, "unfree ships make unfree goods," authorizing them to seize U.S. property found on British ships.) An exasperated Jefferson lectured Genêt that according to the "general law of nations," as opposed to specific conventions, "free ships make free goods" did not apply.⁹

Jefferson must have been comforted by the knowledge that in reining in Genêt, he was actually helping France. The kind of benevolent U.S neutrality that Genêt favored would sooner or later have brought a heavy-handed British reaction. Jefferson tried, as usual, to see a silver lining. Dumouriez's invasion of the United Provinces had been repulsed by the British and Austrians at Neerwinden in March 1793, and the defeated general had arrested the commissioners sent from Paris to investigate. But for Jefferson, the subsequent refusal of Dumouriez's soldiers to march with him on Paris to restore a constitutional monarchy was proof that the French could not "be shaken in their republicanism." The "scoundrel" Dumouriez had gone over to the Austrians, Britain was on the edge of financial collapse, and only famine could destroy the Revolution. Jefferson wrote Madison on June 29, "Hunger is to be expected; but the silence of the late papers on that head, and the near approach of harvest" were reasons for optimism.¹⁰

And there was still hope that he could reason with Genêt. That their personal relations remained cordial is clear from Genêt's desire to communicate delicate information to Jefferson on July 5, "not as Secretary of State but as Mr. Jefferson." Genêt disclosed a vital part of his mission in the form of his instructions to the noted botanist André Michaux to organize insurrections in Canada and Louisiana (the latter in conjunction with a French naval force). Genêt proposed that Kentuckians under the retired American generals George Rogers Clark and Benjamin Logan (willing to undertake the task for three thousand pounds) rendezvous outside U.S. territory, attack the Spanish, and set up an independent state linked by trade to the United States and France.¹¹

Jefferson, who was familiar with French plans, and looked on them with sympathy, told Genêt that U.S. officers who made war on Spain would surely go to the gallows. Aside from that, however, Jefferson said he "did not care what insurrections should be excited in Louisiana." Furthermore, according to Genêt's account,

he [Jefferson] gave me to understand that he thought a little spontaneous irruption of the inhabitants of Kentucky into New Orleans could advance matters; he put me in touch with several deputies of Kentucky, notably Mr. Brown.... He [Brown] showed me ways of acting with success, gave me the addresses of many dependable men, and promised he would apply all his influence to the success of our plans.

Several weeks before, Genêt had asked Jefferson for an exequatur for Michaux to become French consul in Kentucky. Jefferson had explained that consuls were not allowed in the back country, lest the area soon be crawling with Spanish and British agents, but agreed to write a letter of introduction for Michaux to Governor Issac Shelby of Kentucky. Genêt now asked Jefferson to rewrite it, styling Michaux not as a simple botanist, but a "French citizen possessing his [Genêt's] confidence." Jefferson readily obliged. He did not disclose to Washington his knowledge of French plans to overthrow Spanish rule until two months later, when the Spanish minister in Philadelphia lodged a formal protest against Genêt.[12]

"Pacificus" Takes up the Cudgels

Jefferson was not the only member of the government feeling the strain of cabinet conflict. Washington came down with a fever in early June. Hamilton was in poor health and forced to rest in the country. On June 21, he wrote Washington: "Considerations, relative both to the public Interest and to my own delicacy, have brought me, after mature reflection, to a resolution to resign the office, I hold, toward the end of the ensuing session of Congress." He planned to stay until then because some propositions necessary to the full development of his "original plan" and of "some consequence" to his reputation remained to be put forward, but also to allow for "the revival and more deliberate prosecution of the Inquiry" into his conduct begun at the end of the previous session. Though physically worn-down and financially pinched, Hamilton was inviting his enemies to take another crack at him, lest his name suffer from the impression that he had something to hide or had quit out of fear.[13]

In the meantime, writing in the *Gazette of the United States* using the pseudonym "Pacificus," Hamilton delivered a series of blows of his own. To the argument that the executive lacked the authority to issue the April 22 proclamation, he answered that it was

the duty of the Executive to preserve Peace till war is declared; and in fulfilling that duty, it must necessarily possess a right of judging what is the nature of the obligations which the treaties of the country impose on the Government; and when in pursuance of this right it has concluded that there is nothing in them inconsistent with a *state* of neutrality, it becomes both its province and its duty to enforce the laws incident to that state of the Nation.[14]

Hamilton proceeded to blast away at the various rationales – legal, strategic, and sentimental – for an alliance he considered obsolete and dangerous. France had initiated the recent conflict, making it by definition an "offensive war," and this alone gave the United States valid grounds for refusing to execute the guarantee. To those who believed France was waging a just war, Hamilton reviewed the aims of the National Convention. Its decree of November 19, 1792, declared that France would "grant *fraternity* and *assistance* to every people who *wish* to recover their liberty" and ordered French generals to aid those peoples and defend "*those citizens who may have been vexed for the cause of liberty*." For Hamilton, it was "justifiable and meritorious" to help an oppressed nation in the act of liberating itself. It was another matter to issue "a general invitation to insurrection and revolution," something that amounted to what France herself had complained of: flagrant interference by one nation in the internal affairs of another.[15]

In a statement to British sympathizers, the Convention had declared, "'*Royalty in Europe is either destroyed or on the point of perishing*, on the ruins of feudality; and the *Declaration of Rights placed side by side of the thrones is a devouring fire which will consume them*.'" Hamilton called this "an open patronage of a Revolution" in Britain and an "offense and injury" to that country. Finally, the French had violated the law of nations by incorporating conquered land without the sanction of treaties, while its expansion "threatened the independence of all other countries." In an early use of what would become a central argument for a pro-British policy, Hamilton invoked the European balance: "It is a principle well agreed & founded on the best reasons, that whenever a particular nation adopts maxims of conduct contrary to those generally established among nations calculated to disturb their tranquillity & to expose their safety, they may justifiably make a common cause to oppose & controul [sic] such Nation."[16]

Machiavelli had written, "Sometimes men are so little prudent that, not knowing how and not being able to defend themselves, they want to take on the task of defending others." "Pacificus No. 3" pointed out that the United States was simply too weak and exposed to be obliged to honor its guarantee of France's possessions. "Self-preservation is the first duty of a Nation; and though in the performance of stipulations relating to war, good faith requires that the *ordinary hazards* of war should be fairly encountered . . . yet it does not require that *extraordinary* and *extreme* hazards should be run."[17]

In "Pacificus No. 4" and "Pacificus No. 5," Hamilton developed the argument about gratitude introduced in his September 1790 Nootka Sound opinion. The basis of gratitude was "a benefit received or intended, which there was no right to claim, originating in a regard to the interest or advantage of the party, on whom the benefit is or is meant to be conferred." Among individuals, disinterested favors sometimes provided an occasion for gratitude. Among nations "the predominant motive of good offices" was the advantage of the performer. France had acted purely in its own interest in advancing American independence, and the reduction of British power constituted "adequate compensation." In any event, continued Hamilton, "If there was any kindness in the [French] decision, demanding a return of kindness from us, it was the kindness of Louis the XVI" and of the old élite.[18]

Anticipating Washington's Farewell Address, "Pacificus No. 6" cautioned against foreign friendships and attachments. "The former will generally be found hollow and delusive; the latter will have a natural tendency to lead us aside from our own true interest, and to make us the dupes of foreign influence. . . . Foreign influence is truly the GRECIAN HORSE to a Republic." As was usually the case, this generic-sounding warning was directed against France and pro-French opinion in the United States. In the last of the series, Hamilton dismissed Jefferson's argument that the administration should have tried to extract concessions before declaring neutrality. "Were the UStates now what, if we do not rashly throw away the advantages we possess, they may expect to be in 15 or 20 years, there would have been more room for an insinuation . . . namely that they ought to have secured to themselves some advantage, as the consideration of their neutrality." But aside from the questionable "justice and magnanimity" of such a policy, it "could only have served to display pretensions at once excessive and unprincipled." Implicitly at least, Hamilton linked America's future greatness to a policy of friendship with the former parent state.[19]

Codifying Neutrality

His hands full with Genêt, and privately admitting the validity of some of Hamilton's charges, the secretary of state assigned the "unwelcome task" of answering "Pacificus" to Madison. Writing as "Helvidius" in a Philadelphia newspaper (between August 24 and September 18, 1793), Madison defended the war-making authority of the legislature but failed to muster the arguments "to cut him [Hamilton] to pieces in the face of the public" as Jefferson had desired. Madison later acknowledged that his performance had been "of no advantage either to the subject or to the author." At the level of intellectual debate, Hamilton was the clear winner. It remained to be seen whether the same would be true of the final battles of the neutrality war in July and August 1793.[20]

The focus of the controversy was now a captured British brigantine with the innocent-sounding name of *Little Sarah*. In flagrant disregard for U.S. policy (as stated in Jefferson's letter of June 5), Genêt had her rechristened the *Petite Démocrate* and equipped as a privateer "under the very nose of the government" in Philadelphia. Prompted by Hamilton, the cabinet asked Governor Mifflin to investigate. Mifflin reported that the ship had increased its armament, including some American cannon, and that Genêt had angrily rejected the midnight request of Pennsylvania Secretary of State Alexander Dallas (like Mifflin, a French sympathizer) to keep the ship in port. Dallas told Jefferson that Genêt had also threatened to appeal over the head of the president to the people of the United States.[21]

The same day, Sunday, July 7, 1793, Jefferson left his country house on the Schuylkill River to pay a dramatic visit to Genêt. Calling on all his charm and residual credibility, Jefferson tried to calm the agitated minister and persuade him to detain the *Petite Démocrate* at least until Washington's return. Genêt continued to assert his right to arm privateers, but indicated through "look and gesture" that the ship "would not be gone before that time." Jefferson pretended at least to be satisfied that, although "the vessel was to fall somewhere down the river, she would not sail." Though he expressly denied it in his report to Washington, as Jefferson told Madison the "hot headed" Genêt had been offensive and disrespectful to the president and had indicated his intention to go over the head of the executive. Jefferson confessed, "Never in my opinion, was so calamitous an appointment made."

He described Genêt's unstable temperament: "He does me justice personally, and, giving him time to vent himself & then cool, I am on a footing to advise him freely, & he respects it, but breaks out again on the very first occasion." The time was fast approaching to unload Genêt, lest he provoke an open split between the Republicans and a still-revered Washington or, worse, an armed confrontation with the French.[22]

The truly explosive question was whether Pennsylvania militia should mount a battery of artillery on Mud Island in the Delaware River to prevent the *Petite Démocrate*'s departure. Hamilton and Knox strongly favored this when they met Jefferson at the State House on July 8. The secretary of state was appalled. The two sides once again put their opinions on paper for the president, who was back in town on July 11. Jefferson professed to trust Genêt's "word" that the ship would stay until the president could speak. In the same breath, he betrayed his fear that she would depart and, with the battery in place and France's West Indian fleet en route to Philadelphia, "bloody consequences" might result. Jefferson vented his own deep anger and frustration. The British, who had carried off more than their share of American cannon and impressed American seamen, would have no cause for complaint if the ship did sail. Force was unthinkable because it was "inconsistent for a nation which had been patiently bearing for ten years the grossest insults and injuries from their late enemies, to rise at a feather against their friends and benefactors; and that, too, in a moment when circumstances have kindled the most ardent affections of the two people toward each other." Jefferson refused to "gratify the combination of kings with the spectacle of the only two republics on earth destroying each other for two cannon; nor would I, for infinitely greater cause, add this country to that combination, turn the scale of the contest, and let it be from our hands that the hopes of man received their last stab."[23]

Hamilton had no hesitation in arguing that cannon be used to stop the Frenchman. The president had already ordered (May 24) state governors to prevent the arming of privateers, if necessary by force. Hamilton concluded:

If war is to be hazarded, 'tis certainly our duty to hazard it with that power, which by injury and insult forces us to choose between opposite hazards – rather than with those powers who do not place us in so disagreeable a dilemma. To adopt as a rule of conduct, that if we are to be involved in the war, it must be *at any rate* against the powers who are opposed to France, and that we ought rather to give them cause for attacking us, *by suffering ourselves to be made an instrument of the hostilities of France*, rather than to risk a quarrel with her, by a vigorous opposition to her encroachments would be a policy as unjust and profligate, as it would be likely to prove pernicious and disgraceful.

It was no coincidence that, two days later, Hamilton demolished Jefferson's "France as benefactor" thesis in "Pacificus No. 4."[24]

Jefferson could breathe easier with news that the *Petite Démocrate* had slipped down the Delaware, beyond range of Mud Island on July 12. A weary president, near the end of his tether with Genêt, met with the cabinet the same day. The time had come to end the dithering and make neutrality a definite system. Basic elements had already been hammered out. Mainly at Hamilton's insistence, the cabinet had decided that no belligerent could arm in U.S. ports. Whether the French vessels armed before the ban could continue to cruise out of U.S. ports and keep their prizes had also been decided, though not to the full satisfaction of either Hamilton or Jefferson. Cabinet members were in accord on the question of whether U.S. citizens joining in the hostilities were punishable, though not exactly for the same reasons. From Hamilton's standpoint, punishing them mainly hurt the French. For Jefferson, without penalties, the country would be drawn into "every maritime war in which the piratical spirit of the banditi in our ports can engage."[25]

Other questions remained, however, and it is misleading to say that all was settled "with a remarkable minimum" of discord. Jefferson, for example, insisted that ships of the warring parties in U.S. ports should be allowed to mount their own, though not U.S.-purchased, guns; Hamilton wanted a total ban. Jefferson would allow privateers to recruit their own citizens on U.S. soil; Hamilton was opposed. Jefferson believed U.S.-built warships could be sold to the belligerents in U.S. ports; Hamilton did not. His positions tended to favor the stronger sea power, while Jefferson's favored France.

Mainly at Jefferson's behest, the cabinet dispatched a list of twenty-nine questions concerning neutrality for consideration by the Supreme Court. In the meantime, Jefferson informed Genêt and Hammond that privateers would be expected to remain in port. "Passing the buck" to the court was a calculated risk for Hamilton. He probably assumed, correctly as it turned out, that the judges would decline to challenge the separation of powers, thus setting another precedent in favor of the executive.[26] By agreeing to query the court, Hamilton may also have hoped to gain cabinet support for his own move on July 12, a request to Paris to recall Genêt.

The advantages of allowing Genêt to remain and continue to discredit the French cause must have occurred to Hamilton. But other considerations took precedence, namely concern for the reputation of the federal government and fear of a clash with the British. If Genêt's recall provoked an armed conflict with France, there were worse outcomes from Hamilton's point of view. On July 15, he recommended purchase of a large quantity of saltpeter. Hammond, after talking to him, reported that the U.S. government saw war with France as "neither improbable nor distant."[27] Visceral partisanship prevented Jefferson from endorsing Hamilton's proposal, but he admitted privately that Genêt's behavior was "indefensible by the most furious Jacobin." On July 12, he proposed that the minister's correspondence be communicated to his government "with friendly observations." In the meantime, he continued to try to reason with Genêt.[28]

In the middle of July, a French fleet arrived in Philadelphia carrying refugees from Saint Domingue. The French colony (modern Haiti) had been in turmoil since the slave revolt of August 1791. Jefferson reminded Genêt that with the fleet available to attack British shipping, he could afford to abandon his "little pickeroons." Genêt promised to halt further armament, but "honor would not permit" him to give up the privateers already fitted out, a position similar to the secretary of state's earlier view. In the same conversation (July 16) Genêt announced that he *had* ordered the sailing of the *Petite Démocrate*. Genêt was further emboldened by the sensational verdict in the case of Gideon Henfield, a U.S. citizen charged by the federal government with breach of the peace for having served on the *Citoyen Genêt*. In the absence (until the Neutrality Act of June 1794) of a precise law prohibiting such activity, a pro-French jury acquitted Henfield in a federal court in Philadelphia on July 29.[29]

The cabinet met on July 29 and 30 to work out a definitive set of rules regarding privateers. After further sparring, Hamilton, Jefferson, Randolph, and Knox submitted a document incorporating the ban on "original arming and equipping" for Washington's approval on August 3, 1793. To accord with the Franco-American treaty, the rules made exceptions on several points for France (France, for example, would have the right to enlist its citizens on U.S. soil who were not U.S. inhabitants). The cabinet also decided to demand restitution of all prizes taken by French privateers fitted out in U.S. ports after June 5 and, failing that, to indemnify the owners out of monies owed to France. This represented a concession by Hamilton, who had "proposed to supress the privateers by military coercion & deliver the prizes to their owners."[30]

The Demise of Genêt

The main issue was now Genêt himself. On August 1, the cabinet agreed that a full statement of his conduct should be communicated to the French government and that his recall be required. Jefferson was convinced of "the necessity of quitting a wreck which could not but sink all who should cling to it." Hamilton made a statement (Jefferson called it "as inflammatory and declamatory as if he had been speaking to a jury") in favor of publishing Genêt's correspondence. When Jefferson and Hamilton debated the issue the next day, Washington seemed to side with the latter. The exasperated president "ran on much on the personal abuse which had been bestowed on him" and denounced "that *rascal Freneau*."[31] In the end, the cabinet agreed on the text of an eight-thousand-word letter (dated August 16, 1793) detailing Genêt's misconduct, but dispensed with the public appeal. The president came around to the secretary of state's view that a shouting match "would work very unpleasantly" both at home and in France. There was probably a "tacit bargain" by which Jefferson would again postpone his retirement for a few months while the president would support Jefferson's handling of Genêt.[32]

Hamilton accepted these arrangements with an equanimity surprising in light of his earlier vehemence. Perhaps he assumed that Genêt's effrontery, especially his threat to appeal over the president's head to the people, would soon be public knowledge. He helped make it so by leaking the information to his friends John Jay and Rufus King, who made the accusation in a New York newspaper. Hamilton also wrote a series of articles under the name of "No Jacobin" that damned Genêt. By late August, however, he had been thrown on the defensive by news of a June 8, 1793, British order-in-council. The order tightened the screws of existing policy by authorizing the seizure and purchase of all wheat and flour bound for France and the condemnation of all ships and cargoes trying to enter blockaded ports.[33]

In early September, Hamilton and many others were suddenly beset by a problem of a different order. An epidemic of the mosquito-borne viral infection, yellow fever, struck Philadelphia. A modern physician has described the course of the disease: "It begins abruptly with fever, headache, and muscle pain. The victim is extremely ill with bleeding and violent episodes of vomiting. Within a few days the pulse slows, blood pressure falls, and the kidneys fail. Blood oozes from every tissue surface. When the infection is severe, half of those affected die." Twenty thousand people, including most of the federal government, fled the city. Hamilton and his wife fell seriously ill, but were successfully treated (with cold baths) by his boyhood friend, the Edinburgh-trained physician Edward Stevens. Between four and five thousand Philadelphians were not so lucky.[34]

If Hamilton was willing to let Jefferson have his way on the method of Genêt's recall, it was fundamentally because the neutrality battle had been won. With or without publication of the correspondence, the request was a major embarrassment to the French cause. A precedent for executive authority, and a form of neutrality favorable to Britain, had been established. With his finger to the wind of public opinion, Jefferson lectured Madison: "I believe that it will be true wisdom in the Republican party to approve unequivocally of a state of neutrality, to avoid little cavils about who should declare it, to abandon G[enêt] entirely." In early September, he wrote Madison:

Hamilton is ill of the fever, as is said.... He had been miserable several days before from a firm persuasion he should catch it. A man as timid as he is on the water, as timid on horseback, as timid in sickness, would be a phenomenon if his courage of which he has the reputation in military occasions were genuine.

Under the circumstances, Jefferson's comment smacked of sour grapes.[35]

Events in France, meanwhile, had once again precipitated. The members of the Girondist faction were expelled from the Convention in June 1793 and became the scapegoats for an increasingly desperate food and military situation. The Jacobins reorganized the Committee of Public Safety in July and, with the Mediterranean naval base of Toulon about to fall to the British, adopted the *levée en masse* or mass conscription. The new masters of Paris readily accepted the American request for Genêt's recall in early October. They hastened to send a four-man commission to the United States with orders to repudiate Genêt's policies and to return him to France as a public enemy. With the Reign of Terror in full swing, Genêt would surely have followed his Girondist sponsors to the guillotine if Washington had not offered him refuge in America. He married the daughter of Governor George Clinton and lived out his days as a gentleman farmer in New York.

In the end, Jefferson's worst enemies in trying to advance the argument that the cause of France was the cause of American liberty turned out to be the French. But Hamilton faced a similar problem in trying to advance the argument that a pro-British stance was in the strategic interest of the United States. In late August, he told Hammond that the recent order-in-council was "a very harsh and unprecedented measure" and that he hoped "a timely explanation" might remove the bad impression. But as the British made preparations for a major military operation in the Western Hemisphere in late 1793, there was much worse to come.[36]

Hamilton and the Crisis of 1794

Introduction

War, in Machiavelli's view of the world, was as natural and necessary an activity to a republic or principality as was breathing to an individual. But this does not mean it was something to be undertaken lightly: "Because anyone can start a war when he wants to, but not finish it, before taking on such an enterprise, a prince must measure his strengths, and govern his conduct on that basis." He was bound to deceive himself, moreover, if he measured his strength simply on the basis of his financial resources, the loyalty of his subjects, or his geographic position – while lacking military forces of his own.[1] Though he was not always so fatalistic on the subject, Machiavelli also warned against the hotheaded propensities of republics. "[T]here is no easier way to destroy a republic where the people possess authority than to take on bold enterprises; because where the people have weight, such enterprises will always be embraced, nor will a contrary opinion do any good." It was an admonition which anticipated that of "The Federalist No. 6": "There have been...almost as many popular as royal wars."[2]

There were times, moreover, when to survive, it was necessary to seek compromise, appease rather than fight, and even submit to disgrace. Faced with the choice of death at the hands of the victorious Sannites or returning home disarmed and under the yoke, a Roman consul observed that

no step could be excluded to save the fatherland; because the life of Rome consisted in the life of the army, it appeared to him necessary to save it by any means; and that the fatherland was well defended regardless of whether it was defended with ignominy or glory. Saving the army, Rome would have time to undo its disgrace; losing it, even if it died gloriously, Rome itself and its liberty would be lost.[3]

The Retirement of Jefferson

As he settled accounts with his old French *maître d'hôtel* and prepared his books and furniture for shipment to Monticello, Thomas Jefferson felt not only enormous relief at laying down the burdens of office but satisfaction over the recent turn of events. The president's own animus toward the British, never far from the surface, combined perhaps with the lingering hope that he might persuade his secretary of state to stay a little longer, had permitted Jefferson a couple of parting victories. Washington had rejected Hamilton's proposal to expel Genêt for his continued meddling in American affairs. And against Hamilton's wishes, the president had agreed to make a public communication of the Hammond–Jefferson correspondence concerning the peace treaty and about recent U.S. protests against the British order-in-council directing the seizure of ships carrying wheat, flour, or meal to France. At a meeting on November 28, the president, according to Jefferson, had taken up the subject "with more vehemence than I have seen him shew."[4]

On December 16, Jefferson finally submitted his long-awaited "Report on Commerce" to Congress. This systematic indictment of British policy had been delayed for various reasons, including the hope that the newly elected third Congress, in which Republicans narrowly controlled the House (though not the Senate), would be more inclined to enact the Jefferson–Madison program of commercial retaliation. Circumstances now seemed opportune. Not only was there widespread anger over the June "provision order," but also the recent British-arranged truce between Portugal and Algiers, which ended a Portuguese naval blockade of the Straits of Gibraltar and allowed Algerine corsairs to attack American shipping in the Atlantic, had provoked more anti-British ire.

Jefferson wrote his daughter on December 22, "The President made yesterday, what I hope will be the last set at me to continue; but in this I am now immovable." The letter continued, "Our affairs with England and Spain have a turbid appearance. The letting loose of the Algerines on us, which has been contrived by England, has produced a peculiar irritation. I think Congress will indemnify themselves by high duties on all articles of British importation. If this should produce war, tho not wished for, it seems not to be feared."[5] On January 3, Madison introduced resolutions in the House calling, *inter alia*, for increased duties against British manufactured goods, increased tonnage duties against British ships, and the banning of West Indian imports carried in British ships.

According to James Thomas Flexner, Jefferson's retirement was nothing less than a "tragedy" for the aging Washington. The president was personally fond of the man he had chosen to replace Jefferson, Attorney General Edmund Randolph. The former Virginia governor was the most worshipful of Washington's original cabinet members, but also an impressionable and vacillating personality who managed to alienate both Republicans and Federalists. (After presenting the "Virginia Plan" at the Philadelphia Convention, he had refused to sign the draft constitution, and then switched back to support it at the state ratifying convention.) He was also chronically broke and, beneath his courtly manners and mellifluous voice, intellectually second-rate. For Flexner, "At this time, when his powers seemed to be weakening, Washington was deserted by one of the two men on whose presence he relied to help to keep the vehicle of state on a central course. It would require tremendous strength to steer straight now that the right wheel was so much larger than the left." Samuel Flagg Bemis goes even further: "Hamilton's influence was now practically unlimited," as if Washington had become a kind of cipher.[6]

Elkins and McKitrick present a strikingly different picture. During the crisis of early 1794, the president was a model of executive autonomy and decisiveness. His inclinations, at least for a time, ran in a direction significantly different from that of Hamilton and the Federalists. "Largely through the weight of his own prestige, Washington was able to establish a precedent [the dispatch of an extraordinary envoy to Britain] . . . and the result was another major step whereby content was added to the American presidency."[7]

Both descriptions are misleading, Elkins's and McKitrick's because Washington was something other than a tower of strength during this critical period; he was tired, hesitating, and never more reliant on outside advice. Flexner is also off the mark. Hamilton, worn down and, like Jefferson, determined to escape the grueling routine of office, did not have a sure grip on the helm in early 1794. He wrote Angelica Church at the end of December:

> The political Campaign [the session of Congress], which is just opening, and which no doubt in the course of it will present some volcanic exhibitions, will put every good man's fortitude and patience to a severe trial . . . But how oddly are things arranged in this sublunary scene. I am just where I do not wish to be. I know how I could be much happier; but circumstances enchain me. It is however determined that I will break the spell. Nothing can prevent it at the opening of the Spring, but the existence of the certainty of a war between this Country and some European Power – an event which I most sincerely deprecate but which reciprocal perversenessness [sic], in a degree, endangers.

Indeed, he threw himself into the battle against Madison's resolutions at a time when Britain's actions threatened to destroy his pro-British foreign policy and hand victory on a silver platter to the Virginians. In March, Hamilton was the object of another investigation for misappropriation of funds, but discovered that Washington did not readily accept his explanations. An impending disaster in Anglo-American relations coincided with a crisis in Hamilton's relationship with his chief.[8]

What of Flexner's suggestion that the country would have been safer if Jefferson had been at Washington's side in the spring of 1794? Despite his

view that war was possible in November 1793, Jefferson had opposed fortifying the country's main harbors and creating a military academy. Even
when war with Britain appeared imminent, Madison and the Republicans
opposed the Federalist program to build a navy. (In March 1794, Congress
nonetheless authorized the construction of four forty-four gun frigates and
two of thirty-six guns.) It seems more accurate to claim that Jefferson "in-
verted Theodore Roosevelt's maxim: he spoke loudly and self-righteously
and carried no stick at all." In fact, his attitude exemplified what Herbert
Croly, a contemporary of Roosevelt, would call "optimistic fatalism." In
effect, Fortune would always smile on America, with or without *virtù*. Had
Jefferson been in the cabinet, he might have facilitated the last-minute effort to avoid war by sending an envoy to Britain, but there is reason to
doubt it. When he heard that Hamilton himself might go, he let fly a typical
comment: "A more degrading measure could not have been proposed.... I
suspect too the mission, besides the object of placing the aristocracy of this
country under the patronage of that [the British] government, has in view
that of withdrawing H. from the disgrace & the public execrations which
sooner or later must fall on the man."[9]

It is difficult not to conclude that Jefferson's resignation was more of a
blessing than a tragedy. With Jefferson out of the picture, Hamilton was
better able to appeal to Washington's instincts and to prevent the ship of
state from sailing into a disastrous confrontation. Some historians have ex-
aggerated Hamilton's role at this point, but he did provide a practically
unique grasp of British psychology and ability to counteract "reciprocal per-
verseness." With a handful of others, he perceived that a seemingly hopeless
situation was ripe for a diplomatic breakthrough. The spring of 1794 may
have been his finest hour.

Hamilton and the Mission to Avert War

Over the course of 1793, the First Coalition against France emerged through
a series of bilateral treaties between Britain and the continental powers:
with Russia, March 25, 1793; Sardinia, April, 25, 1793; Spain, May 25,
1793; Prussia, July 14, 1793; Naples, July 25, 1793; Austria, August 30,
1793; and last but not least Portugal, September 26, 1793, which led to the
short-lived Portuguese–Algerine truce. Following the example of his father
during the Seven Year's War, the younger Pitt chose to subsidize Britain's
continental allies (paying Prussia fifty thousand pounds a month to keep
sixty-four thousand men in the field), while directing British efforts at the
capture of France's American possessions. The main target was chaos-ridden
Saint Domingue, where French planters, beleaguered by the slave revolt, had
appealed for British help.

The major crisis in Anglo-American relations was an unintended by-
product of Pitt's controversial strategy. By 1793, Samuel Eliot Morison

writes, "famine, disorganization, and blockade [had] raised the price of American provisions to unheard-of figures" throughout the West Indies. Preparing to attack, the British knew that the Caribbean would be swarming with Yankee merchantmen drawn by the prospect of once-in-a-lifetime profits. Some would be carrying food for the starving islands, while others would carry island produce bound for France or for U.S ports. To coincide with Admiral Sir John Jervis's West Indian operation, the British government promulgated the order-in-council of November 6, 1793. It was issued secretly and published in London only on December 26 in order to trap unsuspecting ships. British commanders, always eager for prize money, were authorized to seize "all ships laden with goods the produce of any colony belonging to France, or carrying provisions or other supplies for the use of any such colony."

This blanket order was replaced – once it had fulfilled its purpose – on January 8, 1794, by a milder order upholding the so-called "Rule of 1756" (adopted by Britain during the Seven Year's War). The "Rule" forbade neutral shippers from taking over in wartime the direct trade between France and its colonies from which they had been excluded in time of peace. In other words, after January 8, the British allowed commerce between the French colonies and U.S. ports in noncontraband products. More significantly, they tolerated what became an enormously profitable reexport trade, whereby U.S. merchants landed French and Spanish colonial goods in U.S. ports and then shipped them to Europe, ostensibly as American property. In the meantime, however, before the issuance of the January order, Royal Navy cruisers and British privateers captured two hundred fifty American merchantmen. One hundred fifty were summarily condemned (and their cargoes confiscated) by local admiralty courts. News of the November order-in-council arrived on March 7, 1794, provoking fury in the United States.[10]

Toward the end of the month, another piece of news ratcheted up the tension. Prompted by the encroachment of Vermont citizens on British territory, and the knowledge that an army under Major General Anthony Wayne was preparing a decisive push against the Indians northwest of the Ohio River, Lord Dorchester, the zealous (and nervous) governor-general of Canada, made a speech to the Indian tribes gathered at Quebec on February 10. Said Dorchester (as it turned out, without London's authorization), "I should not be surprised if we are at war with the United States in the course of the present year, and if we are, a line must be drawn by the warriors." On March 26, a version of the speech appeared in the U.S. press.[11]

Bemis's lapidary judgment has long influenced our view: the peace mission to Britain and subsequent "Jay treaty" were the work of Hamilton, "to whom in the last analysis any praise or blame for the instrument must be given.... More aptly the treaty might be called Hamilton's Treaty." For another scholar, "The Jay treaty...was peculiarly Hamilton's doing. He proposed it...chose John Jay for the mission, and drew Jay's instructions."

For yet another, "Jay's treaty was Hamilton's treaty more than that of any other man." For the authors of an authoritative account of the 1790s, "The leading role in the devising of Jay's instructions, as has always been known, was played by Alexander Hamilton." Yet not all of these claims rest on solid ground.[12]

To be sure, Hamilton had begun to consider the prospect of an Anglo-American war even before the shocking news from the West Indies. In "Americanus No. 1," published in a Philadelphia paper, he dismissed the Republican line that the Jacobin cause was the cause of liberty and that the United States could help France. The depredations of U.S. privateers and the loss of trade would make a war "seriously distressing" to Britain, but could not have a decisive impact. U.S. action could not "arrest her career or overrule those paramount considerations [of national interest] which brought her into her present situation."[13] In a second piece, Hamilton spelled out the consequences of war for the United States. "All who are not wilfully blind must see and acknowledge that this country at present enjoys an unexampled state of prosperity." The war-related boom in U.S. trade and shipping had become a key Federalist argument against Madison's program of anti-British retaliation. But American commerce would be "in a great degree annihilated by a war." Added to this was the fact that nine tenths of federal revenues were derived from commercial duties. "To abandon public Credit would be to renounce an essential mean of carrying on the war, besides the sacrifice of the public Creditors and the disgrace of a National bankruptcy."[14]

Hamilton also debunked the popular Republican argument that France's enemies planned to attack the United States. Many Britons, "not improbably a majority, would see in the enterprise a malicious and wanton hostility against Liberty," unless, that is, the United States were foolish enough to thrust itself into the war. "Once embarked, Nations sometimes prosecute enterprises which they would not otherwise have dreamt of. The most violent resentment would no doubt in such case be kindled against us for what would be called a wanton and presumptuous meddling on our part." In effect, Hamilton postulated a kind of strategic standoff between Britain and the United States. Neither side could reduce the other, nor provide much help to its hypothetical allies. If either were misguided enough to provoke the other, it would end up doing serious damage to *itself*. Barring a spiral of reckless, perverse behavior, the premises for a settlement were at hand.[15]

Hamilton's first instinct upon hearing of the November order-in-council was to try to shape the president's reaction. He could well imagine Washington's sense of outrage. Indeed, Washington shared a widespread perception that Britain was trying to provoke war with the United States. Hamilton tried to influence him much as he had during earlier crises: by taking a position that contained more backbone than that of his opponents but also offered greater hope for conciliation. He immediately (March 8, 1794) suggested fortifying the main ports, raising twenty thousand auxiliary troops, and vesting the president with the power to impose an embargo on exports. As an additional thought, it might "also deserve consideration whether the Executive ought not to take measures to form some concert of the Neutral Powers for common Defense." Hamilton's logic echoed Washington's in a recent address to Congress: "If we desire to avoid insult, we must be able to repel it; if we desire to secure peace, one of the most powerful instruments of our rising prosperity, it must be known, that we are at all times ready for War." Soon after, Federalist Congressman Theodore Sedgwick of Massachusetts introduced resolutions resembling Hamilton's advice.[16]

On March 10, a caucus of Federalist senators from sea-faring states, Oliver Ellsworth of Connecticut, George Cabot and Caleb Strong of Massachusetts, and Rufus King of New York, met in King's Philadelphia office to devise a similar program. It contained a key suggestion absent from Hamilton's memo: "an Envoy extraordinary should be sent to England to require satisfaction for the loss of our Property, and to adjust those points which menaced a War between the two Countries." On March 12, Ellsworth called on the president and suggested that Hamilton should be the man. It may be that this idea had originated with Hamilton: declining to nominate himself, he had it done by his friends. But it is equally possible that Ellsworth and company acted on their own. Washington (according to King), "was at first reserved – finally more communicative and apparently impressed with Ellsworth's representation." Washington did, however, express doubts concerning Hamilton. The treasury secretary "did not possess the general confidence of the Country." Painfully aware of Republican loathing of Hamilton, Washington hesitated to make him the top choice.[17]

This was even more the case after House investigators pounced on the revelation that Hamilton had deposited in the Bank of the United States a portion of funds earmarked by a 1790 statute for the repayment of European loans. Hamilton reminded the president that he had received verbal permission to do this. But following the advice of Randolph, and lacking documentation, Washington declined to confirm Hamilton's story. Nor did he immediately make up his mind about the peace mission. On March 26, he endorsed a joint resolution of Congress calling for a thirty-day embargo on ships leaving U.S. ports. (He advised his estate manager at Mount Vernon "to grind no more wheat until you hear further from me.") Federalists saw an embargo as preferable to continued British confiscation of U.S. ships and to truly provocative proposals like federal government sequestration of debts owed by private U.S. citizens to British creditors.[18]

Washington's decision in favor of the mission can be traced to several factors. On March 28, news arrived that the November 6 order had been superseded by the more liberal policy of January 8. Through a private source, King learned that Pitt had responded to the complaints of London merchants about the wholesale condemnation of U.S. cargoes by promising "the most ample compensation." London, typically, had not foreseen the American reaction to its initial move. On April 3, a message from Thomas Pinckney arrived containing reassuring words from Foreign Secretary Grenville about the future treatment of U.S. ships. News had also arrived of the French recapture of Toulon, thanks to the artillery tactics of Napoleon Bonaparte, on December 19. If, as Washington suspected, the British had been planning war with the United States, they must be having second thoughts.[19]

Hamilton's attempt to resolve the crisis came in the form of a long, unsolicited letter to Washington. Historians, as usual, disagree as to its significance. Elkins and McKitrick do not deem it worthy of citation, whereas for McDonald it is one of the most important letters of Hamilton's life and for Bemis it "made up Washington's mind." Two facts are beyond dispute. The letter is one of the most cogent and penetrating, even if least known, of Hamilton's career. For whatever reason, Washington did make up his mind the day after he received it.[20]

Hamilton identified three parties on the U.S. side, one in favor of military preparations but not reprisals (such as the sequestration of debts and a total cutoff of trade) pending a good-faith effort to gain reparations and a settlement, one calling for reprisals in order to provoke hostilities, and one favoring reprisals on the assumption that London would climb down to avoid war. Hamilton did not need to name names: the latter two parties were, respectively, the hotheaded Republicans represented in the anti-administration press and in the French-style "Democratic Societies" that had sprung up in the wake of Genêt, and the more moderate Republicans led by Madison in the House. Hamilton reminded Washington that wars more often proceeded "from angry and perverse passions than from cool calculations of Interest." If this was true for the British, why, he asked, echoing "The Federalist No. 6," don't we admit it about ourselves?[21]

Those two parties were driven, in effect, by the old "Virginia syndrome." "In hostility with Britain they seek the gratification of revenge upon a detested enemy with that of serving a favourite friend.... Those even of them who do not wish the extremity of war consider it as a less evil than a thorough and sincere accommodation" with the British. Yet it would be a mistake to assume that the country at large would back a war begun before a sincere effort had been made to avoid it, while a war with the country divided could "scarcely end in any thing better than an inglorious and disadvantageous peace." It would be equally incorrect to think that Britain was intent on war or that France enjoyed the upper hand. As Hamilton wrote the president, "To you, Sir, it is unnecessary to urge the extreme precariousness of the events of War.... This Country ought not to set itself afloat upon an ocean so fluctuating so dangerous and so uncertain but in a case of absolute necessity."[22]

Britain's recent conciliatory behavior (Hamilton might have mentioned as well the underlying strategic standoff) suggested that the moment was "peculiarly favourable" to attempt a settlement. The three American parties now ostensibly agreed on a peace mission. Those who truly favored its success wished to give Britain an honorable way out. Those who did not wanted reprisals first and then negotiations. But it was obvious that Britain could not settle under such pressure "without renouncing her pride and dignity." And anyone who understood Britain's psychology could see that "she would be less disposed to receive the law from us than from any other nation – a people recently become a nation, not long since one of her dependencies, and as yet, if a Hercules – a Hercules in the cradle." The wise course was to negotiate while taking defensive measures rather than to antagonize one's negotiating partner at the outset while neglecting to prepare for war. "'Tis as great an error for a nation to overrate itself as to underrate itself" – especially one as dependent on British credit and British-generated revenues as the United States. "'Tis our error to overrate ourselves and to underrate Great Britain." This was a reference to Republican bravado born out of recent French victories: "We forget how little we can annoy how much we may be annoyed." In closing, Hamilton urged the president to make a clear and immediate choice between defensive steps and a peace mission unhampered by prior reprisals, on one hand, and coercion accompanied by a pro forma demand for redress, on the other. There was no middle course.[23]

It was a meticulously argued attempt to prevent a costly, unnecessary war brought on by a combustible mix of American resentment and British pride. In a dramatic coda to the letter, Hamilton stated that he was taking himself out of the running as a possible envoy. He was aware of Washington's feelings, of the "collateral obstacles which exist," and assured the president that he would be completely satisfied with the choice of someone else. He did not let the occasion pass, however, to add that there was only one other person (someone he knew Washington was already considering) "in whose qualifications for success there would be thorough confidence," namely Chief Justice John Jay.[24] Washington had been leaning in favor of the mission, but it was probably this letter that clinched the decision. Its sobering logic and call for prudence were incontestable. It also spared Washington the embarrassment of having to veto Hamilton. Though temporarily estranged from him and doubtful of his political suitability, Washington was sensitive to Hamilton's feelings. Before the April 14 letter, he must have felt reluctant to deny him something that he knew the younger man both wanted and deserved. Hamilton had taken Washington off the hook.

On the morning of April 15, Washington offered the envoyship to Jay. Hamilton, Strong, Ellsworth, Cabot, and King met with Jay the same afternoon. Jay agreed, writing his wife, "No appointment ever operated more unpleasantly upon me; but the public considerations which were urged, and the manner in which it was pressed, strongly impressed me with a conviction that to refuse it would be to desert my duty." The Senate approved the appointment on April 19, 1794.[25]

Simultaneously, Hamilton delivered a message to the other party in the dispute. George Hammond, his nerves frayed by popular hostility to Britain, approached Hamilton with the "very conciliatory explanations" that Grenville had provided for the behavior of the Royal Navy. The young minister was "much suprized [sic]" that his confidant did not receive them "with the cordiality" he had expected and "entered into a pretty copious recital of the injuries" suffered by American merchants. Although pointedly not insisting on "free ships make free goods," Hamilton made it clear that the United States expected compensation where cargoes had been condemned without conclusive proof that the seized property was French or where appeals had been impossible. Hammond answered that one should not scrutinize too closely the inevitable inconveniences to neutral shipping, especially "in a war like the present, in which (*as he had often agreed with me*) all the dearest interests of society were involved, and which was a contest between government and disorder." The British had no intention of allowing neutrals to enjoy a commerce that "however, advantageous it might be to them, would be perhaps more beneficial to our enemy." Hamilton interrupted "with some degree of heat" to say that, in fact, "a very powerful party" might emerge in Britain in sympathy with American grievances. Indignant and a little nonplussed, Hammond changed the subject. Increasingly embittered, isolated, and ineffective, he would be recalled later in the year.[26]

Hamilton did agree with Hammond on the stakes involved in the war. Unlike most Americans, moreover, he appreciated that Britain's use of sea power was determined by what it considered a state of absolute necessity. At the same time, he was angry and disgusted with the British for running roughshod over U.S. rights, in the process damaging his credibility and perpetuating an "unnatural quarrel." The basic message to Hammond was that a community of interests could not be built on any basis other than British respect for the United States. If Britain wished to enjoy the benefits of peace with America, it would have both to make amends and recognize that there was a clear line that it could not cross.

Advising Jay

Hamilton did not dictate Jay's marching orders as is often suggested. Their preparation was a collective effort (they went out under Randolph's signature) in which he played a leading role. The Federalist conclave of Hamilton, King, Cabot, and Ellsworth laid out guidelines on the evening of April 21. Compensation for the spoliations in the West Indies, the explosive question of the moment, must come first. If Britain agreed to this, and to execute the peace treaty, the U.S. government should be willing to compensate Britain for losses to its creditors dating from the war. Jay himself played an active part in these discussions.[27]

Hamilton's contribution emerges from a comparison of two late-April memoranda (requested by Washington) with Jay's official instructions. The first priority was "indemnification for the depredations . . . according to a rule to be settled." The "desirable" rule was obviously that only contraband, narrowly defined to exclude provisions (e.g., wheat), be subject to confiscation. But the United States would have to be flexible, insisting, for example, only that provisions be exempt when going to a port not actually blockaded and that, when seized, they be paid for at full value. "In the last resort," he was willing to accept British policy as laid down on January 8, 1794, in effect prohibiting American involvement in the direct trade between France and its colonies but allowing it between the colonies and U.S. ports. With respect to the peace treaty, he foresaw an exchange of British withdrawal from the posts and indemnification for abducted slaves in return for U.S. indemnification of British creditors. Hamilton's main desiderata in a commercial treaty were access by relatively small U.S. ships (sixty to eighty tons) to the British West Indies, to Britain's European dominions on the same basis as other foreigners, and to the British East Indies. If it proved necessary to accept a short-term treaty maintaining the status quo in order to gain satisfaction for the spoliations and the execution of the peace treaty, such a deal would be "consistent with the interests of the UStates."[28]

Jay's instructions, drafted by Randolph and signed on May 6, 1794, incorporated Hamilton's main points but were not identical to the above-cited memoranda. Indeed, Hamilton later described Jay's instructions as "a crude mass" but said that "the delicacy of attempting too much reformation in the work of another head of Department, the hurry of the moment, & a great Confidence in the person to be sent" had prevented his trying to change them.[29] The top priority was compensation for injuries resulting from the order of June 8, 1793, on the grounds that provisions could not generally be considered contraband and from those resulting from the November 6, 1793, order on the further grounds that U.S. ships had been entrapped and their cargoes summarily condemned. Here, the instructions were somewhat vaguer than Hamilton had been as to the "rule" to be insisted on. The second priority was the peace treaty. Jay was to resolve the questions of British debts and the posts, but once again the instructions were less clear than in Hamilton's memoranda. They said nothing about indemnifying British creditors. They did not suggest, nor did they forbid, Jay's eventual approach: to agree to disagree rather than insist on winning the argument over who had first violated the treaty.

If the two main points were accomplished, Jay was free to discuss a commercial treaty. The instructions contained a long list of "desirable" but not necessarily "expected" objects: "free ships make free goods," "provisions never to be contraband, except in the strongest possible case, as the blockade of a port," and "in case of an Indian war, none but the usual supplies in peace shall be furnished." The status quo, plus access to the West Indies for ships of a certain size (left unspecified) "would afford an acceptable basis of [a] treaty" – but there must be no treaty that did *not* satisfy this demand. The instructions bore Randolph's own stamp in at least two places. Jay was authorized to sound out the ministers of Russia, Denmark, and Sweden in London on the possibility of joining an armed neutrality in defense of neutral rights. (Hamilton had not pursued the idea after his mention of it to Washington of March 8.) Second, Jay was to reject any British attempt to "detach" the United States, making it clear that we would "not derogate from our treaties and engagement" to the French.

Other than this last proviso, and the one on the West Indies, the instructions left Jay considerable leeway. He was to "consider the ideas, herein expressed, as amounting to recommendations only, which in your discretion you may modify, as seems most beneficial to the United States."[30] Arguably, this reflected Hamilton's influence: it allowed him to steer Jay through a set of informal instructions – a "few loose observations" on strategic priorities – that he sent him the same day. As important as the objects of the mission were, Hamilton warned Jay, "it will be better to do nothing than to do any thing which will not stand the test of the severest scrutiny and especially which may be construed into the relinquishment of a substantial right or interest." The "*mere appearance* of indemnification" was not enough. But in his eagerness to settle, Hamilton repeated that he was willing "in the last resort" to accept the January 8, 1794, order-in-council as the "line" deciding who should be indemnified and governing future behavior.

Looking to the future, Hamilton was prepared to suggest that if Jay could settle the peace treaty issues and secure a "truly beneficial" commercial treaty, he might even drop the demand for indemnification and let the United States government pay off the aggrieved American merchants. Above all, Jay should open British eyes to the fact that America was an indispensable supplier of the British West Indies (now expanding in size through conquest) and of Britain itself, as well as the largest (and constantly growing) consumer of British goods. "How unwise then in G Britain to suffer such a state of things to remain exposed to the hazard of constant interruption & derangement by not fixing on the basis of a good treaty the principles on which it should continue?" Opening the Mississippi was an "object of immense consequence" politically and commercially to the United States, and the British could share in the benefits. As an added incentive, Hamilton proposed that Jay offer something not in his instructions: a U.S. prohibition of the sequestering of private debt.[31]

One view of this private letter is that Hamilton, "to preserve peace and national credit" was "willing in the face of British sea power, to acquiesce in a complete reversion or suspension of the liberal principles incorporated in the American treaties with France, Sweden, Holland, and Prussia" (namely "free ships make free goods" and a narrow definition of contraband).[32] This is technically true but misleading and a little disingenuous. For one thing, Hamilton supported the current goals, if not the methods, of British sea power. Principles *were* involved, but at a practical level the choice was between a disastrous war to uphold the right of American shippers to their windfall profits and a peace preserving a still-immensely lucrative commerce. Jefferson himself had seen the futility of insisting on liberal principles in his dealings with Genêt. In any event, it was absurd to think that the United States was acting from a position of strength. If ever appeasement was called for, this was the time.

Hamilton, moreover, had in mind something greater than trying to preserve peace and federal revenues – "a whole new Anglo-American system."[33] It was a system not unlike the kind of unrestricted interdependency that had existed before 1776 and that might have been restored had Lord Shelburne and the West Indian planters prevailed in 1782–83. This time, in contrast to the unreliable Morris, Hamilton had the right man for the job. No one was more associated with the vision of a liberal Anglo-America than John Jay and, aside from John Adams, no one had had more more diplomatic experience. It is probable that the leeway in his orders was there because Jay had insisted that it be there. On a well-known occasion, he had patently ignored his government's instructions. He had no regrets about having done so, but it was an episode he preferred not to repeat.

The Jay Treaty

Education of an Envoy

John Jay has been called "the lost founding father," someone who, although a member of the inner circle, did not quite make it into the pantheon of heroes. One reason may be his personality. Many found him cold, aloof, and vain in a prudish sort of way. His portrait by Joseph Wright shows him stiff-necked and sporting a slightly supercilious frown, though with a thoughtful, sensitive pair of eyes. He was a stickler on matters concerning his own, and his country's, dignity, though for a select few he had his droller side. As president of the Continental Congress, he wrote Washington of his unruly charges, "there is as much intrigue in this state House as in the Vatican, but as little secrecy as in a boarding school."[1] There were striking affinities between Jay (born in 1745) and Hamilton. Jay was of Huguenot stock, scion of a family of La Rochelle merchants who had been forced to leave France for England and America after the revocation of the Edict of Nantes in 1685. Like Hamilton, he studied at King's College (where he was suspended for refusing to tattle on fellow students who had smashed a table), became a successful lawyer, and made a politically consequential marriage, in his case to Sarah "Sally" Livingston, daughter of the New Jersey Whig leader William Livingston.

As a delegate to the Second Continental Congress in June 1775, Jay penned a draft of the so-called Olive Branch Petition to the king, including the passage (later deleted) "That altho the People of North America are determined to be free they do not wish to be independent and beg leave again to assure his Majesty that they mean not to question the Right of the British Parliament to regulate the Commercial Concerns of the Empire...." Elected to the New York Provincial Congress, he was not in Philadelphia for the crucial vote on July 2, 1776. After the Declaration of Independence, he threw himself into the war effort, but old attachments died hard. When news arrived of the French alliance, Jay wrote Gouverneur Morris: "If Britain would acknowledge our Independence and enter into a liberal Alliance with us, I should prefer a Connection with her, to a League with any Power on Earth.... The Destruction of old England would hurt me. I wish it well: it afforded my Ancestors an Assylum from Persecution."[2]

Unlike Hamilton, Jay was deeply rooted in New York and serenely confident of his place at the apex of its social pyramid. He lacked Hamilton's frenetic drive but possessed a more natural gravitas. While still in his thirties, Jay had been minister to Madrid, peace commissioner in Paris, and secretary for foreign affairs. As a diplomat, he had acquired the reputation for doing things his way. In 1781, the Continental Congress had ordered him to modify American insistence on free navigation of the entire Mississippi as part of a U.S.–Spanish treaty of alliance. He did so, but added an unauthorized time limit within which the Spanish court would have to take or leave the offer. (They refused it.) In June 1781, Gouverneur Morris wrote him that he had been appointed to the five-man commission charged with making peace, but that Congress wanted France to supervise the negotiations. Morris commented, "when you come to find by your instructions that you must ultimately obey the dictates of the French minister, I am sure there is something in your Bosom which will revolt at the Servility of the Situation." That something was his proud Huguenot heart, similar to Morris's own.[3]

After Jay arrived in Paris in mid-1782 to assist his unwell colleague Benjamin Franklin, he saw that the French were willing to end the war on terms that would deny America's claim to a Mississippi border (France and Spain preferring a small and weak America) and limit its postwar fishing rights in the Atlantic. Without consulting Foreign Minister Vergennes, he pursued separate talks with the British, insisting that the official commission of Richard Oswald, the Shelburne government's negotiator, be changed to accord immediate recognition of American independence. The British agreed, and Jay and Oswald proceeded to negotiate and sign the preliminary peace on November 30, 1782. Both the preliminary and final terms established the border on the Father of Waters, with the United States and Britain to enjoy free navigation of its entire length. (It was Jay's hope that the British would conquer West Florida and thus control the lower stretches of the right bank at the end of the war.) Jay's proposal for complete commercial reciprocity was slated for inclusion in a separate treaty which, due to Shelburne's fall, did not materialize. Jay, Adams, and Franklin were criticized by Congress, but no one could deny that they had pulled off a major coup.[4]

His mission accomplished, Jay spent several months in England trying to collect a legacy left by a deceased relative and taking the cure at Bath. He wrote his wife, "America has many excellent Friends in England, and I may also say, many implacable Enemies. This People is immersed in Pleasure, and yet very far from being happy." The reality of Georgian society did not measure up to the simpler "old England" idealized from afar. As his physical ailments and the British hard line persisted, he wrote, "let us retaliate fully and firmly. This nation like many others, is influenced more by its feelings than reasonings." But Jay's attitude toward Britain could not be compared to the Puritanism of a John Adams, who condemned the "universal spirit of Debauchery, Dissipation, Luxury, Effeminacy and Gaming," as well as the "Prodigality, in Furniture, Equipage, Apparell and Diet." Jay retained his hope, as he later wrote Shelburne, that peace would "draw a veil over the injuries of war." As secretary for foreign affairs and chief justice, he took the position that the United States had violated the treaty on prewar debts and that the British, in effect, were justified in holding onto the posts. The 1794 mission was the culmination of his earlier efforts to foster reconciliation, based on reciprocity and mutual trust.[5]

Drawing a Veil on the Past

Jay sailed from New York on a fast American vessel in mid-May, landing at Falmouth on June 8, 1794. He settled into the Royal Hotel in Pall Mall on Sunday morning, June 15. As he explained to Secretary of State Randolph when trying to collect his expenses, renting a house would have suggested that he was in no great hurry to finish his business. Staying in a hotel, moreover, allowed him to get by with a skeleton staff: a hired footman and coachman and one servant brought from home. The Royal Hotel, he wrote, was "the first, but the most expensive in London. My reasons for preferring the first must be obvious to you and need not be particularized."[6]

Most historians give little credit or blame to Jay himself for the conduct of his mission. According to Bemis, Hamilton was pulling the strings from across the Atlantic. Britain feared war and America held high cards, but thanks to Hamilton, it failed to play them. Somewhat inconsistently, Bemis also argues that Jay was outmaneuvered by his thirty-five-year-old counterpart, Foreign Secretary Grenville. An able and experienced official (he had been home secretary, in charge of Canadian affairs) with an "astonishing" capacity for work, Grenville "shrewdly manipulated" Jay by flattering his sense of his own importance. An alternative view is that the British, surprised by Jay's arrival, were too busy dealing with other problems to pay more than passing attention to him. "It was not the sort of negotiation likely to engage on their part a very high degree of concentration or imagination." Even if it had been, the British did not share the Hamilton–Jay vision of the future. This was a "fundamental weakness" of Jay's approach.[7]

That the British government had other matters on its plate no one would deny. The channel fleet under Admiral Richard Howe had defeated a French squadron (capturing six ships of the line) on June 1, 1794, and Port-au-Prince had fallen to the British invasion force around the same time. But the sacrifice of the French navy had permitted a convoy carrying some twenty-four million pounds of American flour to reach France. Affairs in the strategically vital low countries (where the French won victories at Turcoing in May and at

Fleurus in June) had gone from bad to worse. Meanwhile, holding the First Coalition together was developing into a diplomatic nightmare for Grenville and Pitt. Distracted by a Polish revolt in March, the Prussians had left their allies in the lurch and the British would soon cut off their monthly subsidy. In Paris, the Jacobin leader Robespierre's days were numbered (the coup of 9 Thermidor occurred on July 27, 1794), but for the time being anti-Jacobin hysteria gripped the British Isles. In June and July, Pitt's government was caught up in complicated negotiations leading to the inclusion in the cabinet of five members of the prowar wing of the opposition Whig party, led by the Duke of Portland.

What seems remarkable is the amount of attention the British *did* pay to Jay. Grenville wrote Hammond on August 8 that Jay's appearance had "led to discussions of much length and importance," and the record bears this out. Jay met Grenville on June 18 and had a long conversation with him on June 20. He wrote Randolph that "No delays, or arts to procrastinate, have been practiced." In a private letter to Hamilton, he mentioned the pause brought about by the negotiations with the Portland Whigs, but also that he had dined with Grenville and the cabinet (with no other foreigners present) and that he had invitations from the Lord Chancellor and Pitt. He met with Grenville on July 31 and August 5 and was cordially received by the king and queen.[8]

On meeting Jay, George III remarked, "Well, sir, I imagine you begin to see that your mission will probably be successful." This was a reference to the British decision to meet U.S. demands on the key issue of compensation for U.S. merchants where redress could not be had "in the ordinary course of law." As Hamilton had predicted, if not provoked in advance, the British were prepared to make amends in order to avoid war. Around the same time, London altered the order-in-council of June 8, 1793, which had authorized the seizure of U.S. ships carrying grain to France. Lord Dorchester was reprimanded for his inflammatory speech to the Indians and for authorizing Lieutenant Governor Sir John Simcoe to send regular troops to occupy Fort Miami on the Maumee River, some twenty miles south of Lake Erie, in anticipation of an American attack on Detroit. Jay told Grenville that Anthony Wayne's forces would not move on the posts, pending the outcome of the negotiations, but warned that any new fortification would probably be attacked.[9]

Grenville later wrote of Jay that his "whole conduct...in the course of this arduous and intricate Negotiation [had] been entirely satisfactory." To Jay himself, Grenville spoke (at a time when flattery would have been useless) of "the sincere esteem and friendship with which your whole conduct has impressed me, and of the high sense which I entertain of your virtues and talents." Compared to the Spanish, Austrian, Dutch, Neapolitan, Russian, and Prussian ministers, dealing with Jay was a relief. Long-winded and stuffy he may have been, but he was also averse to settling scores.[10] With the initial

British concessions in hand, Jay understood (he did not need Hamilton's guidance) that it would be counterproductive to try to take further advantage of London's fear of war. The key to success was his decision at this point to "draw a veil over the injuries of war." There is no reason to think, *pace* Elkins and McKitrick, that Grenville did not share Jay's goal of a new era in Anglo-American relations, even if the foreign secretary could not deliver on some key details.[11]

Each side presented its time-worn position on the peace treaty, but Jay did little more than go through the motions. The time had come "to try and agree on such a set of reciprocal concessions as (balancing each other) might afford articles for a treaty, so beneficial to both parties as to induce them to bury in it all former questions and disputes." Jay gave Grenville a working paper on August 6. Its points included evacuation of the posts by June 1, 1795, British compensation of the injuries to U.S. shipping, U.S. compensation to British creditors injured by legal impediments, and access by U.S. ships of up to one hundred tons to the West Indies (though no U.S. reexport of British West Indian products). U.S. ships and goods were to be treated in all other British ports as if they were British and vice versa for British ships and goods entering the United States. No captured British ships would be sold in the United States and vice versa, and no privateering would be permitted in an Anglo-American war. Additionally, the sequestration of private debts was to be banned, and border disputes involving the upper Mississippi and the St. Croix River (in Maine) were to be settled by mixed commissions. Jay suggested a deadline to end negotiations of around November 1.[12]

Grenville replied with draft treaties of his own on August 30. There was substantial agreement (for example, on the compensation issues), but Britain would withdraw from the posts by June 1, 1796, and with indefinite free access and trading rights in the ceded territory for the Indians and its own subjects. Grenville wished to draw the upper Mississippi border to accord with the peace treaty commitment (as he interpreted it) giving Britons access to the river without having to pass through U.S. territory. His draft granted access to the West Indies for U.S. vessels of up to seventy tons to last until two years after the end of the present war. With respect to tonnage duties and tariffs, the British offered mutual most-favored-nation treatment in place of Jay's more radical approach.[13]

Jay's reaction belies his image as a diplomatic pushover. "The present occasion is great," he told Grenville, "and, though critical, yet auspicious to the establishment of confidence and friendship between the two countries. With the magnitude and importance of these objects, the projects in question [Grenville's drafts] really do not strike me as being commensurate." Jay rejected a cession of land on the mistaken assumption that the peace treaty had intended the British to be able to embark on the Mississippi without crossing U.S. territory. Grenville conceded the possibility of letting a mixed commission decide the border (as was to be the case). The two talked for several hours on September 6. Jay's notes indicate the questions he raised about the British drafts: reciprocal rights for U.S. citizens involved in the Indian trade, the definition of contraband, the need to allow the sale by France of British prizes for the duration of the war, and numerous other points.[14]

Word had now arrived of the effusive reception given the new American minister to Paris, Jefferson's protégé, James Monroe. Grenville wrote Jay on September 7: "I do not believe that you personally will envy Mr. Monroe the honor of the fraternal kiss which he received: and if such an exhibition is thought not to degrade an American minister I know not why it should not become a matter of complaint on the part of the British Government." But the news did not stop Grenville from pressing on with the treaty. On the definition of contraband, he proposed a verbatim passage from Vattel: wheat, grain, and provisions could be considered contraband when there was "an expectation of reducing the enemy by the want thereof," but in such cases cargoes must be paid for at full value (as per the British order of June 8, 1793). Grenville would have to consult the cabinet on the Indian issues, but his message was conciliatory. It gives the impression that, as his troubles with the First Coalition mounted, Grenville grew all the more determined that his American treaty should succeed.[15]

Jay assessed the situation in a September 17 letter to Hamilton. He too was irritated with Monroe:

These things are not favorable to my mission. A speedy conclusion to the negotiation is problematical, though not highly improbable. If I should be able to conclude the business on admissable terms, I shall do it and risk consequences, rather than by the delay of waiting for and governing myself by opinions and instructions, hazard a change in the disposition of this court; for it seems our country, or rather some part of it, will not forbear asperities.

As in 1782, Jay's instincts told him to make a deal while there was a well-disposed British government to deal with. As in 1782, he rankled at the idea of following instructions reflecting a pro-French bias in the United States.[16]

On September 30, Jay submitted a new draft treaty to Grenville. Bemis discovered a copy in Britain in the early twentieth century, but it is nowhere to be found in the American archives. The explanation, for Bemis, is that the final treaty, signed November 19, 1794, represented a "stupendous retreat" from the September draft. He systematically compares the two documents. Among the September 30 provisions Jay later abandoned were those banning armed vessels on the Great Lakes and moving to disarm the borders; the outlawing of alliances with the Indians in case of an Anglo-American war and of arming Indians to fight the other; "free ships make free goods"; limiting the size of naval boarding parties; food, naval stores, and raw materials *not* to be considered contraband (though they could be taken and paid for in some cases as per the order of June 8, 1793).[17]

This list may not be the "avalanche of neutral rights and other American propositions" that Bemis claims it is, but with the exception of the last point, their inclusion would have dramatically improved the treaty from the U.S. point of view. Why, then, did Jay advance them and then fail to insist? Bemis himself does not hazard an explanation. For Elkins and McKitrick, they were not points that his instructions had made indispensable, "and it may be doubted whether Jay himself expected to get very far with them." He knew perfectly well that "free ships make free goods" was a nonstarter. And he must have realized that along with giving up the seven posts, the British were not prepared to disarm Canada altogether in the face of a potentially powerful and aggressive United States. This suggests that Jay's inclusion of the provisions was a formality in order to be able to say, if asked, that he had not forgotten them. There is another possibility: remembering the precedent of 1782, Jay was trying against the odds for another diplomatic coup. If the draft was not to see the light of day at home, what did he have to lose?[18]

Bemis makes another famous suggestion in his classic telling of the story: Grenville's rejection of Jay's September 30 provisions was connected to news he had received ten days earlier. This was Hamilton's "amazing revelation" to Hammond that the United States had no intention of joining the Armed Neutrality of Denmark and Sweden, an alliance to enforce a liberal definition of neutral rights, signed March 27, 1794. Relieved of his anxiety on that score, Grenville could take a hard line with Jay. There is no question that Grenville had been concerned about this French-sponsored project. When he heard that the Swedish minister in London had approached Thomas Pinckney about it, Grenville (May 10, 1794) had ordered Hammond to exert himself "to the utmost to prevent the American government from acceding to the measure now proposed to them." Grenville would have been further concerned to know that Jay's instructions authorized him to pursue the matter and that Washington had insisted, at least according to Randolph, that Jay ascertain how far Sweden and Denmark were prepared to go with the United States if "we are driven into a war."[19]

As soon as he received Grenville's orders, Hammond went to see Hamilton. Hamilton assured the minister that

in the present conjuncture, it was the settled policy of this government in every contingency even in that of an open contest with Great Britain, to avoid entangling itself with European connexions [sic], which could only tend to involve this country in disputes, wherein it might have no possible interest, and commit it in a common cause with allies, from whom in the moment of danger, it could derive no succour.

It is hard to know what to make of Hamilton's earlier mention of joining an armed neutrality. Perhaps it had been merely a passing thought. His statement to Hammond, in any case, reiterated his long-standing position of "ostensible neutrality," that is, opposition to anti-British alliances, couched as a generic rejection of European entanglements. It is also a striking instance of his presuming to speak on questions of high policy without consulting Washington on the grounds that he knew best and the president (as was the case) would go along.[20]

Bemis is correct that Hamilton's message was good news for Grenville. But it is hard to believe that Grenville was seriously concerned about the Armed Neutrality by September 1794, that the news came as a surprise, or that it affected his reaction to Jay's September 30 draft treaty. Neither Sweden nor Denmark had the naval power necessary to put teeth into a liberal definition of neutral rights. The United States had little to add of its own, and unlike the Armed Neutrality of 1780 (as Bemis himself points out), neither Russia nor Prussia was on board. If the United States had been interested, Jay would have had serious contacts in London, and the observant British would have known. Jay did talk to the Swedish minister there, but nothing more. By September, London was allowing large shipments of materials Hamilton had sought to buy in Britain for the construction of the American frigates, including bunting and pure copper for the ships' bottoms. This was not a government worried about a war with the United States. Finally, given the substance of Jay's September 30 proposals, Grenville would have rejected them regardless of whether America was planning to join the Armed Neutrality. Indeed (and as Hamilton surely understood), if the Americans had shown an interest in the alliance, the British might well have reacted to such a bid to pressure them by taking a harder line.[21]

The Jay Treaty: Could There Have Been a Better Deal?

The second coup of Jay's career was not in the cards. Grenville made his predictable objections to the September draft. By early November, the two sides were nonetheless close to agreement, and Grenville delayed the sailing of the American mail packet in the final stages. The treaty was signed and copies were immediately sent to America on November 19, 1794. Jay dashed off a half-dozen letters. To Oliver Ellsworth, he wrote, "In my opinion we have reason to be satisfied.... Further concession on the part of Great Britain cannot, in my opinion, be attained." With Hamilton, he struck a more pessimistic note: "If this treaty fails, I despair of another." For Randolph he prepared a hasty article-by-article exegesis. To all his correspondents, he emphasized that current British good will was genuine and that the moment must be seized. Jay was basically satisfied but not without apprehensions. "*I have no idea,*" he wrote Washington a few months later, "*that the treaty will meet with anti-federalist approbation.* Besides men are apt to think of what they wish to have, than what it is in their power to obtain." It was just as well, he may have thought, that he had a good reason not to escort the treaty to Philadelphia. He wrote Rufus King, "my mind is at ease. I wish I could say as much for my body, but the rheumatism will not permit me." Jay lingered in London rather than face the severity of a winter's voyage.[22]

With a partial exception, the soon-to-be-excoriated treaty did fulfill the essential purposes of Jay's mission. The principle of compensation for the outrages in the Caribbean was recognized through the creation of a mixed commission to hear the cases of American merchants. The issue threatening war was defused on terms that preserved American honor, at least as far as Federalist maritime interests were concerned. A second capital objective, the return of the posts, was also in hand. With the posts came control of a vast territory and the federal government's ability to retain the loyalty of the settlers there, which otherwise would have been in doubt. Jay also obtained reciprocal trading privileges with the Indians in Canada (albeit excluding the area controlled by the Hudson's Bay Company), a mixed commission to settle the northeastern border, a joint survey of the upper Mississippi to be followed by "amicable negotiations," and for the first time direct trading privileges with the British *East* Indies, a major boon to the United States.[23]

A less foreseen but highly significant benefit was the impact on Madrid. Fearing that the treaty portended an Anglo-American alliance against them, the Spanish soon gave in to U.S. demands for free navigation of the Mississippi and a port of deposit at New Orleans. Those provisions, along with the abandonment of Spanish claims in the Old Southwest (east of the Mississippi and north of West Florida), were included in the Treaty of San Lorenzo el Real (or "Pinckney's treaty," after Thomas Pinckney who negotiated it), signed October 27, 1795.

The partial result concerned the West Indies. For Jay, Article 12, providing access to ships of up to seventy tons until two years after the war (the question then to be reexamined) but banning reexport from U.S. ports in U.S. ships of molasses, sugar, cotton, coffee, and cocoa, was a way "to break the ice" of the British navigation laws. But even Federalists considered it useless or harmful, and the Senate, in consenting to the treaty, made an exception to this part of Article 12. They could do so on the presumption that, with the British islands ever more dependent on American grain, lumber, cattle, and other supplies, the local authorities would allow access to American ships, with or without Article 12. The most important benefit of the treaty, finally, was that it secured peace and the uninterrupted trade, growth, and flow of customs revenues that peace guaranteed. Failure to settle with the British would have meant conflict on the high seas, ruining American commerce, and the necessity to take the posts by force. If the treaty "violated the spirit if not the letter of the 1778 treaties" with France, as well as Jay's instructions (inserted by Randolph) on that point, for the Federalists this was a small price to pay.[24]

Grenville had his own reasons to be satisfied. Britain, like America, secured the benefits of peace, implicitly accepting Hamilton's argument that the harm done by war would have been far out of proportion to the gain. Specifically, the treaty secured British participation in the fur trade south of the border after withdrawal from the posts. The issue of abducted slaves was effectively buried. British creditors could seek compensation for losses due to legal impediments via another mixed commission. Britain would also receive compensation for spoliations by French privateers illegally fitted out in U.S. ports, something previously denied. British privateers could now enter U.S. harbors with their prizes, and neither side was to receive privateers or prizes of the other's enemies. This article (25) contained the ambiguous (and disingenuous) proviso that nothing in the treaty shall "be construed or operate contrary to former and existing public treaties" with other states. Britain received a guarantee that the United States would not levy discriminatory tariff and tonnage duties during the operation of the treaty, nicely scuttling Madison's commercial strategy. Lastly, though a passage of Article 12 said that the question would be reopened two years after the war, the United States acquiesced in the British definition of neutral rights. Article 17 authorized the British to confiscate enemy property on neutral ships; as per Grenville's proposal, Article 18 provided that food and provisions could at times be considered contraband, though in such cases they would be paid for in full.

The question soon to be debated in America, and ever since by historians, was could the United States have obtained a better deal? Henry Adams wrote, "That Mr. Jay's treaty was a bad one few persons even then ventured to dispute" and that "there has been no moment since 1810 when the United States would have hesitated to prefer war rather than peace on such terms." (Among the treaty's backers, he apparently forgot, were his great-grandfather the vice president, and his grandfather John Quincy Adams, U.S. minister to The Hague, who went to London to exchange ratifications in October 1795.) Critics have always been especially offended by the position on neutral rights – conveniently forgetting Jefferson's position in 1793. Bemis also takes Jay to task for conceding too much power to the mixed debt commission, rather than insisting on the jurisdiction of the U.S. Supreme Court, and for not pushing harder on Indian issues and the new frontier regime. Bemis may be right on the first point. On the second, Jay, better than Bemis, grasped the British perception of their own weakness following the surrender of the posts.[25]

A question Bemis surprisingly does not ask is how, if it had arrived in time, news of the battle of Fallen Timbers, near Fort Miami on the Maumee, might have affected the Jay–Grenville negotiations. On August 20, 1794, Wayne's regular infantry and mounted Kentucky riflemen crushed a force of some thirteen hundred Wabash and Miami Indians dug in behind a barricade of trees uprooted by a violent storm. The brief, bloody encounter changed the balance of power in the Northwest Territory decisively in favor of the United States. A clash with the British was averted because the small force of redcoats garrisoning the fort did not come to the aid of the Indians. It is doubtful, in any event, whether the news of the rout of its tribal allies would have put the British government in a more conciliatory frame of mind.[26]

Bemis's point about the leverage thrown away by Hamilton through his contacts with Hammond is dubious. He may be right that Jay could have gained a point or two by taking a stronger stand on the abducted slave issue, but admits that the United States did not have much of a moral leg to stand on in insisting on the slaves' return. Bemis's vigorously written critique concludes with an intellectually honest whimper. It would have been "hopeless" to expect the British to change their position on neutral rights. Peace, the supreme priority, was preserved. Jay's (or Hamilton's) treaty was worth the price. Jay's "one great lapse" was Article 12 on the West Indies, though there had been a struggle over the issue in the British cabinet, and it would have been practically impossible to gain more. Lord Hawkesbury, Grenville's main opponent on the question, later wrote that the foreign secretary had been "perfectly duped by Jay"![27]

All this begs the question of whether Hamilton himself could have done a better job. No doubt, he would have hit it off with the suave, slightly younger Grenville. And he might have enjoyed London society, starting with the company of his sister-in-law, more than Jay. (One wonders how Jay, with his son-cum-secretary in tow, managed to fill his idle hours.) Hamilton's imperiousness and limited patience compared to Jay's might have inclined him to force the pace of the negotiations. It might not have been beneath his dignity, as it was Jay's, to make greater tactical use of the existence of pro-French popular opinion in the United States. These factors, along with his authoritativeness in the administration, might have won him concessions around the edges. But it is hard to imagine that the British would have conceded him anything of substance that they were not prepared to give to Jay. It is hard to imagine, given his views, that Hamilton would have tried to drive a harder bargain on neutral rights, though his negative reaction to Article 12 suggests that he might have chosen to dispense with the commercial treaty altogether. Whatever Hamilton might have gained, moreover, would have been offset by the political damage at home done by his direct association with the project. The treaty's tortured fate on reaching American shores suggests that Hamilton was wise to let Jay take primary responsibility and content himself with an uncharacteristic adjunct role.[28]

PART IV

INFORMAL ADVISER TO THE PRINCE

Return to Not-So-Private Life, 1794–1795

Rebellion and Retirement

At the end of May 1794, Hamilton wrote the president that he had delayed his resignation because of the recent crisis but was prepared to depart immediately if Washington so desired. The president answered, "I am pleased that you have determined to remain at your Post until the clouds over our affairs, which have come on so fast of late, shall have dispersed." In June, the House of Representatives cleared Hamilton of the charge of misappropriation of funds. His troubled relations with Washington were back on an even keel.[1]

In fact, as new clouds gathered, Washington's reliance on Hamilton was destined only to increase. After mid-1794, the administration's main concern was no longer war with Britain or the Indians, but unrest of a different sort. Infuriated by a federal excise tax on the universal practice of distilling whiskey and forced to defend themselves against violations in a federal court in far-off Philadelphia, hard-bitten, hard-drinking Scotch-Irish settlers in the four westernmost counties of Pennsylvania took the law into their own hands. On July 16, 1794, some five hundred members of local militia units attacked and destroyed the lightly defended estate of the Pittsburgh-area excise inspector. The stills of those who dared to pay the tax went up in flames. Federal authority in the region temporarily collapsed.

After some vacillation, the Washington administration adopted a two-pronged approach. A three-man federal commission was sent to investigate and offer amnesty to cooperating tax evaders. This was followed by a major show of force: the dispatch of some fifteen thousand militiamen (the regular army was still occupied in Ohio) with Washington riding at their head for the Carlisle-Bedford portion of the way. Temporarily running the War Department (with Knox ill) as well as the treasury, Hamilton was at the center of the preparations. He left Philadelphia to join the troops on September 30, returning only at the end of November 1794.

In retrospect, the resistance mounted by the "whiskey rebels" seems rather pathetic, and the force sent to suppress them ridiculously out of proportion to the threat. Perhaps Hamilton sensed this when he wrote flippantly from his Bedford encampment: "I am thus far my dear Angelica on my way to attack and subdue the wicked insurgents of the West." At the same time, he characteristically rejected a middle course and hoped to use the opportunity to strengthen the federal government's authority. His reaction to the rebellion reflected what he had said during the war about dealing with New York Loyalists:

The advice given by a certain general to his son, when the latter had the Roman army in his power, was certainly very politic. He advised him either to destroy them utterly or to dismiss them with every mark of honour and respect. By the first method says he you disable the Romans from being your enemies, by the last you make them your friends. So with respect to the Tories I would either disable them from doing us any injury, or I would endeavor to gain their friendship by clemency.

This observation, in turn, might have come straight from the *Discourses*: "a government is nothing other than keeping subjects so that they cannot and must not offend you: this is done either by insuring yourself totally by taking away every means they have to injure you, or else by benefitting them so that it is unreasonable for them to want to change their fortunes." In *The Prince*, Machiavelli put it more picturesquely: potential enemies "must be either coddled or eliminated."[2]

The administration's reaction to the Whiskey Rebellion also reflected its shaken nerves and sense of insecurity in the nasty political climate of 1794. As one observer usefully reminds us, "conspiracies were afoot in the 1790s." Washington, Hamilton, and many others connected the defiance of federal authority with the pernicious influence of the pro-French Democratic Societies, especially active in Pennsylvania. Washington wrote Henry Lee, "I consider this insurrection as the first *formidable* fruit of the Democratic Societies, brought forth I believe too prematurely for their own views, which may contribute to the annihilation of them." The rebellion had no connection to foreign policy *per se*, but it heightened the Federalists' sense of the country's vulnerability to French meddling in U.S. affairs. The determination to overawe the rebels arose partly from the desire to uphold the government's authority and prestige in European eyes.[3] Shortly before his last Christmas in the capital, Hamilton was approached by Hammond to learn if there had been any change in the government's attitude toward the Armed Neutrality. The answer was that there had not. Among the reasons Hamilton gave was that the country was "generally in too unsettled a state, to admit of its entangling itself in connexions [sic], which might eventually have a tendency to add a participation in the disputes of Europe to the internal causes of agitation." In fact, the disputes of Europe were themselves a source of internal agitation, as the coming year would show.[4]

Hamilton's Pennsylvania expedition was one of his final acts as a minister in Washington's government. On December 8, he wrote Angelica, "*Having contributed to place the finances of the Nation on a good footing, I go to take a little care of my own; which need my care not a little.*" He retired on Saturday, January 31, 1795. His hand-picked successor was Oliver Wolcott, Jr. of Connecticut, a Yale-educated lawyer who shared a birthday with Hamilton (he was born on January 11, 1760). Wolcott had been comptroller of the Treasury and would remain Hamilton's loyal executor. In a characteristic letter he wrote, "You know . . . that I shall do the best in my power, & that intimations from you will always be thankfully recd." But he was not lacking courage (he was one of a handful of federal officials who stayed in Philadelphia during the 1793 epidemic), ability, or, as will be seen, a mind of his own.[5]

Shortly before Hamilton's departure, Washington wrote him, "In every relation, which you have borne to me, I have found that my confidence in your talents, exertions and integrity, has been well placed. I the more freely render this testimony of my approbation, because I speak from opportunities of information which cannot deceive me, and which furnish satisfactory proof of your title to public regard." He did not say what information, but he wished to wipe the slate clean concerning early 1794. The letter concluded,

you may assure yourself of the sincere esteem, regard and friendship of
Dear Sir   Your Affectionate   Go: Washington

Hamilton answered the next day, "As often as I may recall the vexations I have endured, your approbation will be a great and precious consolation." He added, "it will be my pride to cultivate a continuance of that esteem regard and friendship, of which you do me the honor to assure me." The day Hamilton and his family left Philadelphia, his old friend James McHenry (a former aide-de-camp to Washington) wrote him, "What remains for you having ensured fame but to ensure felicity. Seek for it in the moderate pursuit of your profession."[6]

Hamilton was incapable of following this advice. It was partly a question of temperament: he did not tend to do anything moderately. It was partly a well-developed appetite for power and influence, something that could not be expected to disappear after years of immersion in public life. It was partly a need for the continued, unconditional approbation of Washington and a not-unfounded belief in his own indispensability. Finally, it was partly a desire to preserve his painfully constructed handiwork from neglect or deliberate sabotage. In short, Hamilton did not depart Philadelphia prepared to rest on his laurels and to turn the other cheek to his enemies, or feeling satisfied with himself.

Just before leaving office, he had submitted a major "Report on a Plan for Further Support of the Public Credit." It has been called "an explicit confession of failure." With American reluctance to pay taxes dramatically evident, the Dutch money market about to close because of a French invasion, and the very notion of a monetized public debt under bitter Republican attack, Hamilton had good reason to doubt whether investor confidence in the credit of the United States could be sustained. To disarm critics of the debt while making its servicing safe from legislative interference, he proposed a new sinking fund that promised – at least in theory – to extinguish the debt in thirty years.[7]

In February, he watched helplessly as the House eliminated his proposal for immediate payment of that part of the domestic debt ($1,561,175 of a total of $62,000,000) incurred by direct borrowing during his tenure. He wrote Rufus King:

The unnecessary capricious & abominable assassination of the National honor by the rejection of the propositions respecting the unsubscribed debt in the House of representatives haunts me every step I take, and afflicts me more than I can express. To see the character of the Government and the country so sported with, exposed to so indelible a blot puts my heart to the Torture. Am I then more of an American than those who drew their first breath on American Ground? Or What is it that thus torments me at a circumstance so calmly viewed by almost every body else? Am I a fool – a Romantic quixot – Or is there a constitutional defect in the American mind? Were it not for you and a few others, I could adopt the reveries of De Paux as substantial truths, and would say with him that there is something in our climate which belittles every Animal human or brute.... I disclose to you without reserve the state of my mind. It is discontented and gloomy in the extreme.

Postretirement depression combined with the sensation of having left behind unfinished business and, worse, unpaid debts. Hamilton had experienced other such "Machiavellian moments" of bitterness and alienation, and he had probably asked himself the questions in the letter in the past. Was he more, or was he less, of an American? Certainly his vision of America as a great power, with close ties to the former Mother Country, was not one that the majority of Americans had embraced. Was he a romantic (if not necessarily a quixot)? If by that he meant someone who saw himself as part of a heroic elite waging a lonely battle for the honor and regeneration of his country, the description was on the mark.[8]

It is not surprising that, two months after leaving Philadelphia, Hamilton was already contemplating his return. He rejected his friend Troup's offer to take part in a speculative business scheme that might expose him to criticism: "Because there must be some *public fools* who sacrifice private to public interest at the certainty of ingratitude and obloquy – because my *vanity* whispers I ought to be one of those fools and ought to keep myself in a situation the best calculated to render service." Probably sooner than he expected, he would be called on to defend his notion of the country's destiny. The two official copies of the Jay treaty en route to America were thrown into the icy waters of the North Atlantic when the French privateer

Lovely Lass (illegally fitted out in Baltimore) accosted the British mail packet *Tankerville* in December 1794. A third copy, entrusted by Jay to a private citizen, reached Secretary of State Randolph's office on March 7, 1795, a year to the day after the news of the notorious British order-in-council of November 6, 1793.[9]

A "Mad Dog" of a Treaty

A distinguished biographer of Washington makes much of the fact that Hamilton – whom he treats with a disdain bordering on the churlish – was out of the picture during this crucial phase of the Jay treaty story. "Washington felt that when Hamilton had left, he had left." After the treaty arrived, Washington "refrained from consulting Hamilton." Hamilton "did not dare offer unasked his advice to Washington – and he was not asked."[10]

It is true that Hamilton was not asked (for the time being), but this was probably because Washington, as usual considerate of Hamilton's feelings, knew he was resting in Albany until the end of May and then would be busy setting up his house and law practice in New York. As Flexner himself points out, moreover, Washington did not even let Treasury Secretary Wolcott, Secretary of War Timothy Pickering (who had replaced the retiring Knox), or Attorney General William Bradford (Randolph's replacement) have a look at the treaty. Sensing that it was loaded with political "dynamite" (Flexner's apt anachronism), the president ordered Randolph to keep it under lock and key until it could be delivered to the Senate. In the event, the Senate convened a special session to consider the treaty on June 8, 1795. On June 24, after eighteen days of heated and secret debate, the Senate approved the treaty (stipulating that the objectionable part of Article 12 be suspended and the matter pursued with the British) by a bare two-thirds majority of twenty votes to ten.[11]

The president's instincts about the treaty were correct. He himself was deeply unhappy with parts of it: the extension of the deadline for withdrawal from the posts until 1796, the sanction of continued British trade south of the border, and the weak deal on the West Indies. If someone of temperate views was far from satisfied, it was obvious that those who objected to any settlement with Britain as tantamount to a betrayal of France would see this one as a groveling surrender. But even Washington was unprepared for the reaction to the treaty's publication in early July 1795.[12]

The official release, authorized by the Senate, was anticipated by an abstract appearing in Benjamin Franklin Bache's rabidly Republican *Aurora* on June 29. This, in turn, was based on a copy supplied to Bache, the great Franklin's grandson, by the new French minister Pierre Auguste Adet. (Adet had either bought it from Virginia Senator Stevens T. Mason or been given it by Randolph.) Mass meetings from Boston to Charleston immediately denounced the treaty and called on Washington to reject it. Protesters broke windows at George Hammond's house and burned a copy of the treaty on his doorstep. A similar mob, reinforced by a group of French sailors, burned a copy on Jay's Manhattan doorstep. Jay, who had returned to learn that he had been elected governor of New York, affected indifference to the news that he was being burned in effigy up and down the Atlantic coast.[13]

Washington wrote, "At present the cry against the treaty is like that against a mad dog." The problem was now very much on *his* doorstep. As he saw it, his government "in relation to France and England may be compared to a ship between the rocks of Scylla and Charybdis. If the treaty is ratified, the partisans of the French (or rather of war and confusion) will excite them to hostile measures or at least unfriendly sentiments; if it is not, there is no foreseeing *all* the consequences which may follow as respects G.B." Washington leaned toward ratifying the Senate's decision. But he was having trouble deciding and did not want to be rushed. On July 3, he somewhat apologetically turned to Hamilton, asking him for a "dispassionate" article-by-article review.[14]

If care and length are any measure of Hamilton's eagerness to impress Washington, his reply a week later (filling fifty pages of his published papers) outdid even his Nootka Sound advice. In the final analysis, Hamilton found only two of the treaty's twenty-eight articles open to real objections: number twelve, on the West Indies, and number eighteen, allowing food to be treated as contraband. His conclusion placed matters in a broader perspective and struck a tone that he knew would appeal to Washington's instincts:

Well considered, the greatest interest of this Country in its external relations is that of peace. The more or less of commercial advantages which we may acquire by particular treaties are of far less moment. With peace, the force of circumstances will enable us to make our way sufficiently fast in Trade. War at this time would give a serious wound to our growth and prosperity. Can we escape it for ten or twelve years more, we may then meet it without much inquietude and may advance and support with energy and effect any just pretentions to greater commercial advantages than we may enjoy. It follows that the objects contained in the permanent articles [those ending the peace treaty controversies] are of real and great value to us.[15]

Washington stated his "great satisfaction" with Hamilton's response. They had a further exchange on whether the treaty, if accepted by Britain without Article 12, would have to return to the Senate. When Hamilton disagreed with Randolph on the point, Washington told the secretary of state to "revise" (probably meaning "review") his opinion and asked Hamilton to contact Randolph directly. Indeed, said the president, it would be a "considerable gratification" to hear from Hamilton on the treaty or "any other interesting subject." Washington was drawing Hamilton back into the game.[16]

Had a complicating factor not suddenly arisen, Hamilton's analysis might have convinced Washington to sign the treaty immediately. On July 7, however, came news of yet another order-in-council (dated April 25, 1795), secretly ordering British commanders to bring in neutral ships transporting grain and other provisions to France. Britain, like France, faced a severe bread shortage, leading to riots up and down the country, and precisely at the moment when final U.S. payments on the French debt had allowed France to make large purchases of wheat in the United States. Necessity dictated that precious American food go to feed starving British rather than French mouths, and the British government paid for what it "stole" in accordance with the as-yet-unratified treaty.

None of this garnered Britain sympathy in the United States. Washington was exasperated and disgusted that "the domineering spirit of Great Britain should revive just at this crisis, and the outrageous and insulting conduct of some of her officers should combine therewith, to play into the hands of the discontented and sour the minds of those who are friends of peace." He was referring specifically to Captain Rodham Home of H.M.S. *Africa*, who had flagrantly violated U.S. neutrality in waters off Newport, Rhode Island, in an attempt to capture the departing French minister, Joseph Fauchet (recalled to France after the execution of Robespierre). The Washington administration could do little to protect Fauchet (in the event his ship slipped away under cover of fog) but revoked the exequatur of the British vice-consul in Newport who had cooperated with Home.[17]

Several days before leaving for the peace and quiet of Mount Vernon, Washington took Randolph's advice that the British minister should be told that the president would ratify the treaty, but only after withdrawal of the latest order-in-council. Randolph duly delivered the message. But when Hammond (who knew that Pickering, Wolcott, and Bradford had advised the president to ratify the treaty unconditionally) asked if this decision were irrevocable, Randolph wavered. He had no instructions on that point. Washington was exasperated with Randolph, but himself apparently unsure of what to do. Perhaps against his better judgment, he agreed with Randolph that the secretary of state should now send a memorial through Hammond to the British government, inviting further negotiations on the contraband issue and other unsatisfactory features of the treaty. In effect, this was a decision not to decide for months to come. Washington and his family fled the heat, political as well as literal, of Philadelphia in a caravan of coaches on July 15, 1795.

A Traitor in Our Midst

Over the next several weeks, a tragicomic drama unfolded whose result was to provide a respite from the Jay treaty agony and indirectly to draw Hamilton further back into the inner circle. The villain, as well as the victim, of the piece was Edmund Randolph, done in by a combination of conniving enemies, his own hapless intriguing, and bad luck. The bad luck began in March 1795, when the British frigate *Cerebus* intercepted the French corvette *Jean*

Bart carrying dispatches from Fauchet to his superiors in Paris, including a "Dispatch No. 10," dated October 31, 1794. This time, a diving sailor fished the jettisoned diplomatic pouch out of the Atlantic. The French dispatch found its way to Grenville, who had it translated and sent to Hammond in Philadelphia. On July 26, 1795, Hammond read parts of it to Oliver Wolcott. Wolcott, once he had obtained a copy, showed it to Pickering and Bradford. The protreaty ministers immediately grasped that they had another piece of political dynamite – but this time a useful one – on their hands.

This was particularly true of Pickering, a dour, hard-line Massachusetts Federalist. Born in 1745, "Tim Pick" had been quartermaster general in the war, postmaster general in Washington's first cabinet, and a skilled negotiator with the Iroquois Indians. He was a charter member of the so-called Essex Junto, a close-knit group of ultraconservative Federalist lawyers and merchant-ship owners-turned-politicians, many of whom hailed from Essex County. (Others included George Cabot, Fisher Ames, Stephen Higginson, and Theophilus Parsons.) His portrait by Charles Willson Peale suggests the kind of thin-lipped Puritan zeal that had made life miserable for suspected witches in his native Salem in the previous century and would drive the abolitionist movement in the next. Pickering wrote to the president on July 31, urging him to return at once to Philadelphia. Washington, who had been planning to come back early anyway, arrived on August 11. Called to the presidential mansion, Pickering found Washington at the dinner table with Randolph. Washington motioned Pickering into another room and asked him what the matter was. Indicating Randolph, the secretary of war replied, "That man is a traitor." He handed Washington a hastily translated copy of the Fauchet dispatch. A shocked and baffled president sat down to read it after Randolph and Pickering had gone home.[18]

Historians have long debated the significance of Dispatch No. 10, written during the Whiskey Rebellion of the previous year. In it Fauchet attributed strongly pro-French and Republican views to Randolph, who had spoken of his "influence ... over the mind of the president." More seriously, it could be read to suggest that Randolph had solicited a bribe from the French in return for ensuring the opposition of Pennsylvania officials and Democratic Societies under his influence to the administration's suppression of the rebels. The evidence was far from conclusive, and Fauchet referred to other relevant dispatches not available to the president. Still, Washington knew that Randolph was strapped for cash, and his recent advice on the treaty could now be seen as motivated by a pro-French bias. Washington seems to have decided on the spot that Randolph could no longer be trusted and that it was time, despite his "very serious doubts," to end the drama. The next day, August 12, after listening once more to the views of his cabinet, he announced that he would ratify the treaty without insisting on the withdrawal of the order-in-council. In that instant, comments Alexander DeConde, Washington "in the eyes of Republicans, fell as had Lucifer."[19]

Conclusion

A week later, Washington, Pickering, and Wolcott gathered in the president's office to confront Randolph with Dispatch No. 10. According to Wolcott's recollection, Randolph admitted that he had asked Fauchet if money in the hands of French flour contractors could not be used to counter Hammond's alleged efforts to "destroy" New York Governor Clinton, Fauchet, and Randolph himself. The secretary of state insisted, and would continue to argue in a caustic if somewhat incoherent pamphlet aimed at Washington, that he had done nothing wrong. But Randolph, who with some reason considered himself the president's most devoted servant, had been humiliated. He ran down the steps of the president's house at the end of the meeting and sent his letter of resignation the same day.[20]

Randolph's disgrace and subsequent personal attack was one of the most distressing episodes of Washington's long career. The aging president – he was not personally close to Wolcott, Pickering, or Bradford – found himself alone in his own government. All of the major officers appointed in 1789 – Jefferson, Hamilton, Knox, and Randolph – were now gone. Though separated by physical distance and the old wall of formality, Washington and Hamilton continued to gravitate back toward each other. In fact, they had never needed each other more; Washington because of the vacuum of trust and reliable counsel and Hamilton because of his unsated ambition, the desire to protect his legacy, and an abiding attachment to his chief.

At the end of August, Washington asked Hamilton to suggest subjects to be taken up in further negotiations with Britain, as recommended by the Senate in approving the treaty. The letter went on,

Altho'you are not in the Administration – a thing I sincerely regret – I must, nevertheless, (knowing how intimately acquainted you are with all the concerns of this country) request the favor of you to note down such occurances as, in your opinion are proper subjects for communication to Congress at their next Session.

Hamilton, whose position on the April 1795 order-in-council had been close to Randolph's, if slightly more conciliatory to the British, replied with a list including the West Indies and the definition of contraband. The letter concluded, "I beg Sir that you will at no time have any scruple about commanding me. I shall always with pleasure comply with your commands.... With the truest respect & the most affectionate attachment...."[21]

The problem of finding qualified ministers while maintaining a sectional balance tormented Washington. "What," he wrote Hamilton on October 29, "am I to do for a Secretary of State?" He confided that he had already offered the job to William Paterson of New Jersey, Thomas Johnson of Maryland, Charles Cotesworth Pinckney of South Carolina, and even the former antifederalist Patrick Henry of Virginia. All had refused. "Would Mr [Rufus] King accept it?" Washington had a similar problem in trying to replace the recently deceased Bradford. Hamilton answered that King had also refused, adding, "The embarrassment is extreme as to Secretary of State." Their mutual friend, the jovial, Irish-born McHenry of Maryland, "would give no strength to the administration but he would not disgrace the Office – his views are good." Unfortunately, "a first rate character is not attainable. A second rate must be taken with good disposition & barely decent qualification. I wish I could throw more light. 'Tis a sad omen for the Government." In the end, a reluctant Washington had to persuade his *sixth* choice, the equally reluctant Pickering, who had taken it on a temporary basis, to keep the job of secretary of state. Charles Lee of Virginia, brother of Henry Lee, became attorney general. McHenry (after Patrick Henry had refused a second time) replaced Pickering as secretary of war.[22]

13

"Camillus" into the Breach

Introduction

Machiavelli dedicated much of his *Discourses* to distilling the lessons of
Roman and recent Italian history for vulnerable and emerging states. "One
of the most prudent practices of men," he observed, "is to abstain from
threatening and insulting someone with words; neither weakens the enemy,
while the one makes him more cautious, and the other makes him hate you
more and study with greater industry how to hurt you." Another lesson was
that: "Princes under assault by much more powerful forces can make no
greater error than to refuse (*recusare*) any agreement, especially when it is
offered to them: for there will never be an offer so empty that it doesn't
contain some benefits for the one who accepts it." As was often the case,
Machiavelli used the example of Florence in 1512. The invading Spanish,
desperate for food and supplies, at one point had dropped their demand
that the Medici family be restored to power and had accepted instead their
return to Florence as private citizens, plus a payment of cash and provisions,
in exchange for evacuating Florentine territory. The Florentines refused the
deal, enraged the Spanish, and lost their republic as a result.[1]

To illustrate his maxims, Machiavelli often invoked the figure of Fu-
rius Camillus, a Roman leader repeatedly called upon to save his city from
calamity. Someone who did not shrink from unpopularity, Camillus had
once been falsely accused of misappropriation of funds and went into temporary exile. His enemies included one Marcus Manlius, who (according to
Plutarch) "took that ordinary course toward usurpation of absolute power,
namely, to gain the multitude, those of them especially that were in debt."
Camillus's most famous exploit had been to rescue Rome from its partial
occupation by the Gauls. Through Camillus, Machiavelli taught that enemies should either be rendered harmless or befriended. Camillus was deeply
admired, and able to overcome his rivals' envy, thanks to his *virtù* as a leader.
But he was also hated because he gave the spoils of conquest to the public

treasury rather than dividing them among the people and seemed arrogant and full of himself. For a political leader to evoke hatred, but for reasons which gained him nothing, was to play with fire.[2]

Hamilton as Camillus

If Hamilton's most important contribution to the prevention of war was his little-known letter to Washington in April 1794, the Jay treaty ratification fight prompted his most sustained literary effort since "The Federalist," the "Camillus" essays. Hamilton composed twenty-eight of them, Rufus King the remaining ten. He wrote the first ("The Defense No. 1," signed "Camillus," appeared in a New York paper on July 22, 1795) during a week when he had refused to duck in the face of his own unpopularity. Defending the treaty at an outdoor meeting in lower Manhattan on Saturday, July 18, he was reportedly struck on the forehead by a stone. The same day he became involved in an argument with a former naval officer, James Nicholson, father-in-law of the Swiss-born financial expert and soon-to-be Republican congressman from Pennsylvania Albert Gallatin. Nicholson called Hamilton "an abettor of Tories" and accused him of having refused his challenge to a duel on a previous occasion. Hamilton waited two days and then challenged Nicholson to meet him at Paulus Hook, New Jersey, in a week's time.

While negotiations proceeded – eventually leading to an apology by Nicholson – Hamilton prepared a will. Appointing Robert Troup his executor, he wrote, "My concerns are not very extensive and of course will not give you much trouble." If his slender assets did not cover his debts, he hoped the loss would fall on his generous brother-in-law, John Church, whom he owed about five thousand pounds. Among his debts were drafts drawn on him by the father he had not seen in thirty years. "Though as I am informed a man of respectable connections in Scotland he became bankrupt as a merchant at an early day in the West Indies and is now in indigence. I have pressed him to come to me but his great age & infirmity have deterred him from a change of climate."[3]

Hamilton's first essay set out the motives of the Jay treaty's opponents: "the vanity and vindictiveness of human nature," in particular, the animosity aroused by the success of the federal system, old-fashioned demagoguery and political ambition, continuing resentment of Britain, and misguided enthusiasm for France. "From the combined operation of these different causes, it would have been a vain expectation that the treaty would be generally contemplated with candor and moderation." In "The Defense No. 2," he repeated his argument that it would have been folly to retaliate against Britain *before* negotiations and that peace was the path to national strength. "A very powerful state may frequently hazard a high and haughty tone with good policy, but a weak State can scarcely ever do it without imprudence. The last is yet our character, though we are the embryo of a great empire."[4]

Another maxim was that "Nations, no more than individuals, ought to persist in error, especially at the sacrifice of their peace and prosperity; besides nothing is more common in disputes between nations, than each side to charge the other with being the aggressor or delinquent." Hamilton defended Jay's decision to compromise rather than persist in Jefferson's futile and erroneous argument that complete blame for the peace treaty violations lay with the British. He took up the British arguments on the slaves and the posts, concluding that they had considerable merit. Jefferson, in his May 1792 letter to Hammond, had failed to discuss whether performance of the articles was to begin with the preliminary or the final peace treaty. In either case, the American failure to implement Article 5 was at least contemporaneous with the British failure to order a withdrawal from the posts.[5] Jay, "because he did not mistake strut for dignity and rudeness for spirit, because he did not by petulance and asperity enlist the pride of the British Court against the success of his mission . . . is represented as having humiliated himself and his nation." Anticipating Theodore Roosevelt's famous motto, Hamilton continued: "It is forgotten that mildness in the *manner* and *firmness* in the *thing* are most compatible with true dignity, and almost always go farther than harshness and stateliness."[6]

Because Republicans railed against the treaty's failure to deal with the impressment of American seamen, Hamilton pointed out:

Everybody knows that the safety of Great Britain depends on her Marine. This was never more emphatically the case, than in the war in which she is now engaged. Her very existence as an independent power seems to rest on a maritime superiority. In this situation can we be surprised that there are difficulties in bringing her to consent to any arrangement which would enable us by receiving her seamen into our employment to detach them from her service?

Hamilton dismissed the Republican view that French victories had weakened Britain to the point that it was ready to make significant concessions. He painted the picture of a defiant John Bull, still possessed of "an immense credit" and triumphant on the seas. The British government possessed "as much vigour" and had "as much national support as it perhaps ever had at any former period of her history."[7]

Among those impressed was Jefferson himself. His view of the Jay treaty episode, as stated in a letter to Philip Mazzei, was that "Men who were Sampsons in the field and Solomons in the council [namely Washington] . . . have had their heads shorn by the harlot England." In September 1795, he urged Madison to take up his pen: "Hamilton is really a colossus to the antirepublican party – without numbers, he is a host within himself. They have got themselves into a defile, where they might be finished; but too much security on the Republican part, will give time to his talents and indefatigableness to extricate them." Madison, remembering that he had not done brilliantly in his 1793 tussle with "Pacificus," turned down the request.[8]

In essay after essay, Hamilton defended the treaty's provisions on the posts, U.S.–Canada trade arrangements, compensation for British creditors, U.S. merchants and British ship owners (the latter for losses to illegal privateers), and the ban on the sequestering of private debt. He even had something nice to say about the notorious Article 12. Britain's Navigation Laws had been breached and it could be "strongly argued that the precedent of the privilege gained was of more importance than its immediate extent." Discussing the treaty's failure to uphold "free ships make free goods," he took pleasure in recalling Jefferson's 1793 sermon on the subject to Genêt. Article 18 contained an admittedly "unpleasant" element, the illiberal definition of contraband, but did not worsen things compared to the situation before the treaty. And "in a war in which it was more than ordinarily possible that the independent existence" of Britain might depend on its naval superiority, it was idle to expect it to give up the right to seize food and naval stores.[9]

Hamilton's final three efforts as Camillus appeared within a week of each other in early 1796. Reminding readers that under the Constitution treaties became "the supreme law of the land," he dismissed the view that the treaty was unconstitutional because the Constitution gave Congress the "power to regulate commerce with foreign nations." That was equivalent to saying that "all the objects upon which the legislative power may act in relation to our Country are excepted out of the power to make treaties." Such a notion was absurd. In the final essay, he challenged Madison, a key member of the 1787 convention who was now preparing to attack the treaty in the House of Representatives, to deny that the framers had intended to give broad and binding treaty-making powers to the executive. Camillus concluded (January 9, 1796) on a note that suggested lingering feelings of betrayal and bitterness toward his former collaborator:

It is really painful & disgusting to observe sophisms so miserable as those which question the constitutionality of the Treaty retailed to an enlightened people and insisted upon with so much seeming fervency & earnestness. It is impossible not to bestow on sensible men who act this part – the imputation of hypocrisy.

Should their doctrines be adopted, "There would be no security at home, no respectability abroad."[10]

By the time Camillus took this parting shot, Hamilton, though theoretically retired, was once again playing a central role in the administration. In November, the president had him prepare his seventh annual address to Congress, delivered on December 8, 1795. Rather than answer, or even acknowledge, criticisms leveled at his conduct, Washington caught the Republicans off guard by emphasizing the positive. Never had he met the legislators "at any period when more than at present the situation of our public affairs has afforded just cause for mutual congratulation; and for inviting you to join with me in profound gratitude to the Author of all good for the numerous and extraordinary blessings we enjoy." He cited the victorious end of the Indian war, consolidated by the Treaty of Greenville (August 3, 1795), a preliminary peace with the Algerines, and news of the imminent treaty with Spain opening the Mississippi. Washington mentioned the Jay treaty next, almost in passing, before a discussion of the orderly and prosperous state of domestic affairs. The speech did not end the treaty controversy, but it was, as Flexner writes, "a brilliant stroke."[11]

From One Crisis to the Next

As Hamilton had foreseen, the final treaty showdown took place in the lower house, the question at issue being the appropriations required to implement the accord. In a last effort to kill the treaty, Republicans demanded that the administration hand over Jay's instructions and correspondence and asserted the House's right to pass judgment, despite Senate and presidential ratification, on the treaty's merits. Supporters believed, with reason, that failure to execute the treaty would mean a major constitutional crisis and war with Britain over the posts and neutral rights.

From New York, Hamilton dashed off his opinion that supplying the documents in question would be "fatal to the Negotiating Power of the Government." To William Loughton Smith he supplied arguments to use on the House floor. The Republican doctrine "would vest the Legislature & each House with *unlimited discretion* & destroy the very idea of a Constitution limiting its discretion." Moreover, after looking again at Jay's instructions, Hamilton wrote that it would be just as well if they remained secret. Among the points likely to provoke clamor was the one authorizing the banning of privateering, while the revelation of other parts would be "a violation of decorum towards G Britain." Hamilton recommended stonewalling the House's demand and sent a draft message outlining the reasons. In the event, Washington did not use it but followed the substance of his advice.[12]

Setting out a series of steps, including confidential assurances to London and the mobilization of the country's merchants, he wrote Rufus King: "In all this business celerity decision & and an imposing attitude are indispensable. The Glory of the President, the safety of the Constitution, the greatest interests depend upon it." In the end, Washington's prestige, together with support not only from Anglophile merchants enjoying a booming business in 1795–96 but also from pro-Republican westerners eager for the return of the posts and afraid of renewed hostilities with the Indians, saved the treaty. On April 30, 1796, the House approved the appropriations by a vote of fifty-one to forty-eight. Although the Republican leader Albert Gallatin had favored postponement of the treaty, Madison rejected any compromise. In effect, he continued to gamble that his alternative policy of commercial retaliation would oblige the British to compromise their vital interests, even though if they did not, the United States would face the choice of war or disgrace. Approval of the treaty was a "heavy blow" for the Virginian and confirmed his earlier decision to retire from the House.[13]

Barely had the administration managed to salvage the treaty when a new crisis threatened to erupt. In early March, Gouverneur Morris, in London, relayed news just arrived from Paris that the French Directory would send a new envoy, backed by warships, to America to demand an explanation for the treaty. When Hamilton communicated this to Washington, the president wrote back, speculating about French intentions. Perhaps they would insist on release from the "free ships make free goods" provision of the Franco-American treaty or U.S. fulfillment of the guarantee of France's West Indian colonies or attempt to render the Jay treaty null and void, but he could not quite believe they would send a fleet to demand the treaty's "annihilation." In any case, "were it not for the unhappy differences among ourselves," his answer to France would be "short & decisive, to this effect. We are an independent Nation, and act for ourselves.... We will not be dictated to by the Politics of any Nation under Heaven, farther than Treaties require of us."[14]

Washington suspected that French hostility to the treaty had been encouraged by the U.S. minister in Paris, in cahoots with his Virginia friends. Indeed, James Monroe had begun to make his pro-Royalist predecessor, Morris, look like a model of restraint. In September 1795, after Washington had signed the Jay treaty, Monroe had recommended to Randolph that the federal government seize British property in the United States, "take the posts, and then invade Canada. This would not only secure to us completely our claims upon Britain, and especially if we likewise cut up her trade by privateers; but by making a decisive and powerful diversion in favor of France, promote, and very essentially, a general peace." In January 1796, the French foreign minister, Charles Delacroix, encouraged by popular opposition to the treaty, prepared a similar, ambitious plan. The new French minister in America, Adet (he had taken up residence in June 1795), would first assist the Republicans in defeating Washington and electing Jefferson to the presidency, after which the United States would renounce the Jay treaty and invade Canada. The previous year, during negotiations leading to the Treaty of Basle (July 22, 1795) and Spain's departure from the First Coalition, the French had tried to persuade Madrid to retrocede Louisiana. In March 1796, Adet dispatched General Victor Collot, a French cartographer, to reconnoiter the Mississippi Valley as far south as New Orleans. The French dream of a second North American empire, including territory *east* of the Mississippi, was very much alive.[15]

One may question how seriously the rest of the Directory took Delacroix's grand design. For months, the French government had paid little attention to the Jay treaty, lodging an official protest only on March 11, 1796. But there is no doubt that the French, with the help of their Republican fifth column, were planning some heavy-handed interference in American politics. The treaty included timber on the list of contraband, allowed food to be seized under some circumstances and failed to uphold "free ships make free goods." It also provided a convenient pretext for a new French policy on the high seas. A French client reported the likelihood of this to Hamilton in mid-June 1796. Although Adet did not inform the U.S. government until the end of October, on July 2, 1796, the Directory issued a decree according to which "The flag of the [French] Republic will treat the flag of neutrals in the same manner as they suffered it to be treated by the English." In other words, French raiders would confiscate British goods found on American merchantmen. Or rather they would take *all* goods carried on American ships headed for British ports, in theory paying for what *they* decided was not British property.[16]

Hamilton wrote his protégé and successor, Wolcott: "This state of things is extremely serious. The Government must play a skilful card or all is lost." His assessment had been foreshadowed in a recent letter to Washington. Sensing the president's anger and agitation, Hamilton had urged a conciliatory and dilatory approach. The French should be given a detailed explanation of the treaty, stressing America's peaceful and friendly intentions. If the French claimed the West Indian guarantee, they should be told – in obvious contradiction with real Hamilton's convictions – that it was up to Congress to decide. As Hamilton noted, "For to gain time is everything."[17]

Hamilton repeated to Washington what he had recommended to Wolcott: a "faithful organ" of the administration, someone at the same time not "obnoxious" to France, should be sent to Paris to explain. He had in mind his other confidant in the cabinet, Secretary of War McHenry. Hamilton was intent on avoiding, if at all possible, a war with France. But his more basic concern now emerges with considerable clarity. To Wolcott he wrote, "Remember always as a primary motive of Action that the favourable Opinion of our own Country is to be secured." To Washington, he emphasized, "It is all important that the people should be satisfied that the Government has made every exertion to avert Rupture as early as possible." He reiterated the point on July 5: it was to be feared that if "no *actual & full* explanation takes place, it will bring serious censure upon the Executive. It will be said that it did not display as much zeal to avoid misunderstanding with France as with G Britain [in 1794]."[18]

Hamilton was deeply irritated with the British knack for complicating the life of their American sympathizers. When the Royal Navy preyed on American commerce during the Jay treaty battle, he called the British government "as great fools, or as great rascals, as our Jacobins." At the same time he impressed on Washington the importance of sending "a man *able and not disagreeable*" to the British to replace the retiring Thomas Pinckney. He wrote a glowing recommendation for Rufus King, the New York Senator who had asked Hamilton to help him obtain the position. King, born in 1755, was the son of a revolutionary-era Loyalist and himself a convert to Anglicanism. Washington duly nominated King. Typically, Hamilton did not share with Washington a more controversial suggestion made contemporaneously to Wolcott:

A [British] frigate or two to serve as Convoys would not be amiss. If the English had been wise they would neither have harassed our Trade themselves nor suffered their Trade with us to be harassed. They would see this a happy moment for conciliating us by a clever little squadron in our Ports & on our Coast. A *hint* might not perhaps do harm.[19]

Also revealing was Hamilton's "Design for a Seal for the United States," composed in May 1796, though apparently consigned to a desk drawer. On the seal would appear America "represented by *Pallas* – a female figure with a firm, composed countenance, in an attitude of defiance," her spear striking and breaking the iron scepter of a "Colossus," representing the French Directory, one of whose feet extended menacingly into the Atlantic. Hamilton added, "It would improve it if it did not render it too complicated to represent the Ocean in tempest & Neptune striking with his Trident the projected leg of the Colossus." Neptune with his Trident represented British naval power. As Hamilton knew, the complication in portraying America and Britain fighting side-by-side was not so much aesthetic as domestic political in nature.[20]

It is clear, in any event, that by "playing a skilful card" Hamilton meant fostering in the public mind the appearance of absolute evenhandedness on the part of the executive with respect to the British and the French. The onus of a possible break must be seen to fall squarely on the shoulders of Paris. Astute management of the situation meant, if not killing the French with kindness, giving them enough rope to hang themselves, as they had nearly done with Genêt. Coinciding and closely interconnected with the French crisis was the delicate question of Washington's upcoming retirement and the selection of a new president. Break or no break, the situation must not be allowed to help the Republicans recover from their defeat on the Jay treaty and advance their fortunes in the elections. Such was the state of Hamilton's mind when Washington asked him to help prepare a valedictory message to the American people, a task that would occupy him for a number of months in 1796.

14

A High-Stakes Game: Washington's Farewell Address, 1796

The Origins of the Farewell Address

The Farewell Address, the most famous state paper in American history, has spawned a vast literature and ongoing controversy. John C. Miller, a discerning scholar, treated Washington and Hamilton as virtual coauthors. Felix Gilbert, in his well-known study, argued that Hamilton left his mark on the central foreign affairs section of the address and turned Washington's notions into a true "political testament" in the eighteenth-century tradition. The view that Hamilton wrote the address was first advanced by his widow and children, backed by documentary evidence. In 1810, six years after Hamilton's death, Judge Nathaniel Pendleton (one of the executors of his estate and his second in the duel with Aaron Burr), was dismayed to discover a draft of the address in Hamilton's handwriting. Pendleton and other Federalists feared that attributing the address to Hamilton would damage Washington's reputation. He entrusted the relevant bundle of papers to Rufus King, who refused to surrender them until 1826, after being sued by the Hamilton family. The "Hamilton as author" thesis, and a whiff of conspiracy surrounding the matter, has persisted ever since.[1]

There has always been a different view. A prominent diplomatic historian argued that Hamilton's contribution to the address had been its "incisive style." For a more recent commentator, the address was "emphatically Washington's at its intellectual core." Flexner, who analyzed the question as carefully as anyone, concluded: "The address could correctly be attributed to Hamilton if it expressed Hamilton's ideas. This it only did insofar as Hamilton's ideas coincided with Washington's." Such was Jay's view during the original controversy: a "careful perusal" of Washington's life would convince the skeptics "that the principles of policy which it [the address] recommends as rules for the conduct of others, are precisely those by which he regulated his own."[2]

Establishing authorship entails tracing the address's peregrinations and the changes it went through at each stage. When Washington was considering retirement in May 1792, he handed a letter to Madison, asking for help in preparing a farewell message. This letter, the core of the future Address, sketched out a set of thoughts that Washington wished to include: that "the spirit of the government may render a rotation in the Elective officers of it more congenial with their [the people's] ideas of liberty & safety," that the country's size and diversity made its parts necessary to each other and "may render the whole (at no distant period) one of the most independent in the world," the importance of cementing the union, and the need for prudence in criticizing public measures and officials. Washington turned to Madison, among other reasons, because Hamilton and Jefferson were caught up in their bitter quarrel. He may also have hoped that the exercise would serve to moderate Madison's own opposition to the administration. In June 1792, Madison sent back a brief draft incorporating, while rephrasing, the president's ideas.[3]

In the spring of 1796, firmly resolved to return to Mount Vernon, Washington once again began work on a farewell message. A draft he showed Hamilton at the end of April in Philadelphia contained three sections. The first consisted of a conspicuous verbatim quotation of Madison's 1792 draft. Gilbert asserts that Washington wished to include this as a demonstration of cooperation with the Republicans, but this is the opposite of what he had in mind. As he later explained to Hamilton, by including the Madison quotation, and showing the public that he had wanted to give up power in 1792, Washington hoped to lessen the "pretentions" of the Republicans to "the patriotic zeal & watchfulness" on which they tried to build their importance and to counter their inevitable "shafts" to the effect that he had decided to retire now because he feared defeat.[4]

The second section of Washington's draft included a pointed discussion of foreign policy. It was his ardent wish that "we may fulfil with the greatest exactitude all our engagements: foreign and domestic... for in public, as in private life, I am persuaded that honesty will forever be found to be the best policy." It was also his wish to "avoid connecting ourselves with the Politics of any Nation, farther than shall be found necessary to regulate our own trade." The dignity of the American nation would be "absorbed, if not annihilated, if we enlist ourselves (further than our engagements may require) under the banners of any other Nation whatsoever." Washington also wished that "we would guard against the Intriegues [sic] of any and every foreign Nation who shall intermeddle (however indirectly and covertly) in the internal concerns of our country – or who shall attempt to prescribe rules for our policy with any other power, if there be no infraction of our engagements." The latter passage was an obvious reference to the French.[5]

As was the following: experience proved that "Nations as well as individuals, act for their own benefit, and not for the benefit of others, unless both interests happen to be assimilated (and when that is the case there requires no contract to bind them together)." Experience also proved that "all their interferences are calculated to promote the former." Accepting foreign favors would necessitate granting favors in return, which "may involve us in disputes and finally in War, to fulfil political alliances." But "if there be no engagements on our part" we would be free to act "from circumstances, and the dictates of Justice – sound policy – and our essential Interests." For all intents and purposes, Washington was repudiating the Franco-American alliance.[6]

At the end of section two, Washington took up some of the themes of his 1792 letter to Madison. It was his hope that "We may be always prepared for War, but never unsheath the sword except in self defence so long as Justice and our essential rights and national respectability can be preserved without it." For if the country could remain at peace "20 years longer…such in all probability will be its population, riches & resources, when combined with its peculiarly happy & remote Situation from the other quarters of the globe – as to bid defiance, in a just cause, to any earthly power whatsoever." He stressed the importance of preserving the union, "the evils and horrors" of political faction, the necessity to avoid encroachment by one branch of government on "the rights and privileges of another," and the dangers of withdrawing confidence from elected officials. However high-minded and disinterested they may seem today, in 1796, these sentiments looked very much like Washington's own shafts aimed at the faction whose latest caper had been to try to kill a duly ratified treaty in the House of Representatives. This was explicitly so of the third section of the draft:

As this Address, Fellow citizens will be the last I shall ever make to you, and as some of the Gazettes of the United States have teemed with all the invective that disappointment, ignorance of facts, and malicious falsehoods could invent, to misrepresent my politics & affections; – to wound my reputation and feelings; – and to weaken, if not entirely to destroy the confidence you had been pleased to repose in me; it might be expected at the parting scene of my public life that I should take some notice of such virulent abuse. – But, as heretofore, I shall pass them over in utter silence.

The president went on to insist on the purity of his motives throughout his career: "To conclude, and I feel proud in having it in my power to do so with truth, that it was not from ambitious views; – it was not from ignorance of the hazard to which I knew I was exposing my reputation; – it was not from an expectation of pecuniary compensation – that I have yielded to the calls of my country."[7]

It is impossible to say how much of this draft Washington had completed, or how much of it Hamilton actually saw, when the two met in April in Philadelphia. If he had read all of it, it is easy to see why Hamilton was eager to begin "redressing" it, as the president had proposed. Far from a dignified "utter silence" in the face of attacks, its coda was more in the nature of a

Nixonesque, "you won't have me to kick around anymore." As a whole, the draft was something other than the "skilful card" that Hamilton was keen to play. His anxiety to get his hands on it comes through in his letter of May 10, 1796, to Washington: "As it is important that a thing of this kind should be done with great care and much at leisure touched & retouched, I submit a wish that as soon as you have given it the *body* you mean it to have that it may be sent to me."[8]

Washington satisfied this wish by sending the draft on May 15, 1796. In a cover letter he explained his reasons for using the Madison quotation. According to Gilbert, it was Hamilton who then devised a way to drop the quotation and its objectionable republican sentiments. In fact, the same cover letter makes clear that Washington himself (who had apparently discussed the issue with his fellow Virginian at dinner on May 12) had decided not to mention Madison by name and now invited Hamilton to cut parts of the quotation. These included Madison's phrase (based on Washington's original May 1792 letter) about "the example of rotation in office." To Hamilton's undoubted relief, Washington also invited him to discard the "egotism (however just they [sic] may be)" and said that he wished to avoid discussing personalities and specific measures and provoking attacks on himself. He told Hamilton either "to throw the *whole* into a new form," in other words, to prepare a new text preserving the ideas of the original, or simply to revise the present draft. Hamilton, as was his wont when he took pen in hand for Washington, would do both.[9]

Machiavelli, Hamilton, and the Farewell Address

The basic message of Machiavelli's *Discourses* is the superiority of republicanism over absolutism. The author adduces many reasons, including the greater military potential and foreign policy dynamism of regimes jealous of their liberty and drawing on popular support. As a rule, moreover, a well-ordered populace would show greater wisdom, steadiness, and susceptibility to reasoned argument (and could wreak less havoc if not well-ordered) than an individual with all power in his hands. Because times changed, but the nature of men did not, another advantage of republics was their adaptability. Fabius Maximus's innate caution suited the times brilliantly when Rome was on the defensive against Carthage, but according to Machiavelli, if he had been king rather than a mere consul, Rome would not have won the war. Fortunately, the republic was able to choose a more aggressive commander, Scipio, when the time was ripe.[10]

In assisting Washington in taking the step, practically unprecedented since ancient times, of voluntarily relinquishing power, Hamilton was affirming the superiority of republicanism and helping to establish the legitimacy of the new regime. But there was a contradiction in Hamilton's action, mirroring a basic tension in Machiavelli's thinking. When it came to the executive, both wanted to have their cake and eat it: the advantages of strong, continuous leadership and the resourcefulness and adaptability of republicanism. Both saw advantages in a kind of republican kingship, with a chief magistrate elected to serve for life. Indeed, there is some evidence that Hamilton would have preferred Washington to remain in office after 1796. To a considerable extent his own influence depended on it, and in his view, circumstances might compel it. In April, he had written King that failing execution of the Jay treaty, "the President will be called upon by regard to his character & the public good to *keep his post* till another House of Representatives has pronounced." On July 5, he wrote Washington that he had "completed the first draft of a certain paper." As to the timing of the announcement, however, Hamilton counseled that "you should *really hold the thing undecided to the last moment* . . . . If a storm gathers, how can you retreat? This is a most serious question."[11]

But whether Washington stayed or left (Hamilton probably did not seriously believe that he could be dissuaded from doing what he had wanted to do in 1792), the consolidation of the still-precarious federal system required that the founding prince retain an aura of "all piety, all faith, all integrity, all humanity, all religion." This is what Hamilton tried to assure with his so-called major draft of the address. Judging from its reception, then and since, he did so with conspicuous success. Washington himself greatly preferred it, except for its excessive length, to other versions, including Hamilton's much simpler, rather wooden reediting of the president's draft. Hamilton's major draft, after extensive rewording and shortening by the president, became the Farewell Address published in *Claypoole's American Daily Advertiser*, a Philadelphia newspaper, on September 19, 1796.[12]

Hamilton set out to write an address that could not fairly be accused of being a Federalist apology or piece of election-year propaganda, even though it was both. As he told Washington, in sending him the draft on July 30, 1796, "It has been my object to render this act *importantly* and *lastingly* useful, and . . . to embrace such reflections and sentiments as will wear well, progress in approbation with time, & redound to future reputation." While mentioning the 1792 effort, Hamilton cut it considerably and did not quote Madison's draft directly, leaving the minimum necessary to prove Washington's point that Madison had indeed collaborated four years earlier. (Only one of Madison's substantive notions found its way into the final version: the American system as an example to the world.) Hamilton included a bit of toned-down "egotism" (which Washington himself then edited out), but eliminated entirely the self-defeating coda. In Hamilton's hands, Washington was no longer a self-pitying victim of the Republican scandal sheets, but a sage and self-effacing patriarch, aware of the "inferiority" of his qualifications and the "inadequateness" of his faculties. His counsels were those "of an old and affectionate friend – counsels suggested by laborious reflection and matured by a various experience."[13]

If readers drew the conclusions that France and its domestic supporters were the real threats to peace and union, and that the French alliance was a dangerous anachronism, so much the better from Hamilton's point of view. But his phraseology did not betray the slightest bias. In the key foreign affairs section of the address, Hamilton's version conveyed the impression of greater coolness and impartiality with respect to Britain and France than Washington's: "nothing is more essential than that antipathies against particular nations and passionate attachments for others should be avoided – and that instead of them we should cultivate just and amicable feelings toward all." It also evinced a somewhat greater deference to the requirements of the French treaty: "The great rule of conduct for us in regard to foreign Nations ought to be to have as little political connection with them as possible – so far as we have already formed engagements let them be fulfilled – with circumspection indeed but with perfect good faith."[14]

Thus Hamilton *did* make an essential contribution to the style and tone of the address. It was that of a Machiavellian "spinmeister" who lent Washington's somewhat raw sentiments a princely dignity and politically efficacious detachment. But what about the ideas? There is truth in Flexner's statement that Hamilton contributed nothing of substance that Washington did not believe independently of Hamilton. In fact, most of the themes appearing in Hamilton's and in the final version were already present in Washington's earlier drafts: the supreme importance of the union, the economic interdependence of the various regions, the danger of faction and of foreign interference, the perils of encroachment by one branch of government on another, the need for respect for elected officials, the folly of expecting disinterested favors, the importance of avoiding emotional and political connections to foreign states, "equal and impartial" commercial policies, and the unrivalled strength of America if it could exploit the advantages of geography and buy time. As both Gilbert and Edmund S. Morgan have pointed out, the theme of steering clear of European disputes is present in Washington's correspondence well before 1796. Washington had talked of defying the world in twenty years' time in a letter to Gouverneur Morris in December 1795. To a considerable extent, Hamilton's draft simply elaborated on these ideas.[15]

But this does not exhaust the question of authorship – first of all, because Hamilton gave some of the ideas a different twist. To be sure, Washington did not accept each and every twist. For example, he eliminated Hamilton's point that in a geographically large republic it could perhaps be said that the popular faction posed a greater threat to liberty than did the rich and well-born faction. He did the same with Hamilton's statement: "In my opinion the real danger in our system is that the General Government organised as at present will prove too weak rather than too powerful." Interestingly, he also crossed out Hamilton's reference to "our Empire," a term that he himself had not employed.[16]

Some of Hamilton's gloss, however, did find its way into the final version. It was Hamilton, not Washington, who made the prophetic link between political factionalism and geographical sectionalism. As the final version puts it: "One of the Expedients of Party to acquire influence, within particular districts, is to misrepresent the opinions & aims of other Districts – You cannot shield yourselves too much against the jealousies & heart burnings which spring from these misrepresentations." In contrast to Washington's unequivocal call for no foreign engagements, Hamilton left the door open to "occasional alliances for temporary emergencies." (Washington then changed "occasional alliances" to "temporary" ones.) As Hamilton knew, in the world of eighteenth-century power politics, alliances were temporary by definition, lasting no longer than the interests of the parties dictated.

Hamilton made the point (harkening back to "The Federalist No. 11") that "Europe has a set of primary interests which have none or a very remote relation to us." Hence America would be unwise to implicate itself in the "ordinary vicissitudes" of European politics. It is hard to believe that Hamilton himself accepted the first point, a kind of intellectual cliché, contradicted by reality, though perhaps useful in promoting national feeling and caution during America's period of weakness. The second point begged the question: what about Europe's extraordinary vicissitudes, the bid for hegemony of a Louis XIV or the current French regime? As Hamilton also knew, American territory had been involved in each such vicissitude since the War of the League of Augsburg at the end of the seventeenth century. Neither Hamilton nor anyone else could foresee that the balance of power prevailing after 1815 would allow the United States to remain detached from Europe for an entire century. Washington's draft spoke of the day (in twenty years or so) when America would be able "to bid defiance, in a just cause, to any earthly power." For Hamilton, "the period [was] not distant... when we may choose peace or war as our interest guided by justice shall dictate." Washington let Hamilton's more explicit language stand.[17] It is clear enough from his own words that Washington was not endorsing what would later be called "isolationism," except as a temporary measure to allow the United States to build up its strength. The effect of Hamilton's changes was to nudge the address toward a prudent, realistic recognition of America's long-term inseparability from the European state system that it otherwise would not have had.

At the same time, and as commentators have usually failed to see, Hamilton's draft included ideas *not* present in any prior draft. Together, they represent the most original part of his contribution. Interestingly, with a partial exception, these ideas have something in common: their Machiavellianism. The partial exception is the nexus between public credit and national "strength and security" and the necessity of tax-based revenue.[18] (Washington kept Hamilton's language on this point nearly intact.) Finance was not a major theme for Machiavelli, though he certainly would have agreed. Hamilton wrote, and Washington retained with minor changes:

To the duration and efficacy of your Union a Government extending over the whole is indispensable. No alliances however strict between the parts could be an adequate substitute. These could not fail to be liable to the infractions and interruptions which all alliances in all times have suffered.

Hamilton was reiterating a Machiavellian idea, as well as a favorite theme of his own: the precariousness of alliances and confederations. Unlike Washington, moreover, Hamilton grounded the arguments about "party spirit" and the "spirit of encroachment" in an explicit view of human nature. Washington accepted this telling addition, and thus his quintessentially American address speaks, echoing Machiavelli, of "that love of power, and proneness to abuse it, which predominates in the human heart."[19]

Hamilton contributed another argument, namely "To all those dispositions which promote political prosperity, Religion and Morality are essential props. In vain does that man claim the praise of patriotism who labours to subvert or undermine these great pillars of human happiness these firmest foundations of the duties of men and citizens." In his passionate iconoclasm and attachment to the classical world, Machiavelli had deplored the effects of contemporary Christianity. But he had insisted on the usefulness of religion, reinforced by official ceremonies, in inspiring discipline, fighting spirit, and loyalty. "There was never as much fear of God" as in the Roman republic "which facilitated whatever enterprise the Senate or those great men of Rome designed to do." Washington included Hamilton's paragraph, with minor changes, in the final text.[20]

One of Hamilton's new arguments that Washington cut in the end was "Cultivate also industry and frugality. . . . Is there not room for regret that our propensity to expence exceeds the maturity of our Country for expence? Is there not more luxury among us, in various classes, than suits the actual period of our national progress?" Here Hamilton went too far in trying to cloak Washington in the mantle of Cincinnatus, whom Machiavelli had singled out for his "generosity of soul" and exemplary poverty. Washington wrote in the margin, "not sufficiently important," but no doubt realized that coming from him, the passage would lack credibility. His liking for a certain ostentation was no secret, and among the few accurate charges made by Republican abusers was that he had overdrawn his expense account.[21]

There was one notable instance where Hamilton eliminated a sentence from Washington's draft, which the president then restored. Perhaps this particular sentence seemed superfluous to Hamilton in the midst of so many similar lofty statements. Or perhaps however much he wished to elevate the tone of the message, it simply jarred with his deepest instincts about the nature of statecraft, and the lessons of personal experience. The sentence in question was: "I hold the maxim no less applicable to public than to private affairs that honesty is always the best policy." It became one of the most characteristic lines of the address.[22]

Who then, in the final analysis, *was* the author of the Farewell Address? It seems fair to say that it was Washington. Certainly that is what Hamilton would have wanted us to believe. He would have been the first to agree with his friends (as opposed to his family) that his role in ennobling Washington's name, while permanently attaching it to Federalist principles, should be concealed from public view. To give credit where credit is due, let us simply say that Hamilton's role in the project showed, beyond any doubt, that he could play a skillful card.[23]

15

Transition to the New Regime, 1796–1797

Introduction

Unfortunately, it could not be said, in Hamilton's view, that the government in Philadelphia was playing a particularly adept game in the fall of 1796. Toward the end of the year, the Federalist administration risked slipping off the moral high ground where he had tried to plant it with the Farewell Address. On October 27, 1796, the French minister Adet wrote Secretary of State Pickering to announce France's new policy toward neutral shipping, adopted in July. Adet correctly pointed out that earlier French protests about U.S. toleration of British impressment of American seamen had gone unanswered by the administration. If the United States had supinely failed to defend its neutrality against British violations, it could hardly complain if France treated it in the same way, taking enemy property found on American merchantmen. In an insulting flourish, Adet leaked his letter to the fanatically pro-French *Aurora*, which published it on October 31. Adet's maneuver, coordinated with Philadelphia Republican leaders, was patently designed to influence the popular election of presidential electors in Pennsylvania, scheduled for November 3.[1]

Hamilton immediately wrote Wolcott that Adet's communication demanded "a very *careful & well managed answer*." In reply to Washington's request for advice, Hamilton suggested that the president greet Adet next time he saw him "with a *dignified reserve*, holding an *exact medium* between an *offensive coldness* and *cordiality*. The *point* is a nice one to be hit," he added, but no one would "know better how to do it" than Washington. The official reply, "one of the most delicate papers that has proceeded from our government," must walk a similarly fine line and "save a great political interest which this step of the French Government opens up to us." If properly handled, in other words, Adet's communication presented a golden opportunity to embarrass the pro-French Republicans. Reply should be made not to Adet, but to the Directory through General Charles

Cotesworth Pinckney, the South Carolina Federalist whom Washington had recently sent to Paris to replace James Monroe. Immediate publication of a reply, moreover, would both be unnecessary and stoop to the level of the other side.[2]

Before Hamilton's advice arrived, however, Washington's cabinet approved immediate publication of Pickering's answer to Adet. Reflecting the character of its author, it was a sharp rebuke in the spirit of Adet's original provocation – exactly what Hamilton had wanted to avoid. He wrote Wolcott, "I regret extremely the publication ... otherwise than through the channel of Congress. The sooner the Executive gets out of the news Papers the better." He implored Washington, "the Card now to be played is perhaps the most delicate that has occurred in your administration. And nations like Individuals sometimes get into squabbles from the manner more than the matter of what passes between them. It is all important to us – first, if possible, to avoid rupture with France – secondly, if that cannot be, to evince to the People that there has been an unequivocal disposition to avoid it." For that reason, it was a mistake not to have paid more attention to France's earlier complaints.[3]

Adet upped the ante in a second letter to Pickering on November 15, 1796, a summary of which soon appeared in the *Aurora*. Declaring the Jay treaty the equivalent of an Anglo-American alliance, he announced that both the commercial relations enshrined in the Franco-American treaty and his own functions as minister were suspended until the American government returned to its true self and embraced its old policy of friendship. The message could be interpreted as a French ultimatum: either elect Jefferson, the Republican candidate for president, or face war with France. Hamilton wrote Washington: "The crisis is immensely important to the glory of the President & to the honor & interest of the Country." The reply "should be managed with the utmost possible prudence & skill – so that it may be a solid justification – an inoffensive remonstrance – the expression of a dignified seriousness reluctant to quarrel but resolved not to be humbled. The subject excites the greatest anxiety."[4]

This time the administration stayed out of the newspapers and avoided the charge that it was playing politics. A calm, reasoned, and meticulous answer to the French (to be delivered by Pinckney) was communicated to Congress on January 19, 1797, after the results of the election were known. In the meantime, however, Hamilton could not resist publishing his own detailed refutation of Adet's complaints in a New York paper. Though Adet's first message undoubtedly helped the Republicans in Pennsylvania, historians generally agree with Hamilton's assessment that blatant French interference in American politics served "in the main" to rally support for a Federalist administration. The French had overplayed their hand. The Federalist candidate for president, John Adams, defeated Jefferson (the latter became vice president under the prevailing electoral system) by a margin of seventy-one electoral votes to sixty-eight (the Federalist Thomas Pinckney received fifty-nine and the Republican Aaron Burr thirty votes).[5]

"An Extreme Anxiety"

During the first months of 1797, Hamilton, in his own words, was "overwhelmed in professional business" with "scarcely a moment for anything else." Yet things were not quite as he described. From his private letters and articles signed "Americus," emerge conflicting preoccupations and emotions. On one hand, he was progressively outraged by reports of French attacks on American shipping and Republican passivity in the face of behavior he considered more egregious than that of the British in 1793–1794. On the other hand, he saw the need to bend over backward to appear evenhanded in the domestic arena, even as the news from Europe fed his fear of war with France. Underlying all this was a nagging uncertainty: would he, under the new dispensation, continue to be part of the game?[6]

The final months of the Washington administration (Adams was inaugurated on March 4, 1797) coincided with the crumbling of the First Coalition against France. Bonaparte's stunning victories over the Austrians at Arcola, Rivoli, and Mantua raised the prospect that France's main continental opponent would be knocked out of the war. In October 1796, the British had proposed peace to France on the basis of the return of Belgium to Austria. Even before their Italian successes, the French had rejected British terms. To further complicate matters, France and Spain were now allies, and the Royal Navy faced the combined fleets of France, Spain, and The Netherlands. The death of Catherine the Great in November 1796 raised the prospect that Russia would also leave the war.

On February 14, 1797, a British squadron under Sir John Jervis and Horatio Nelson inflicted crippling losses on the Spanish navy off Cape St. Vincent, near Cadiz. But the end of February brought shocking news: the Bank of England had been forced to suspend gold payments on its obligations (King reported this to Hamilton on March 8). The long-predicted (and, by Jefferson and his friends, long-hoped-for) collapse of the British financial system appeared to be at hand. At the very least, it was hard to see how Britain, if the Austrians managed to fight on, could continue to subsidize them. In December, Hamilton had closed a letter to his friend, the new American minister in London: "We are labouring hard to establish in this country principles more and more *national* and free from all *foreign ingredients* – so that we be neither 'Greeks nor Trojans' but truly Americans." The message was to encourage the British not to take the United States for granted in its present troubles with France or make life difficult for those who might see a coincidence of interests with them. Two months later, there was a real possibility that Britain, the only real barrier to French aggression against the United States, might be brought to its knees.[7]

"I trust my Dear Sir," Hamilton wrote Pickering in February, "*effectual measures* are taking to bring us to some issue with France to ascertain whether her present plan is to be persisted in or abandoned." In effect, he had answered the question himself in "The Warning No. I" (January 27, 1797). That article demolished the argument that recent depredations were simply a reaction to the Jay treaty. French attacks on U.S. and other neutral ships carrying British property were part of a systematic policy to destroy British commerce, driven "by a spirit of universal domination." In the second of the series, he considered the implications. "The question now is whether she [France] shall be aggrandized by new acquisitions, and her enemies reduced by dismemberments, to a degree, which may render her the Mistress of Europe, and *consequently* in great measure of America." So much for the view that Europe and America were separate systems whose vicissitudes had no connection with one another. Hamilton later spelled out what he meant to McHenry:

If things shall so turn that Austria is driven to make peace & England left to contend alone – who can guarantee us that France may not *sport* in this country a *proseliting* [sic] army? Even to get rid of the troops, if it fails, may be no bad thing to the Government of that country. There is a *possible* course of things which may subject us even to an internal invasion by France. Our calculations to be solid should contemplate the possibility.

He was not arguing for American participation in the war and hoped "to defer a resort to arms 'til a last effort of negotiation shall have demonstrated that there is no alternative.... But if unhappily this period shall ever arrive, it will impose a sacred and indispensable duty to meet the contest with firmness, and relying on a just providence confidently to commit the issue to the God of battles." "The honor of a nation," declaimed "The Warning No. III," "is its life. Deliberately to abandon it is to commit an act of political suicide.... The Nation which can prefer disgrace to danger is prepared for a master and deserves one."[8]

While "Americus" gave vent to Hamilton's feelings of indignation and defiance, in private he took the tack he had suggested to Washington at the end of January: an extraordinary mission to France. "As an imitation of what was done in the case of Great Britain, it will argue to the people equal solicitude." There was, however, to be a crucial difference – the French mission would be a three-man affair. Pinckney, a middle-of-the-road figure already in France, should be joined by a prominent opposition leader, preferably Madison, accompanied, in turn, by a Federalist expert on maritime affairs. Hamilton thought Senator George Cabot of Massachusetts, who had amassed a fortune privateering during the Revolution, would fit the bill. The mission would try to settle matters with France, including redress for recent spoliations, but would do nothing inconsistent with the Jay treaty and would avoid extending political relations. In fact, as he explained to Theodore Sedgwick, Hamilton wished to "get rid of that [the French] Treaty by mutual *consent*" or, failing that, to replace the guarantee with a more limited commitment, and one nonoperable in the present war.⁹

A three-man commission, combined with defensive preparations, became Hamilton's fixation, an apparent means of fending off the charge that he was biased toward the British, as well as a test of his ability to have his way. Even the news that the French had kept Pinckney cooling his heels, and then ordered him out of the country (he left Paris for Amsterdam in February), did not dampen his ardor for the idea. If France refused to receive the commission, he wrote McHenry, still "the great advantage results of shewing in the most glaring light to our people her unreasonableness – of disarming a party of the plea that all has not been done which might be done – of refuting completely the charge that the *actual* administration desires War with France." If the Republicans favored the mission, "'Tis the strongest reason for adopting it. This will meet them on their own ground & shut their mouths." To Pickering, he wrote that he had "not only a strong wish but an *extreme anxiety*" that the measure be adopted.¹⁰

Part of Hamilton's anxiety had to do with his friends' reaction to his plan. He must have been taken aback to learn from Wolcott that on March 3, Adams had actually proposed to Jefferson that he go to France but that two days later Wolcott himself had pleaded with the president to abandon the idea. Wolcott cited French insolence to Pinckney, Madison's alleged hobnobbing with Adet, and the likelihood that the three commissioners would disagree among themselves. Hamilton reminded Wolcott not to let the strength of his feelings, "the companions of energy of character," stand in the way of the flexibility that circumstances demanded. Perhaps it occurred to him that Wolcott's uneasiness about being seen as one of Hamilton's men in the new administration may have influenced his reaction to Hamilton's proposal. It may also have occurred to him that his own strong feelings, as expressed through "Americus," seemed in tune with Wolcott's own.¹¹

If, as Hamilton wrote William Loughton Smith, his plan was "ever...to combine *energy* with *moderation*," perhaps it was time for more of the latter. For Smith, his closest friend in the House, he composed a sober overview of his plan. He began with what had always been a fundamental premise: "it is of the utmost consequence to us that our progress to that degree of maturity which puts humanly speaking our fortunes absolutely in our hands shall not be retarded by a premature war." Moreover, "the state of affairs externally and internally" suggested "the strongest imaginable auxiliary motives to avoid, if possible, at this time" a break with France. That power was triumphant on the continent while Britain and Austria might be on their last legs. Should France turn its attention to America, there could be no doubt that "she will be governed by a spirit of *domination* and *Revenge*."¹²

One by one, he took up his friends' objections to the three-man commission. Many felt that France had been so violent and insulting that the United

States would disgrace itself by making a further effort to negotiate. Hamilton observed, "It is often wise by some early *condescension* to avoid the danger of future *humiliation*." There were times – as he had consistently maintained – when appeasement was necessary. "Our Country is not a military one. Our people are divided.... But this is not all. The measure will tend to *unite* and *fortify*.... It may beget the noble resolution to die in the last ditch." As for Madison's alleged unreliability, Hamilton noted, "It goes further in ascribing *Turpitude* to the character in question than perhaps is warrantable." In any case, the Virginian would be chaperoned by the other commissioners. Hamilton stressed the need to alter the French treaty: "It is bad to be under obligations which it will be a violation of good faith not to perform" and which would "certainly compromit [sic] the peace of the Country to perform." He concluded the main part of his argument with an appeal to political self-interest: "The plan of the Government and of the Federal party has been to avoid becoming a party in the present War. If any measure it has taken is either the cause or pretext of a War with France, the end will be lost. The credit of preserving peace will not exist. The confidence in the Government will be shaken. The adverse party will acquire Reputation & influence of superior foresight.... Hence it is all important to avoid War if we can – if we cannot to strengthen as much as possible the Opinion that it proceeds from the *Unreasonableness* of France."

There followed specific recommendations: an increase in government revenue, including a loan of five million dollars, completion of three of the frigates (the *United States*, *Constitution*, and *Constellation*) authorized in 1794 and the purchase of smaller warships, a general embargo ("The President to grant licenses to sail, if the Vessels go themselves armed or with Convoys either of our own or of any foreign Nation"), fortification of the main ports, additional regular cavalry and artillery, and a provisional army of twenty thousand infantry as a precaution against a French invasion. If negotiations failed, the U.S. minister in London should attempt to buy or borrow two ships of the line and three frigates. Britain had more ships than it could man, whereas American seamen "employed in them will increase the force to be employed against the common enemy."

Hamilton ended with a reflection similar to the one he had placed near the end of the Farewell Address:

A philosopher may regard the present course of things in Europe as some great providential dispensation. A Christian can hardly view it in any other light. Both these descriptions of persons must approve a national appeal to Heaven for protection. The politician will consider this an important mean of influencing Opinion, and will think it a valuable resource in a contest with France to set the Religious Ideas of his Countrymen in active Competition with the Atheistical tenets of their enemies. This is an advantage which we shall be very unskilful, if we do not improve to the utmost.... I am persuaded a day of humiliation and prayer besides being very proper would be extremely useful.[13]

A Loss of Touch?

Hamilton could be forgiven for thinking his political brief was one of the most concise and persuasive of his career. But it did not have the hoped-for effect. Early in June, Smith introduced resolutions in the House incorporating most of Hamilton's military measures, but not the peace mission. Pickering wrote that, on that subject, "much difficulty occurs." Smith pointed out what had been an obvious, if not fatal, weakness all along: he doubted if either Jefferson or Madison "would go on this business, unless as Sole Envoy; certainly not, unless as Senior Commissr." In fact, Vice President Jefferson had made his intentions clear to Adams during their March 3 conversation: "without considering whether the Constitution will allow it or not, I am so sick of residing in Europe, that I believe I shall never go there again." Adams himself later wrote of his offer: "I would not do it again, because, upon more mature reflection, I am decidedly convinced of the impropriety of it .... The nation must hold itself very cheap, that can choose a man one day to hold its second office, and the next send him to Europe, to dance attendance at levees and drawing rooms, among the common major-generals, simple bishops, earls, and barons, but especially among the common trash of ambassadors, envoys, and ministers plenipotentiary."[14]

What Jefferson did not say to Adams was that he had no intention of walking into what must have looked like a trap. Negotiating on behalf of the administration would have meant endorsing the hated Jay treaty (in his view the main cause of the troubles with France), while a successful mission would enhance Federalist prestige. In fact, Jefferson's 1797 advice to the French through their consul general in Philadelphia was to temporize in dealing with Adams, who would not be around forever. Above all, he urged, France should get on with the conquest of Britain itself, one of the benefits of which would be the end of the Franco-American conflict on the high seas.

Hamilton probably surmised Jefferson's attitude and does not seem to have taken the idea of his going to France very seriously. But Madison was a different matter. A pair of historians exaggerate in saying that Hamilton at this point "had no doubt of Madison's patriotism or of his care for the national interest." But he does seem to have thought that his former collaborator, now retired from the House, was not a totally lost cause. He had hinted at this to Smith and wrote McHenry, "it is possible too much may be taken for granted with regard to Mr. Madison." In reality, however, Madison was no more eager than Jefferson to be put in a position where he would be confronting the French and taking Federalist chestnuts out of the fire. To have calculated otherwise was a symptom of wishful thinking and a certain loss of touch with events.[15]

Hamilton's digestion had been in poor shape in late 1796, and his friends had taken him on a rare, five-day grouse-shooting expedition to Long Island to restore him. Early in the new year, he was laid up with a bad leg after taking part in nocturnal patrols in Manhattan aimed at stopping a mysterious rash of fires. In February, he told King that he was "overwhelmed in professional business." In fact, he was immersed in one of his most demanding cases, *Louis Le Guen v Issac Gouverneur and Peter Kemble*. En route to Albany to argue it before the state supreme court, he wrote his wife that he had forgotten his brief in New York. "Request one of the Gentlemen to look for it and send it up to me .... Beg them not to fail."[16]

The one political bright spot, seemingly, was the president himself. On March 25, 1797, Adams issued a call for a special session of Congress to deal with the French crisis and would soon embrace the idea of a three-man commission including Pinckney. On April 8, Hamilton wrote King, "I believe there is no danger of want of firmness in the Executive. If he is not ill-advised he will not want prudence. I mean that I believe that he is himself disposed to a prudently firm course." It was reassuring to Hamilton that McHenry, who looked gratefully to him for guidance, was in a position to advise Adams. In April, Hamilton supplied McHenry with answers to questions that Adams had submitted to the secretary of war regarding negotiations and defensive measures.[17]

Hamilton's observation to King suggests that it is groundless to argue that since it seemed to Hamilton that his advice was "being followed implicitly" by Adams, he considered the president "a weakling who could be easily dominated through his Cabinet." But he did apparently fail to fathom the hostility that the president felt toward him personally. For this attitude, Hamilton himself bore a degree of responsibility. Arguably, his Machiavellianism had not served him well. Or perhaps this is a case where he had not been sufficiently Machiavellian. To determine which, we must retrace our steps to the presidential election of 1796.[18]

FIGURE 1. Alexander Hamilton statue
Located on the south side of the Treasury Department in Washington, D.C., the statue was erected by the Warren G. Harding administration in 1923. The 1920s were the last decade in which Hamilton was an important symbol for the Republican Party. *Source:* Courtesy of the Library of Congress.

FIGURE 2. Niccolò Machiavelli (1469–1527)
This is the best-known portrait of Machiavelli, even though it was painted by the
Tuscan artist Santi di Tito (1536–1603) long after its subject's death in 1527. It hangs
today in Florence's Palazzo Vecchio, where Machiavelli worked as an official of the
Florentine republic from 1498 until his abrupt dismissal in 1512.
Source: Alinari/Art Resource, NY.

FIGURE 3. Alexander Hamilton, October 1781
An unknown artist's rendering of Hamilton during the siege of Yorktown, Virginia, where he led a battalion of New York infantry in an attack on a British redoubt. Hamilton began the war in 1776 as the captain of a company of New York provincial artillery. From early 1777 to early 1781, he was an aide-de-camp to General George Washington and part of the commander-in-chief's military "family."
Source: Courtesy of the Library of Congress.

FIGURE 4. Elizabeth Schuyler Hamilton (1757–1854)
Engraving from the original painting by Ralph Earle. The second of four daughters of the Hudson Valley magnate General Philip Schuyler, "Eliza" Hamilton stood by her husband through thick and thin, bore him eight children, and outlived him by fifty years.
Source: Courtesy of the Library of Congress.

FIGURE 5. Alexander Hamilton, 1792

Oil on canvas, by John Trumbull. Hamilton was appointed secretary of the treasury by President Washington on September 11, 1789. He carried out his major projects, including the funding of the national debt and the creation of a national bank, while actively poaching in the realm of foreign affairs.

Source: Courtesy of the Library of Congress.

FIGURE 6. James Madison (1751–1836)
Engraving after the painting by Thomas Sully. As the leader of the Republican opposition in the House of Representatives, Hamilton's former collaborator waged a bitter battle against the Washington administration's fiscal and foreign policies. His fingers poised on a copy of the U.S. Constitution, he seems to be saying, "This is my handiwork."
Source: Courtesy of the Library of Congress.

FIGURE 7. "George Washington in Consultation with Thomas Jefferson and Alexander Hamilton"
Painting in the U.S. Capitol by Constantino Brumidi (1870–1873). In this Italian-born artist's rendering of the most famous cabinet triangle in U.S. history, Washington (seated at right) appears to be telling his recalcitrant ministers to put aside their personal and political rivalry for the good of the country.
Source: Courtesy of the Library of Congress.

FIGURE 8. George Washington, 1795
Engraving after the oil painting (the so-called Vaughn portrait) by Gilbert Stuart.
Washington began to sit for this portrait in Philadelphia in March 1795, shortly
after Hamilton's retirement as secretary of the treasury and with the political battle
over the Jay treaty about to begin. Finding himself without trusted collaborators in
his cabinet, Washington soon turned to his old aide for help.
Source: Courtesy of the Library of Congress.

FIGURE 9. Alexander Hamilton, 1796
Oil portrait by James Sharples. Said to be his family's favorite likeness of him, this picture portrays Hamilton around the time when he was assisting Washington in the preparation of the Farewell Address and on his way to becoming one of the most successful lawyers in New York.
Source: Courtesy of the Library of Congress.

FIGURE 10. John Adams, 1783
Oil painting by John Singleton Copley. As this portrait, executed in London at the
end of the War of Independence suggests, Adams liked to think of himself as a man
of the world. A seasoned diplomat, though without military experience, he would
come to view Hamilton and his ideas with suspicion and contempt.
Source: Courtesy of the Library of Congress.

FIGURE 11. Alexander Hamilton in his final years
Oil painting by Ezra Ames, *circa* 1810, based on his earlier painting from life of Hamilton, done in 1802. Ames's original portrait, painted not long after the death of Hamilton's eldest son, Philip, in a duel, captured the characteristic expression of his final years.
Source: Courtesy of the Schaffer Library, Union College, Schenectady, New York.

FIGURE 12. "Duel Between Burr and Hamilton"

Contemporary engraving. For Burr, the last straw in his troubled relationship with Hamilton was a derogatory statement the latter reportedly made when Burr was running for governor of New York in 1804. Their fatal meeting occurred in a small clearing just above the Hudson River, near Weehawken, New Jersey, on the morning of July 11, 1804.

Source: Courtesy of the Library of Congress.

FIGURE 13. Alexander Hamilton for the ages
Oil painting by John Trumbull, *circa* 1806. Discovering that there was a demand
for youthful pictures of Hamilton after his death, the Connecticut artist produced
several portraits based on one of his earlier portraits done from life.
Source: Courtesy of the Library of Congress.

PART V

A PRINCE IN HIS OWN RIGHT?

16

Hamilton and Adams: The Background

Introduction

John Adams, born on a modest farm in Braintree, Massachusetts, on October 19, 1735, was twenty years Hamilton's senior. It is difficult to dispute Adams's view of himself as a political-intellectual heavyweight and Washington's rightful heir. A graduate of Harvard College and a distinguished lawyer in colonial times, he had demonstrated his "almost rabid" independence by successfully defending British soldiers accused of murder following the 1770 "Boston Massacre." As a delegate to the Continental Congress, he had served on the drafting committee of the Declaration of Independence. With the exception of Jay, he had more diplomatic experience than any American alive in the late 1790s, having helped to negotiate the Franco-American treaties, the peace with Britain, and loans from the Dutch. He had resided in Europe (where Hamilton had never set foot) for many years, including his unsuccessful mission to Britain (1785 to 1788). During the free time his public life had afforded (in London it had afforded much), Adams produced such monuments to erudition as *Thoughts on Government*, *Defense of the Constitutions of Government of the United States of America*, and *Discourses on Davila*.[1]

There is little trace of animosity, for that matter, of any kind of relationship, between Adams and Hamilton before 1796. Adams was the prototype of American vice presidents, coveting the top position, but scrupulously loyal and prepared to suffer in silence as the president and cabinet more or less ignored his existence. He was also the first to deal with a common vice presidential dilemma, how to seem the dutiful and worthy successor of a revered chief while demonstrating a strong will of his own. Adams's characteristic solution would be to leave Washington's cabinet in place, but later to fire a pair of ministers in a kind of delayed volcanic eruption after more than three years on the job.

The absence of friction between Adams and Hamilton also stems from the fact that their outlooks were not dissimilar. Hamilton had no quarrel with Adams's view that "It is fashionable to charge wars upon kings, but I think '*le peuple souverain*' is as inflammable and as proud, and at the same time less systematic, uniform, and united, so that it is not easy for them to avoid wars." Both supported the Constitution of 1787. Both deplored the utopianism of the French intellectuals and the excesses of the Revolution. Both were appalled by the antics of the "Jacobin" faction in the United States, including its attempt to kill the Jay treaty. When the Republicans tried to force Hamilton from office for alleged corruption, Adams called him a "faithful servant" and supported him as an *ex-officio* trustee of the Treasury Sinking Fund.[2]

Hamilton was familiar with Adams's political arguments, and some of them struck a responsive chord. Adams believed that human beings were creatures of passion as well as reason and driven to seek distinction vis-à-vis their fellow men. All societies were naturally divided into aristocratic and democratic elements, each intent on domination. To avoid the tyranny of one or the other, the constitution maker must divide the power to legislate and create an autonomous executive holding the balance of power between the two. Even more than Washington, Adams believed that the president must be a powerful, nonpartisan figure above the fray.

Under the influence of Jean Louis de Lolme's *The Constitution of England*, which he read in the 1780s, Adams had come to admire the British constitution. It was "both for the adjustment of the balance and the prevention of its vibrations, the most stupendous fabric of human invention; and . . . the Americans ought to be applauded instead of censured, for imitating it as far as they [had] done." Adams was censured for his prediction-cum-preference that it might be desirable to adopt a hereditary rather than an elected executive and upper house:

Mankind have universally discovered that chance was preferable to corrupt choice, and have trusted Providence rather than themselves. First magistrates and senators had better be made hereditary at once, than that the people should be universally debauched and bribed, go to loggerheads, and fly to arms regularly every year. Thank Heaven! Americans understand calling conventions; and if the time should come, as it is very possible it may, when hereditary descent shall become a less evil than fraud and violence, such a convention may still prevent the first magistrate from becoming absolute as well as hereditary.[3]

Despite the affinities, however, Hamilton had reservations about Adam's character and views. During the war, Adams had favored short-term troop enlistments and annual rotation of the position of commander-in-chief. Hamilton later cited these "visionary notions" as proof that Adams "was far less able in the practice, than in the theory, of politics." He gave due credit to Adams for the peace negotiations, but Adams's European diary (sent by error to the Continental Congress) suggested that its author was a self-important windbag. According to the diary, the French foreign minister's wife had told Adams: *"vous êtes le Washington de negociation."* Adams commented that the French "have a very pretty knack of paying compliments." Hamilton's comment was that they also had "a very dexterous knack of disguising a sarcasm."[4] During the Nootka Sound crisis, Hamilton's closely reasoned opinion, should the British ask permission to cross U.S. territory, had been to grant it. But if after marching *without* permission the British encountered U.S. forces, the avoidance of humiliation required war. From a far more superficial analysis, Adams had concluded that the government should deny the British permission if they asked for it, but evaded the issue of what to do if they defied the United States. If the British moved without asking permission, Adams argued, the United States should not fight, but send a minister to "remonstrate," once again evading the question of what to do if the British defied the United States.[5]

As their famous 1791 conversation at Jefferson's house suggested, Adams admired an abstract version of the British system, Hamilton the real thing. "Purge that constitution of its corruption," Jefferson recorded Adams as saying, "and give to its popular branch equality of representation, and it would be the most perfect constitution ever devised." Purge it of its corruption (the king's use of patronage), Hamilton had replied, and it would not work. The two also parted company on fiscal and banking matters. Adams had supported funding and the assumption of state debts, but deplored a British-style financial system. He thought a national bank of deposit was constitutional and necessary but opposed paper money and profit-making operations by Hamilton's or any bank. He later wrote: "every bank of discount, every bank by which interest is to be paid or profit of any kind made by the deponent, is downright corruption. It is taxing the public for the benefit and profit of individuals." For Hamilton, these were the views of a financial crank.[6]

Contemporaries naturally asked whether Adams did not have more in common with the vice president, an old comrade though now his ostensible adversary, than with Hamilton, a mere acquaintance, though his supposed ally. Adams had become more conservative in the 1780s and distrusted Jefferson's deviousness. His grandson Charles Francis Adams's description of the so-called Sage of Monticello as "cautious, but not discreet, sagacious, though not always wise, impulsive, but not open" reflected Adams's own view.[7] Still, the two shared a basic preference, traceable to their rural roots and the views of the French Physiocrats, for an agriculture-based society. As young men, they had been steeped in the radical Whig critique of the British state and had favored early on a complete break with the crown. Adams took a certain pride in his English roots, but his attitude toward the British elites who had treated him with "supercilious neglect" was akin to Jefferson's – the opposite of forgive and forget. To his wife, Abigail, he spoke of British "insolence, which you and I have known and felt more than any other Americans." The British acted toward America not simply out of perceived interests, but of "jealousy, envy, hatred, and revenge, covered under pretended contempt." If he were not mistaken, he wrote in 1795, "it is to be the destiny of America one day to beat down his [John Bull's] pride."[8] His philosophy of foreign affairs, as he later described it, consisted of three points:

(1) That neutrality in the wars of Europe is our truest policy; and to preserve this alliances ought to be avoided as much and as long as possible. But, if we should be driven to the necessity of an alliance,
(2) Then France is our natural ally; and
(3) That Great Britain is the last power, to which we should, in any, [except] the last extremity, resort for any alliance, political or military.[9]

Adams would eventually brand Hamilton "the most restless, impatient, artful, indefatigable and unprincipled intriguer in the United States." Jefferson would not have disagreed. Hand in hand with a detestation of Hamilton's policies went a loathing of the flesh-and-blood individual. In Jefferson, Hamilton evoked Virginia snobbery, together with a self-defensive impulse to demean the kind of masculine *virtù* that Jefferson did not possess. In Adams, Hamilton evoked contempt arising from a fundamentally Puritanical view of humankind. The first of New England's advantages over the rest of America (and of the known world), Adams had once written, was that "The people are purer English blood; less mixed with Scotch, Irish, Dutch, French, Danish, Swedish, &c., than any other; and descended from Englishmen too, who left Europe in purer times than the present, and less tainted with corruption than those they left behind them." Not only was Hamilton the product of a sinful sexual relationship, as a Scotch-French West Indian, he was a lower breed of human being.[10]

A Not So Clever Hand

Hamilton could hardly be blamed for Adams's unendearing qualities: his vanity and irascibility, his nativism, his tendency to nurture rather than to act upon his myriad of resentments – what modern psychologists would call "passive-aggressive" behavior. Nor could Hamilton have been aware of the extent to which Adams disliked his program and him personally – Adams had kept it mostly to himself. But he could have imagined that Adams would bear a grudge against someone who had tried to thwart his ambition to attain the highest office. That is exactly what Adams came to think. On December 12, 1796, shortly after the presidential electors of the various states had cast their ballots, Adams wrote to his wife:

I am not enough of an Englishman, nor little enough of a Frenchman, for some people. These would be very willing that [Thomas] Pinckney should come in chief.... There have been manoeuvers [sic] and combinations in this election that would surprise you. . . . There is an active spirit in the Union who will fill it with his politics wherever he is. He must be attended to, and not suffered to do too much.

That Hamilton plotted to have Pinckney elected is what a majority of historians have taken for granted ever since.[11]

The plot thesis is connected to the nature of the electoral system. Before the twelfth amendment to the Constitution, each presidential elector cast a vote for a candidate for president and one for vice president, but without being able to designate which was which. The candidate with the highest number of votes became president; the one with the second highest became vice president. It was possible for the winner to be of one political coloration and the runner-up of a different one – as happened in 1796. It was also possible, through the scattering of ballots and/or voting for favorite sons, that the person intended by his supporters to be president might end up with fewer votes than the person intended to be vice president.

This is what Hamilton and others feared might happen when Washington ran unopposed for president, and Adams virtually unopposed for vice president, in 1789. Hamilton had written James Wilson, "Suppose personal caprice or hostility to the new system should occasion half a dozen votes only to be witheld from Washington – what may not happen?" He admitted that "to avoid disgust to a man who would be a formidable head to Antifederalists – it is much to be desired that Adams may have the plurality of suffrages for Vice President," but recommended that a handful of votes be diverted to other candidates for that office so that Adams did not outpoll Washington. In the event, the "plan" worked even better than Hamilton had imagined it would. South of New England, a number of vice presidential votes were scattered or given to John Hancock or John Jay. Washington ended up with sixty-nine votes, Adams a mere thirty-four. Disgust is exactly what Adams felt. He wrote his friend Dr. Benjamin Rush, "Is not my election to this office, in the scurvy manner in which it was done, a curse rather than a blessing? Is this Justice?" Nothing similar occurred in 1792, when Adams was challenged for the vice presidency by Hamilton's political enemy, Governor George Clinton. Hamilton wrote before the elections, "Mr. Adams whatever objections may be against some of his theoretic opinions is a firm honest independent politician." Adams had no reason to complain.[12]

The essence of the 1796 plot thesis is that Hamilton and his friends, although ostensibly supporting Adams for president and the South Carolinian Thomas Pinckney for vice president, tried to have Pinckney come in first. The alleged reason is that Adams was not a "politically correct" Federalist and too feisty to be controlled. The execution of the plot was simple. Hamilton would persuade New England electors to support Pinckney equally with their native son Adams while trying to make sure that Pinckney would outpoll Adams in the South, thus giving him more votes overall. But the case for the plot is hardly an open-and-shut one. Why would Hamilton choose Congressman Robert Goodloe Harper to do his "dirty work" in South Carolina, as Elkins and McKitrick allege, rather than his friend William Loughton Smith? Moreover, what "dirty work" could Hamilton do, or was it necessary for him to do, in the Palmetto state? With no involvement of Harper or Hamilton, their political opponent, the Low Country notable Edward Rutledge, successfully sponsored a slate of electors supporting Pinckney for president and Jefferson for vice president. Why, in New York, did all twelve electors vote loyally for Adams instead of throwing away a vote or two to be safe?[13]

Why, moreover, did the "plot" fare so poorly in New England? To outpoll Adams nationally, Pinckney needed to receive at least thirty-four of thirty-nine votes destined for him there (giving him a total of seventy-two to Adams's seventy-one). Instead he got only twenty-one of thirty-nine. Had he been the "zealot for the Pinckney scheme" one scholar claims he was, Hamilton's friend Wolcott, son of the Federalist governor of Connecticut, might have tried harder to prevent Federalist electors from throwing away votes for Pinckney. Although they were fearful of a Jefferson victory, there is little evidence that the Wolcotts' wanted Pinckney to finish first. In the event, Oliver Wolcott, Sr. supported the expedient of scattering five of Connecticut's nine votes intended for Pinckney in order to reduce the chances that the South Carolinian would be the winner.[14]

One of the few indications of Hamilton's intentions is a letter to New England friends, dated November 8, 1796. In it, he expressed his fear that New England Federalist electors might withhold votes from Pinckney out of concern that the South Carolinian would beat Adams – exactly what happened in Connecticut. This would be "a most unfortunate policy" because it "would be to take one only instead of two chances against Mr. Jefferson, and well weighted, there can be no doubt that the exclusion of Mr. Jefferson is far more important than any difference between Mr. Adams and Mr. Pinckney." According to Hamilton's (accurate) calculation, Jefferson was close to beating Adams, whereas "Pinckney has the chance of some votes southward and westward, which Adams has not." Several weeks later, he repeated, "My chief fear is that the attachment of our [north] eastern friends to Mr. Adams may prevent their voting for *Pinckney* likewise, & that some irregularity or accident may deprive us of *Adams* & let in Jefferson.... 'Tis therefore a plain policy to support Mr. Pinckney equally with Mr. Adams."[15] It is easy to assume that Hamilton's real aim was to help Pinckney at Adams's expense. But the context of the November 8 letter was Jefferson's unexpected win in Pennsylvania (giving him fourteen of the state's fifteen votes), and Wolcott's warning to Hamilton two days earlier: "There are still hopes that Mr. Adams will be elected, but nothing more. I hope Mr. *P* will be supported as the next best thing which can be done." It was Wolcott who urged Hamilton (not vice versa) to write "our Eastern friends" to that effect.[16]

It is possible, in other words, that after the Pennsylvania shock, and in light of Adams's unpopularity in the south, Hamilton simply thought Pinckney had a better chance to beat Jefferson and acted on that belief. There is no evidence that Hamilton urged New England electors to back Pinckney equally with Adams *before* the news from Pennsylvania. On December 16, he wrote Rufus King:

Our anxiety has been extreme on the subject of the Election for President. If we may trust our information . . . it is now decided that neither *Jefferson* nor *Burr* can be President. It must be either *Adams* or *Pinckney*, the *first most probably*. By the throwing away of votes in New England lest *Pinckney* should outrun *Adams*, it is not unlikely that Jefferson will be *Vice President*. The event will not a little mortify *Burr*.

If Hamilton had been hoping to elect Pinckney, one would expect such a letter to contain at least a trace of disappointment at the result.[17]

A pair of letters from Stephen Higginson, a prominent Boston merchant and trusted ally, raise additional questions about the "plot." Higginson reported to Hamilton on December 9 that a majority of Massachusetts electors had at first been inclined to throw away their votes for Pinckney, but most had been persuaded to do otherwise. Higginson thought Pinckney would win, but his reaction was not that of a happy coconspirator. "Should Pinckney be elected care must be taken early to guard him against Adet &c, who have strong hopes, I know, of attaching him to their Views & party." As Rutledge's support in South Carolina showed, Pinckney was no more a "politically correct" Federalist than Adams. Higginson was even more alarmed by another consequence of a Pinckney victory: "Mr Adams & many of his friends will be very clamorous. They will swear the union of Pinckney with him was a trick to prevent his election." Higginson saw that Pinckney's election would divide the Federalist party. It is hard to believe that Hamilton did not see this, too.[18]

Higginson also had bad news following Adams's narrow victory:

The blind and devoted partisans of Mr. Adams, instead of being satisfied with his being elected, seem to be alarmed at the danger he was in of failing; & they have the folly to say, that this danger was incurred wholly by the arrangement of pushing him & Pinckney together. They go further & say, that this arrangement was intended to bring in Pinckney & exclude him.

At the head of the alleged "Junto" determined to control Pinckney and exclude Adams were Hamilton and Jay. Higginson added, "These sentiments, however foolish & impudent," were entertained and communicated not only by Adams's friends but also, it was believed, by the new president himself. They might even lead him to attach himself to Jefferson rather than to the Federalists.[19]

Higginson's letter gives rise to yet another question about the alleged plot: was it a coincidence that those propagating the idea that Hamilton had tried to steal the election from Adams were the same as those promoting a Federalist split and an Adams–Jefferson rapprochement? These included contributors to Republican papers like the *Aurora* and the Boston *Chronicle* and some of Adams's friends referred to by Higginson, above all, the former Massachusetts Congressman Elbridge Gerry. Gerry wrote Abigail Adams on January 7 as follows:

I have been long acquainted with Mr. Jefferson & conceiving that he and Mr. Adams have had a mutual respect for each other: conceiving also that he is a gentleman of abilities, integrity, altho not entirely free from a disposition to intrigue, yet in general a person of candor & moderation, I think it is a fortunate circumstance that he is Vice President & that great good is to be expected from the joint election.

Gerry continued,

The insidious plan to bring a third person into the presidential chair arose from a corrupt design of influencing his administration, as is generally conceived. Whether his want of experience will justify the expectation, I will not pretend to say, but sure it was from good information that the supporters of Mr. Jefferson give Mr. Adams a decided preference as well for his abilities as his independent spirit.[20]

Not surprisingly, the purveyors of the plot included Jefferson himself. On December 28 he penned an ingratiating letter to Adams, averring his wish that the vice president be elected to the top position. Yet it was "possible that you may be cheated of your succession by a trick worthy of the subtlety of your arch-friend of New York." Jefferson sent the letter first to Madison, asking him to decide whether delivering it would be politic under the circumstances. In the event, Madison decided that it would not be. One reason, he explained to Jefferson, was that Adams presumably knew of "the trick aimed at by his pseudo-friends of N.Y." and might suspect Jefferson of wanting to use him (Adams) to avenge himself against Hamilton. Moreover, Madison presciently pointed out, the Republicans might have to oppose Adams's policies, in which case it would be embarrassing if the president had written evidence of Jefferson's initial friendliness and confidence. An Adams–Jefferson entente was not in the cards.[21]

It may have been the obvious utility of the plot rumors to the Republicans that raised Adams's own doubts. On February 13, 1797, he tried to reassure Gerry:

I believe they honestly meant to bring in me; but they were frightened into a belief that I should fail, and they, in their agony, thought it better to bring in Pinckney than Jefferson, and some, I believe, preferred to bring in Pinckney president rather than Jefferson should be Vice-President. I believe there were no very dishonest intrigues in this business.

This was exactly what Hamilton and his friends were saying. It must have been clear to Adams, moreover, that the humiliating closeness of his victory over Jefferson (seventy-one to sixty-eight) was the result of the outcomes in Pennsylvania and the South rather than anything Hamilton could have engineered. But prone as he might have been to rationalize things, Adams's suspicions of Hamilton continued to eat at his mind while the rumors did not fade away. As Stephen Kurtz aptly reminds us, the Republicans "would not let Adams forget."[22]

And indeed, there *are* several pieces of evidence that cast doubt on Hamilton's defense. The first is a November 15, 1796, letter from Robert Troup to Rufus King: "I am inclined to think ... that Mr. Adams will not succeed; but we have Mr. Pinckney completely in our power if our [north] eastern friends do not refuse him some of their votes under an idea that if they vote for him unanimously, they may injure Mr. Adams."[23] Troup's letter was written in light of the Pennsylvania result, but an earlier missive from Hamilton to King (May 4, 1796) does suggest that Hamilton had been scheming against Adams for many months. During the House debate over the Jay treaty, Hamilton (with King's apparent knowledge) had asked the Richmond-based Federalist lawyer John Marshall to sound out Patrick Henry on the idea of running alongside Adams in 1796. The idea was to use Henry, enormously popular in the South, to undercut Jefferson. Henry had told Marshall, who in turn wrote King, that he was not interested. King then suggested a new idea: why not capitalize on the popularity of Pinckney, who had recently negotiated the treaty with Spain opening the Mississippi? Hamilton answered on May 4, "I am intirely of opinion that P.H. declining Mr. P___ ought to be our man. It is even an idea of which I am fond in various lights. Indeed on latter reflection, I rather wish to be rid of P.H., that we may be at full liberty to take up Pinckney."[24] The question is "take up Pinckney" to do what? The answer may have been to elect him vice president. Or perhaps they simply wanted a candidate who would be able to beat Jefferson if Adams, as turned out to be the case, was weaker than expected in the North.

Another, seemingly unequivocal, piece of evidence is a letter from Troup to King dated November 16, 1798. Relations between Adams and Hamilton had by then soured, and Troup gave one of the reasons:

During the last election for President, Hamilton publickly [sic] gave out his wishes that Pinckney should be elected President. These wishes were communicated both privately and publickly [sic] to the President, and have occasioned, I suspect, more than a coolness on the part of the President. I blamed Hamilton at the time for making the declarations he did, and I foresaw that evil would arise from them.[25]

Yet even this letter raises as many questions as it answers. Why had Troup changed his story after telling King immediately after the elections that the Federalists had simply been taking a "double chance" in supporting Adams and Pinckney equally? (Forrest McDonald argues that Troup's "memory was faulty" when he wrote King in 1798.) Why would a New York political insider like King have been left in the dark after proposing Pinckney in the first place? King, who sailed for England with his wife and four sons on June 20, 1796, was perfectly placed to brief Pinckney on the "plot," if there was one. There is no evidence that he did so when he saw Pinckney in London in August. In November, King wrote John Quincy Adams, "I feel little doubt that the choice of a successor [to Washington] will fall where it is eminently merited, where you & I must wish it."[26]

Finally, there is Hamilton's *own* account, written in mid-1800. He spoke of a "plan" generally agreed on by Federalists to support Adams and Pinckney equally in 1796, with the overriding aim of excluding Jefferson. But he admitted, "It is true that a faithful execution of this plan would have given Mr. PINCKNEY a somewhat better chance than Mr. ADAMS; nor shall it be concealed that an issue favorable to the former would not have been disagreeable to me; as indeed I declared at the time, in the circles of my confidential friends." (He mentioned Troup – confirming the soundness of the latter's memory – and his brother-in-law, New York Lieutenant Governor Stephen Van Rensselaer.) Hamilton's position was "that if chance should decide in favor of Mr. PINCKNEY, it would not be a misfortune; since he, to every essential qualification for the office, added a temper far more discreet and conciliatory than that of Mr. ADAMS." Hamilton added that his preference for Pinckney "had resulted from the disgusting egotism, the distempered jealousy, and the ungovernable indiscretion of Mr. ADAMS's temper, joined to some doubts of the correctness of his maxims of Administration."[27]

Here, it would seem, is the proverbial "smoking gun." Or is it? It is difficult to believe that Hamilton's hostility toward Adams was actually as intense in 1796 as he said it was in this 1800 statement. Indeed, one of the reasons for that claim was presumably to neutralize the charge that his hostility toward Adams had arisen from sour grapes over the president's handling of the French crisis and other events during 1798–99. Needless to say, expressing a personal preference to a handful of friends does not constitute much of a plot. There is no extant evidence that he actively campaigned for Pinckney before Jefferson's victory in Pennsylvania. Hamilton's assumption that Pinckney had a better chance of beating Jefferson than Adams did was an eminently reasonable one. Indeed, it was only thanks to a completely unexpected vote from Virginia, and one from North Carolina, that Adams was able to eke out his win.

* * *

Four centuries before Murphy's law, Machiavelli had taught that when it comes to political conspiracies, if something can go wrong, the chances are that it will. All plots, he pointed out in a famous chapter of the *Discourses*, consist of three distinct phases: preparation, execution, and aftermath.

History showed that "it is almost impossible to get through all of them successfully." In general, the more people involved and the more time between conception and execution, the more likely it was that the plot would be foiled. Even successful plotters exposed themselves to attempted revenge by the family and friends of the victim.[28] At the end of the day, two things can be said with certainty about Hamilton's role in the 1796 elections. The first is that if he *was* trying to make Pinckney president, he was flagrantly ignoring Machiavelli's teachings on the subject. There was too much time involved, and far too many necessary principals, including thirty-nine presidential electors spread across New England. If there was a plot, it was based on faulty calculations, half-heartedly carried out, and it ended in utter failure. Had it "succeeded," it would have hastened a showdown between Hamilton and his opponents and raised doubts among his friends.

If, as seems more likely, Hamilton preferred Pinckney without working for him very assiduously and was mainly concerned with stopping Jefferson, he managed to create a different impression. What was worse, Hamilton compounded that perhaps unavoidable mistake by failing to make an effort to cultivate Adams after the election (as Higginson, for one, suggested he should to do). To King in mid-February, Hamilton wrote of the president's "real good sense and integrity." The final puzzling question is why he did not reach out to Adams to prevent the poisoning of their relationship. The reasons may include the pressures of business and his belief in Adams's reasonableness. Or he may have thought that, because they seemed to see eye to eye on foreign policy, the election would soon be forgotten. But he should have taken human nature (not to mention his own advice about coddling or destroying opponents) into account and made a more overt gesture of alliance. Instead, distractedly and overconfidently, he took the middle path. It was not a clever hand.[29]

The Reynolds' Redux

As if Hamilton did not have enough on his mind in mid-1797, including his demanding law practice and the developing French crisis, Elizabeth Hamilton was in the advanced stages of pregnancy. (William Stephen Hamilton would be born on August 4.) Then, out of the blue, he was thrown into a state of agitation by the revival of a serious threat to his reputation. In June and July, the Republican gutter journalist James Thomas Callender published a set of pamphlets, appearing in book form as *The History of the United States for 1796*. Callender, a Scot who had fled Britain to avoid arrest for sedition, revived the accusations of peculation against Hamilton made in late 1792 by James Reynolds and his partner, Jacob Clingman.[30] He published supposedly incriminating letters that Reynolds had given Frederick Muhlenberg, Abraham Venable, and James Monroe, who had been investigating

Hamilton at the time. According to Callender, recent attacks on Monroe for his conduct in France were ungrateful, because the Virginian had shown the "greatest lenity" to Hamilton in the past.

Hamilton was beside himself. The Republican politicians had privately told him in 1792 that they were fully satisfied with his explanation that the correspondence concerned payment of blackmail to the husband of his lover, Maria Reynolds, and that the matter would not be pursued. Naturally, Hamilton wondered how the likes of Callender had obtained the suppressed correspondence. The culprit, in all likelihood, was Callender's crony John Beckley, the Virginia-born former clerk of the House of Representatives and an architect of Jefferson's recent Pennsylvania victory. In 1792, Beckley's own clerk had made a copy of the correspondence before Monroe deposited the originals with "a respectable character in Virginia," in all probability Jefferson. Beckley, an inveterate gossip-monger and schemer in a supposedly nonpartisan position, had been removed as clerk through Federalist efforts after the elections and was taking his revenge. Hamilton's suspicions, however, fell upon Monroe.[31]

He had no sooner written Muhlenberg, Venable, and Monroe (July 5, 1797), asking them to make a declaration equivalent to the one made to him in December, 1792, than he was stunned by the publication of another pamphlet. It included a December 16, 1792, memo in which the same trio averred that they had merely left Hamilton "under an impression" that their suspicions of him had been removed. The second pamphlet also included a note by Monroe recording a January 2, 1793, conversation with Clingman in which the latter, backed by the testimony of Maria Reynolds (by then Clingman's lover) called Hamilton's version of events a "fabrication." Both Venable and Muhlenberg replied to Hamilton's request for a denial, but he heard nothing from Monroe.[32]

Hamilton arranged to confront the future president, who happened to be in New York, on the morning of July 11, 1797. Both came with friends, respectively, Hamilton's brother-in-law John Church, and David Gelston, a local merchant and politician. During an hour-long meeting, Monroe denied having had anything to do with the leak to Callender, but Hamilton found his version of the story "totally false." If so, Monroe replied, Hamilton was a "scoundrel." According to prevailing notions of honor, those were fighting words. The two rose to their feet and indicated a readiness to settle the issue on the spot. After their friends had intervened, Hamilton agreed to Monroe's and Gelston's suggestion that Monroe consult Venable and Muhlenberg in Philadelphia, to be followed by a joint reply.[33]

Muhlenberg and Monroe (Venable had left town) duly wrote Hamilton affirming that they had indeed believed the version of events he had given them on December 15, 1792, but this did not end the affair. Hamilton also wanted Monroe to deny that, in recording his January 1793 conversation with Clingman, he had meant to give credence to Clingman's charges. Monroe's refusal either to confirm or deny this triggered an increasingly acrimonious exchange of letters. When Monroe wrote that he remained agnostic on the issue of guilt or innocence, pending Hamilton's "defense," Hamilton threatened that a publication he was about to make of "the whole affair" would expose Monroe's "malignant and dishonorable" motives. Hamilton's friend, Major William Jackson, who delivered this message to Monroe in Philadelphia, reported that Monroe was ready to say with Muhlenberg and Venable that they had not given credence to Clingman. Jackson urged Hamilton to suspend his publication.[34] In reality, however, Monroe refused to pretend that Clingman's words had made "no impression" on him. For Hamilton it was totally "inadmissable" that *his* word could be called into question by that of a petty criminal like Clingman. Although claiming that he had no wish to do Hamilton a "personal injury," Monroe refused to budge and was prepared to meet a direct challenge if that was what Hamilton had in mind.[35]

As former officers, bound by a code of honor, neither man was prepared to shrink from a challenge. But other considerations impelled both to try to avoid a duel. It must have occurred to Hamilton that killing or wounding Monroe would not really serve to prove the all-important point regarding his veracity. A publication of "the whole affair," though extremely painful, might accomplish before the court of public opinion what a resort to pistols would leave in doubt. For his part, Monroe was hard at work on a defense of his conduct in Paris, hence the ensuing minuet in which each man expressed his readiness to fight while declining to take the initiative. Through Jackson, Hamilton queried Monroe if his latest note was meant as a challenge, while Monroe engaged his friend Aaron Burr to ascertain from Hamilton if he (Monroe) was being called out.

As was often the case, the seconds played a crucial role. Jackson assured Hamilton that, having been called "malignant and dishonorable," Monroe was the injured party and that it was up to *him* to challenge. Burr, asked by Monroe to help avoid or postpone a showdown, advised his future adversary, Hamilton, on the wording of a letter to Monroe in which he (Hamilton) acknowledged Monroe's disavowal of an intention to challenge. Burr recommended to Monroe that he and Muhlenberg issue a certificate reiterating their belief in Hamilton's version of the facts, though Monroe declined to follow this advice. Months later, after completing his pamphlet, and lest the impression persist that he had been afraid to fight, Monroe considered reviving the controversy, but his friends advised him to do otherwise. Thus the dispute had no clear resolution – it was allowed to fade away.[36]

In the meantime, Hamilton published an exhaustive reply to Callender's pamphlets. He dismissed the charges of corruption as implausible and ridiculous while confessing his "amorous connection" with Maria. He attached an encyclopedic appendix, including his recent exchanges with Monroe.[37] He may have been hoping that his threat to publish that correspondence, which cast the Virginian in an unflattering light, would extract a disavowal from Monroe. As that was not the case, he saw no choice but to proceed. In any case, his readiness to expose his marital infidelity to remove all doubts about his professional conduct was testimony both to his obsession with his reputation and his eagerness to strike back. Few of Hamilton's friends saw the publication as either wise or necessary. After all, his intellectually honest opponents (Muhlenburg and Burr, for example) had not believed the charges in the first place, while the rest would continue to believe them in the face of clear evidence to the contrary. Elizabeth Hamilton seems to have been deeply shocked, though determined to cope, in her typically Spartan way. In what appears to be the only reference to the affair in his correspondence with her he wrote, "I rely on your promise to compose your dear heart; and to be as happy as you can be."[38]

Hamilton's enemies reveled in what the Germans call *Schadenfreude*: they rejoiced to see him drag himself through the mud. (One of them, at least, would have his comeuppance. The same Callender whom he had abetted as a tool against Hamilton, and whom he would commission to write a vicious attack on Adams before the 1800 elections, later published a story about Jefferson's sexual relationship with his slave girl, Sally Hemmings. For once, as it transpired two centuries later, Callender had gotten his story right.) Hamilton's list of confirmed enemies did not, at this point, include the president, but it is hard to imagine that Adams did not receive the revelation with disgust. Everyone had known that Hamilton was the natural offspring of a philandering peddler. For Adams, someone who made up his mind with his viscera, the Reynolds affair was but more proof of his bad blood.

17

Hamilton's "Grand Plan"

Introduction

Though he probably entertained doubts about Adams's choice of Elbridge Gerry, a former antifederalist, as one of the three envoys, Hamilton could only applaud the president's decision in the spring of 1797 to seek satisfaction for French seizures of U.S. ships and to make a final effort to settle Franco-American differences. Gerry, together with the astute, stalwart John Marshall and the dull, dignified Charles Cotesworth Pinckney, formed the three-man commission Hamilton had favored all along. The mission, he knew, was a diplomatic long shot. The French decree of March 2, 1797, had authorized a kind of licensed piracy. All British goods found on U.S. ships were subject to confiscation; U.S. citizens found serving on British ships would be treated as pirates, even if they had been impressed into service; U.S. ships lacking a French-model crew and passenger list, or *role d'équipage*, would be legitimate prizes. The destination of the U.S. commissioners (they arrived in Paris in early October 1797) has been described as a "catacomb of traffickers, warlords, and bravoes." Prominent among the traffickers was the mission's presumed negotiating partner, Talleyrand, who had returned from four years of exile in England and America in 1796. Upon becoming foreign minister in July of 1797, through the influence of a former lover, he laid out his program: "I have to make an immense fortune out of it, a really immense fortune." When it came to such serious matters, Talleyrand was a man of his word.[1]

After the *coup de force* of 18 Fructidor (September 4, 1797), the French Directory and its henchmen were little more than a glorified gang engaged in the plunder of a growing list of conquests and client states. With the backing of General Pierre Augereau, sent by Napoleon from Italy, the hard core of the Directory (Paul Barras, Jean-François Reubell, and Louis Marie de Larevellière-Lépeaux) had ousted their moderate colleagues (Lazare Carnot and François Barthélemy) and arrested scores of members of the Council of the Five Hundred (the lower chamber under the Constitution of 1795) said to favor restoration of the Bourbons, peace, or both. Napoleon, whose Italian campaign was itself "a *razzia* or looting raid on an epic scale," was about to wring terms from France's main continental enemy, Austria. The Treaty of Campo Formio, signed October 17, 1797, established France's eastern frontier on the Rhine (Austria was to cede Belgium) while erasing the Most Serene Republic of Venice from the map. Not for the first or the last time in its history, Britain stood alone.[2]

Rumors that the U.S. commissioners had not been properly treated in Paris reached Philadelphia in January 1798, prompting Adams to write his cabinet. In the case of the mission's failure, what should the commissioners do? Should there be an immediate declaration of war, or perhaps an embargo? But "above all what will policy dictate to be said to England?" Although he was ostensibly consulting his ministers, Adams's view was obvious:

Will it not be imprudent in us to connect ourselves with Britain in any manner, that may impede us in embracing the first favourable moment of opportunity to make a separate peace? What aids or benefits can we expect from England, by any stipulations with her, which her interest will not impel her to extend to us without any? On the brink of the dangerous precipice on which she stands will not shaking hands with her, necessitate us, to fall with her, if she falls? On the other hand, what aid could we stipulate to afford her, which our own interest would not oblige us to give without any other obligation?[3]

Adam's position, in effect, prefigured that of those many Americans between 1939 and 1941 who held that by actively trying to help Britain, the United States would only be injuring itself and who implicitly rejected the argument that Britain's defeat by Germany would fatally compromise the security of the Western Hemisphere.

Courtesy of McHenry, Adams's letter was soon in the hands of Hamilton. His reply (which according to a regular procedure became McHenry's answer to Adams) marks the beginning of his involvement in the crisis of 1798–99. Rather than formal hostilities in case of the mission's failure, he favored "a truly vigorous defensive plan, with the countenance of a readiness still to negotiate." The public was strongly averse to war, from which, moreover, there was nothing desirable (trade or territory) to be gained. Building on his May 1797 memo to William Loughton Smith, he called for the arming of merchant vessels, the acquisition ("in case of open rupture") of ten ships of the line, possibly from Britain, the suspension of the French treaties, the raising of a "substantial regular Force of 20,000" and an "auxiliary *provisional* army" of thirty thousand men. "In addition to these measures Let the President recommend a day to be observed as a day of fasting and humiliation & prayer. On religious ground this is very proper – On political, it is very expedient." As he put it to Theodore Sedgwick, "We must oppose to religious fanaticism religious zeal."[4]

On the key question, Hamilton is worth quoting at length:

As to England it is believed to be best in any event to avoid *alliance*. Mutual interest will command as much from her as Treaty. If she can maintain her own ground she will not see us fall a prey – if she cannot, Treaty will be a feeble bond. Should we make a Treaty with her and observe it we take all the chances of her fall. Should France endeavour to detach us from a Treaty if made, by offering advantageous terms of Peace it would be a difficult & dangerous Task to our Government to resist the popular cry for acceptance of her terms. Twill be best not to be entangled.

So far the reasoning was similar to Adams's. This was probably not a co-incidence. To influence the president, Hamilton had to adapt himself, to a point, to the latter's views. But he added the following:

Nothing therefore seems proper to be done than through Mr. King to communicate the measures in Train – to sound as to cooperation in case of open Rupture, the furnishing us with naval force – pointing the cooperation to the Floridas Louisiana & South American possessions of Spain [France's ally], if rupture as is probable shall extend to her. To prevail on Britain to lodge in her Minister here ample authority for all these purposes; but all this without engagement or commitment in the first instance. All on this side of the Mississippi must be *ours* including both Floridas.[5]

His basic approach was thus in place before the arrival on March 4, 1798, of the American commissioners' first dispatches. In a decree announced January 11, 1798, the Directory had further tightened the screws on American trade with Britain and its possessions. Secretary of State Pickering related more sensational news on March 25: a trio of Talleyrand's agents, identified by Marshall as messieurs "X," "Y," and "Z," had communicated the preconditions for a negotiation: the disavowal of the president's speech of May 16, 1797, censuring French conduct; U.S. government liability for all of France's unpaid bills to American suppliers, as well as for possible indemnities for French attacks on American shipping; an immediate loan in the form of the purchase of worthless Batavian (Dutch) Republic paper to the tune of thirty-two million florins (twelve million eight hundred thousand dollars); and last but not least, a payment of fifty thousand pounds sterling for the "private use" of Talleyrand and the Directory. As one of the agents put it, "*Il faut de l'argent – il faut beaucoup d'argent.*" And let Venice's fate be a lesson. On April 3, an outraged Adams laid Marshall's dispatches before the House of Representatives, at its request. Abigail Adams commented that the news, flashing throughout the country, "has been like an electrical shock."[6]

Hamilton's January 1798 memo contained the kernel of what Adams's grandson, anticipating many modern accounts, called his "grand plan" to place himself at the head of a conquering army. Though not advocated at the outset, an alliance with Britain was "distinctly contemplated" as a consequence of the execution of the scheme. The Hamiltonian Federalists, moreover, wanted war for two additional reasons: "1. The preponderance which an appeal to the patriotic feeling of the people was giving to the party. 2. The great military organization which it was throwing into their hands. With the aid of these forces, they trusted to procure modifications in the laws, and even in the constitution itself" such as would allow them to exclude the opposition from power on a permanent basis. Fortunately, President Adams's instincts told him that the methods needed to place Hamilton at the head of the army were of the kind intended to give him, "and in certain contingencies, perhaps, to the country itself, A MASTER." Hamilton's penchant for intrigue and worship of "the false idol of honor" could be traced, in the final analysis, "to a deficiency in early moral foundations." The 1798–99 episode, in effect, was the climax of a morality tale which had begun with his illicit issue from the womb of Rachel Faucett years before.[7]

Naturally, Hamilton's partisans have told a different tale. According to one, intrigue was no part of Hamilton's character. For another, Hamilton was not pursuing juvenile dreams of glory at age forty-one but rather following the dictates of duty. During the anti-French hysteria provoked by the "XYZ" revelations, he was an isolated voice of moderation. His goal was "to keep the country independent of Europe at a time when isolation from Europe was impossible." Another argues that Hamilton was assuredly not a militarist, even if, under the circumstances, "he was doomed to be misconstrued as one." Rather, he was "an American Churchill warning of a gathering storm about to vent its fury on the Western Hemisphere," and exemplifying the virtues of prudence and responsibility.[8]

Where does the truth lie? What *was* Hamilton thinking? For the moment, let us concern ourselves with what was on his mind during the first half of 1798.

Geopolitics or Glory?

A convincing case can be made that geopolitical anxiety trumped dreams of personal triumph. The fear was that the fall of Britain – for Hamilton and other Federalists its fleet was now America's de facto first line of defense – would allow a French invasion of the United States: "Great Britain once silenced, there would be no insuperable obstacle to the transportation [of French armies]." It was not a new scenario, but after Campo Formio, one which seemed even more plausible than before. Hamilton wrote in the margin of his January memo, "I think the overthrow of England & the Invasion of this Country very possible so possible that any other calculation for our Government will be a bad one." Bonaparte was in fact looking for a new outlet for his energies. Even before the XYZ affair, it was clear that the Directory looked on the United States as a potential satellite and milk cow to be controlled through the local pro-French party, if possible, but punished for its impudence if need be.[9]

To compound the security threat, Spanish control over New Orleans and Louisiana appeared to be collapsing. Pickering reported that Madrid was no longer in a position to resist French pressure to retrocede Louisiana and was about to evacuate its small garrisons on the Mississippi. (In reply, Hamilton said he would accept a preemptive Spanish cession, even if temporary, to the United States). Still more harrowing, Hamilton argued, was the possibility that with the acquisition of Louisiana, "the foundation will be laid for stripping her [Spain] of South America and her mines; and perhaps for dismembering the United States." Recent French designs along those lines were common knowledge. The War of the Spanish Succession at the beginning of the century had been fought to avoid the union of French and Spanish power. The previous April, none other than John Quincy Adams, U.S. minister at The Hague, had written his father that France was planning to invade the United States and carve out a client state in the South and West. By early 1798, the fear of a French invasion, combined with the outbreak of slave revolts like the one that had devastated St. Domingue, was rife in the southern states.[10]

The case can also be made that Hamilton was not eager to be entangled with the British and had his eye squarely on safeguarding American independence. In answering a letter from Lafayette, he wrote on April 28, "I shall only assure you that a disposition to form an intimate connection with Great Britain, which is charged upon us forms no part of the real Cause [of a probable break with France], though it has served the purpose of a party to impose the belief of it on France. I give you this assurance on the faith of our former friendship." On June 8, he wrote Pickering, "I take the liberty to express to you my opinion that it is of the true policy as well as of the dignity of our Government to act with spirit and energy as well toward G Britain as France.... It will evince that we are neither *Greeks* nor *Trojans*." He suggested to Pickering that a U.S. frigate be sent to Charleston to control the British frigate H.M.S. *Thetis*, said to be attacking American commerce in the area.[11]

But in Hamilton's annoyance with the British, and protestations of impartiality, it is also possible to see a frustrated desire for closer Anglo-American cooperation. It is well to recall that he had never been touchier, or more on the defensive, concerning his reputation. As Troup wrote King in June 1798, "For this twelvemonth past this poor man – Hamilton I mean – has been most violently and infamously abused by the democratical party." In October 1797, he had appealed to the British government, through the British minister in Philadelphia, Robert Liston, to avoid asking the U.S. administration to do anything "which might add strength to that imputation of partiality to Great Britain which has of late been cast upon them by the Democratic [i.e., Republican] Party." In an essay which remained unpublished, he lashed out: "There is a set of men whose mouths are always full of the phrases *British faction, British agents, British Influence* .... The truth is, that there is in this Country a decided *French Faction* but no other foreign faction." Hamilton was sick to death of the charge.[12]

He was also mortified that the British, in classic fashion, seemed to be undermining the possibility of collaboration and hurting the position of their supporters. With their order-in-council of January 25, 1798 (revoking that of January 8, 1794), albeit a reaction to the recent French order, they seemed to be giving free rein again to unscrupulous and predatory commanders like Captain Cochrane of *Thetis*. "How unfortunate," Hamilton wrote King, that just as indignation was growing against France, news of the British orders should arrive. "Why are weapons to be furnished to our Jacobins?" "I scarcely think it possible," he told Pickering, "that the British Administration can have given the orders" that reports attributed to them.[13] All this does not mean that Hamilton was simply lying to Lafayette and in fact working toward an alliance. Common sense dictated that there was no point in a formal connection if Britain were on the verge of collapse. If Britain held its own, domestic politics and the president's inclinations rendered an alliance problematical and made talk of one embarrassing to the Federalists. Some of Hamilton's most pointed remarks were directed at Pickering, the most incautiously pro-British member of the cabinet. Prone to zealotry himself, Hamilton was wary of it in Pickering and sought to stay his hand.

But it is evident that Hamilton *was* working toward closer cooperation with Britain. He had advised Adams (through McHenry) to have King take the initiative in pursuing possible joint action against the Spanish empire. On March 27, he wrote Pickering, "I am against going immediately into alliance with Great Britain." This did not rule one out at a later date. Hamilton viewed the unfolding situation through the lens of his longer term thinking and aspirations. Since the days of his clandestine talks with Beckwith (well before the Jacobins and the Directory), he had favored disentanglement from France and deeper economic interdependence with Britain – a de facto reversal of alliances. Advising Washington in 1790, he had contemplated joint U.S.–British action. If Madrid continued to bar the Mississippi, he argued, war was to be preferred to a detachment of the western settlements. "In an event of this sort we should naturally seek aid from Great Britain. This would probably involve France on the opposite side, and effect a revolution in the state of our foreign affairs." In 1792, he had proposed an Anglo-American alliance to open the river and end Spanish support for the Indians.[14]

Later in the decade, Hamilton had had occasional talks with the Venezuelan soldier and conspirator Francisco Miranda, encouraging him to believe that the United States might act with Britain to liberate South America. In early 1798, Miranda was in contact with both Hamilton and the British along those very lines. Hamilton was aware, finally, that Britain had been instrumental in maintaining the European equilibrium on which U.S. independence ultimately depended. As he wrote in April 1798:

History proves, that Great Britain has repeatedly upheld the balance of power there [in Europe], in opposition to the grasping ambition of France. She has no doubt occasionally employed the presence of danger as the instrument of her own ambition; but it is not the less true, that she has been more than once essential and an effectual shield against real danger.

It is hard to imagine that it did not occur to him that in cooperating with Britain, the United States would be helping it to play this historic role. His approach prefigured the view of those twentieth-century Americans who, although recognizing the domestic political obstacles and strategic risks involved in helping Britain, saw U.S. security as tied to Britain's fate.[15]

What kind of personal role did Hamilton envision? Was he a reluctant warrior? A grasping glory seeker? Or perhaps some combination of the two? Not surprisingly, the evidence is not clear-cut. In mid-April, Governor John Jay appointed him to the seat of a retiring U.S. senator. In declining, Hamilton wrote, "This situation you are too well acquainted with to render it necessary for me to enter into explanation. There may arrive a crisis when I may conceive myself bound once more to sacrifice the interest of my family to public call. But I must defer the change as long as possible." Around the same time, in the first of a provocative and emotional newspaper series, "The Stand No. I," he *ruled out* accommodation with Paris: "the inexorable arrogance and rapacity of the oppressors of unhappy France bar all the avenues to reconciliation as well as to redress, accumulating upon us injury and insult till there is no choice left between resistance and infamy." Among America's many assets were "experienced officers ready to form an army under the command of the same illustrious chief who before led them to victory and glory, and who, if the occasion should require it, could not hesitate again to obey the summons of his country."[16] As usual, he was presuming to speak for Washington. On May 19, he approached the former president directly. If it came to a rupture with France (a "great probability"), "the public voice will again call you to command the armies of your Country." Washington, himself, was more optimistic ("I cannot make up my mind, *yet*, for the expectation of *open War*; or, in other words, for a formidable Invasion, by France") and not keen to be cast as Cincinnatus. Among other things he wanted to know beforehand was "who would be my coadjutors, and whether you would be disposed to take an active part, if Arms are to be resorted to."[17]

Hamilton's answer on June 2 echoed his letter to Jay. He was relieved to hear that Washington had not ruled out active service. As to his own plans: "I have no scruple about opening myself to you on this point. If I am invited *to a station in which the service I may render may be proportioned to the sacrifice I am to make* – I shall be willing to go into the army." In fact, he had in mind a specific station: "If you command, the place in which I should hope to be most useful is that of Inspector General [in charge of recruitment, doctrine, and organization] with a command in the line." He took it for granted that "the services of all the former officers worth having may be commanded & that your choice would regulate the Executive."[18]

The writer of this letter sounds less like a person ready to exchange his law briefs for the baton of the conquering hero than one weighing conflicting considerations and wanting to play a careful hand. In his early forties, Hamilton still possessed tremendous drive but was prone to physical ailments. He wrote King, "my professional avocations occupy me to the extent of the exertions my health permits." For the first time in his life, he was making a considerable amount of money, and able to banish the thought that, like his father, he might not be able to take care of his dependents. He had grown closer to his family following the Reynolds revelations, but the evidence suggests that Elizabeth was still suffering from the blow. He wrote her on June 3, 1798: "I have been extremely uneasy, My beloved Eliza, at the state of health and state of mind in which you left me [to go to Albany]." A few days later, he wrote, "In proportion as I discover the worthlessness of other pursuits, the value of my Eliza and of domestic happiness rises in my estimation."[19]

But the author of these words was still ambitious, unsatisfied with a life of "avocations," and recoiling from the prospect of a placid middle age. Between the two letters to his wife, he dashed off a list of recommendations to Wolcott, including the immediate raising of noncommissioned officers for an army of fifty thousand and "half a million of secret service money" (for purposes he did enumerate – perhaps the subversion of Spanish territory). He knew that the opportunity, if that is what it was, to undertake a crowning enterprise, possibly to achieve the kind of battlefield renown that had eluded him in the previous war, and to silence his enemies and belittlers, would not come again. Although it is obviously far-fetched to see him as a would-be Caesar, Cromwell, or Napoleon seeking sole power for himself, it is inconceivable that Hamilton did not compare himself to his fellow former artillery officer and look on his exploits with envy and admiration. In April, he called Napoleon "that unequalled conquerer, from whom it is painful to detract; in whom one would wish to find virtues worthy of his shining talents." It would have been equally out of character if Hamilton did not imagine that on a wave of military success, he might even be propelled to the country's highest office, out of the shadow of Washington, a kind of prince in his own right.[20]

18

Hamilton and His Army, Part One, 1797–1798

Introduction

Machiavelli's supreme example of severe and stirring leadership was Titus Manlius. In 340 B.C., Titus and his fellow consul commanded the Roman army in what Machiavelli called the most important battle in the city's early history. Facing a Latin force of identical size, training, and determination, whose victory would have meant Rome's enslavement, Titus instilled a decisive extra degree of resolve and discipline in his troops by having his own son decapitated for disobeying his orders. (The son had engaged in unauthorized single combat.) Titus's harsh standards served to restore old *virtù* and breathe new life into original principles – for Machiavelli a prerequisite of republican vitality and longevity. Though revered for his character, Titus was not a popular general and therefore not in a position to use the army for private purposes. His extraordinary reputation rested, finally, on the fact that he had continually renewed it through decisive action at different stages in his life.[1]

From the Romans, Machiavelli acquired a preference for brief, intense wars that would help to pay for themselves through the spoils they provided. He believed that it was better to invade than to be invaded: "he who assaults comes with greater spirit than he who waits; moreover, he takes away many advantages from the enemy." And it was better to obtain territory by force than by money: "things acquired with gold, one doesn't know how to defend with iron." A military leader, moreover, with a hastily improvised force "who sees that for lack of funds or friends the army cannot be held together for long, is mad not to try his luck before it falls apart: waiting he will surely lose, trying he could win." As Machiavelli memorably put it:

it is better to be impetuous than respecting, because fortune is a woman, and to hold her down, it is necessary to beat and jolt her. She more often lets herself be won over by those who do this than those who proceed coldly; and as a woman, she is always a friend of the young, because they are less respectful, more ferocious, and command her with greater audacity.

Ultimately, this preference for the impetuous approach to war and statecraft can be traced to his view of human nature and of the consequent state system. The republic's well-being and security required expansion: states will either molest or be molested, and in the latter case they will develop the desire and necessity to molest. To think otherwise, or to put one's faith in friends, fortune, or providence, was to lose one's independence – and to deserve to lose it.[2]

As a Florentine official, Machiavelli found himself in the middle of a "military revolution," the traumatic turn that began when Charles VIII overran the peninsula in 1494. Geoffrey Parker observes,

the military revolution of early modern Europe possessed a number of separate facets. First, the improvements in artillery in the fifteenth century, both qualitative and quantitative, eventually transformed fortress design. Second, the increasing reliance on firepower in battle...led not only to the eclipse of cavalry by infantry in most armies, but to new tactical arrangements that maximized the opportunities of giving fire. Moreover these new ways in warfare were accompanied by a dramatic increase in army size.

Machiavelli witnessed the beginnings of all of these changes. What impressed him most was the growing obsolescence of the temporizing maneuvers and skirmishes of Italian Renaissance warfare and of armies based on heavy cavalry. The fearsome Swiss (in the French and Papal service) and Spanish formations who fought in Italy showed that "the nerve of armies, without doubt, is the infantry." And "the end of making war is to combat each enemy in the field and to be able to win the day," in other words, a commander must seek the decisive encounter.[3] Machiavelli favored a citizen militia on the Roman republican model, but the target of his polemic was less military professionalism, than reliance on mercenaries who might prove dangerous to their employers and ineffectual in the face of modern armies. His writings are full of contempt for the princelings and ruling oligarchies who had allowed old virtue to decay by abolishing the citizen militias of medieval times and risked losing their independence for fear of arming their own people.

Machiavelli was a practitioner before he was a theorist. He took a leading role in recreating a Florentine militia, a permanent fighting force conscripted from countryside districts under Florence's dominion, eventually numbering some twenty thousand men. In December 1506, Machiavelli was made secretary, or executive officer, of a newly created magistracy, "the Nine officers of the Florentine ordinance and militia." The militiamen were drilled in the Swiss manner, wore a white cap and doublet, a pair of half-white and half-red trousers, and an iron breastplate, and were primarily armed with the pike. They played an indispensable part in the latter stages of the campaign against Pisa. The rebellious city's surrender to Florence in June 1509, after fifteen years of war, was a triumph for Machiavelli and his ideas.[4]

And yet his project was dogged by basic contradictions. Not only was it seen as risky to draft men from restive cities under Florentine rule like Arezzo or Pistoia (hence conscription began in more reliable, rural areas like the Mugello and the Casentino), there was deep suspicion of his definite (though understated) aim of eventually rearming the citizens of Florence itself, lest such a force become the tool of oppression. According to Federico Chabod, such was the distrust of standing military forces on the part of the old patrician opposition to Soderini and Machiavelli, that if the latter had proposed rearming the Florentines, "they would have been accused of wanting to reestablish the dictatorship." Modern scholars stress that Machiavelli was an inspiration to seventeenth- and eighteenth-century Anglo-American opponents of standing armies. They fail to realize that in his own day Machiavelli, in effect, was on the opposite side of the debate.[5]

Aside from the problem of the fear of tyranny, was it really possible to make god-fearing Roman warriors of sixteenth-century Tuscans? Or did such a project grow out of a kind of noble naiveté? On the other hand, what was to prevent the virtuous and therefore successful state from sooner or later becoming the victim of its own expansion through the corrosive effects of wealth on society, financial and strategic overextension, or the emergence of a Sulla or a Julius Caesar? Among the other reasons for the end of the Roman republic, according to Machiavelli, was that increasingly distant wars necessitated placing armies under the command of the same consuls for periods longer than had once been considered prudent. Under those circumstances, soldiers tended to become the partisans of their generals rather than of the state. Machiavelli had no formula for the perpetual life of the republic except the contradictory notion of a frequent return to first principles – meaning the cultivation of *virtù* and thus exposure again to the pitfalls of success.[6]

* * *

Washington's final annual address to Congress, drafted by Hamilton, called for the creation of a military academy, invoking "that evident maxim of policy which requires every nation to be prepared for war while cultivating peace and warns it against suffering the military spirit & knowledge wholly to decay." In none of Hamilton's major memos did he neglect to point out the usefulness of religion in inspiring patriotism and discipline. He had nothing but contempt for those who undermined preparedness or seemed ready to sacrifice the country's independence in the name of an ideological obsession with standing armies. Military forces, like munitions factories, must be in existence in advance of emergencies. To behave otherwise was tempting fate.[7]

When making his public call to arms in 1798 ("The Stand" series), the pseudonym Hamilton adopted was none other than Titus Manlius. (One wonders where he learned Titus's story; Plutarch, his usual source, does not tell it.) During the war against Britain, Hamilton had expressed frustration with a Fabian strategy: "I hold it an established maxim, that there is three to one in favour of the party attacking." His preference for an impetuous, preemptive approach in case of war with France and Spain, aiming to take control of New Orleans and the Floridas, was clear from the beginning of the crisis.[8]

The military revolution of Hamilton's own day, though arguably a continuation of the transformation which had begun around 1500, was the one carried forward by revolutionary France, and later analyzed by Carl von Clausewitz, with its divisional organization (a division combining infantry, cavalry, and artillery under a single commander), huge increases in manpower, and unprecedented concentrations of force. With Napoleon, the doctrine of the decisive battle once again replaced the more civilized, temporizing warfare of the preceding era, and fixed fortifications proved of little use. Infantry was once more the "queen of battle," as it had been in Machiavelli's and in Roman times. In the summer of 1798, Hamilton contemplated an American army of unprecedented size and composed a detailed "Plan for a Legion" (each legion containing infantry, dragoons, and artillery, with "two legions to constitute a "grand Division").[9]

And yet Hamilton's project was beset by contradictions not dissimilar to those that had bedeviled Machiavelli's. Standing forces, and the debt and taxes required to pay for them, released familiar demons in the minds of much of the political establishment. Fear of tyranny, and thus internal opposition to a professional army (especially one intended for offensive purposes), would be intense. Moreover, if it had been difficult during the war for independence to inspire Americans (as Hamilton had then put it) with "the natural enthusiasm of republicans," it would be a daunting task to fill the army's ranks in a time of relative prosperity and domestic tranquility. Military success, finally, would bring with it the risks of overextension and of an overweening central government. Hamilton may have been confident that, over the long run, the American republic would be able to avoid this last pitfall. But meanwhile, the others lay in his path.[10]

Seizing the Helm Again

By early summer 1798, the outpouring of patriotic and anti-French feeling released by the XYZ revelations showed few signs of slackening. John Adams found himself riding the crest of the wave. He spent hours each day writing replies to hundreds of patriotic petitions and memorials delivered by the postman. The notion of president as arbitrator, above the political fray, had proved more theoretical than practical. Adams, "for a brief dizzying period became widely popular for the first and only time in his life."[11]

By July, a Federalist campaign in Congress had borne important fruit. Some of the legislation Adams actively supported, some of it he did not.

All of it he signed into law. In the first category, were provisions for new warships and harbor fortifications, the creation of a Navy Department (Benjamin Stoddert, an energetic Maryland merchant, became secretary), formal abrogation of the French treaties, an embargo on trade with France, and the authorization for U.S. warships to attack French ships cruising against American commerce, creating a state of "quasi-war" between the two countries. In the second category were a set of measures destined to undermine national unity, aid the Republicans, and mar Adams's historical reputation, despite his later wish to disavow them. The Naturalization Act of June 16, 1798, raised the residency requirement for naturalization from five to fourteen years. The Alien Act of June 25, 1798, allowed the president summarily to expel foreigners deemed "dangerous to the peace and safety of the United States." Among its main targets were the pro-French Irish refugees – the "Wild Irish" – whom it was feared might flood American shores (and fill Republican ranks) after their uprising against Britain in 1798. The Sedition Act of July 14, 1798, made it a crime to speak or print "any false, scandalous, and malicious writing or writings against the Government of the United States . . . with intent to defame . . . or to bring them . . . into contempt or disrepute." The least that can be said is that Adams's own feverish rhetoric helped to pave the way for the passage of these laws. Ten people were eventually convicted under the sedition law, including James Thomas Callender. Adams signed three warrants for deportation under the Alien Act, though the individuals in question departed on their own.[12]

Also in the second category of measures were laws expanding the military establishment. On May 28, 1798, after a long and heated debate, a bill became law creating a "provisional army" of ten thousand men, though only to be called into service in the event of a declaration of war, French invasion, or imminent danger thereof, "before the next session of Congress." (The bill's Federalist sponsors had wanted at least twenty thousand men; Hamilton, thirty thousand.) The same law authorized the president to appoint a commander-in-chief with the rank of lieutenant-general. On July 2, Adams nominated Washington, and the Senate unanimously approved this the next day. On July 16, a bill became law augmenting the existing regular army of four infantry regiments by an additional twelve and adding six troops of light dragoons. (The twelve regiments became known as the "new army.") It provided for two major-generals and an inspector general with the rank of major-general. Because Washington was sure to devolve much responsibility upon his subordinates, the ranking of the three major-generals became an important question.

Hamilton looked on with a mixture of expectation and trepidation. There was now too much at stake for the country and for himself to permit mismanagement, but that is what he feared. He was not enthusiastic about the wave of repressive measures, warning Wolcott that a bill sponsored by an extremist Federalist, Senator James Lloyd of Maryland, to redefine treason might provoke civil war. And it was at this point that Hamilton began to

develop his serious doubts about Adams's temperament and political strategy. The president's popularity seemed to have gone to his head. Adams's
reply to one of the patriotic addresses struck Hamilton as inflammatory.
"This will do harm to the Government, to the cause & to himself. Some hint
must be given for we must make no mistakes."[13]

For Hamilton, characteristically, the only way to avoid disaster was to
seize the helm. In early July, he went to Philadelphia. Learning there of
Washington's nomination, he urged him on July 8 to accept and to involve
himself directly in "the arrangement of the army." Adams had "no *relative*
ideas & his prepossessions on military subjects" were "of the wrong sort."
This was a thinly veiled way of saying that not only was Adams not a strong
supporter of the army, but (as Pickering had already written Washington on
July 6) he did not want Hamilton to be second-in-command.[14] This letter,
and subsequent maneuvering, are classic examples of how Hamilton tried to
steer Washington, as well as additional nails (after the 1796 election) in the
coffin of relations between Hamilton and the president. But it must also be
said that, once the decision to raise the "new army" had been made, logic
dictated giving effective command to the best available candidate. This logic
Adams did his best to resist.

After nominating Washington, Adams sent McHenry to Mount Vernon
on July 11 to talk to the former president. On July 17, McHenry arrived
back in Philadelphia with Washington's choices for major-general, listed in
the following order (the same list was contained in a personal letter from
Washington to Hamilton, dated July 14): Hamilton (also to be inspector
general), Charles Cotesworth Pinckney (now on his way home from France),
and Henry Knox (former head of artillery and secretary of war). The problem
was that at the end of the war in 1783, General Knox had ranked first,
General Pinckney second, and Colonel Hamilton a distant third. On July 18,
Adams submitted the list to the Senate in the order in which Washington had
composed it and the Senate approved it the next day. He then left Philadelphia
for an extended stay at his home in Quincy without signing the commissions.
He would later claim that he had acted in hopes that the vexing question of
rank might be settled among the principals "by agreement or acquiescence,"
but also in the belief that previous service should be decisive. In August,
when Knox, who hailed, like Adams, from the Bay state, reacted angrily to
the prospect of being ranked third, Adams supported him and insisted that
the order must be Knox, Pinckney, and Hamilton. Adams warned McHenry,
"You may depend on it, the five New England States will not patiently submit
to the humiliation that has been meditated for them."[15]

Hamilton, interestingly, had anticipated the Knox problem and (as he
told Pickering) was prepared to serve under him if necessary. Knox was an
old friend, and would presumably defer to him, as he had as a member
of the cabinet. Washington had raised another problem in his recent letter
containing the list of major-generals. If, he wrote, the French "should be

so mad as to invade this Country," they would do so south of Maryland in order to be closest to their American supporters and their strategic objectives of Louisiana and the Floridas. In that case, Washington wondered whether the South Carolinian Pinckney, whose "services and influence" in the South would be important, would be willing to "serve under one whom he will consider a Junr. Officer." Washington concluded, "my wish to put you first, and my fear of losing him, is not a little embarrassing. But why? for after all it rests with the President to use his pleasure."[16]

This was not simply a minor hitch. If Pinckney ranked above him, he and not Hamilton might lead the army in the field against the French and Spanish. Hamilton told Pickering that he would not accept the "principle that every officer of higher rank in the late army who may be appointed is to be above me." Writing Washington, he found it hard to conceal his frustration and did his best to promote his own qualifications, including the support of leading Federalists. Biting his tongue, he crossed out the sentence: "General [Nathanael] Greene once told me that Pinckney was more of a *martinette* than an efficient officer." If necessary, Hamilton "stood ready to submit our relative pretentions to an impartial decision and to wave the preference," though he did not say by whom. He added that in Philadelphia he had witnessed the spectacle of their friend McHenry foundering under his responsibilities. He had tried to make himself useful, but "the idea has been thus far very partially embraced" and he was returning to New York. Before departing, Hamilton asked McHenry that he be called into immediate service as inspector general in charge of recruiting, tactics, and discipline. To Washington, he was tempted, but decided not to confess his problem with Adams. He crossed out the passage, "In my situation I could not if so disposed make any communication to him. The idea that I favoured the choice rather of [Thomas] Pinckney than of himself in the late Election has hitherto been an obstacle to free communication."[17]

The ranking of the generals now escalated into a monumental clash of egos. McHenry enlisted Hamilton to draft letters to Knox, but Adams refused to send them. On August 29, the president wrote McHenry that his decision to place Knox first and Hamilton third was final. "There has been too much intrigue in this business both with Washington & me. If I shall ultimately be the dupe of it, I am much mistaken in myself." McHenry protested his innocence and offered to resign. He also sent Adams's letter to Hamilton, asking him to acquiesce.[18]

Acquiescing was the last thing Hamilton had in mind. In response to an August letter from Washington, he had said that he would cheerfully accept whatever his old chief decided, but it did not "seem necessary to precipitate any thing," pending Pinckney's return. Around the same time, though probably confident of Washington's preferences, he engaged Pickering to tell Washington that New England preferred Hamilton to Henry Knox. When he received McHenry's letter asking him to capitulate, he reflected for twenty-four hours and then answered on September 8: "My mind is unalterably made up. I shall certainly not hold the commission on the plan proposed [by Adams]." At this point McHenry and Pickering decided to call on the heavy artillery: Treasury Secretary Wolcott, a New Englander who retained credibility with Adams, and Washington himself.[19]

It may be, as some claim, that it was Wolcott's long and cogent brief that caused Adams to see the handwriting on the wall. Wolcott reminded Adams that, because he had requested Washington's opinion and then submitted his list to the Senate, both Washington and the public expected Hamilton to be second-in-command. Regulations to which Knox had appealed were "wholly inapplicable to the present state of things." And if the issue boiled down to having the services of either Knox or Hamilton, given Washington's preference, was there really any choice? Flexner, whose account does not mention Wolcott's letter, shows that around the same time he received it, Adams learned from McHenry that Washington would probably resign if he did not have his way. It is clear, in any event (from an unsent reply to Wolcott, dated September 24), that Adams had surrendered before hearing directly from Washington. He decided to sign and date the three commissions on the same day and let Washington and the three major-generals "come to some amicable settlement." (On September 30, Adams signed the commissions and sent them to the secretary of war.)[20]

Washington's own letter to Adams, which arrived in Quincy on October 8, merely rubbed salt in the wound. Washington wrote that although he had made his choices clear, Adams had "been pleased to order the last to be first and the first to be last." Why, he wondered, had Adams not changed the order *before* submitting the list to the Senate? This was a good question. Adams's handling of the matter had been maladroit, to say the least. He would have been better off challenging Washington's preferences from the start. Of Hamilton, Washington's letter observed: "That he is ambitious I shall readily grant, but it is of that laudable kind which prompts a man to excel in whatever he takes in hand. He is enterprising, quick in his perceptions, and his judgment is intuitively great; qualities essential to a military character and therefore I repeat that his loss will be irreparable." The reluctant Cincinnatus did not say that his own services were contingent on having Hamilton as his number two. He knew that Adams already knew this to be the case.[21]

The "Grand Plan" in the Balance

Hamilton had won the first battle over the army, but the cost of his victory was by no means entirely clear. Though Adams had rejected McHenry's request to call him and Knox into immediate service (and he had told McHenry that he must remain in New York for the time being), Hamilton began to take an active interest in the new army in July and August. He sent McHenry thick sheaves of names of candidates for appointments with comments on their qualifications and political reliability. He found time to place Philip Church (son of Angelica and John Church) as a captain in the infantry and his Scottish cousin, Robert Hamilton, as a lieutenant in the navy. In Church's case, he wrote Adams to ask it as a "personal favour." Perhaps he was trying to break the ice with the president, still did not fathom the nature of Adams's feelings toward him, or both. Adams's prompt, affirmative answer contained no trace of hostility, only the writer's "great esteem."[22]

Hamilton also surveyed the broader picture. In Rufus King, he had a strong supporter of a bold, offensive strategy. The U.S. minister sent periodic reports to Pickering concerning a possible British attack on the Spanish colonies. At the end of February, King had reported that Pitt's cabinet had settled on a policy regarding South America:

If Spain is able to prevent the overthrow of her present Government and to escape being brought under the entire controul [sic] of France, England . . . will at present engage in no scheme to deprive Spain of her possessions in Sth. America. But if, as appears probable, the [French] army destined against Portugal, and which will march thro' Spain, or any other means which shall be employed by France, shall overthrow the Spanish Government, and thereby place the resources of Spain and her Colonies at the disposal of France, England will immediately commence the execution of a Plan long since digested and prepared for the compleat independence of S. America.

If Britain engaged in the plan, its minister at Philadelphia would "propose to the U.S. to co-operate in its execution." The president "may therefore expect the overture of England, and will, I am persuaded, act upon it, under the influence of that wise and comprehensive Policy, which, looking forward to the destinies of the New World, shall in the beginning by great and generous Deeds lay deep and firm the foundations of lasting accord between its rising Empires."[23]

In June, Grenville informed Robert Liston that, because Franco-American tensions "must ultimately lead to a state of general and open War," London would agree to "naval cooperation" with the United States on the basis of reciprocity (British ships and officers to be provided in return for American seamen). The British government would cordially consider other proposals for joint action and "much wished" King to be fully instructed in that regard. In response to Liston's report that U.S. ministers were considering the conquest of Florida and Louisiana, Grenville observed that this would "certainly be Matter of Satisfaction to this Government, and in that State of Affairs it is also easy to see the Advantage which America would derive from seeing Santo Domingo in the Hands of His Majesty rather than of any other European Power."[24]

As these dispatches suggest, the fate of Hamilton's "grand plan" was now in the hands of two protagonists. The first was the French regime, including Napoleon. Unless France tried to take control of Spain and South America, the British overture King spoke of would probably not be forthcoming. And it was largely up to Paris to decide whether a state of war between France and the United States would materialize as well. On May 19, 1798, a large fleet carrying Napoleon and thirty-five thousand troops slipped out of Toulon bound for an unknown destination. Following orders from Philadelphia, Marshall and Pinckney had demanded their passports in April, but Adams's friend Gerry had inexplicably stayed behind in Paris. Pickering had written to summon him home on June 25.

Throughout the summer, King kept Hamilton posted on the French expedition. On July 2, he wrote, "We are still at a loss where Buena parte [sic] is bound.... My opinion has been that Ireland was his object. At present it seems to be the general Opinion that he never intended to leave the Mediterranean." Admiral Nelson and a force of ships-of-the line were in hot pursuit. Several days later, King reported that Malta had surrendered to Napoleon without firing a shot. "We are left to conjecture what are his ulterior Plans." On July 14, he wrote that "the fate of Europe is as uncertain and difficult as at any period of the war." Two months later, he wrote Pickering that "strange as it will appear we are still ignorant of the ultimate destination and views of Buonaparte." King stressed the necessity of a "bold and active" approach, a clear reference to South America. On July 31, perhaps beginning to despair of a British démarche, he wrote, "we have a Right, and it is our Duty to deliberate, and to act not as secondaries, but as Principals."[25]

On August 22, Hamilton replied to several of King's letters and to one from Francisco Miranda urging U.S. cooperation. His intentions could not have been more explicit. Hamilton wrote King: "With regard to the enterprise in question I wish it much to be undertaken but I should be glad that the principal agency was in the UStates–they to furnish the whole land force necessary. The command in that case would very naturally fall upon me." He wrote Miranda that it was now too late in the year, "the Winter however may mature the project." "The plan in my opinion ought to be, a fleet of Great Britain, an army of the ustates." The United States, he wrote, was raising a force of about twelve thousand men. "I am appointed second in command." On an earlier letter from Miranda (dated February 7, 1798), Hamilton had noted, "I shall not answer because I consider him as an intriguing adventurer." Perhaps he chose to answer this time (though he told King to decide, depending on circumstances, whether to deliver it) because he was confident that he, and not the Venezuelan, would be in command.[26]

On the future of the Spanish colonies, Hamilton wrote King, "The independency of the separated territory under a *moderate* government, with the joint guarantee of the cooperating powers, stipulating equal privileges in commerce would be the sum of the results to be accomplished." Charles Francis Adams commented on these words, "An [Anglo-American] alliance was assumed to be inevitable in the South American project." In fact, Hamilton was not contemplating a formal alliance (something both unnecessary and out of the question politically). But his scheme does resemble the kind of joint Anglo-American tutelage over the former Spanish empire proposed a quarter of a century later by British Foreign Secretary George Canning and rejected by Secretary of State John Quincy Adams (son of John and father of Charles Francis) and President James Monroe.[27]

The second protagonist on whom Hamilton's plan depended, naturally, was the president. Adams had been no enthusiast of the new army, and Washington's return, even before the command controversy, had done nothing to endear him to the idea. There is no evidence for saying that Adams appointed Washington in July 1798 in order to preempt Hamilton, but there is truth in Flexner's observation that Adams was "in all probability the man who had for the longest time been most deeply jealous" of the first president. Washington had completely overshadowed him for eight years and then stolen the show (in Adams's view) at his own inauguration. Now, at the height of his popularity, Adams would be forced to share the stage with "the father of his country" once again.[28] As for the West Indian emigrant, Adams's feelings on the verge of his capitulation on the command issue emerge from his unsent letter to Wolcott:

If I should consent to the appointment of Hamilton as second in rank, I should consider it as the most responsible action of my whole life, and the most difficult to justify. Hamilton is not a native of the United States, but a foreigner, and, I believe, has not resided longer, at least not much longer, in North America than Albert Gallatin. His rank in the late army was comparatively very low. His merits with a party are the merits of John Calvin,–

'Some think on Calvin heaven's own spirit fell,
While others deem him instrument of hell.'[29]

In rapid succession, Adams had swallowed the new army, Washington's return, and Hamilton as second-in-command. To add insult to injury, the Senate had rejected the nomination of his son-in-law, Colonel William S. Smith, to be adjutant general. Pickering had lobbied senators against Smith, citing chicanery connected to his upstate New York land dealings. Pickering's real motive may have been that Smith "would have been an Adams spy in an otherwise purely Hamiltonian force."[30] Ensconced in Quincy (where Abigail lay bedridden with a mysterious illness), Adams would have plenty of time to nurse his wounds and reflect on his mistakes. The least that could be expected was that he would do everything in his power to prevent Hamilton from having his splendid little war. Commenting on the repressive legislation of 1798, Elkins and McKitrick write that for Adams, "the entire parcel was pure bad luck." That is an odd conclusion because Adams had not opposed the laws, but would be helped in his later efforts against the High Federalists by the public outrage they engendered. Adams, however, was about to be showered with some pure *good* luck, and from a most unlikely source.[31]

19

Hamilton and His Army, Part Two, 1798–1799

Taking Back the Helm

The last thing one expects to find in Adams's writings is a word of praise for an action of the British government. The number of such instances scattered throughout his vast *oeuvre* are so rare that they can probably be counted on the fingers of a single hand. One of them was on New Year's Day, 1799. Looking back at 1798, Adams wrote his wife: "The English have exhibited an amazing example of skill and intrepidity, perseverance and firmness at sea."[1]

Napoleon's destination (as Rufus King was finally able to report in September and early October), was Egypt, where he had landed with his army on July 1 and thence probably India. Adam's first stroke of luck came courtesy of the British navy and the "Nelson touch." On August 1, 1798, in a rash, brilliant nighttime attack, Nelson's squadron destroyed most of the French Mediterranean fleet at anchor in Aboukir Bay, leaving Napoleon marooned in the Levant. A second coalition against France, including Britain, Turkey, Russia, and in March 1799, Austria, began to form. In a lesser known action on October 11, 1798, the Royal Navy captured or dispersed a number of French men-of-war carrying troops and ammunition to assist the Irish rebellion against British rule. The French, it seemed, *were* mad enough to attempt almost anything. One of Napoleon's biographers comments on the Egyptian campaign, "The whole enterprise was so preposterous that it remains an enigma." But it was clear that they could not, for the time being, seriously threaten America. Though Adams was not prepared to admit it, the British navy *was* part of America's first line of defense. His position in the fall of 1798 toward the European antagonists anticipated that of those Americans who believed that, after the British sinking of the battleship *Bismarck,* Hitler's invasion of the Soviet Union, and the containment of the German submarine menace in mid- to late 1941, the United States could safely adopt a stance of live and let live with the Reich.[2]

Along with the suspense surrounding Napoleon's expedition, the mystery of Elbridge Gerry's activities in France was also dispelled in late 1798. He arrived in Boston on October 1 and promptly rode out to Quincy. Adams's next piece of luck came thanks to Talleyrand and his legendary opportunism. After failing to extort money from the Americans, the foreign minister had played on Gerry's fear of war with France to persuade him to continue a dialogue. His departing colleague Pinckney wrote King, "I never met a man of less candor and so much duplicity as Mr. Gerry." Such was the typical Federalist view, and Adams himself was none too pleased. To his credit, however, Gerry had refused to negotiate on his own and had become a source of information on French policy toward the United States.[3]

Having overplayed his hand, Talleyrand now told Gerry that France was ready to strike a deal and would curb its West Indian-based privateers. Though Talleyrand carried little weight, it was obvious to the Directory that simply going through the motions of a negotiation would undermine preparedness efforts in America and raise the fortunes there of France's beleaguered friends. Talleyrand opened another channel through William Vans Murray, U.S. minister at The Hague. In dispatches reaching Adams in October, Murray, a moderate Maryland Federalist, wrote that the French were concerned about a possible Anglo-American naval agreement. In fact, American merchant ships were already sailing under Royal Navy protection and the United States was seeking to buy British munitions. By the fall of 1798, the French also knew that the U.S. Navy's heavy frigates, *Constellation*, *United States*, and *Constitution*, were patrolling the Atlantic coastline. Late in the year, Secretary Stoddert would concentrate their speed and firepower in the Lesser Antilles and in particular against the main French privateering base at Guadaloupe.[4]

King reported in September that it was "more and more plain that the Directory will endeavour to avoid an open rupture with America." A dramatic letter to Hamilton opened with the words, "You will have no war!" But the American minister did not give up on the South American operation. On receiving Hamilton's August 22 letter, he replied, "things are here, as we could desire: there will be precisely such a cooperation as we wish, the moment *we* [the U.S. government] *are* ready." "What we know is favorable; but if we are to be betrayed by France, the glorious opportunity will be lost." King wrote Pickering, "You are silent concerning South America . . . . As England is steady [ready?], she will furnish a fleet and military stores, and we should furnish the army." The thrust of King's message was that the British government would respond positively to an American initiative.[5]

King was right to suspect that the plan was in trouble. Robert Liston, after receiving his orders to approach the Americans, had actually traveled to Quincy to see Adams. The president had politely made it understood that, although it would be folly not to secure aid in the case of war, he was not interested in discussing military or naval cooperation at the time.

Francisco Miranda, naively, had also contacted Adams. England, he said, had decided that its "future health and happiness depend[ed] absolutely on an alliance and an intimate attachment with America." Adams's laconic, loaded comment on this letter (he had also seen King's earlier dispatches on the subject) to Pickering read in part: "We are friends with Spain. If we were enemies, would the project be useful to us? It will not be in character for me to answer the letter." No answer was ever sent.[6]

Years later, Adams claimed that he had not known that Hamilton was in contact with Miranda and could not have cared less if he had. His concern (perhaps recalling the costly British siege of Havana in 1762) was the prospect of

Seven thousand men and two thousand horses, crowded into transports in the Gulf Stream, bound to South America, two thirds of them, within a fortnight after their landing, dead with the rot, the jail fever, the yellow fever, or the plague, and their fathers and mothers, wives and children, brothers and sisters, weeping and wailing their losses, and cursing John Adams as a traitor to his country, and a bribed slave to Great Britain, – a Deane, an Arnold, a devil!

Such a ghastly scene probably did cross Adams's mind, but it strains belief to claim (as Charles Francis Adams did) that he did not suspect Hamilton's involvement. Adams had read Hamilton's – ostensibly McHenry's – January 1798 memo. He knew when he reacted to Miranda's letter who would be in charge of the army and that the Venezuelan had also written to Hamilton and Knox.[7]

Adams also presumably realized that cold-shouldering Miranda and the British did not rule out a military adventure. French aggression might still lead to hostilities. Despite, or rather because of, the apparent French bid for détente, the Federalists might take the initiative and declare war or else attach conditions to negotiations that would be unacceptable to France. At the height of the anti-French frenzy, Adams himself had declared (on June 21, 1798) that he would never send a minister to France "without assurances that he would be received with the respect due to the representative of a great, free, independent, and powerful nation." Adams now moved cautiously but systematically to close off all avenues that might allow Hamilton to march.[8]

On October 20, Adams sent two questions to Pickering to be discussed before the convening of Congress in December. The first was the expediency of a declaration of war, the second, whether the president "may not say, that in order to keep open the channels of negotiation, it is his intention to nominate a minister to the French republic" as soon as satisfactory assurances were in hand.[9] According to Charles Francis Adams, "the symptoms of hesitation, visible in the second question, and still more in the reasoning of the letter, seem to have burst like a clap of thunder" over the cabinet. This seems a bit of an exaggeration, but the president had sent an unmistakable signal. He intended to put the declaration of war issue on the table and to kill it. (The previous summer a majority of Federalist senators had favored a resolution to declare war, but when Representative John Allen of Connecticut had introduced one in the House, it had fallen short.) The cabinet discussed the questions before Adams's return to Philadelphia on November 23. McHenry alone recommended declaring war, though thought Congress should take the initiative. Pickering and Wolcott, whose answer to Adams reflected a kind of cabinet consensus, did not think a declaration was expedient. Adams had correctly guessed that no one was prepared to press the issue, especially in the face of his own opposition. After he had met the cabinet, the declaration of war issue dropped from view.[10]

On the second question, a draft speech prepared for Adams by Wolcott and Pickering read, "the sending a new minister to make a new attempt at negotiation would, in my opinion, be an act of humiliation to which the United States ought not to submit without extreme necessity. No such necessity exists. It must, therefore, be left with France, if she be indeed desirous of accommodation, to take the requisite steps." *La grande nation*, as France now styled itself, would have to come to the United States. Adams's own version of the speech, solemnly delivered to Congress on December 8, 1798, stated that sending a new minister *"without more determinate assurances that he would be received*, would be an act of humiliation." In place of the suggestion that France would have to send a minister to America, he substituted, *"And with a sincere disposition on the part of France to desist from hostility, to make reparation for her injuries heretofore inflicted on our commerce, and to do justice in the future, there will be no obstacle to the restoration of a friendly intercourse."* In defiance of his cabinet, Adams had laid down conditions for negotiations that the French, if only for tactical reasons, might well decide to accept.[11]

"Our Game Will Be to Attack"

The question of what Hamilton actually planned to do with "his army," perhaps the main controversy dogging his historical reputation, centers on the period from late 1798 to late 1799. His defenders have argued that he acted prudently in response to a plausible external threat and had no intention of tampering with the U.S. political system. A variation on this argument is that neither the liberation of South America nor the conquest of Louisiana and the Floridas "was ever more than a faint possibility, and nobody was more aware of this than Hamilton himself, much as he might have wished otherwise." As for the possible internal use of the army, the urges the Hamiltonians "may have felt in their sleepless hours, or blurted out in their private letters, was one thing; a readiness and commitment to act on them was quite another." In the end, the Federalists did not know what they wanted to do with the army. "Perhaps they need not use it for anything at all – but they wanted it, just to have it there."[12]

In sharp contrast is the view that Hamilton and his cohorts not only entertained grandiose dreams of conquest but actually tried to realize them. At the same time, Hamilton's letters suggest to some that the new army was intended mainly for domestic purposes and that he was prepared to provoke a major rebellion in the south. This was the view, by and large, not only of Adams, Jefferson, and their epigoni, but of the supposedly authoritative Gouverneur Morris. Morris wrote that Hamilton "well knew that his favorite form (of government) was inadmissible, unless as the result of civil war; and I suspect that his belief in that which he called 'an approaching crisis' arose from a conviction that the kind of government most suitable in his opinion to this extensive country, could be established in no other way."[13]

A third, and rather more subtle, view is that Hamilton must have known that Adams would never permit offensive action against the Floridas or Louisiana. With regard to the army's alleged domestic purpose, there were "no contingency plans, no troop dispositions, no evidence of discussions for interfering with elections, nothing." The only logical explanation of Hamilton's plans, therefore, is that he hoped to become the permanent head of an American standing army. The basic purpose of such an army, like that of analogous European forces, would be to intimidate the pro-French Republican opposition, deter sedition, and embody the conservative values of hierarchy, discipline, and patriotism. Once created, its supporters did not think it would actually have to be used – its mere existence would do the trick. Hamilton, according to this argument, was quite simply "the personification of American militarism."[14]

The truth, as is often the case, lies somewhere between these various positions. To put it another way, all sides of the argument are partly right and partly wrong. And one must distinguish between what, on one hand, Hamilton and his friends simply imagined and, on the other, what they considered feasible, as well as desirable, and tried to carry out. Those who doubt that Hamilton not only imagined but also considered possible and sought to advance an offensive, Machiavellian strategy need only reread his correspondence with King, starting with his letter of August 22, 1798. He asked King, "Are we yet mature for this undertaking? Not quite – But we ripen fast, and it may (I think) be rapidly brought to maturity, if an efficient negotiation [with Britain] for the purpose is at once set on foot upon this ground." On October 2, he wrote that the enterprise

has been acted upon by me from the very moment that it became unequivocal that we must have a decisive rupture with France. In some things my efforts succeeded, in others they were disappointed – in others I have had promises of conformity to lay the foundations of future proceeding the performance and effect of which promises are not certainly known to me. The effect cannot yet be known.

Though in the dark as to the government's intentions, Hamilton was optimistic: "There are causes from which delay and feebleness are experienced.

But difficulties will be surmounted and I anticipate with you that the Country will ere long assume an attitude correspondent with its great destinies majestic efficient, and operative of great things. A noble career lies before it." He wrote McHenry a week later, "To organise & to raise the army are the immediate *desiderata*."[15]

Delay and feebleness were to be the leitmotifs of the next twelve months and Hamilton's correspondence indicates his growing frustration. His mood was due partly to poor health and partly to the realization that, in the nearly two decades since he had donned a uniform, he had grown accustomed to a different lifestyle. Shortly after arriving in Philadelphia to come to grips with the army's organization, he wrote Elizabeth, "I discover more and more that I am spoiled for a military man." It grated that for months he received no compensation for his services while, in the meantime, his normal income had fallen by half. After being closeted (November 9–December 15, 1798) in the capital on army business, he wrote McHenry that, although it was disagreeable to talk about money, "a man past forty with a wife and six Children, and a very *small* property beforehand, is compelled to wave [sic] the scruples which his nicety would other wise dictate." It seems highly unlikely, moreover, that Elizabeth Hamilton had much enthusiasm for her husband's new career. It must have been acutely troubling, in light of the barely composed turmoil of 1797, that she and the children would immediately pay a price. To console her, he wrote from Philadelphia, "I have formed a sweet project, of which I will make you my confident [sic] when I come to New York." This was a reference to the house Hamilton would build in the countryside of northwest Manhattan, known (after his grandfather's Ayrshire seat) as "The Grange."[16]

It is probable, though there is no definitive evidence, that McHenry's recommendation of a declaration of war on France had been coordinated with Hamilton, who was in Philadelphia at the time. If so, here was another setback. And it would be surprising if a premonition of failure did not flash through Hamilton's mind as he sat next to Washington, listening to Adams's speech on December 8. After that date, and especially after Adams's subsequent move in February, his "grand plan" was sustained by the commonest of palliatives: believing in his own wish. Despite the feeling at times that he was engaged in the work of Sisyphus, however, Hamilton desired, presumed, planned for, and tried to hasten a conflict with France and Spain.

A question that can hardly be avoided is whether he was reasonable to do so and whether he was acting consistently with his long-held policy of strength through peace. Hamilton (here he saw eye to eye with Madison as well as Washington) had always believed that control of the mouth of the Mississippi was crucial to the survival of the American union. A foreign power in a position to close the river, and to use threats and blandishments to influence American settlers, was pointing a gun at the back of the United States. It was well known that France, now in possession of the world's strongest army, had long intended to put itself in that very position. Jefferson himself would later argue that if the French occupied New Orleans, the United States would be obliged to make an alliance with Britain to force them out. No prudent person would have predicted that five years later, facing other exigencies, France would suddenly change its plans. The policy of strength through peace applied as a practical matter to Anglo-American relations and had never been synonymous with a policy of peace at any price. If there were ever a case where the republic must molest to survive, or be molested, control of the Mississippi and the Gulf coast was such a case. France's Egyptian adventure, it is true, reduced the near term threat to U.S. territory. Arguably, however, France's momentary distraction elsewhere was an opportunity to be seized.

* * *

Meeting in Philadelphia, Washington, Hamilton, and Pinckney (on his return, the South Carolinian had readily agreed to serve under Hamilton) tackled the job of vetting long lists of candidates to staff the still-theoretical army. As political opponents were quick to charge, they did so according to criteria of "Federal correctness" as well as military credentials. Sick to death of the Jeffersonian opposition, Washington was convinced that officers recommended by Republican congressmen would "poison" the army.[17] The lion's share of this administrative work fell as usual to Hamilton. Washington asked him to prepare written answers not only to his own questions but also to McHenry's questions to him. McHenry then converted Hamilton's answers into official reports to the president – giving Adams (who took no part in the discussions) ample opportunity to drag his feet.

Two reports (in Washington's name) to McHenry dated December 13, 1798, were Hamilton's last major efforts on behalf of his erstwhile chief. "Though it may be true that some late occurrences have rendered the prospect of invasion by France less probable, or more remote," the "rapid vicissitudes" of events counseled "a spirit of self-dependence" and the effort "by unremitting vigilance and exertion under the blessing of providence to hold the scales of our destiny in our own hands." In contemplating the possibility of war, it would "be wise to anticipate that frequently the most effectual way to defend is to attack. There may be imagined enterprises of very great moment to the permanent interests of this Country which would certainly require a diciplined force." The raising and training of the army, which would probably take at least a year, should begin at once. Hamilton recommended that Brigadier General James Wilkinson, commanding the "Western Army" (the four regiments of regulars stationed on the Canadian and Spanish borders) be called east for consultations. Arms and munitions should be stocked for an army (estimated at forty thousand infantry, two thousand riflemen, four thousand artillerymen, and four thousand cavalry, for a total of fifty thousand) sufficient to resist "the most serious invasion of the most powerful

European nation." This report served to place Washington's imprimatur on the notion of offensive action in case of war.[18]

Hamilton provided a detailed overview of the army's structure and organization. For reasons of economy and selectivity, the army, in case of war, should decrease the number of officers with respect to the rank and file. "The proportion of officers to men ought not to be greater than is adequate to the due management and command of them.... This conclusion will be assisted by the idea that our fundamental order, in conformity with that of the nations of Europe generally, ought to place our infantry in three ranks." As has been pointed out, the army was "to be capable tactically and strategically of waging the new warfare then sweeping Europe." Hamilton did not neglect the details: The uniform of the infantry and artillery would consist of "a blue Coat with white buttons and red facings white under cloath and cocked hats," and the cavalry would wear green. General officers would wear blue coats with buff facings, with a white plume adorning the commander-in-chief's tricorned hat and a blue one the inspector general's. Washington, who left most matters to Hamilton, took an interest in the subject of uniforms and insignia. He attempted to have his own uniform made by a Philadelphia tailor in time for his step-granddaughter Nelly Custis's wedding at Mount Vernon on February 22, but for lack of gold thread, it had to be sent to Europe for completion. Rather than the black cockade worn by Federalists and the British, and a symbol of anti-Jacobinism, he suggested attaching a small eagle. The final decision was for the black cockade with a small white eagle in the center. On this not irrelevant detail, the old general left his mark.[19]

There is no evidence from succeeding weeks that Hamilton saw reason to deviate from his basic strategy. In a letter to the militia general and U.S. senator from Georgia, James Gunn, he argued that in view of various factors, including "a prospect of peace... again presented by the temporizing conduct of France," he did not yet recommend augmenting the barely nascent army. But he did favor preparing for conscription (in case of an invasion) and renewing the now expired authority for a "provisional army" in order to provide his desired pool of fifty thousand men. (He proceeded to draft a bill for McHenry.) In addition to those mentioned in his recent report to Washington, there were "some other objects of supply equally essential." These included fifty ten-inch mortars, essential for siege warfare. "This you will perceive looks to offensive operations. If we are to engage in war our game will be to attack where we can. France is not to be considered as separate from her ally [Spain]. Tempting objects will be within our Grasp." A post script read, "This is communicated *in confidence.*"[20]

In January 1799, with the possibility of a new negotiation hanging over the army project, Hamilton wrote Lafayette, hoping to nip in the bud the idea that his old friend might be sent as minister to America. What more insidious choice, he must have wondered, could France make? To Massachusetts Congressman Harrison Gray Otis, chairman of the House committee on defense, he recommended a law empowering the president, in case negotiations had not begun by August 1, or had begun but ended in failure, to declare that a state of war existed and to send U.S. forces into action. "If France is really desirous of accommodation, this plan will accelerate her measures to bring it about." When had the Directory, he must have asked himself, ever complied with an ultimatum from a country like the United States? But if France did not want a deal, "it is best to anticipate her final vengeance, and to throw whatever weight we have into the Scale opposed to her." At any moment, Madrid might retrocede Louisiana to Paris. The executive must be equipped with the power "to meet and defeat" such a plan, in other words, to take possession for the United States. Hamilton wrote, "I have been long in the habit of considering the acquisition of those countries as essential to the permanency of the Union, which I consider as very important to the welfare of the whole." He continued, "if universal empire is still to be the pursuit of France, what can tend to defeat the purpose better than to detach South America from Spain, which is the only Channel, through which the riches of *Mexico* and *Peru* are conveyed to France? The Executive ought to be put in a situation to embrace favorable conjunctures for effecting the separation."[21]

Asked by McHenry for his opinion on command arrangements (Washington intended to remain inactive unless a war started), Hamilton answered: "This is a delicate subject for me – yet, in the shape in which it presents itself, I shall wave the scruples." Pinckney should command south of Maryland, himself to the north. The delicate part was the Western Army. Hamilton recommended that it be under his direct control, admitting "that there are objections to this plan. I am not sure that it ought to be adopted." Not surprisingly, it was. McHenry issued orders assigning Hamilton command of forces north of and including Maryland (eight of the twelve new infantry regiments), as well as the Western Army. Hamilton promptly opened a direct line to General Wilkinson at his remote Loftus Heights (near Natchez), Mississippi Territory, headquarters, ordering him to come east at once. "The actual and probable Situation of our public affairs in reference to foreign powers renders this step indispensable."[22]

James Wilkinson, born in 1757, in Calvert County, Maryland, was himself a delicate subject. The energetic, ingratiating Continental Army veteran had acquired a practically unique familiarity with the Western frontier, where he had served since 1791, as well as a reputation for "lying, scheming and carousing." He was a former aide-de-camp to Washington's old enemy, Horatio Gates, and had recently conducted a smear campaign against Anthony Wayne in an attempt to replace him as ranking officer in the army. He had accomplished this on Wayne's death in December 1796. Not only did Wilkinson have ties to congressional Republicans, he was widely believed to be in the employ of the Spanish government. In fact, the opening of Spanish records in the nineteenth century would reveal that he was on a two-thousand-dollar-per-year stipend and had received a total of twenty-six thousand dollars from

Madrid by 1796. (For purposes of comparison, the annual salary of the president of the United States in the 1790s was twenty-five thousand dollars.)[23] Hamilton's letter suggested his intention to handle Wilkinson with a combination of flattery and firmness. If, Hamilton wrote, as was probable because of his long experience, Wilkinson had been given discretionary powers to act on the frontier, such powers should not be transferred to subordinates in his absence. "Care must be taken that the Nation be not embroiled, but in consequence of a deliberate policy."[24]

Enemies Foreign and Domestic

If, as seems clear, Hamilton planned to use the army against France and Spain, and did not consider the chances of such use to be remote, the question remains as to whether he also intended to use it against his domestic enemies. If, as he told Otis, he saw the chance to realize his long-held objective of taking New Orleans and the Floridas, did he also see an opportunity to enact changes in the U.S. political system? The evidence is not unambiguous, and the temptation was surely there, as it had been during the Newburgh conspiracy, "to be not good." Hamilton was also working from something similar to the Machiavellian assumption that internal tumults might actually be turned to the advantage of the republic. Be that as it may, this is a case where Hamilton's defenders are basically correct.[25]

Hamilton had been troubled by the drift of Federalist policy during the war fever of mid-1798. Far from welcoming an internal upheaval, he had feared that broadening the definition of treason as part of the sedition law might "endanger civil war." Hamilton warned, "Let us not establish a tyranny. Energy is a very different thing from violence. If we make no false step we shall be essentially united; but if we push things to an extreme we shall then give to faction *body* & solidarity."[26] To be sure, there was much water over the dam by early 1799. In the face of the repressive legislation, the army project, and noxious accompanying taxes on land, salt, and even stamps, hopes of remaining united had fallen by the wayside. On November 13, 1798, the Virginia legislature adopted the so-called Virginia Resolutions, written secretly by Madison, condemning the Alien and Sedition Acts. On December 24, the Kentucky legislature adopted the longer "Kentucky Resolutions," penned secretly by Jefferson. The resolutions asserted the duty of the states to stop the federal government from the dangerous exercise of powers not explicitly granted by the constitution and, in this case, expressly forbidden by the Bill of Rights. The other fourteen state legislatures were called upon to join (as the Kentucky text put it) "in declaring these acts void and of no force."

No state took up the call, and Madison and Jefferson did not favor a resort to violence. Rumors of a coming armed conflict were rife nonetheless. The Virginia Republican John Nichols publicly accused the Old Dominion of planning civil war. To many Virginians, it seemed self-evident that the purpose of the new army was to crush their state. On January 23, 1798, the state legislature passed an Armory Law calling for the stockpiling of weapons. Such defensive steps, in turn, were seen by Federalists as proof of Virginia's rebellious plans. The Richmond Federalist William Heth reported to Hamilton that a bill had been introduced to give state courts power over persons charged under the federal sedition statute. This would lead to a confrontation with the federal marshal, "[a]nd thus, the signal of Civil War will be given."[27]

The main evidence that has been used to damn Hamilton is a letter to Senator Theodore Sedgwick, dated February 2, 1799. "What, My Dear Sir," it began, "are you going to do with Virginia? This is a very serious business." Hamilton proposed a two-pronged approach. A special committee of Congress should prepare a report defending the alien and sedition laws and demonstrating "the tendency of the doctrines advanced by Virginia and Kentucke [sic] to destroy the Constitution." "The Government must not merely defend itself but must attack and arraign its enemies. But in all this, there should be great care to distinguish the people of Virginia from the legislature and even the greater part of those who may have concurred in the legislature from the Chiefs." Indeed, the report should propose better safeguards against abuse of the laws. "Concessions of this kind adroitly made have a good rather than a bad effect." In the meantime, however:

the measures for raising the Military force should proceed with activity . . . . When a clever force has been collected let them be drawn towards Virginia for which there is an obvious pretext–& then let measures be taken to act upon the laws & put Virginia to the test of resistance. This plan will give time for the fervour of the moment to subside, for reason to resume the reins, and by dividing its enemies will enable the Government to triumph with ease.[28]

It must be asked whether Hamilton's "stick" would not have defeated the purposes of his "carrot," fuelling the fervor rather than allowing it to subside. But his approach was based on the experience of the Whiskey Rebellion rather than a desire to provoke civil war. In 1794, the combination of a commission of inquiry and the mere news of an approaching army had led to the isolation of the ringleaders and the collapse of the insurrection. Hamilton spoke of drawing the force toward, but not necessarily into, Virginia. Joseph Ellis cannot be serious when he writes that Hamilton "hoped to march his conquering army through Virginia" and then all the way to Peru, offering the intervening territories "membership in an expanded American republic." Measures "to act upon the laws" referred to federal enforcement of the Alien and Sedition Acts. It is obvious that Hamilton's purpose was to give the federal government a quick and advantageous victory. After all, the army might be needed to fight the French and the Spanish. That he did not see the need or likelihood of serious trouble in Virginia is clear from his letter to King of

February 6: "If well managed this affair will turn to good account. In my apprehension it is only disagreeable not formidable. The general progress of things continues in the right direction."[29] In the event, there were no overt signs of defiance from Virginia, and no troops were dispatched. The Federalists fought back impressively in April congressional elections, sending John Marshall to Congress at the expense of the Republican firebrand William Giles.

Trouble, when it came, was not in Virginia but Northhampton County, Pennsylvania, where angry German farmers led by militia captain John Fries liberated eighteen fellow citizens from a jail where a U.S. marshall held them for resisting federal property taxes. The Federalist reaction to "Fries's rebellion" threw the proadministration Germans into the opposition camp and helped to elect a Republican governor in Pennsylvania. Infantry and cavalry drawn mainly from Philadelphia "volunteer companies" marched into the traditionally law-abiding area and arrested sixty people. (The volunteer companies had been authorized by the 1798 provisional army law, for all intents and purposes renewed by the "Eventual Army Act" of March 2, 1799.) After an initial mistrial, Fries was convicted of treason and sentenced to hang (Adams later pardoned him) by a federal court. Hamilton's advice to McHenry was "Beware, my Dear Sir, of magnifying a riot into an insurrection, by employing in the first instance an inadequate force. 'Tis better far to err on the other side. Whenever the Government appears in arms it ought to appear like a *Hercules*, and inspire respect by the display of strength." If Hamilton's tactics were questionable, his aim, to use Machiavellian imagery, was to channel the flood and to employ it for constructive purposes, not to provoke a civil war.[30]

Indeed, Hamilton hoped significant, though not radical, changes might be coaxed out of the current conflict. In a letter to New Jersey Senator Jonathan Dayton (the editors of his papers date it October–November 1799), Hamilton said he was disturbed by the possibility of armed resistance and thought it would be an unpardonable error if the Federalists did not use the powers in their hands "to surround the constitution with new ramparts and to disconcert the schemes of its enemies." He recommended new judges and justices of the peace to enforce federal law, as well as "laws for restraining and punishing incendiary and seditious practices." Writings libelous under common law, if leveled against federal officials, should be cognizable in federal courts. At the same time, the construction of new roads and interstate canals, and the creation of a federally funded society for the promotion of "Agriculture and the arts" would enhance the central government's influence and popularity.

Hamilton's most provocative idea was perhaps that sections of existing states containing at least one hundred thousand people could constitute themselves into separate states. For years, he had believed that the big states would always feel a rivalry with, and would "often be disposed to machinate against," the central government. Their breakup ought to be a "cardinal point" of federal policy. While controversial, this fell well short of his call in June 1787 for the virtual elimination of the states. Though convinced of the constitution's inadequacy, and alert to the opportunity of reforming it, he did not want to push things too far. Carving new states out of old ones was only a suggestion. He admitted that it would be "inexpedient & even dangerous" to attempt it at the time.[31]

The letter sheds light, finally, on the controversial issue of Hamilton and a standing army. According to one historian, Hamilton pressed Dayton "to make the New Army perpetual." This is basically correct, and the view was not Hamilton's alone. Hamilton recommended to Dayton that the army be kept on its present footing for the time being, with a provision for five-year reenlistments in the case of a Franco-American settlement. In the case of a general European peace, he favored keeping the new army at a skeleton level of twenty privates per company (full strength was about one hundred). A corps of sergeants for the "eventual army," as the provisional army was now called, should be enlisted and trained in advance and a military academy established. At the same time, if (like Richard Kohn) one defines "militarism" as the advocacy of a permanent new army for mainly *domestic* purposes, Hamilton cannot be considered a militarist. Moreover, and as Kohn's useful account shows, by the late 1790s, knowledgeable Republicans had themselves moved beyond radical Whig exaltation of the militia to endorse a small, permanent military establishment and the superiority of regular troops.[32]

Killing Two Birds with One Stone, 1799

Karl-Friedrich Walling writes that the approach of Hamilton and the Federalists to internal dissent from 1798 to 1799 reflected an "essentially Machiavellian psychology of empire: combine fear with love to produce loyalty; but if one is compelled to rely on fear, then take great care to avoid producing hatred for the authority one seeks to establish." Walling's is a shrewd observation. Unfortunately, however, from the point of view of their enemies, the Federalists seemed to be following a too-literal reading of *The Prince*: in situations where one cannot be both, "it is much more secure to be feared than loved." And they would have done well to pay greater attention to the dictum from the same chapter: "men more quickly forget the death of a father than the loss of their property."[1]

If mistakes like these were avoidable, Hamilton can be more easily forgiven for failing to understand John Adams's capacity for self-delusion. For months, the president had been determined to cut Hamilton and his army down to size. In early 1799, he asserted (as Gerry noted after speaking with him in March) that the Federalist plan was "to get an army on foot to give Hamilton the command of it & then to proclaim a Regal Government, place Hamilton at the Head of it & prepare the way for a Province of Great Britain." At the same time, Adams was remarkably lucid when it came to the army's growing political consequences. The widely reviled project was giving help on a silver platter to the Republican party, which would oppose him in 1800. Having taken a preliminary step in December, Adams now prepared what has inexplicably been called "perhaps the bravest" move of his career. In reality, it was a move calculated to recoup his personal authority and popularity while crippling his two political opponents, Hamilton and Jefferson, in a single blow.[2]

When it came, Adams's move seems to have caught the Federalist camp completely by surprise. This is itself a little surprising because Adams had given a number of hints as to what he was planning. In the middle of January, he directed Pickering to prepare a draft treaty with France and released

Gerry's correspondence with Talleyrand. On February 6, 1799, Adams told Sedgwick (as the latter reported to Hamilton):

'As to the Virginians, sir, it is weakness to apprehend any thing from them, but if you must have an army I will give it to you, but remember it will make the government more unpopular than all their other acts. They have submitted with more patience than any people ever did to the burden of taxes which has been *liberally laid on*, but their patience will not last always.'

The president was outraged by Federalist plans to award Washington a fourth star and the rank of general. Said Adams: "'I have not been so blind but I have seen a combined effort, among those who call themselves the friends of government to annihilate the essential powers given by the president.'" McHenry, who saw Adams the following day, found that he was in no hurry to approve orders for the distribution of army commands. Hamilton wrote Washington, "I more and more discover cause to apprehend that obstacles of a very peculiar kind stand in the way of an efficient and successful management of our military concerns. These it would be unsafe at present to explain."[3]

For months, Adams had carefully collected evidence of a shift in French policy. In addition to Gerry's, there was the testimony of the Philadelphia Quaker Dr. George Logan, who had returned from Paris with reports of the Directory's pacific intentions. Washington inadvertently provided Adams with ammunition by sending him a report he had received along similar lines from the Connecticut poet and radical Republican Joel Barlow. At the end of January, Adams received a dispatch from William Vans Murray (dated October 7, 1798) enclosing a September 28 letter from Talleyrand to the head of the French legation at The Hague, in which the French foreign minister accepted the conditions for new negotiations that Adams had stipulated the previous June. If the United States sent a minister, he would be received "with the respect due to the representative of a free, independent, and powerful nation." On February 18, 1799, Adams announced the nomination of Murray as the new U.S. minister plenipotentiary to the French Republic. His message to the Senate indicated that Murray would not depart without "direct and unequivocal assurances" that he would be properly received, but because Talleyrand had already given assurances indirectly, the French would presumably do what was required.

The shocked Federalists, rather than reject a peace mission out of hand and precipitate an open break with Adams (or even Adams's resignation, saddling them with Jefferson!), prevailed on him to nominate a three-man commission of Murray, Patrick Henry, and Oliver Ellsworth, Connecticut Federalist and chief justice of the Supreme Court. A three-man commission (in the event Henry declined and was replaced by William R. Davie, the Federalist governor of North Carolina) would be safer than sending Murray alone but from the point of view of the army project and the strategic design attached to it, the damage had been done.[4]

On February 19, 1799, Adams wrote Washington to inform him of his decision to nominate a minister and to acknowledge receipt of the Joel Barlow letter. In passing, he referred to the Republican opposition's behavior and made a telling observation: "In elective governments, peace or war are alike embraced by parties, when they think they can employ either for electioneering purposes." In embracing peace, Adams acted on the basis of a number of interrelated considerations. High on the list was hatred of Hamilton and fear of his personal ambition. Another concern was the repugnant prospect of military cooperation with the British and that they might make a separate peace, leaving the United States in the lurch. Perhaps most important of all was the factor Adams had confessed, advertently or otherwise, to his predecessor: upcoming congressional elections, not to mention the presidential contest less than two years away.[5]

Hamilton and Wilkinson

Around the time he received Adams's letter, Washington recorded his impressions of the new army's prospects: "The zeal and enthusiasm which were excited by the Publication of the Dispatches from our Commissioners at Paris (which gave birth to the Law authorising the raising of twelve Regiments &c) are evaporated." Given the public mood, "none but the riff-raff of the Country, & the Scape gallowses of the large Cities will be to be had."[6]

Hamilton's dedication to his project was such that he was not prepared to accept this gloomy assessment. "At length," he wrote Washington at the end of March, "we are on the point of commencing the recruiting service in five of the states, Connecticut, New York, New Jersey, Pennsylvania & Delaware." Against the odds, he worked out of his New York law office at 69 Stone Street with a tiny staff to organize a force able to carry out both defensive and offensive operations. The odds included not only the negative public mood, but the confused state of affairs in Philadelphia. Wolcott reported that Pennsylvania Governor Mifflin was drunk every day, usually before noon, and that with the close of Congress in early March, the president himself had disappeared. Indeed, Adams had retreated into to his cocoon at Quincy, whence he would conduct official business by mail for the following six months. McHenry was doing his best, "yet his operations are such as to confirm more and more a belief of utter unfitness for the situation," and not surprisingly Adams showed "no disposition to apply any correction." What Wolcott did not say was that he, too, was basically opposed to the new army and attendant fiscal measures and doing little to fill the vacuum of leadership.[7]

Wolcott's letter was appropriately dated April 1. Though McHenry had successfully reorganized the tiny regular army after 1796, he was too good-natured and politically inept to cope with the demands of a major mobilization, and his relations with army suppliers and Hamilton bordered on the comic. Clothing for the army was late in arriving and was shoddy and contrary to specifications. Finding that hats for the Twelfth Regiment could be cocked only on one side instead of three and lacked loops and cockades, Hamilton berated his friend, "Nothing is more necessary than to stimulate the vanity of soldiers. To this end a smart dress is essential. When not attended to, the soldier is exposed to ridicule and humiliation." At the end of May, Hamilton lectured McHenry: "The returns from every quarter shew that desertion prevails to a ruinous extent." In June, he lamented: "the management of your Agents as to the affair of supplies is ridiculously bad." The men the army did manage to enlist and clothe, it had trouble paying. In September, a regimental colonel in Virginia wrote Hamilton: "I really think that a Supply of money for the Troops is absolutely Essential." The recruits were starting to grow restless, having been told by "the enemies of Government" that they were not to be paid at all.[8]

At the end of June, Hamilton wrote McHenry that he was prepared to come to the capital to work out a much needed "general plan" for the use of the armed forces. "Certainly there ought to be one formed without delay. If the Chief is too desultory, his Ministers ought to be the more united and steady and well settled in some reasonable system of measures." Hamilton continued, "we ought certainly to look to the possession of the Floridas & Louisiana – and we ought to squint at South America." Notwithstanding the view of Elkins and McKitrick that a "Gang of Three" (McHenry, Pickering, and Wolcott) were at Hamilton's beck and call in Philadelphia, it appears that none of them was ready to take up his offer and to defy Adams. Hamilton could no more automatically have his way through his friends in 1799 than he could in the spring of 1797. What influence he exerted with Adams depended, in the final analysis, on Washington's sponsorship, and that connection had proved to be a two-edged sword.[9]

With the raising of the new army perhaps hopelessly stymied – in fact, less than half the authorized manpower would ever be enlisted – Hamilton devoted increasing attention to the organization of the existing Western Army under General Wilkinson. For this he has been harshly criticized. According to one biographer, "Despite his vigilance against admitting Republican subversives into the army, Hamilton failed to detect a real traitor when he saw one. In a long career of duplicity and treachery, James Wilkinson deceived many others besides Hamilton, but probably his greatest triumph was in hoodwinking the West Indian." By "long career" is meant Wilkinson's later role in Aaron Burr's conspiracy to attack Mexico and/or create a separate nation in the west. According to another author, "Hamilton went through phases of believing (wrongly) that he could manipulate intriguers: hence his desire to promote Wilkinson [from brigadier to major-general]." When Hamilton recommended promotion, McHenry agreed, but begged him "most earnestly to avoid saying any thing to him" about action against Spanish territory. Ignoring this advice, Hamilton held exhaustive discussions with Wilkinson when he arrived in New York by ship from New Orleans in early August. On their agenda was "The best mode (in the event of Rupture with Spain) of attacking the two *floridas*."[10]

Hamilton's dealings with Wilkinson are another instance in which he was prepared "to be not good." But there is little evidence that Wilkinson either hoodwinked Hamilton or harmed U.S. interests while the latter was second-in-command of the army. Hamilton handled him in textbook Machiavellian fashion. Lacking definite proof of Wilkinson's treason, he held out a promotion to gain his confidence and cooperation. Otherwise, Hamilton told Washington, "he will be apt to become disgusted . . . and through disgust may be rendered really what he is now only suspected to be." (Washington agreed, with slight reservations.) If Wilkinson *was* a Spanish agent, Hamilton must have reasoned, he (Hamilton) was still dependent for the time being on the brigadier general's expertise.[11] In fact, Hamilton absorbed much from talking to Wilkinson and had him put his recommendations concerning the Western frontier on paper. Wilkinson did not, as has been claimed, favor an American attack on New Orleans. His principal worry was that local "French fanatics" would topple the weak Spanish government in New Orleans and, with the help of Indians and French regular troops, mount a river-borne attack on U.S. territory. Loftus Heights, the U.S. post near the border, had a garrison of only two hundred men. Wilkinson's main recommendation was that three of the four regular infantry regiments, three artillery companies, and two troops of cavalry be concentrated in a defensive posture in the Southern Mississippi area, leaving a lone infantry regiment and two artillery companies to cover the entire Ohio valley and Great Lakes.[12]

The purpose of Wilkinson's proposal was evidently to deter a French seizure of Louisiana and an attack upriver, and it may well have reflected the fears and assumptions of his Spanish employers. Had Hamilton been gulled by Wilkinson, he might have shown more regard for this plan. Historians have unaccountably ignored the fact that, after consulting Washington, Hamilton imposed a very different deployment on Wilkinson. Hamilton's plan assigned more or less equal quantities of infantry and artillery to the forts on the Great Lakes, the Ohio, and the Mississippi, with a substantial mobile strike force to be stationed just below the falls of the Ohio at Louisville, Kentucky. Hamilton's wish to have the Western Army's center of gravity further north did not reflect concern about an attack from Canada (he assumed the "probability of a continuance of good understanding with Great Britain for some time") but rather other considerations, including the Indians and the possible need to prevent or suppress an internal insurrection. More importantly, however, Wilkinson's plan was at cross-purposes with Hamilton's offensive strategy.[13] As Hamilton told Washington, a force deployed as Wilkinson had recommended would be both vulnerable to attack from downriver and too small to guarantee a successful move on New Orleans. Its deployment near the border might cause the Spanish to reinforce their own defenses. (Wilkinson's Spanish employers wanted to persuade Madrid to do just that.) Keeping the mobile force far upriver, but able to make a lightning descent, would be less likely to alarm the Spanish while preserving a degree of surprise. Hamilton noted that "concerted and combined operations may insure efficacy," a reference to a simultaneous British attack from the sea.[14]

The final version of Hamilton's plan (October 12, 1799) called for the preparation at the mobile reserve's Ohio River base of boats for transportation downriver "of Three thousand men with baggage stores provisions Artillery and other apparatus." The fort at Loftus Heights would be strongly reinforced, but the overall number of U.S. troops on the lower Mississippi would actually be reduced. An unstated assumption was perhaps that the new disposition of forces might actually tempt the French to carry out the very operation Wilkinson wished to deter, giving Hamilton a pretext to attack New Orleans. Having reversed the logic of Wilkinson's plan, Hamilton removed its author from the vicinity of his suspected employers. After returning to pick up his wife and sons at Loftus Heights, Wilkinson was transferred to the Ohio to establish the new base.[15]

The Moment of Truth: Trenton, October 1799

Adams said in later life that he wanted nothing on his gravestone save the inscription, "Here lies John Adams, who took upon himself the responsibility of the peace with France in the year 1800." There is no reason to doubt that he was sincere when he wrote those words, but peace with France does *not* appear to have been his overriding concern in 1799. To this day, Adams scholars debate the reasons for his delay in ordering the American negotiators to France after he had nominated them early in the year. A popular account of his life suggests that Adams intended to send the mission all along and that suspending it did not occur to him. But this is clearly not the case.[16]

In March 1799, British minister Liston quoted Adams as saying that he did not believe the French were serious about negotiating and would now call their bluff: "We shall be up with them, we shall outwit them." Certainly, he was determined to proceed carefully with the hyperslippery Talleyrand and to avoid a farcical (and politically fatal) repetition of the XYZ affair. He could also reckon that the United States had now established naval superiority over France in the Caribbean. In the most important single engagement of the "quasi-war" (February 9, 1799), the *Constellation*, commanded by Captain Thomas Truxtun, had battered the *Insurgente*, forcing the French frigate to strike her colors. Meanwhile, with Napoleon still stranded in Egypt, Russian and Austrian armies were scoring impressive victories on the continent. Above all, simply by announcing the intention to parley, Adams had achieved two of his main objectives: further undermining domestic support for the new army and countering Republican attacks on his administration. Adams was in no hurry to put his negotiators to the test.[17]

Thus it did not matter if obtaining ironclad assurances that the envoys would be properly received was a leisurely process. Pickering wrote to Murray at The Hague, who wrote Talleyrand, who in turn sent assurances back to Murray. Murray's letter to Pickering containing Talleyrand's arrived in Philadelphia on July 30. Adams received it in Quincy on August 5. Satisfied, Adams wrote Pickering, ordering him to draw up a final version of the envoys' instructions. After the cabinet's review, this would have to go to Quincy for approval and thence back to the seat of government. By the end of August, however, Navy Secretary Stoddert, the one cabinet member Adams himself had appointed, was growing uneasy about this mode of conducting business. He wrote the president on August 29 that he had better be on hand personally if events in Europe counseled changes in the instructions or the mission's postponement.[18]

Adams brushed off this advice. For one thing, the seat of government was now Trenton, New Jersey, where the cabinet had gone to escape yet another outbreak of yellow fever. According to Adams, accommodations there were beneath the dignity of the president of the United States. He had said to Pickering (August 6), "Although I have little confidence in the issue of this business, I wish to delay nothing, to omit nothing." Now, however, he wrote Stoddert that he had "no reason nor motive to precipitate the departure of the envoys." Events might well necessitate a suspension. "France has always been a pendulum." In a passage tending to confirm Liston's point that Adams saw himself engaged in a battle of wits not only with the Hamiltonians but with a diabolical foreign opponent, the president said that he had always "considered this manoevre of the French as the deepest and subtlest, which the genius of the Directory and their minister has ever invented for the division of our people." Caution was the order of the day.[19]

Pickering, who thought negotiations would be a disgrace and was looking for ways to prevent them, received welcome news from Murray on August 26: there had been another shake-up in the French government. In June, a coalition of conservatives and Jacobins in the Council of Five Hundred had ousted some of the same members of the Directory (Reubell, Treilhard, Larevellière, and Merlin) who had provided the recent assurances to the United States. Though Pickering did not yet know it, Talleyrand himself (foreseeing the end of the Directory) had resigned in late July. With the agreement of the cabinet, Pickering advised Adams to consider suspending the peace mission. Adams readily agreed, telling Pickering that in light of the news, there was no need to rush off the envoys.[20] Pickering's letter (September 11) to Adams was pointedly silent on the subject of Adams's coming to Trenton. But Stoddard wrote a second time (September 13) to reiterate his message. The Navy secretary did not openly say so, but he believed that Adams's absence was undermining his standing with the Federalist party and the public. Whether the mission was confirmed or suspended, he reminded Adams, the president must be at the helm to lend authority and solemnity

to such an important decision. Stoddert mentioned two additional considerations, one of which probably did not overly concern Adams and one of
which prompted him to change his travel plans.[21]

The first was a dangerous drift in Anglo-American relations. Stoddert attributed this partly to the decision to nominate the peace envoys and partly
to an acrimonious deadlock within the Philadelphia-based mixed commission stipulated by the Jay treaty to adjudicate the prewar claims of British
creditors in America. Cruisers on the Royal Navy's West Indian station had
resumed attacks on American shipping, with a large number of condemna-
tions in British admiralty courts. Stoddert believed that the president must
take personal charge of the matter. His clinching argument, however, was
the following: "I have been apprehensive that artful designing men might
make such use of your absence from the seat of government, when things so
important to restore peace with one country, and to preserve it with another,
were transacting, as to make your next election less honorable than it would
otherwise be." In other words, get a firm grip on things or you may not be
the Federalist candidate in 1800. Not long after receiving this letter, Adams
departed Quincy, stopping in Windsor, Connecticut, to consult with one of
the envoy-designates, Oliver Ellsworth. He reached Trenton on October 10,
1799.[22]

If there is a point in the Hamilton–Adams saga when one laments the lack
of a modern presidential taping system, it is the week following Adams's arrival in the temporary capital. Rarely has an important decision been so
poorly documented. Indeed, the protagonists' accounts leave a cloud of uncertainty, even mystery, hanging over what transpired. To make a long story
short, during a meeting of Adams and his cabinet on October 15, the envoys' instructions were discussed and approved. The next morning, Adams
ordered Pickering to arrange for the envoys to sail for France by November
1. But he had apparently arrived in town intending to suspend the mission.
That is what he had told Ellsworth on October 3. Why did he change his
mind? The only detailed explanation is Adams's own, published ten years
after the event. According to Adams, he held extensive discussions with his
ministers but was surprised and unconvinced by their main argument for
delaying the mission, namely the likelihood of France's military collapse and
the imminent restoration of the monarchy. Both Wolcott and Stoddert questioned Adams's memory: the cabinet had not discussed the merits of sending the mission, only the details of the instructions. According to Stoddert,
Adams had confused a cabinet meeting with a conversation with someone
else: General Alexander Hamilton.[23]

Another confused claim is that Hamilton left his troops encamped at
Newark in a desperate and insubordinate bid to lobby Adams. In fact, he
came to Trenton from New York (arriving a day before Adams) as previously arranged with Wilkinson and McHenry to finalize the deployment of
the Western Army. He had not even known that the president would be

in town. For Adams, however, Hamilton's presence could not have been a mere coincidence. Here is an excerpt of his account of what happened when Hamilton came to see him:

I received him with great civility, as I always had done from my first knowledge of him. I was fortunately in a very happy temper, and very good humor. He went over the whole ground of the victories of [the Russian general] Suwarrow [sic] and Prince Charles [of Austria], and the inflexible determination of the two courts, in concert with Great Britain, to restore the House of Bourbon to their Kingdom. That there was no doubt the enterprise was already accomplished, or at least would be, before the end of the campaign. That Mr. Pitt was determined to restore the Bourbons. That the confidence of the nation in Mr. Pitt was unbounded... [Hamilton's] eloquence and vehemence wrought the little man up to a degree of heat and effervescence like that which General Knox used to describe in his conduct in the battle of Monmouth, and which General Lee used to call his *paroxysms* of bravery but which he said would never be of any service to his country.

Adams disputed Hamilton on every point, adding,

I treated him throughout with great mildness and civility; but after he took leave, I could not help reflecting in my own mind on the total ignorance he had betrayed of every thing in Europe, in France, England, and elsewhere.[24]

Hamilton left no corroboration of this conversation (or conversations), except for a pair of passing references in which he said that Adams had thought there would be a "general peace" in Europe during the coming winter, whereas he had taken a different line. Assuming this was the gist of the exchange, both men were mistaken. With France in a desperate situation, it was reasonable to think so, but the monarchy was not about to be restored. Instead, Napoleon returned home from Egypt, seized power in the *coup d'état* of 18 *Brumaire* (November 9, 1799), and set off again to defeat the Austrians in Italy. Nor was there to be a "general peace" until March 1802 (the Treaty of Amiens), and then one lasting little more than a year. What is striking, in any case, is that Adams and Hamilton had *both* believed, even if for different reasons, when they came to Trenton that the mission should not be sent to France for the time being. It is hard to avoid the conclusion that one of the reasons, if not the main one, why the president ordered it to leave immediately was Hamilton's unexpected appearance. That confirmed in Adams's mind that "artful designing men," and who presumed to understand Europe better than *he* did, were attempting to profit by delay.[25]

His motives aside, did Adams make the right decision? It is certainly understandable if he (unlike Hamilton) gave a literal reading to the Farewell Address, to the effect that the United States had little or no stake in Europe's quarrels. And he was correct to think that there was very limited public support for a policy of military confrontation, let alone of preemptive action, against the Spanish and the French. Indignation toward France had cooled considerably, while hostility toward Hamilton's army was still intense. Adams's decision had the advantage of testing Paris's intentions and of uniting the country in case further trickery necessitated war. But the arguments on the other side of the ledger seem at least equally compelling. Making peace with the power that threatened the European balance, like making war on Britain in 1812, was dubious from the standpoint of basic U.S. interests. Unbeknownst to Adams, one of Napoleon's motives in wanting to settle was to smooth plans for the new American empire, which, had it materialized, would have threatened the United States. Strictly from the standpoint of Adams's own political interests, the peace mission would prove highly questionable. The French undoubtedly calculated – Jefferson was telling them as much at the time – that a conciliatory attitude and a new negotiation would not only prevent Hamilton's army from marching on New Orleans, it would help to split the Federalist party and enhance the chances of the candidate whom their heavy handed efforts had failed to elect in 1796.[26]

A Seal upon His Glory

If Adams's February decision had left a sliver of hope for Hamilton's offensive strategy, after Trenton its fate was sealed. Informing Washington of the October 16 decision, Hamilton disconsolately observed, "All my calculations lead me to regret the measure. I hope that it may not in its consequences involve the United States in a war on the side of France with her enemies." A possible war with Britain had apparently not been one of his arguments to Adams, but it weighed on his mind. Washington himself opposed Adams's policy, writing McHenry that he had been "stricken dumb" by the president's latest move.[27]

The next blow in store for Hamilton was kind of a symbolic confirmation of the recent turn of events. In November, he continued to occupy himself writing long memos on a military academy, the formation of regiments for battle and exercise, and elements of infantry tactics. On Thursday, December 12, Washington wrote Hamilton expressing support for the military academy proposal. The same day, the former president spent five hours touring his farms, despite driving rain and snow. Washington, in good health at age sixty-seven, contracted what modern experts believe was acute epiglottis, a bacterial infection of the flap at the back of the throat. He died in his bed on the second floor of his house at Mount Vernon on Saturday evening, December 14, 1799. His letter to Hamilton had been the final one of his life.[28]

It is impossible to say exactly how and when first reports of Washington's death reached Hamilton, but his reaction can only have been one of shock and dismay. Answering a message from the general's secretary, Tobias Lear, Hamilton wrote that the news, which he had already received, had filled his heart with bitterness. "Perhaps no man in this community has equal cause with myself to deplore the loss. I have been much indebted to the kindness of the General, and he was an Aegis very essential to me." He added philosophically: "For great misfortunes it is the business of reason to seek consolation. The friends of General Washington have very noble ones. If virtue can secure happiness in another world he is happy. In this the Seal is now put upon his Glory. It is no longer in jeopardy from the fickleness of Fortune." If only, Hamilton must have been thinking, he could say the same thing about himself.[29]

PART VI

THE LESSER OF EVILS

2 I

1800 and After

Introduction

There are times when fortune inflicts wounds that simply won't heal, when the story of a life breaks into two distinct sections, a before and an after. Those who experience this sort of caesura discover that from a certain day on they are no longer the same person, they suffer an anguish they have never felt before, they discover personal resources they did not know existed, and they see the world and their fellow humans in a new and chilly light. They may find they are stronger; they may find that they are more vulnerable; in any case they find that they are different.

This is how a biographer describes the impact on Machiavelli of the events of late 1512.[1]

Abandoned by its ally, Florence felt the wrath of France's enemies, Pope Julius II and the Spanish, who aimed to oust Machiavelli's patron, Piero Soderini and to restore the Medici family to power. At the end of August 1512, a force of five thousand hardened Spanish troops broke through the walls of Prato, twelve miles northwest of Florence. After the militiamen defending the city threw down their arms and ran, the half-starved Spaniards went on a rampage, killing several thousand people. Panic-stricken Florence yielded to the will of the Medicis. In mid-September, a general assembly, or *parlamento*, controlled by their supporters sent Soderini into exile and abolished the Great Council and the Nine Officials of the Ordinance and Militia.

Following the humiliation of the republic and the dissolution of his prized militia, Machiavelli was abruptly removed from office. In subsequent weeks, he was banned from the Palazzo Vecchio, except to answer charges of financial malfeasance, and forbidden to leave Florentine territory. (Investigators could find nothing to pin on him.) After his name was discovered on a list of anti-Medici conspirators – he was not involved but several acquaintances were executed – he spent several months in a stinking, rat-infested cell. Half-a-dozen times he was subjected to a routine torture known as the *strappado*, or pendulum, by which the prisoner, hands tied behind the back, was raised by a rope and dropped to within a short distance of the floor, violently dislocating the shoulders.

After his release in March 1513, Machiavelli was consigned with his wife and four children to a new life on his small estate south of Florence, known as the *Albergaccio*, the "rundown hotel." Overseeing his farm and family, cards at the local *osteria*, an occasional love affair, and, above all, reflection and writing amused him and diverted him from his bitterness and despondency. He continued to wear the ironic trace of a smile we see in Santi di Tito's portrait of him hanging today in the Palazzo Vecchio. As Maurizio Viroli describes it, Machiavelli's was a "smile of determination and challenge; it dies on the lips without warming the soul, without loosening the grief that clamps tight to the heart."[2]

Hamilton's transition from "before to after" was less traumatic than Machiavelli's, but no less marked in its effects. Ezra Ames's first portrait of him, done in 1802, shows Hamilton with a similar shadow of a smile, suggesting strength suffused with an enormous sadness and sense of loss. For contemporaries, it was the characteristic expression of his final years.

Choosing the Lesser of Evils

As Hamilton summed up the state of affairs in early 1800,

Vanity and Jealousy exclude all counsel. Passion wrests the helm from reason. The irreparable loss of an inestimable man removes a controul [sic] which was felt and was very salutary. The leading friends of the Government are in a sad Dilemma. Shall they risk a serious scism [sic] by an attempt to change? Or shall they annihilate themselves and hazard their cause by continuing to uphold those who suspect or hate them, & who are likely to propose a course for no better reason than because it is contrary to what they approve?[3]

As the Federalists contemplated their dilemma, Adams and de facto Republican allies took the offensive against the army. On February 20, a Federalist-sponsored compromise was adopted, suspending enlistments rather than decreeing immediate dissolution. On May 14, however, Adams signed a bill discharging the men of the new regiments on June 14, 1800. After a final review of the "Union Brigade" at Scotch Plains, New Jersey, Hamilton confessed to his wife, "at the bottom of my soul there is more than the usual gloom."[4]

Hamilton was heavily engaged in his law practice and routine army business in early 1800, but even so, he seems to have been following politics with less than his usual care. In a typical letter, he wrote to Elizabeth, "While all other passions decline in me, those of love and friendship gain new strength."

That summer he would buy the first of three plots of land overlooking the Hudson River and Harlem Valley, where he built his modest country house. ("A garden," he later said, "is a very usual refuge of a disappointed politician.") In February 1800, he penned a quick note to Theodore Sedgwick to ask about plans for nominating a presidential candidate. Untypically, he proposed nothing and added, "Unless for indispensable reasons I had rather not come [to Philadelphia]." When he did send advice, it was after Federalists had already caucused on the issue.[5] Until the last minute, Hamilton does not seem to have played an active part in the New York State Assembly elections of spring 1800, whose outcome would determine the choice of the state's twelve presidential electors. Henry Adams called the New York City elections, decisive for the statewide vote, "the turning-point of American political history in that generation." Hamilton's correspondence does not mention them until the above-cited May 4 letter to Sedgwick, written after the results were known.[6]

The results were a shock. The Republicans took control of the assembly (including all twelve New York City seats), dealing a body blow to Federalist chances of retaining the presidency. The Republicans owed their victory to the astute and innovative management of Hamilton's fellow attorney (bidding again to become vice president) Aaron Burr. Unlike the Federalists – someone quipped that they managed to run "two grocers, a ship chandler, a baker, a potter, a bookseller, a mason, and a shoemaker" – Burr recruited candidates with name recognition, including the former governor, George Clinton, and the "hero of Saratoga," General Horatio Gates. With the backing of a recently founded Republican bank, an engaging newspaper, and teams of door-to-door campaigners, Burr fashioned a machine to bring in the vote.[7]

The Republicans' stunning victory obliged Hamilton to face up to his dilemma: either support Adams or back someone else and split the Federalist party. There had never been much doubt in his mind. The party, after all, had already split into pro- and anti-Adams factions over the army, the French mission, and Adams's basic competency (some would have said sanity). In his letter to Sedgwick, Hamilton urged the Federalists to make a solemn agreement to support Adams and Charles Cotesworth Pinckney equally, as "the only thing that can possibly save us from the fangs of *Jefferson*." In fact, this is what the Federalists, meeting the same day as the bad news from New York, had agreed to do. Ostensibly, Adams was their choice for president, but most assumed that if the agreement were strictly adhered to in New England, Pinckney would outpoll Adams by picking up more votes in the South. By insisting on equal support for the two, Hamilton and his friends were working for Pinckney. In contrast to 1796, they would make little attempt to conceal their hand.[8]

Whether, without New York's electoral votes, *anyone* could defeat Jefferson was another question. Hamilton's approach to that problem did not mean, as is sometimes suggested, that he had become unhinged in the absence of Washington's guidance. He believed, as he always had, that there were situations requiring the statesman "to be able to be not good." As he put it to Governor Jay, "in times like these in which we live, it will not do to be over scrupulous. It is easy to sacrifice the substantial interests of society by a strict adherence to ordinary rules." Hamilton urged Jay to call into session the outgoing Federalist-controlled assembly to adopt a measure taking the power to pick New York's presidential electors away from the new Republican-controlled body and giving it to the people voting in districts. In effect, he wanted a new election, after having changed the rules of the game.[9]

Jay apparently never answered Hamilton's letter. At the bottom of it, he wrote that it proposed "a measure for party purposes wh. I think it wd. not become me to adopt." In fact, Hamilton must have known that his suggestion had little chance of adoption and that Jefferson's victory was nearly a foregone conclusion. He wrote to Sedgwick on May 10:

For my individual part my mind is made up. I will never more be responsible for him [Adams] by my direct support – even though the consequence should be the election of *Jefferson*. If we must have an *enemy* at the head of the Government, let it be one whom we can oppose & for whom we are not responsible, who will not involve our party in the disgrace of his foolish and bad measures. Under *Adams* as under *Jefferson* the government will sink. The party in the hands of whose chief it shall sink will sink with it and the advantage will all be on the side of his adversaries.

He seemed resigned to a Jefferson victory, and if it eliminated Adams and helped to restore party unity, there might be a silver lining in defeat.[10]

Hamilton, in other words, had probably decided on his main objective – stopping Adams – before the latest news from Philadelphia. Apprised of the New York assembly results and the Federalist decision to back him and Pinckney equally, Adams had thrown a temper tantrum, leavened by a healthy dose of self-serving calculation. Somehow seeing Hamilton's hand (rather than Burr's) behind the New York results, and determined to put political daylight between himself and the sinking High Federalists, Adams bullied McHenry into resigning and fired a defiant Pickering.[11]

To say that McHenry's account of these events confirmed Hamilton's determination to end Adams's career would probably be an understatement. Adams had called McHenry to his Philadelphia sitting room on May 5. After some War Department small talk, Adams launched into the evening's business:

Hamilton has been opposing me in New York. He has caused the loss of the election. No head of Department shall be permitted to oppose me.... You [McHenry] are subservient to him, Sir. It was you who biased General Washington's mind (who hesitated) and induced him to place Hamilton on the List of Major Generals, before Generals Knox and Pinckney.... Even General Washington's death and the

Eulogiums upon him have been made use of as engines to injure and lower me in the eyes of the public, and you know it, Sir.

McHenry defended himself as best he could, but there was no stopping Adams's tirade:

Hamilton is an intriguant – the greatest intriguant in the World – a man devoid of every moral principle – a Bastard, and as much of a foreigner as Gallatin. Mr. Jefferson is an infinitely better man; a wiser one, I am sure, and, if President, will act wisely. I know it and would rather be Vice president under him, or even Minister Resident at the Hague, than indebted to such a being as Hamilton for the Presidency.... You are subservient to Hamilton, who ruled Washington, and would still rule if he could....

The monologue degenerated into an attack on McHenry's management of his department, the first time the president had ever directly criticized him. A shaken, incredulous McHenry gave his resignation on the spot.[12]

A "Letter From Alexander Hamilton Concerning the Public Conduct and Character of John Adams"

Even for friendly observers, Hamilton's subsequent role in the presidential campaign, culminating in his notorious attack on Adams, is evidence of a self-destructiveness and loss of equilibrium for which the Federalist party paid the price. For one historian, the "calamitous attack on President John Adams is impossible to excuse, difficult to explain." For another, it "backfired, destroying his reputation." For still others, the letter was "the most lunatic political act of his life." It "led to the sad conclusion that Hamilton's once formidable influence in the councils of Federalism was at an end."[13]

The explanation, at least, would seem to be obvious. For the previous eighteen months, Adams had systematically thwarted Hamilton's ambitions while acting against his view of the national interest in the case of France. Now he had allowed his hatred and contempt to come into the open, bruiting about Hamilton's illegitimacy, figuratively spitting in his face. On top of this came another provocation. On August 1, 1800, Hamilton wrote Adams demanding an explanation for reports that Adams and his friends were calling Hamilton a member "of a *British faction* in this Country." Receiving no answer, Hamilton wrote Adams again, calling the charge "a base wicked and cruel calumny." Adams had managed to touch two of the rawest nerves in Hamilton's makeup. It is inconceivable that someone with his hypersensitivity regarding questions of honor would not have replied.[14]

Inconceivable, but also suicidal for the Federalists? Here the answer is more complicated. As noted earlier, by early May the party was already divided and had slim hopes of retaining the presidency. Hamilton spent three weeks in New England in June, urging Federalists not to do what some had done in 1796 – throw away votes for the ostensible number-two man on the ticket – but he knew he was powerless to persuade all of them to support Pinckney. His old friend Robert G. Harper wrote that in South Carolina, some Federalist electors would quietly drop Adams at the last minute, but from what Hamilton could see of both the Northern and Southern situations, he wrote in early August, "our prospects are not brilliant. There seems to be too much probability that Jefferson or Burr will be President." This certainly did not incline him to hold off on his attack.[15] To be sure, his friends warned him to tread carefully. Although they did not tell him to ignore Adams's charges, seasoned New England politicians like George Cabot and Fisher Ames urged him not to sign anything and, above all, not to ask electors to violate the agreement to support Adams and Pinckney equally. That would be inviting pro-Adams Federalists to drop Pinckney and then blame Hamilton for Jefferson's election. Ames had a piece of advice that might have struck a responsive chord: "The question is not I fear how we shall fight, but how we and all Federalists shall fall – that we may fall like Anteus [sic] the stronger for our fall."[16]

Hamilton paid lip service to the electoral agreement but insisted on signing his attack on Adams in his own name. He was eager to establish the purity of his motives in opposing the president to Federalist electors while at the same time vindicating himself against scurrilous Adamsite attacks. Unfortunately, these two objectives were contradictory, and the letter dated October 24, 1800, did not succeed on either count. The first part was a long rehearsal of Adams's foibles, designed to prove his unfitness for the presidency and the unreasonableness of his hostility toward Hamilton. This was followed by an extended critique of Adams's foreign policy, the thrust of which was that he should have insisted that France send an envoy (rather than vice versa) and had improperly and dangerously ignored his cabinet. But in tiptoeing around the real reasons for his hostility, and in pretending that he was not motivated by "private resentment," Hamilton managed to be both dull and disingenuous. He did not mention that Adams had deliberately undermined the army and had failed to see the advantages of offensive action. Cabot later told Hamilton that some New Englanders had complained that the letter was too soft on Adams. They had expected Hamilton to use Adams's "designs to involve the country in war with G B," his "pernicious jealousy" of Washington, and other choice arguments.[17]

Toward the end of the letter, where he recounted Adams's firing of McHenry and replied to the charge of membership in a British faction, Hamilton acknowledged that he *did* have "causes of personal dissatisfaction." Here the polemic was more pointed and effective, but it shattered the pretense of objectivity. And although he was scrupulous in setting out his foreign policy positions, including support for preparedness against Britain in 1794 and conciliation of France in 1797, it was unconvincing to suggest that he had been evenhanded. His concluding call to support Adams and Pinckney equally can only have struck electors as insincere. The document could more logically be read as an appeal to throw away votes destined for

Adams while supporting Pinckney in order to do what he had failed to do in 1796.[18]

Originally intended for a select group of Federalist notables, the text fell into the hands of Republican editors (probably through Burr's machinations), who published excerpts to the delight of their readers. Hamilton then authorized publication of the entire letter by a Federalist paper in New York. It had no effect on the outcome of the presidential election. With the exception of one Rhode Island elector, New England Federalists stuck to the agreement and supported the candidates equally. After the loss of New York, the Federalists' slim hopes of beating Jefferson rested on South Carolina. But on October 15, *before* the appearance of the letter, the state elected a Republican-controlled legislature. Even if Republicans there had given their second vote to Pinckney instead of Burr, the South Carolinian would not have beaten Jefferson. In the event, Republican electors stuck to their own agreement to support their candidates equally. The overall result was Jefferson and Burr tied at seventy-three; Adams with sixty-five; Pinckney, sixty-four; and John Jay, a single vote.

The letter *did* have an effect on Hamilton's reputation and party standing. Robert Troup wrote King that in its wake, Hamilton's usefulness would be "greatly lessened." Cabot wrote Hamilton, "I am *bound* to tell you that you are accused by respectable men of Egotism, & some very worthy & sensible men say you have exhibited the same *vanity* in your book [letter] which you charge as a dangerous quality & great weakness in Mr. Adams."[19] But the letter did more to confirm the decline in Hamilton's authority than it did to cause it. Since the end of 1799, Hamilton had seen his public career as closing, if not essentially over. This was reflected in his ineffectual role in the New York assembly elections. He could hardly expect to have great influence in national councils once he had proven unable to deliver the electoral vote of his own state. Nor did the letter episode have much effect on his ability to influence the Federalist position on the next dilemma facing the party. Well before its appearance, Cabot had observed that Federalists, if forced to swallow one or the other, seemed to prefer the ambitious Burr to the Jacobin Jefferson. Contemplating that question around the same time, Hamilton wrote of the man who had outmaneuvered and humiliated the New York Federalists (his correspondent was James A. Bayard, the lone congressman from Delaware) that Burr, as president, would "certainly attempt to reform the Government *a la Buonaparte*. He is as unprincipled and dangerous a man as any country can boast; as true a *Cataline* [sic] as ever met in a midnight conclave."[20]

The Lesser of Evils Once Again

Aaron Burr, Jr., born in 1756 in Newark, New Jersey, was Hamilton's nearly exact contemporary, and the similarities did not end there. Burr had been left parentless early in life, risen to the rank of colonel in the Continental Army, and become a fixture of the New York bar. Small in stature (his nickname was "little Burr"), he was endowed with an outsized charm and razor-sharp intelligence. So too were there differences: if Hamilton was self-made American gentry, Burr, grandson of the Puritan divine Jonathan Edwards and son of a president of the College of New Jersey, was to the manor born. (He graduated from Princeton with distinction at age sixteen.) Burr was vastly cultivated but lacked Hamilton's prodigious powers of concentration. Hamilton had anchored himself in his relationships with Washington and his family, while Burr, though happily married for a time, was a free spirit living a private rebellion against conventional morality. If he was a "deviant type" in the eyes of contemporaries and historians, it is partly because his model of personal behavior was more European than American: "A gentleman is free to do whatever he pleases so long as he does it with style" and "so long as no ill-will was intended."[21] When it came to politics, if Hamilton was leery of popular rule, Burr was a prototype of the aristocrat as democrat, the model later perfected by his fellow New Yorker, FDR.

The paths of the two men had crossed many times before 1800. Burr had left Washington's staff after brief service and had sided with Gates during the wartime feud. In 1791, Burr allied with the antifederalists to remove Philip Schuyler from the U.S. Senate and had been the Republican candidate for vice president in 1796. The following year, Schuyler had won back his seat from Burr. Although they were on friendly terms personally, Hamilton had long considered Burr, if not a nemesis in the making, a dangerous political adversary, whose antecedent was to be found in Roman history:

Mr. Burr's integrity as an Individual is not unimpeached. As a public man he is one of the worst sort – a friend to nothing but as it suits his interest and ambition.... 'Tis evident that he aims at putting himself at the head of what he calls the 'popular party'.... In a word, if we have an embryo-Caesar in the United States 'tis Burr.

Burr's New York coup seems to have convinced Hamilton that he was no longer dealing with an embryo-Caesar but a full-fledged Catiline – the bold and dissolute aristocrat who had tried to seize control of the Roman republic in 63 B.C.[22]

Once the 1800 election had been thrown into the House of Representatives (where each state delegation had one vote), Hamilton was not alone among Federalists in fearing Burr. A minority, including Jay and Morris, agreed with him. But Hamilton's opposition was of an entirely different order. In a spate of letters, he described Burr as a gifted demagogue and cunning operator with (as in Catiline's case) a special appeal to the young. He was a gambler without political principles, except permanent power for himself. The Federalists were foolish to think that they would control him after voting for him. He would control *them*, and they would take the blame for his disastrous policies.[23] If all this were not bad enough, Burr was a well-known Francophile and heavily in debt. This, in fact, was the crux of the problem: Burr would be bought by the French and take the United States into the war: "He is bankrupt beyond redemption except by the resources that grow out of war and disorder or by a sale to a foreign power or by great peculation. War with Great Britain would be the immediate instrument. He is sanguine enough to hope every thing – daring enough to attempt every thing – wicked enough to scruple nothing."[24]

In fact, the prospect of Burr entering the White House coincided with the debate over the settlement with France negotiated by Adams's commissioners, the so-called Convention of Môrtefontaine (signed September 30, 1800). Like most Federalists, Hamilton found it highly unsatisfactory. Although it confirmed the end of the 1778 treaties, it failed to secure the central objective of indemnities for French attacks on U.S. shipping and required the United States to return naval vessels captured during the "quasi-war." At the same time, he reasoned to Morris,

The mania for France has in a great degree revived in our country and the party which should invoke a rupture would be likely to be ruined.... If the present Convention be ratified our relations to France will have received a precise Shape. To take up the subject anew and mould it into a shape better according to Jacobin projects will not be as easy, as finding the whole business open to give it that shape. I think it politic therefore to close as far as we can.

The Senate first rejected the convention and then ratified a revised version of it in February 1801.[25]

Forced again to choose the lesser of two evils, Hamilton again opted for Jefferson, someone who was "by far not so dangerous a man" as Burr and with "pretensions to character." In one of several letters to Congressman Bayard, who was emerging as a key player in the deadlocked House, Hamilton wrote of his historic enemy:

I admit that his politics are tinctured with fanaticism, that he is too much in earnest in his democracy, that he has been a mischevious enemy to the principal measures of our past administration, that he is crafty and persevering in his objects, that he is not scrupulous about the means of success, nor very mindful of the truth, and that he is a contemptible hypocrite. But it is not true as is alleged that he is an enemy to the power of the Executive.

Hamilton could already see what Henry Adams would observe with the benefit of hindsight. As president, Jefferson "could no more resist the temptation to stretch his powers than he could abstain from using his mind on any object merely because he might be drawn upon ground supposed to be dangerous."[26]

Nor, continued Hamilton (no doubt recalling Jefferson's handling of Genêt), was he zealot enough to do anything in pursuance of his principles which will contravene his popularity, or his interest. He is as likely as any man I know to temporize – to calculate what will be likely to promote his own reputation and advantage; and the probable result of such a temper is the preservation of systems, though originally opposed, which being once established, could not be overturned without danger to the person who did it.[27]

Hamilton advised the Federalists to seek assurances from Jefferson on four points: preservation of the fiscal system, adherence to neutrality, preservation and gradual increase of the navy, and continuance of Federalist appointments in office, except at the cabinet level. But most Federalists were no longer listening. To the odious Virginian, they preferred Burr.[28]

Arriving in the new capital of Washington, D.C., members of the House found that only the Senate wing of the Capitol building had been completed, obliging them to meet in temporary quarters known as "the Oven." The surrounding neighborhood, according to Albert Gallatin, consisted of "seven or eight boarding-houses, one tailor, one shoemaker, one printer, a washing-woman, a grocery shop, a pamphlets and stationery shop, a small dry-goods shop, and an oyster house." Between February 11 and 17, 1801, the congressmen conducted thirty-five ballots, each resulting in eight votes for Jefferson and six for Burr, with Maryland and Vermont deadlocked and voting for neither candidate. With sixteen states voting, it took nine votes to win. The key to the election turned out to be the role played by Bayard and a handful of small-state (Maryland, Delaware, and Vermont) Federalists. They had agreed among themselves to support Burr until it became clear that he could not win and then to allow a Jefferson victory rather than provoke a constitutional crisis. On the thirty-sixth ballot, Maryland, Vermont, Delaware, and South Carolina Federalists cast blank ballots, putting their states in the Jefferson column. Jefferson became president by a margin of ten states to four.[29]

The result could be seen as a moral victory for Hamilton, but had he actually contributed to it? The answer is perhaps and to a degree. Bayard wrote him afterward, "Your views in relation to the election, differed very little from my own, but I was obliged to yield to a torrent [of anti-Jefferson sentiment] which I perceived might be diverted, but could not be opposed." Bayard was no doubt familiar with the terms of the deal Hamilton had wished to make with Jefferson. In fact, though Jefferson would later deny it, before changing his vote Bayard had received assurances through Jefferson's friend, Congressman Samuel Smith of Maryland, similar to those Hamilton had proposed.[30]

But Bayard, as he recounted to things Hamilton, had also sought assurances from Burr. Burr's reaction had been puzzling. Though the Jeffersonians later insisted that the New Yorker had tried to steal the election, Burr had refused to betray Jefferson by making a deal with the Federalists. As several scholars have pointed out, Burr considered himself a gentleman and wished to be seen as a man of his word. At the same time, he was not about to admit that he did not want to be, or was not competent to be, president. At the critical juncture, the alleged Catiline was paralyzed by the conflicting demands of honor (which he knew some questioned) on one hand and ambition and self-esteem on the other. Bayard's conclusion was telling: "The means existed for electing Burr but they required his cooperation.... He will never have another chance of being President of the U.states and the little use he has made of the one which has occurred gives me but a humble opinion of the talents of an unprincipled man."[31]

Burr's behavior begs the obvious question: were there reasonable grounds for Hamilton's extraordinary hostility toward him? The answer is yes, but more than reason was involved. Burr's political abilities were far from ordinary. His extravagant lifestyle did leave him chronically in debt and liable to bribery. In 1799, Burr and John Church had fought a duel over Church's charge that Burr had taken a payoff from a New York land company. After shots were fired, Church apologized, but the fact remained that Burr had received a "loan" that he never repaid. It would have been difficult to reopen relations with France after Senate approval of the Convention of Môrtefontaine, but Burr might have taken the country (as Napoleon hoped) into the new League of Armed Neutrality, including Russia, Sweden, Denmark, and Prussia, thus putting the United States on a collision course with Britain. Above all, Burr's later involvement in a conspiracy to attack Mexico and perhaps to carve an independent state out of U.S. territory (he was acquitted of treason for lack of evidence) suggests that there *was* reason to consider him an adventurer and a rogue.[32]

Yet this does not quite explain why Hamilton could write in January 1801, "There is no circumstance which has occurred in the course of our political affairs that has given me so much pain as the idea that Mr. Burr might be elevated to the Presidency by the means of the Federalists." The pain was searing and acutely personal. It was simply intolerable that Burr, a man who, in his view, was not only dangerous and unprincipled but also whose achievements in public life paled in comparison to his own, might put his hands on the prize which Hamilton could no longer hope to obtain. Not only that, but if Federalist votes elected Burr, he would "become *in fact* the man of our party," the effective leader of the political formation Hamilton had done as much as anyone to create. In defeat, Hamilton saw the looming shape of a rival prince and moved with his remaining strength to block his path.[33]

"Nothing to Do but to Prophesy"

Thomas Jefferson was sworn in as the third president of the United States on March 4, 1801. John Adams became not only the first one-term president in

American history, but the first to refuse to attend his successor's inauguration. Albert Gallatin, Jefferson's treasury secretary-designate, wrote his wife on March 5, "Mr. Adams left the city yesterday at four o'clock in the morning. You can have no idea of the meanness, indecency, almost insanity, of his conduct, specially of late. But he is fallen and not dangerous. Let him be forgotten." And so for many years he was.[34]

For Hamilton, the arrival in power of the lesser evil was small compensation for the defeats he had endured since 1799. Jefferson, once in the White House, proved anything but grateful for his "help." One of his first acts as president was to direct Gallatin "to ransack the Treasury records in search of evidence of Hamilton's turpitude. The fact that Gallatin found none struck Jefferson not as proof of the innocence of the former Secretary of the Treasury but of his skill in concealing the evidence of his wrongdoing." When Hamilton sent Secretary of State James Madison a letter he had received containing the grave news of Spain's retrocession to France of the Louisiana Territory, Madison returned it without so much as a word of thanks. (The retrocession treaty, a key step in the execution of Napoleon's American strategy, had been signed in Madrid on October 1, 1800, one day after the Convention of Môrtefontaine.) Divided and demoralized, the Federalists were practically spent as a national force. Some, like Pickering, were pursuing the misguided project of northern secession from the rule of the south.[35]

Hamilton wrote to King, "Truly, My Dear Sir, the prospects of our Country are not brilliant. The mass is far from sound. At headquarters a most visionary theory presides." In reality, Jefferson, although he would abolish the hated excise, kept the navy and left the Bank of the United States, and a modified version of the sinking fund, in place. King, who retired from his London post in 1803 (Jefferson replaced him with James Monroe), observed of his friend:

Hamilton is at the head of his profession, and in the annual rect. of a handsome income. He lives wholly at his house 9. miles from town .... I don't perceive that he meddles or feels much concerning politics. He has formed very decided opinions of our System as well as of our administration, and as the one and the other has the voice of the country, he has nothing to do but to prophesy![36]

Prophesying had its own pitfalls. In March 1803, not long after Jefferson had sent Monroe to France to assist the U.S. minister, Robert Livingston, in trying to buy New Orleans and the Floridas, Hamilton wrote, "There is not the most remote probability that the ambitious and aggrandizing views of Bonaparte will commute the territory for money." Hamilton proposed taking New Orleans and the Floridas by force in cooperation with the British, and then negotiating. On April 30, however, France sold New Orleans and the entire Louisiana Territory (over eight hundred thousand square miles), though not much-coveted West Florida, to the United States for eleven million two hundred fifty thousand dollars, plus the assumption of French debts to U.S. citizens amounting to about three million five hundred thousand dollars. It could have been of little comfort to Hamilton that his long-standing recommendation of offensive action had been a perfectly reasonable one. Napoleon had abandoned his plan for an American empire centered in Saint Domingue and Louisiana only because yellow fever and an army of former slaves had inflicted heavy losses on a French expedition and because general war, allowing Britain to seize New Orleans, was about to resume. Jefferson acquired Louisiana not through any merit, or even any intent, of his own. It essentially fell onto his lap.[37]

Fortune, meanwhile, had another blow in store. On the evening of November 20, 1801, the eldest of the Hamiltons' seven children, high-spirited, nineteen-year-old Philip, and a friend had become involved in a shouting match with one George Eacker at the Park Theatre in New York. The youths, both recent graduates of Columbia, challenged Eacker, a Republican lawyer who had attacked Philip's father in a Fourth of July speech. The friend's duel ended without bloodshed, but Eacker fatally wounded Philip Hamilton at Powles Hook, New Jersey, on the afternoon of November 23. Hamilton, according to the testimony of another friend of Philip's, had told his son to hold his fire and allow his antagonist to shoot first. Robert Troup reported to King, "Never did I see a man so completely overwhelmed with grief as Hamilton has been. The scene I was present at, when Mrs. Hamilton came to see her son on his deathbed (he died about a mile outside the city) and when she met her husband and son in one room, beggars all description!" It was not long after Philip's death that Ames's portrait captured Hamilton's now-characteristic smile.[38]

* * *

Chapter 7 of *The Prince* recounts the story of the rise and fall of Cesare Borgia, the illegitimate son of Pope Alexander VI and Machiavelli's exemplary "new prince." On his personal flag, Borgia had emblazoned the motto, *Aut Caesar, aut nullus* – "Either Caesar, or nothing." Machiavelli had known Borgia personally, carefully observed him in action, and had been much taken for a time by his all-or-nothing boldness. In the final analysis, however, Machiavelli wrote that the younger man had "acquired and lost the state through the fortune of the father, even if he did everything a prudent and virtuous man must do to put down roots of his own."[39] In fact, Borgia's star fell almost as quickly as it had risen after his father's sudden death in August 1503. He tried to manipulate, but was eventually outmaneuvered and ruined by his father's successor, Pope Julius II. As a Florentine envoy, Machiavelli was on hand at the papal court to witness Borgia's last attempts to salvage his position. It was not a pretty sight. Machiavelli wrote, "One can see that his sins have brought him little by little to penance." "And so, inch by inch, the Duke [Borgia] slips into the tomb."[40]

Not surprisingly, the parallel between Borgia and Hamilton occurred to an implacable enemy, John Beckley, the Republican political operator and Jefferson protégé. Commenting on the publication of Hamilton's letter against Adams in late 1800, Beckley wrote, "Vainly does he essay to seize the mantle of Washington .... His career of ambition is passed .... As a political nullity, he has inflicted upon himself the sentence of '*Aut Caesar, aut Nullus.*'" Cruel and unflattering though it was, the comparison contained more than a grain of truth.[41]

From Fortune into Providence

Introduction

The last episode of Machiavelli's career coincided with the decisive show-down in the Franco-Spanish struggle for control of Italy, which had begun in 1494. In May 1521, Pope Leo X (Giovanni 'de Medici) had allied the papacy and Florence with the Emperor Charles V (he became king of Spain in 1516 and was elected Holy Roman Emperor in 1519). Charles had subsequently defeated the French, forcing them to evacuate the Duchy of Milan. The reversal of alliances had therefore paid dividends, but as fortune would have it, the pope died in December 1521. Clement VII (Giulio 'de Medici), indecisive and naive compared to the astute gambler Leo, made the fatal decision to return to Florence's traditional alliance with France. On February 24, 1525, Charles's forces had routed the French at Pavia, just south of Milan, capturing King Francis I on the field of battle. After years of a kind of semirehabilitation, Machiavelli was called into service by the Medicis to help to defend the city against the threatening armies of the emperor. In April 1526, Florence created a new magistracy to supervise the reinforcement of the city walls. Machiavelli was named its secretary and returned to the Palazzo Vecchio after an absence of fourteen years.

His return proved to be short-lived. In May 1526, France, Florence, Venice, and Pope Clement formed a new league to oppose Charles V and his Spanish and German armies. Despite the efforts of Machiavelli and his friend Francesco Guicciardini, lieutenant-general of Florentine troops, the alliance proved vacillating and ineffectual. In early May 1527, Imperial soldiers sacked Rome, forcing the feckless pope to flee to Orvieto. Italy's humiliation was complete. As in 1494, Medici authority collapsed, and the Florentine republic, with its Great Council, was restored. The final indignity of Machiavelli's life was that, though he was a sincere republican and had worked tirelessly to defend the honor of Florence and Italy, the new (as it transpired, short-lived) government looked on him as a Medici lackey. He died a few weeks later, apparently of peritonitis, on June 21, 1527. It is doubtful whether Machiavelli, as his grandson later claimed, was or became "a fit and devout and religious person" or whether, like Cesare Borgia, his sins brought him to penance in the end. But he confessed himself to a priest before dying and was buried in the church of Santa Croce in the center of Florence. One of his final compositions was a prayer, the "Exhortation to Penitence." There cannot be much doubt that he had taken to heart the words of the poet Petrarch with which the prayer ended: "worldly joy is just a fleeting dream."[1]

* * *

Hamilton's religious turn grew out of the worldly disappointments and personal tragedy that overwhelmed him in his final years. On the occasion of the death of his mother-in-law, he exhorted his wife, "Arm yourself with resignation. We live in a world full of evil. In the later period of life misfortunes seem to thicken round us; and our duty and our peace both require that we should accustom ourselves to meet disaster with christian fortitude." To James Bayard, he proposed the creation of a "Christian Constitutional Society," a network of clubs whose purpose would be to counter the Republicans' successful manipulation of popular passions. The project (which went nowhere) combined his long-standing belief in the political usefulness of piety with his newfound religious faith.[2]

In the spring of 1804, Hamilton advised a friend as follows:

Arraign not the dispensations of Providence – they must be founded in wisdom and goodness; and when they do not suit us, it must be because there is some fault in ourselves, which deserves chastisement, or because there is a kind intent to correct in us some vice or failing, of which, perhaps, we may not be conscious; or because the general plan requires that we should suffer partial ill.

In Machiavelli's humanist world, Christian Providence had been transmuted into the pagan Goddess of Fortune, whom the man of *virtù* could aspire to control. For most of his career, Hamilton had disdained Providence and grappled manfully with the fickle deity. In his final view of life, Fortune was transformed once again into Providence, from whose decrees there was no possibility of escape.[3]

The Interview at Weehawken

Shortly after seven o'clock in the morning on Wednesday, July 11, 1804, Hamilton and Burr faced each other on a narrow, tree-shaded ledge about twenty feet above the Hudson River, near Weehawken, New Jersey. They were accompanied by their seconds, Nathaniel Pendleton and William P. Van Ness, respectively, and by Hamilton's physician, Dr. David Hosack. The two men were separated by ten paces; each held a loaded smoothbore pistol in his right hand. Upon a signal, a shot rang out, followed a few seconds later by another. The .54-caliber ball fired from Burr's weapon tore a gaping hole in Hamilton's right side. Striking a rib, it passed through the liver and lodged in the second lumbar vertebra. Burr made a gesture as if to approach his stricken adversary, but Van Ness hustled him off to their waiting barge. Hamilton was rowed across the river to lower Manhattan and carried to the house of a friend. He remained there in agonizing pain, despite large doses of laudanum, until the following afternoon. Sometime after 1 P.M. on July 12, Hamilton repented his sins in the presence of Benjamin Moore, the Episcopal bishop of New York and president of Columbia College. According to Moore, Hamilton said, "I have no ill will against Col. Burr. I met him with a fixed resolution to do no harm. I forgive all that happened." At his request, and for the first time in his life, Hamilton received the Holy Communion. He died in the presence of members of his family and of the bishop at about 2 P.M.[4]

More than one mystery surrounds the "interview at Weehawken." In a "Statement on Impending Duel with Aaron Burr," written shortly beforehand, Hamilton avowed: "I have resolved . . . to *reserve* and *throw away* my first fire, and I *have thoughts* even of *reserving* my second fire – and thus giving a double opportunity to Col Burr to pause and reflect." If so, why then did Hamilton apparently try out a firearm before the duel and – at least according to Van Ness – put on a pair of glasses and practice aiming just before the signal to fire? Moreover, who fired the first shot? According to Pendleton, and most historians sympathetic to Hamilton, it was Burr; Hamilton fired in the air as the result of an involuntary reflex after being hit. According to Van Ness, however, Hamilton fired first and missed. After flinching, Burr coolly waited four or five seconds as the smoke cleared and then took his fatal shot.[5]

A recent, careful consideration of the case plausibly concludes that Hamilton did fire first, but probably with the intention of missing his antagonist. This interpretation takes seriously Pendleton's claim that he returned to the site the next day and discovered that Hamilton's ball had passed through the limb of a cedar tree well over Burr's head and four feet to his right. Unless one assumes that Hamilton lost his nerve and fired wildly, he had no intention of hitting Burr. Burr, ignorant of Hamilton's intentions, fired a few seconds later. Contrary to what was commonly assumed at the time, he may not have intended to kill Hamilton. According to the so-called *code duello*, vindicating one's honor did not require that one kill or be killed, and such affairs often ended with the parties unscathed or slightly wounded. Not only did Burr show concern for his wounded adversary, he had also remarked to Van Ness before the duel that Dr. Hosack "is enough, & even that unnecessary."[6]

Exactly what happened on July 11, 1804, will remain forever shrouded in uncertainty. The underlying causes of the Hamilton–Burr collision, however, are clear enough. The latest round in Hamilton's singular campaign against Burr, dating back until at least 1792, had occurred earlier in the year. The vice president, after being shunned by Jefferson and the Republicans, had tried to have himself elected governor of New York with Federalist support. Fearing that Burr aimed to become the leader of a Northern secession from the union, Hamilton urged New York Federalists to back a Republican candidate and renewed his attacks on the man of "talents intrigue and address."[7] Burr was soundly defeated in the gubernatorial race, his political career effectively at an end.

The 1804 episode, understandably, was the last straw for Aaron Burr. When a letter published in an Albany newspaper came to his attention after the election, he saw no choice but to call Hamilton to account. The author of the letter, one Charles D. Cooper, claimed to have heard Hamilton say during the campaign that he considered Burr "a dangerous man," adding, "I could detail to you a still more dispicable opinion which General HAMIL-TON has expressed of Mr. BURR." After the duel, Burr wrote to a friend, "It is too well known that Gen. H had long indulged himself in illiberal freedoms with my character." He claimed (though there is no confirming evidence) that Hamilton had twice come forth with apologies in the past. Burr had declined to challenge Hamilton, "always hoping that the generosity of my conduct would have some influence on him. In this I have been consistently deceived, and it became impossible that I could consistently with self-respect again forbear." On June 18, Burr threw down the gauntlet, demanding "a prompt and unqualified acknowledgement of the use of any expressions which could warrant the assertions of Dr Cooper."[8]

Hamilton had no wish to be drawn into a confrontation, but nor was he prepared to submit to disgrace. In fact, his reply to Burr ended on a note of defiance:

I stand ready to avow or disavow promptly and explicitly any precise or definite opinion, which I may be charged with having declared of any Gentleman. More than this cannot fitly be expected from me; and especially it cannot be reasonably expected, that I shall enter into an explanation upon a basis so vague as that which you have adopted. I trust, on more reflection, you will see the matter in the same light with me. If not, I can only regret the circumstance, and must abide with the consequences.

Burr, considering this letter evasive (and probably patronizing), answered with one which Hamilton found "rude and offensive." Burr now asked, in effect, for what Van Ness characterized at a later stage as "a general disavowal of any intention on the part of Genl Hamilton in his various conversations to convey impressions derogatory to the honor of Mr Burr." As Burr put it to Van Ness, "more will now be required than would have been asked [to settle without a fight] at first." Hamilton obviously could not comply.[9]

Hamilton's thoughts during the final days of his life emerge from his fascinating "Statement" on the impending duel. For a series of reasons, he was "certainly desirous" of avoiding it: "My religious and moral principles are strongly opposed to the practice of Duelling.... My Wife and Children are extremely dear to me, and my life is of the utmost importance to them, in various views ... I feel a sense of obligation to my creditors ... I am conscious of no *ill-will* to Col Burr, distinct from political opposition." And yet the duel "was, as I conceive, impossible for me to avoid it. There were *intrinsick* difficulties in the thing, and *artificial* embarrassments, from the manner of proceeding on the part of Col. Burr."[10]

By "intrinsic difficulties," Hamilton meant that he had indeed provoked Burr: "it is not to be denied, that my animadversions on the political principles character and views of Col Burr have been extremely severe." He and others had made "very unfavourable criticisms on particular instances of the private conduct of that Gentleman. In proportion as these impressions were entertained with sincerity and uttered with motives and for purposes, which might appear to me commendable, would be the difficulty ... of explanation or apology. The disavowal required of me by Col Burr, in a general and indefinite form, was out of my power." By "artificial embarrassments," Hamilton meant that he believed that it was improper for him to submit to be questioned in an open-ended manner by Burr. Moreover, Burr appeared to him "to assume, in the first instance, a tone unnecessarily preemptory and menacing, and in the second, positively offensive." Thus, apology or explanation was out of the question and Burr's manner had fatally complicated the affair.[11]

Hamilton had not changed his basic opinion of Burr. But the use of the qualifying words "in proportion as" suggests that he was aware that his own motives and conduct may not have been above reproach. He did not, he continued, wish "to affix any odium on the conduct of Col Burr, in this case." Burr had doubtless heard "animadversions of mine which bore very hard on him.... He may have supposed himself under a necessity of acting as he has done." The decision, wrote Hamilton, to reserve and throw away his fire arose directly from his "general principles and temper" with regard to duelling – the death of Philip must have weighed heavily on his mind – but also from a realization: "it is possible that I may have injured Col Burr." In other words, Hamilton was prepared to put his life on the line not only to preserve his honor, but because he knew he was partly in the wrong.

He made a final observation:

To those, who with me abhorring the practice of Duelling may think that I ought on no account to have added to the number of bad examples – I answer that my *relative* situation, as well in public as private aspects, enforcing all the considerations which constitute what men of the world denote honor, impressed on me (as I thought) a particular necessity not to decline the call. The ability to be in future useful, whether in resisting mischief or effecting good, in those crises of our public affairs, which seem likely to happen, would probably be inseparable from a conformity with public prejudice in this particular.[12]

Hamilton's death was eloquent of his life's commanding passions: to embody "what men of the world denote honor," and to be useful in preserving the union from internal and external peril. Facing his nemesis, his frame of mind was not self-destructive or vindictive but proud and penitent. Providence, in bringing him to the duel, had indicated that "there was some fault in ourselves, which deserves chastisement." Hamilton, in the end, was prepared to admit and to pay for his mistakes, something that cannot be said of Madison, Jefferson, Adams, or most of the other great men of the age.

Conclusion: Hamilton Then and Now

Hamilton's fundamental teaching for his time and posterity is that the United States is (one would have said, "are" in his day, reflecting the reality of disunion) in and of the old, continental European world of power politics. Geography and national character offer no escape from the inexorable decree of human nature. As Machiavelli put it, "the nature of men is ambitious and suspicious." It was Hamilton who wrote into Washington's Farewell Address, the Sermon on the Mount of American statecraft, an explicit presumption of the "love of power, and proneness to abuse it, which predominates in the human heart." In such a world, there is no choice but "to molest or be molested." To think otherwise, to place one's faith in Providence, "American exceptionalism," or some other product of human fancy, rather than one's own devices, is to lose one's liberty and to deserve to lose it. For Hamilton, as for Machiavelli, "It was the test of a good political order to grow, to expand and to absorb other political societies, even to ward off decline for a while."[1]

To pass the test, organized societies must choose leaders and design institutions capable of bringing to bear *virtù* – that bundle of qualities including steadfastness, adaptability, boldness, guile, and dexterity at arms – in their relations with the external world. Institutionalized *virtù* does not guarantee survival or mastery of *fortuna* (contingency), but without it there is no hope. From Girolamo Savonarola to Thomas Jefferson, the moral authority of the "unarmed prophet" has never sufficed to protect the state. Just as Machiavelli looked for inspiration to the quasi-miraculous rise of the Roman republic, Hamilton looked for lessons in the experience of the most dynamic and remarkable generator of *virtù* in his day, the Britain of the elder and younger Pitts. Given the provincialism, and distrust of power, of the majority of his adopted countrymen, Hamilton's program for creating a similar state in eighteenth-century America proved to be nearly as fabulous as Machiavelli's vision for early sixteenth-century Italy. As in all great creative projects, there was an element of almost childlike idealism and naiveté in its breathtaking reach and scale.

But the kernel of Hamilton's system, despite its vicissitudes, survived his political defeat in 1799–1800: the kind of basic financial infrastructure with its monetized national debt, secure federal revenues, and national bank, needed to promote economic development and to mobilize wealth for military purposes. Though the ideas were bitterly contested in his own day, Hamilton's legacy also includes the kind of minimum standing forces, peacetime cultivation of the military arts and sciences, and defense-industrial preparedness that would allow the United States not simply to survive, but to thrive, in war. It includes the kind of strong and assertive president (if not exactly the republican prince he favored) who set a key precedent in 1793 by declaring neutrality without consulting Congress and who has been able to act decisively and autonomously in the realm of foreign and military affairs. It includes the idea of the Union itself, which survived the trial of the Civil War – an event which would not have surprised Hamilton – thanks to the greatest of his disciples, Abraham Lincoln. Finally, his legacy includes the theory and practice of reason of state. Thanks partly to Hamilton's example, Machiavelli's teaching that the statesman must "learn to be able to be not good" in the defense of the polity, if not as American as apple pie, became as American as Hamilton himself.

To be sure, not only his enemies but Hamilton, harbored doubts on that very question. Near the end of his life, he observed to a man he called a fellow "exotic," Gouverneur Morris:

Mine is an odd destiny. Perhaps no man in the UStates has sacrificed or done more for the present Constitution than myself – and contrary to all my anticipations of its fate, as you know from the very beginning I am still labouring to prop the frail and worthless fabric. Yet I have the murmurs of its friends no less than the curses of its foes for my rewards. What can I do better than to withdraw from the Scene? Every day proves to me more and more that this American world was not made for me.[2]

Like the centaur Machiavelli evoked to describe the prince, and like Machiavelli himself, Hamilton was a hybrid: Part of him was thoroughly American, part belonged to another time and place. But even if his ambitions remained unfulfilled during his own lifetime, Hamilton is entitled to share with Washington the "double glory" of the new prince who gives rise to a new state, "adorning it and reinforcing it with good laws, good arms, and good examples." (By the same token, Machiavelli pointed out, a chief executive who inherits power and then proceeds to lose it deserves "double shame.")[3]

Strikingly, much of Hamilton's prolific foreign policy advice in the 1780s and 1790s belies the image of an aggrandizing Machiavellian preoccupied with the cultivation and projection of *virtù*. Many of his most characteristic axioms emphasize realism and self-restraint. He warned, for example, that "There can be no time, no state of things, in which credit is not essential to a nation." Like the so-called declinists of the late twentieth century, he reminds us of the permanent nexus between financial stability and national security. Or: "Not only the wealth: but the independence and security of a Country, appear to be materially connected with the prosperity of manufactures. Every nation...ought to...possess within itself all the essentials of national supply." The state, in other words, must promote the health of industry, especially defense-related industry, regardless of the dictates of the free market.[4]

Nothing could be more typical of Hamilton than the following observation: "Wars more often proceed from angry and perverse passions than from cool calculations of Interest." The statesman should always allow for the role of emotion, and especially of injured pride, in the behavior of potential adversaries. Or: "[M]ildness in the *manner* and *firmness* in the *thing* are most compatible with true dignity, and almost always go farther than harshness and stateliness." In the same spirit, Hamilton advised, "It is often wise by some early condescension to avoid the danger of future humiliation." Going more than halfway to settle disputes – appeasement of the other party – may be a way to buy time or to avoid needless and costly conflicts. Finally, Hamilton observed that "Evil is seldom as great, in the reality, as in the prospect." External threats often do not turn out to be as urgent and dreadful as they are thought to be, and one should avoid actions which fulfill one's own gloomy prophecies.[5] Running through these axioms is the assumption that a distinction must always be made between what the country *needs* to do to survive and what it might *want* to do in the world if it had the luxury to decide.

Hamilton's foreign policy in the 1790s, as has often been said in this book, was a policy of strength through peace, as well as peace through strength. The great achievement of Federalist diplomacy was to guarantee the fragile and hemmed-in republic's survival, to ensure that the "Hercules in the cradle" would not be strangled like the Florentine republic before it could develop its potential power.[6] War with Britain would have meant the destruction of American commerce, the collapse of public credit, a bloody and uncertain campaign to take the frontier posts, and perhaps the breakup of the country along sectional lines, as nearly occurred during the War of 1812. Under the circumstances of the 1790s, Hamilton helped to craft a definition of American neutrality that although it did not gain the (unenforceable) right to be allowed to supply Britain's enemies with impunity, secured the benefits of peace. That it was also a definition precluding cooperation with France and helpful to Britain was part of its appeal. Hamilton and his friends recognized well before their Jeffersonian rivals that preventing the rise of a European hegemony was a basic American interest. In effect, British power was the first line of defense against a continental colossus that harbored designs on the Mississippi Valley and threatened the territorial integrity of the United States. Hamilton's policy of peace with a pro-British bias was consolidated by the Jay treaty, which in turn helped to secure an equally vital interest, Spain's recognition of the U.S. borders laid down in 1783 and its opening of the Mississippi to American navigation.

Hamilton's basic philosophy, arguably, is as valid in the early twenty-first century, a time of finite resources and probably fleeting unipolarity, as it was two hundred years ago. In this reading, Hamilton becomes the patron of a robust, but also prudent, realist, and cautiously accommodationist approach to the world. But finally to grasp Hamilton, it is necessary to ask whether *he* would believe that his 1790s advice is appropriate for the United States today. A clue to the answer may lie in his observation: "A very powerful state may frequently hazard a high and haughty tone with good policy, but a weak State can scarcely ever do it without imprudence. The last is yet our character, though we are the embryo of a great empire."[7] When Hamilton and Washington spoke in the Farewell Address about taking advantage of America's "detached and distant situation," they were talking about conditions in 1796. Hamilton, at least, expected that as the country became stronger, and as distances grew shorter due to improvements in ocean transport, it would join the ranks of the world powers. One had only to look at what the British had achieved and at America's power base compared to theirs. Hamilton never spelled out exactly what he meant by an American "empire," but in addition to gradual absorption of the West, he presumably thought that the United States, by virtue of its commercial and naval power, would come to exercise hegemony (if not necessarily direct control) over other portions of the globe.

Now that the United States has brilliantly passed the test of a "good" political order and become (or so it is often claimed) the strongest power on earth since the Roman Empire, it seems appropriate to ask what Hamilton would have to say about the challenges that lie ahead. Should the United States, for example, systematically try to prevent the emergence of "peer rivals" even at the risk of exhausting itself in the process? It is conceivable that he might argue, in the spirit of his 1790s advice, that the United States should appease China by granting it naval supremacy on its own doorstep, just as the British prudently conceded U.S. naval supremacy in the Western Hemisphere one hundred years ago. He might argue that the United States should gracefully accept, even abet, the rise of a powerful united Europe, just as Britain accepted, more or less gracefully, the rise of a powerful United States. As someone who pointed out that there had been nearly as many popular as royal wars, Hamilton would probably argue that the notion of the "democratic peace," seen by liberals and conservatives alike as a pillar of U.S. global leadership, is in reality a slender reed. As someone who rejected permanent alliances not to pursue an illusory freedom of movement, but in favor of closer ties to Britain rather than France, and who insisted on the supremacy of treaties over domestic law, he would probably look on the doctrinaire defenders of American sovereignty in Washington today with amused contempt. As a statesman with the rare capacity to see his country through the eyes of an outsider, he would no doubt warn of the risks of deluding oneself, and of failing to fathom the impact of one's actions on others, in dealing with terrorism and the so-called rogue states of the world. As a student of history, and a witness to the formation of two coalitions dedicated to the curbing of France's ambitions, he might well point out the futility of plans for world dominion on the part of any state.

And yet it seems equally likely that Hamilton's geopolitical instincts, akin to those of British statesmen, would prompt him to oppose the emergence of a single power center on the European continent capable of challenging the United States. It would be in the spirit of his fatalistic vision of American greatness to argue that, of course, you have no choice but to keep allies and client states in line (lest they climb on someone else's bandwagon) and potential rivals down. As Pericles (whose name Hamilton once used as a pseudonym) told his fellow Athenians, "Your empire is now like a tyranny: it may have been wrong to take it; it is certainly dangerous to let it go." As an acute modern observer put it, "Great power status is lost, as it is won, by violence. A great power does not die in its bed." Hamilton's temperament was not distinguished by a sense of balance or *mesure*. And what little meliorism one detects in his view of international politics was based on his faith in American (or Anglo-American) economic and military might.[8] It was this confident, defiant, imperial side of Hamilton that captivated Theodore Roosevelt and his followers a century ago, in the heyday of Social Darwinism, and that appeals today to some of those who believe it is America's destiny to run the world. It is perfectly conceivable, finally, that the general who favored, nearly to the point of obsession, an impetuous, preemptive strategy to secure the homeland against what he considered the great threat of the late 1790s, who advised that adversaries should be either crushed or coddled, and who coveted the laurels that he and his party expected to win with a lightening victory, would favor a similar approach today.[9]

The basic, unanswered question at the heart of Hamilton's outlook is once you have succeeded in creating institutions and pursuing policies that generate the *virtù* necessary to survive, what is to prevent you at a later stage from overreaching yourself abroad and endangering liberty at home? Is it really possible to be rich and austere, powerful and moderate, imperial and republican at the same time?

The foreign policy legacy of Thomas Jefferson is fundamentally ambiguous because his message can be read to support the notion not only of America as passive exemplar of liberal values but also of America as crusader, with a mission to reform the world. It would be comforting to be able to conclude that Hamilton is different, that he leaves us with a clear set of prescriptions and that his legacy is the rightful property of one side or the other – either the prudent realists or the bold hegemonists – in the contemporary debate. But this is not the case. In the end, Hamilton's message, like Jefferson's, is ambiguous. One basic part of it, preoccupied with survival and consolidation, is prudence, solvency, and the creative role of the state. The other part, preoccupied with power and glory, is the "imperial temptation": the impulse to cut Gordian knots with military force and to eschew painstaking diplomacy, the tendency toward hubris, and the loss of self-control.[10] Hamilton's ideas and achievements entitle him to a sustained revival of interest in his life, a rank second to none in the national pantheon, even a monument of his own. But his career also counsels scepticism and vigilance toward those who invoke the prerogative "to be not good" in the name of national security, or who propose open-ended predominance as a compelling national goal.

It seems only fitting to ask how the Florentine himself might view contemporary America. The answer is undoubtedly with considerable admiration, tempered by a typical dose of wry skepticism. For one thing, the United States, though in many ways a prize pupil, cannot be said to have "a lean citizenry and a fat treasury" of the kind he would have preferred.[11] Machiavelli would probably remind those who compare the United States today to Rome that a basic premise of the republic's success in its dynamic phase was popular support and involvement – the plebes had their say through the tribunate, the army was a citizen army, and the people had a direct voice and a direct stake. He might point out that Rome never managed to bring under its control large parts of the known world, including the lands beyond the Rhine and the Danube, and the Parthian empire, corresponding roughly to present-day Iran. At the height of their power, the Romans suffered major military setbacks, losing three legions at the hands of German tribesmen in the Teutoburg Forest in 9 A.D. Finally, to those who contend that the United States enjoys the luxury of choosing war to satisfy its wants – as opposed to its needs – he would no doubt repeat his adage: "Because anyone can start a war when he wants to, but not finish it," a prince must have enough prudence not to deceive himself as to his strengths.[12] In sum, Machiavelli's message would be that fortune smiles on the well-situated, the enterprising, and the courageous but not on the overconfident, the reckless, and those who willfully ignore the past.

Notes

Introduction

1. Hamilton's statue, interestingly, is less visible to passersby than the one on the north side of the building dedicated to his longtime critic, Jefferson's treasury secretary Albert Gallatin.

2. See, among other works by these authors, Bowers, *Jefferson and Hamilton: The Struggle for Democracy in America* (Boston: Houghton Mifflin, 1925); Malone, *Jefferson and His Time* (6 vols.) (Boston: Little, Brown: 1948–81); Boyd (longtime editor of Jefferson's papers), *Number 7: Alexander Hamilton's Secret Attempts to Control American Foreign Policy* (Princeton: Princeton University Press, 1964); Peterson, *The Jefferson Image in the American Mind* (New York: Oxford University Press, 1960); Koch, *Jefferson and Madison: The Great Collaboration* (New York: Knopf, 1950). To help sort out Hamilton's changing "image in the American mind," I have consulted Stephen F. Knott's useful and long overdue study, *Alexander Hamilton & the Persistence of Myth* (Lawrence: University Press of Kansas, 2002).

3. See Rossiter, *Alexander Hamilton and the Constitution* (New York: Harcourt, Brace, and World, 1964); McDonald, *Alexander Hamilton: A Biography* (New York: Norton, 1979).

4. On President John Adams's view of Hamilton, see Chapters 16–20 of this book. Russell Kirk wrote, "Alexander Hamilton, the financier, the party-manager, the empire-builder, fascinates those numerous Americans among whom the acquisitive instinct is confounded with the conservative tendency, and they, in turn, have convinced the public that the 'first American businessman' was the first eminent American conservative." *The Conservative Mind from Burke to Santayana* (Chicago: Henry Regnery, 1953), 64–5. See also Charles Francis Adams, ed., *The Works of John Adams, with a Life of the Author* (Freeport, NY: Books for Libraries Press, 1969; first published, 1850–9) (hereafter Adams, *Works*, vol. no.). The historian Henry Adams's animosity toward Hamilton was such that when his friend Henry Cabot Lodge's biography of Hamilton appeared, Adams wrote him, "Much as I want to read your Hamilton, the subject repels me more than my regard for you attracts." See Knott, *Alexander Hamilton &*

nce of Myth, 73. See also, Manning J. Dauer, *The Adams Federalists* The Johns Hopkins University Press, 1953); Stephen G. Kurtz, *The of John Adams: The Collapse of Federalism* (Philadelphia: University *rania* Press, 1957); John Ferling, *John Adams: A Life* (Knoxville: University of Tennessee Press, 1996); David McCullough, *John Adams* (New York: Simon & Schuster, 2001). To this list could be added Richard H. Kohn, *Eagle and Sword: The Federalists and the Creation of the Military Establishment in America, 1783–1802* (New York: Free Press, 1975).

5. Recent critical treatments of Jefferson include Conor Cruise O'Brien, *The Long Affair: Thomas Jefferson and the French Revolution, 1785–1800* (Chicago: University of Chicago Press, 1996); Robert W. Tucker and David C. Hendrickson, *Empire of Liberty: The Statecraft of Thomas Jefferson* (New York: Oxford University Press, 1990); Joseph Ellis, *American Sphinx: The Character of Thomas Jefferson* (New York: Knopf, 1997); Pauline Maier, *American Scripture: Making the Declaration of Independence* (New York: Knopf, 1997); Anthony F. C. Wallace, *Jefferson and the Indians: The Tragic Fate of the First Americans* (Cambridge, MA: Belknap Press, 1999).

6. These include Morton J. Frisch, *Alexander Hamilton and the Political Order: An Interpretation of His Political Thought and Practice* (Lanham, MD: University Press of America, 1991); Harvey Flaumenhaft, *The Effective Republic: Administration and Constitution in the Thought of Alexander Hamilton* (Durham, NC: Duke University Press, 1992); John Steele Gordon, *Hamilton's Blessing: The Extraordinary Life and Times of Our National Debt* (New York: Penguin, 1997); Richard Brookhiser, *Alexander Hamilton: American* (New York: The Free Press, 1999); Karl-Friedrich Walling, *Republican Empire: Alexander Hamilton on War and Free Government* (Lawrence: University Press of Kansas, 1999). Walling, like several of the scholars in this group, of Straussian lineage, is concerned to establish that Hamilton was "foremost a modern liberal" (8) and to challenge Richard Kohn's argument that he was a militarist.

7. Not all the recent offerings are favorable to Hamilton, but see, for example, Michael Lind, ed., *Hamilton's Republic: Readings in the American Democratic Nationalist Tradition* (New York: The Free Press, 1997); Arnold A. Rogow, *A Fatal Friendship: Alexander Hamilton and Aaron Burr* (New York: Hill and Wang, 1998); Roger G. Kennedy, *Burr, Hamilton and Jefferson: A Study in Character* (New York: Oxford University Press, 1999); Thomas Fleming, *Duel: Alexander Hamilton, Aaron Burr, and the Future of America* (New York: Perseus Books, 1999); Stuart A. Kallen, *Alexander Hamilton* (Minneapolis: Abdo, 1999); James H. Read, *Power versus Liberty: Madison, Hamilton, Wilson, and Jefferson* (Charlottesville: University Press of Virginia, 2000); Joseph J. Ellis, *Founding Brothers: The Revolutionary Generation* (New York: Knopf, 2000); Knott, *Alexander Hamilton and the Persistence of Myth*; Lawrence S. Kaplan, *Alexander Hamilton: Ambivalent Anglophile* (Wilmington: Scholarly Resources, 2002); Willard Sterne Randall, *Alexander Hamilton: A Life* (New York: Harper, Collins, 2003).

8. The last full-length, narrative study devoted to Hamilton's foreign policy role to appear was Gilbert L. Lycan, *Alexander Hamilton and American Foreign Policy: A Design for Greatness* (Norman: University of Oklahoma Press, 1970).

9. Among those historians who tend to minimize the differences between the foreign policy objectives of Hamilton and Jefferson (see discussion below of the 1790 Nootka Sound crisis, and the 1793 controversy over American neutrality) are Lycan, *Alexander Hamilton and American Foreign Policy*; Ellis, *American Sphinx: The Character of Thomas Jefferson*; Stanley Elkins and Eric McKitrick, *The Age of Federalism: The Early American Republic, 1788–1800* (New York: Oxford University Press, 1993); Kaplan, *Alexander Hamilton: Ambivalent Anglophobe*. Kaplan writes, for example (162), that "in the vital area of foreign relations, the divisions between Jefferson and Hamilton were always more apparent than real."

10. Hamilton's birth date is still a matter of dispute. Hamilton himself, his family, and historians for many years said it was January 11, 1757. In the twentieth century a probate court document (relating to his mother's death) was found in the Danish archives indicating that he had been born on January 11, 1755. See H. U. Ramsing, "Alexander Hamilton og Hans Modrene Slaegt," *Personalhistorisk Tidsskrift*, 6ode Aargang, 10. R, 6 Bd., 3–4 H. (Copenhagen, 1939), 22570. See also Harold Larson, "Alexander Hamilton: The Fact and Fiction of His Early Years," *William and Mary Quarterly* 9 (April 1952): 139–51. Most modern biographers, for example, Broadus Mitchell, follow Ramsing and Larson, and accept 1755. Some, like Forrest McDonald (who perhaps wishes to emphasize Hamilton's precociousness), dispute the accuracy of the court document and stick with 1757. See Mitchell, *Alexander Hamilton: Youth to Maturity, 1755–1788* (New York: Macmillan, 1957), 12; McDonald, *Alexander Hamilton: A Biography*, 366, n. 8.

11. Jefferson quoted in Tucker and Hendrickson, *Empire of Liberty*, 82. On the Napoleon connection, see also Kaplan, *Alexander Hamilton: Ambivalent Anglophobe*, 6, 23.

12. This issue is further discussed in Chapter Two. The editions of Machiavelli's main works used in this book are: *Discorsi sopra la prima deca di Tito Livio* (Turin: Bollati Boringhieri, 1993) (in English, *Discourses on Livy*; hereafter cited as NM *Discorsi*); *Il Principe* (*The Prince*) (Turin: Bollati Boringhieri, 1992). All translations from the Italian are the author's. Machiavelli was born May 3, 1469; Napoleon, Aug. 15, 1769.

13. Isaiah Berlin, "A Special Supplement: The Question of Machiavelli," *The New York Review of Books*, Nov. 4, 1971 (http://www.nybooks.com/articles, 1–24). See also Leo Strauss, *Thoughts on Machiavelli* (Glencoe, IL: Free Press, 1958).

14. J. G. A. Pocock, *The Machiavellian Moment: Florentine Political Thought and the Atlantic Republican Tradition* (Princeton: Princeton University Press, 1975). Among the prominent works of Straussian inspiration are Paul Rahe, *Republics Ancient and Modern* (Chapel Hill: University of North Carolina Press, 1992), especially, 10–11, 34–41, 260–7, and Harvey C. Mansfield, *Machiavelli's Virtue* (Chicago: University of Chicago Press, 1998), especially, 258–80.

15. Berlin, "The Question of Machiavelli," 7. Berlin calls it a choice between the Christian and the "pagan," but Roman republican seems more to the point. For a similar argument, see Federico Chabod, *Scritti su Machiavelli* (Turin: Einaudi, 1993), 383–4.

16. See Pocock, *The Machiavellian Moment,* ix, Chapters 12–15. One cannot do justice in such a summary to the complexity and richness of Pocock's argument. Suffice it to say for now that I will emphasize a different Machiavelli than Pocock's inspirer of Country party ideology, namely a Machiavelli hostile to mercenary but not to permanent national military forces, favoring urban capitalist development rather than a land-based economy, and seeing a dynamic, expansionist foreign policy as necessary and unavoidable for the republic.

17. See Arnold Wolfers and Laurence W. Martin, eds. *The Anglo-American Tradition in Foreign Affairs: Readings from Thomas More to Woodrow Wilson* (New Haven: Yale University Press, 1956), xxi; Robert Kagan, "Power and Weakness," *Policy Review,* June–July 2002, 7; Henry Kissinger, *Diplomacy* (New York: Simon & Schuster, 1994); Francis Fukuyama, *The End of History and the Last Man* (New York: Free Press, 1992).

18. Walter Russell Mead, *Special Providence: American Foreign Policy and How It Changed the World* (New York: Knopf, 2001), 34–55, 77, 101, 103.

19. Even in light of Mead's disclaimers that he did not intend to write a conventional history of the Hamiltonian outlook, it is striking that his discussion of the subject contains no reference to Hamilton's own extensive writings, nor even (except for a passing mention of Henry Cabot Lodge's late-nineteenth-century biography) to the secondary literature on Hamilton. In effect Mead's is Hamiltonianism *sans* Hamilton. See *ibid.,* Chapter 4.

20. See Alexander Hamilton (hereafter, AH) to Henry Knox, March 14, 1799, in Harold C. Syrett and Jacob C. Cooke, eds., *The Papers of Alexander Hamilton* (New York: Columbia University Press, 1961–87) (hereafter *PAH*, vol. no.: page numbers), 22: 535; Felix Gilbert, "Machiavelli: The Renaissance of the Art of War," in Peter Paret, ed., *Makers of Modern Strategy: From Machiavelli to the Nuclear Age* (Princeton: Princeton University Press, 1986), 17. On Machiavelli as a passion-driven thinker, see also Chabod, *Scritti su Machiavelli,* 250.

21. Strauss, *Thoughts on Machiavelli* (Glencoe, IL: Free Press, 1958), 1. On God's authority, see Max Savelle, *Seeds of Liberty: The Genesis of the American Mind* (Westport, CT: Greenwood, 1981), 179 (first published 1948). On Adams and Machiavelli, see C. Bradley Thompson, "John Adams's Machiavellian Moment," *The Review of Politics* 1995, vol. 57, n. 3, 389–417. I say Machiavelli's presumed atheism because it is difficult to read Sebastian de Grazia's exhaustive, if not in the end convincing, study of Machiavelli's religious views without feeling some doubts about the conventional view of him as a strict nonbeliever and materialist. See *Machiavelli in Hell* (Princeton: Princeton University Press, 1989), esp. Chapter 3.

22. Walling, *Republican Empire,* 302, n. 38 (emphasis added). He adds, however, "In all probability, Hamilton's debt to Machiavelli is indirect, through the teachings of Locke, Hume, Montesquieu, and other modern theorists, who [Harvey] Mansfield demonstrates, owed enormous debts to Machiavelli." *Ibid.* See also, Paul Rahe, "Thomas Jefferson's Machiavellian Political Science," in *The Review of Politics* 1995, vol. 57, n. 3, 451. Several major studies have noted in passing the similarities between Machiavelli and Hamilton. These include John C. Miller, *Alexander Hamilton: Portrait in Paradox* (New York: Harper Bros., 1959); Gerald Stourzh, *Alexander Hamilton and the Idea of Republican Government* (Stanford: Stanford University Press, 1970); and Lance Banning, *The*

Sacred Fire of Liberty: James Madison and the Founding of the Federal Republic (Ithaca: Cornell University Press, 1995). Banning observes (310), for example, "A Hobbesian or Machiavellian in his conception of the world, the secretary [Hamilton] faced toward the Atlantic and envisioned an arena of competing empires into which America must enter much like any other state."

Of all those positing a Machiavelli–Hamilton link, Walling is the most systematic and penetrating, and I would like to acknowledge my debt to his important book. This is not to say that I agree with his uniformly favorable assessment of Hamilton, and I find his treatment of Machiavelli and of the Hamilton–Machiavelli connection at times inconsistent. Walling writes (15–16), "The essential yet paradoxical truth is that Hamilton was much more like Machiavelli than commonly believed and was at the same time fundamentally opposed to the kind of politics that we usually call Machiavellian. Following Machiavelli, Hamilton believed there was no viable alternative to transforming the United States into a great empire; unlike Machiavelli he meant to found the American empire by means of consent rather than through the force and the fraud that the former assumed were the only effectual foundations of political authority in his efforts to found the world's first republican empire." But he also writes (125), "As both Hamilton and Machiavelli knew quite well, innovation is no less necessary to a republic's survival than stability. For both men, the great task for republics was to change according to the predictable necessities and unpredictable fortunes of war while preserving the principles of consent and the rule of law that kept a republic free."

Chapter 1

1. In addition to Florence, the main political subdivisions of Italy around 1500 were the Duchy of Milan, the Venetian Republic, the Kingdom of Naples, and the Papal domains. The Franco-Spanish struggle did not really end until the Treaty of Cateau-Cambrésis in 1559, but the Spanish were in effective control of Naples and Milan by the end of the 1520s. The Medicis had preserved the appearances of Florence's traditional republic but had ensured that key office holders were friends or clients of the family.

2. On Machiavelli's family, see Roberto Ridolfi, *The Life of Niccolò Machiavelli* (Chicago: University of Chicago Press, 1963), 2–4; Felix Gilbert, "Machiavelli: The Renaissance of the Art of War," in Paret, ed., *Makers of Modern Strategy: From Machiavelli to the Nuclear Age*, 16; Maurizio Viroli, *Niccolò's Smile: A Biography of Machiavelli* (New York: Farrar, Straus and Giroux, 2000), 6, 108. De Grazia presents evidence that Bernardo Machiavelli was a natural child, though legitimated on his father's deathbed. See de Grazia, *Machiavelli in Hell*, 5.

3. NM, *Discorsi*, Book I, Chapter 6: 50. On "passions," see Machiavelli's essay "Del Modo di Trattare I Popoli Della Valdichiana Ribellati" ("On The Way To Treat The Rebellious Peoples of The Valdichiana") (1503) in Corrado Vivanti, ed., *Opere* (Torino: Einaudi-Gallimard, 1997), 1: 24. See also NM, *Discorsi*, III, 43: 155. Machiavelli completed the bulk of this work after 1513.

4. NM, *Discorsi*, I, 29: 122; I, 37: 146.

5. NM, *Il Principe*, 25: 133–6. He made a similar point in the *Discorsi*, II, 30: 356–9. On *fortuna* see Chabod, *Scritti su Machiavelli*, 62.

6. Felix Gilbert, *Machiavelli and Guicciardini* (New York: Norton, 1984), 179; Mansfield, *Machiavelli's Virtue*, 8, 19, 26, 31, 36, 40–1, 212. (One should note the double sense of Mansfield's title.) See also Pocock, *The Machiavellian Moment*, 37, 167.

7. On the link between necessity and *virtù*, see Mansfield, *Machiavelli's Virtue*, 14–16. NM, *Discorsi*, II, 12: 275; I, 2: 28.

8. See Fred Anderson, *Crucible of War: The Seven Year's War and the Fate of Empire in British North America, 1754–1766* (New York: Vintage, 2000), 315. After Spain entered the war in 1762, Britain seized and plundered Havana.

9. For family history, see Mitchell, *Alexander Hamilton: Youth to Maturity*, Chapter 1; Allan McLane Hamilton, *The Intimate Life of Alexander Hamilton* (New York: Scribner's, 1910), 6–19; McDonald, *Alexander Hamilton: A Biography*, Chapter 1.

10. For Hamilton on human nature, see "Federalist No. 6," in Alexander Hamilton, James Madison, John Jay, *The Federalist Papers* (New York: Bantam, 1982), 22.

11. McDonald, *Alexander Hamilton: A Biography*, Chapter 1. On the hurricane, see the AH letter to the *Royal Danish American Gazette*, St. Croix, Sept. 6, 1772, *PAH*, 1: 36–7. See also Douglass Adair and Marvin Harvey, "Was Alexander Hamilton a Christian Statesman?" *William and Mary Quarterly* (April 1955), 308–29. The answer given in this unsympathetic, but on this point convincing, treatment of Hamilton's career is no, until political defeat and the death of his eldest son prompted a conversion around 1801. Convention anecdote reported in Miller, *Alexander Hamilton: Portrait in Paradox*, 175; Joseph Ellis, "The Big Man: History vs. Alexander Hamilton," *The New Yorker*, Oct. 29, 2001. It should be said that at least one historian dismissed this story as "palpable nonsense." See Catherine Drinker Bowen, *Miracle at Philadelphia: The Story of the Constitutional Convention, May to September, 1787* (Boston: Little, Brown, 1966), 127.

12. Quentin Skinner, *Machiavelli* (New York: Hill and Wang, 1981), 25–7.

13. James Thomas Flexner, *The Young Hamilton: A Biography* (New York: Fordham University Press, 1997) (first published in 1978), 4, 26–7. For a similar view, see Robert Hendrickson, *Hamilton I (1757–1789)* (New York: Mason Charter, 1976), Jacob E. Cooke, *Alexander Hamilton* (New York: Charles Scribner's Sons, 1982), 2–3, and Arnold A. Rogow, *A Fatal Friendship: Alexander Hamilton and Aaron Burr*, Chapter 1. AH to John Laurens, Apr. 1779, *PAH*, 2: 35; AH to William Jackson, Aug. 26, 1800, *PAH*, 25: 88–90.

14. McDonald convincingly disputes Flexner's view of Rachel Faucett's character and role. See McDonald, *Alexander Hamilton: A Biography*, 366–7, n. 8. Mitchell, *Alexander Hamilton: Youth to Maturity*, 7, 17, 28.

15. Flexner and Hendrickson suggest that Rachel abandoned James; McDonald the reverse. For observation, see AH, "A Full Vindication," Dec. 15, 1774, *PAH*, 1: 75. See also AH to William Jackson, cited note 13. In this letter Hamilton refers to the "marriage" of his parents, but also says that it was not "lawful" because of the nature of his mother's divorce. Hamilton's 1774 remark about the law might also refer to the fact that his mother's (albeit modest) estate was

inherited by her legitimate son, Peter Lavien, leaving Alexander and his brother, James Hamilton, Jr., with nothing.

16. In his letter to Jackson (cited note 13) AH said of his birth: "On this point as on most others which concern me, there is much mistake – though I am pained by the consciousness that it is not free from blemish." See also John Adams to Thomas Jefferson, July 12, 1813, in Lester J. Cappon, ed., *The Adams–Jefferson Correspondence: The Complete Correspondence between Thomas Jefferson and Abigail and John Adams* (Chapel Hill: University of North Carolina Press, 1959), 354. NM, *Il Principe*, 24: 131.

17. On James Hamilton's character, see Allan McLane Hamilton, *The Intimate Life of Alexander Hamilton*, 13. AH to his brother James, June 22, 1785, *PAH*, 3: 617–18. He added, "Should he be alive inform him of my inquiries, beg him to write to me, and tell him how ready I shall be to devote myself and all I have to his accommodation and happiness." See also AH to Jackson, cited note 13; McDonald, 7.

18. On Ann Lytton Mitchell's help, see *PAH*, 20: 456, n. 1. See also AH to Elizabeth Hamilton, July 10, 1804 (the day before AH's duel with Aaron Burr), *ibid*. 26: 307. In this letter AH called Ann Lytton Mitchell "the person in the world to whom as a friend I am under the greatest Obligations." Flexner, in *The Young Hamilton*, eager to show the coolness of AH's relations with his mother and her family, writes, "His mother's rich relations were neither generously disposed nor stable." As regards ALM, this is an obvious error.

    See also Mitchell, *Alexander Hamilton: Youth to Maturity*, 33, 44, 72–3. On the uncertainty surrounding the date of AH's departure from St. Croix, see Larson, "Alexander Hamilton," 149–50. On "principles" see AH to his Scottish uncle William Hamilton, May 2, 1797, *PAH*, 21: 77. See also AH, "A Full Vindication of the Measures of the Congress," Dec. 15, 1774, *PAH*, 1: 105.

19. On "joy," see Thaddeus Maccarty, quoted in Gordon S. Wood, *The Creation of the American Republic, 1776–1787* (Chapel Hill: The University of North Carolina Press, 1969), 102. See also ibid., 79–80. AH later wrote, "The present law of inheritance making an equal division among the children, of the parents['] property, will soon melt down those great estates, which if they continued, might favour the power of the *few*." AH, "Second Letter From Phocion," Apr. 1784, *PAH*, 1: 553.

20. The conventional view, for which there is very little evidence, is that the College of New Jersey rejected Hamilton's request that he be allowed to pursue an accelerated course of study. Flexner points out that Hamilton was very well connected through his New Jersey friends and that exceptions to the rules were made for others, for example, James Madison. Flexner, *The Young Hamilton*, 56, 58, 63, 80.

21. On the eighteenth-century idea of "character," see Gordon S. Wood, *The Radicalism of the American Revolution* (New York: Vintage, 1991), 39–40; Joanne B. Freeman, *Affairs of Honor: National Politics in the New Republic* (New Haven: Yale University Press, 2001), xx; Elkins and McKitrick, *The Age of Federalism*, 37; Flexner, *The Young Hamilton*, 22. For mention of his father as a "gentleman" and of his own "Character," see AH to Edward Stevens, Nov. 7, 1769, *PAH*, 1: 4; AH to Jackson, cited note 13.

22. On ancestry, see *ibid.*
23. AH to Edward Stevens, Nov. 11, 1769, *PAH*, 1: 4. NM, *Il Principe*, 14: 88.
24. Gilbert, "Machiavelli: The Renaissance of the Art of War," in Paret, ed., *Makers of Modern Strategy*, 17.
25. Skinner, *Machiavelli*, 7.
26. To complicate matters, Pisa was opportunistically supported by Venice, who attacked Florentine territory from the northeast. On these events, see Ridolfi, *The Life of Niccolò Machiavelli*, Chapters 3–4; Viroli, *Niccolò's Smile: A Biography of Machiavelli*, 20–4, 39–40, 42–3, 52, 123–4. The Florentine florin, containing fifty grains of fine gold, was in circulation throughout Europe.
27. Skinner, *Machiavelli*, 7–8. On French character, see NM, *Discorsi*, III, 43: 529. See also II, 15: 283. On the pitfalls of seeking outside help see III, 26: 479. On citizen as opposed to mercenary forces, see NM, *Il Principe*, 12: 78–83, and numerous passages of the *Discourses*.
28. Washington to AH, Sept. 1, 1796, *PAH*, 20: 311. On AH's national outlook, see Saul K. Padover, ed., *The Mind of Alexander Hamilton* (New York: Harper's, 1958), 9, 27. For a different view, stressing the self-interest of conservatives in creating a national government that would control the western lands and pay off creditors, see Merrill Jensen, "The Idea of a National Government during the American Revolution," *Political Science Quarterly* 58 (1943), 356–79.
29. Mitchell, *Alexander Hamilton: Youth to Maturity*, 94; Flexner, *The Young Hamilton*, 134–5. The Hamilton–Washington personal relationship is discussed in Chapter 3.
30. AH to George Clinton, Feb. 13, 1778, *PAH*, 1: 425–8; AH to Duane, Sept. 3, 1780, *ibid.*, 2: 400–18; AH, "The Federalist No. 15," in AH et al., 69.
31. My use of the expression should not be confused with that of J. G. A. Pocock in his *The Machiavellian Moment*. Hamilton's grandson observed, "He undoubtedly possessed that form of nervous instability common to many active public men and characterized by varying moods, which was sometimes expressed by alternating depression on one hand and gayety on the other." Allan McLane Hamilton, *The Intimate Life of Alexander Hamilton*, 43.
32. AH to Lt. Col. John Laurens, Jan. 8, 1780, *PAH*, 2: 255. He told his fiancée: "I was once determined to let my existence and American liberty end together." AH to Elizabeth Schuyler, Sept. 6, 1780, *ibid.*, 2: 423. He added, "My Betsey has given me a motive to outlive my pride."
33. See Pay Book notes from Plutarch's *Lives*, also from Malachy Postlethwayt's *The Universal Dictionary of Trade and Commerce*, *PAH*, 1: 373–411. On the Enlightenment view of human nature see, R. G. Collingwood, *The Idea of History* (New York: Oxford, 1946), 82. See also McDonald, *Alexander Hamilton: A Biography*, 36–9. AH quotes Hume's essay, "Of the Independency of Parliament," in "The Farmer Refuted," *PAH*, 1: 95. On venality and rectitude, see "The Federalist No. 76," in AH et al., 387. In "The Federalist No. 72," AH spoke of "the love of fame, the ruling passion of the noblest minds." *ibid.*, 367. In "The Federalist No. 85" he called Hume "a writer, equally solid and ingenious." *Ibid.*, 449.
34. NM, *Discorsi*, I, 3: 35. See also *ibid.*, I, 9–10, on lawgivers. Skinner, *Machiavelli*, 30.

35. NM, *Discorsi*, I, 4: 37–40; I, 58: 214–15. See also I, 6: 50; II, *proemio*, 223; II, 2: 233; II, 19: 309.

36. AH, "The Farmer Refuted," Feb. 23, 1775, *PAH*, 1: 99, 129–30. This pamphlet was a reply to one written by the New York Loyalist spokesman Samuel Seabury, alias "the Westchester Farmer."

37. On the evolution of the federative idea and the colonial position from 1774 to 1775, see Savelle, *Seeds of Liberty*, 338–42; Wood, *The Creation of the American Republic*, 270–1; 352–3. Franklin had written that "America, an immense territory, favoured by Nature with all advantages of climate, soil, great navigable rivers, and lakes, must become a great country, populous and mighty" and that the "foundations of the future grandeur and stability of the British Empire" lay in the colonies. Quoted in James Hutson, "Intellectual Foundations of Early American Diplomacy," *Diplomatic History* 1 (Winter 1977), 10–11. Adams quoted in *ibid.*, 15.

38. AH, "The Farmer Refuted," Feb. 23, 1775, *PAH*, 1: 155–64. See also Lycan, *Alexander Hamilton and American Foreign Policy*, 47.

39. AH to George Clinton, June 1, 1783, *PAH*, 3: 370. AH was advising Governor Clinton that American obligations under the peace treaty to restore Loyalist rights and property must be fully carried out. If not, the British would have a pretext to violate the treaty by continuing to occupy the frontier posts that controlled the St. Lawrence River valley and the fur trade of the west.

40. The words quoted are Lodge's, used approvingly by Rossiter in *Alexander Hamilton and the Constitution*, 15. Samuel Flagg Bemis, *Jay's Treaty: A Study in Commerce and Diplomacy* (New Haven: Yale University Press, 1962) (first published in 1923), 190. Charles Ritcheson, *Aftermath of Revolution: British Policy toward the United States, 1783–1795* (Dallas: Southern Methodist University Press), 109, echoes Bemis's judgment: "It was not Anglophilia or 'monarchomania'... which caused Hamilton and his friends to struggle so desperately to preserve amity with Britain; it was the acknowledgement of Britain's preponderant role in America's trade and, hence, in furnishing the federal government with the revenues which were the means of life." For a similar view see McDonald, *Alexander Hamilton: A Biography*; Lycan, *Alexander Hamilton and American Foreign Policy*; Helen Vivian Johnson, "Alexander Hamilton and the British Orientation of American Foreign Policy, 1783–1803," Ph.D. dissertation, University of Southern California, 1963; and most recently, Kaplan, *Alexander Hamilton: Ambivalent Anglophobe*, 18, 71, 80, 82, 85, 90–3.

    I am closer to the position of Stanley Elkins and Eric McKitrick, who argue that an Anglophile "predilection was organic to Hamilton's entire experience and temperament." Russell Kirk wrote: "All his revolutionary ardour notwithstanding, Hamilton loved English society as an English colonial adores it." He should have said a Scottish-Huguenot colonial, but he was basically on the mark. Elkins and McKitrick, *The Age of Federalism*, 128; Kirk, *The Conservative Mind*, 67.

    A leading critical historian who stresses AH's Anglophilia is Julian Boyd, *Number 7: Alexander Hamilton's Secret Attempts to Control American Foreign Policy*. On France's and Spain's support of American independence, AH wrote: "In this their calculations and their passions conspired." *PAH*, 7: 44.

41. Thomas Jefferson referred to England as "the harlot" in a famous letter to his Italian friend Philip Mazzei, Apr. 24, 1796, quoted in Elkins and McKitrick, *The Age of Federalism*, 869, n. 82.

42. AH speech to the Philadelphia Convention, June 18, 1787 (from James Madison notes), *PAH*, 4: 192. On "Country versus Court," see Elkins and McKitrick, *The Age of Federalism*, Introduction, who rely, in turn, on Lance Banning, *The Jefferson Persuasion: Evolution of a Party Ideology* (Ithaca, NY: Cornell University Press, 1978). The classic exposition of the influence of the English opposition mentality on the American revolutionaries is Bernard Bailyn, *The Ideological Origins of the American Revolution* (Cambridge, MA.: Harvard University Press, 1967). Pocock, *The Machiavellian Moment*, 425.

43. Greene to AH, Jan. 10, 1781, *PAH*, 2: 532; AH to Robert Morris, proposing the creation of a national bank, Apr. 30, 1781, *ibid.*, 2: 635.

44. On AH's dislike of Catholicism, see AH, "Remarks on the Quebec Bill," parts one and two, *PAH*, 1: 165–76. Talleyrand quoted in Allan McLane Hamilton, *The Intimate Life of Alexander Hamilton*, 255. On Vergennes and Beaumarchais, see Samuel Flagg Bemis, *The Diplomacy of the American Revolution* (Bloomington: Indiana University Press, 1957), Chapter 2. The king of France approved of the sum of one million *livres* in military aid to America in May 1776, even before an American delegation had arrived in France to ask for money.

45. Flexner, *The Young Hamilton*, 158. AH to Laurens, May 22, 1779, *PAH*, 2: 53; AH to Laurens, Feb. 4, 1781, *ibid.*, 26: 407.

46. On close Franco-American ties, see AH to the Vicomte de Noailles, Apr. 4, May 18, May 24, 1782, *PAH*, 26: 424–8. On Shelburne's offer, see AH to GW, Mar. 17, 1783, *PAH*, 3: 291.

47. On pro-French party, see AH, "Letter From Alexander Hamilton, Concerning the Public Conduct and Character of John Adams, Esq. President of the United States," Oct. 24, 1800, *PAH*, 25: 188.

Chapter 2

1. For description of Elizabeth by Hamilton's fellow aide-de-camp Tench Tilghman, see Flexner, *The Young Hamilton*, 277. She was born August 9, 1757.

2. On AH's preparation for the bar, see Julius Goebel, Jr., ed., *The Law Practice of Alexander Hamilton, Documents and Commentary* (New York: Columbia University Press, 1964), 1: 47–54.

3. Emmerich de Vattel, *The Law of Nations; or Principles of the Law of Nature, Applied to The Conduct And Affairs of Nations and Sovereigns* (London: S. Sweet, Stevens & Sons, A. Maxwell, 1834), lxii. AH used a 1760 English edition. For examples of his citations of Vattel, see *PAH*, 3: 492; and 4: 132. On AH and Vattel, see also McDonald, *Alexander Hamilton*, 52–6, though he emphasizes different features than those discussed here.

4. Vattel, *The Law of Nations*, lx. See also Andrew Linklater, *Men and Citizens in the Theory of International Relations* (London: Macmillan, 1990), 81–2.

5. AH, *The Farmer Refuted* (Feb. 1775), *PAH*, 1: 88, 122.
6. AH speech to the Philadelphia Convention, June 18, 1787, *PAH*, 4: 185. Vattel, *The Law of Nations*, lxi (emphasis in original). Vattel (195–98) says that treaties give rise to a "perfect obligation" and therefore a "perfect right" to compel adherence. But treaties that are "pernicious" (or judged to be) are null and void, while countries are excepted from duties whose performance would do harm to themselves. On the importance of Vattel to eighteenth-century American thought see Daniel George Lang, *Foreign Policy in the Early Republic: The Law of Nations and the Balance of Power* (Baton Rouge: Louisiana State University Press, 1985). See also Stourzh, *Alexander Hamilton and the Idea of Republican Government*, 134.
7. Vattel, *The Law of Nations*, 5, 6, 34, 37, 199–200, 311, 313.
8. The school's members included Gatien de Courtilz, Jean Rousset de Missy, Jean-Louis Favier, and Charles de Peyssonel. Felix Gilbert, *To the Farewell Address: Ideas of Early American Foreign Policy* (Princeton: Princeton University Press, 1961), 162–3. According to Gilbert (111), a list of AH's readings for 1778 indicates his acquaintance with works from the school. He provides no citation, however, and the names of the above-mentioned authors discussed by Gilbert do not appear in Hamilton's published papers. On this subject see also Friedrich Meinecke, *Machiavellianism: The Doctrine of Raison d'Etat and Its Place in Modern History* (New Haven: Yale University Press, 1962), Chapters 6, 10, 11, and 12.
9. Quotations from Frederick's political testament of 1768, in Meinecke, *Machiavellianism*, 303, and 315, respectively. On Frederick's writings, see Allan McLane Hamilton, *The Intimate Life of Alexander Hamilton*, 74.
10. On Christianity, see NM, *Discorsi*, I, 12: 76 and II, 2: 235. On NM's hostile, cynical view of Savonarola, see Chabod, *Scritti su Machiavelli*, 268–73. See also NM, *Il Principe*, 6: 51–51. On "being able to be not good," see *ibid.*, 15: 91–3. See also *ibid.*, 18: 104, where NM advises the prince "not to depart from good, if able, but to know how to enter evil, if necessitated." His verse on Soderini is quoted in Ridolfi, *The Life of Niccolò Machiavelli*, 203. Sebastian de Grazia, intent on demonstrating NM's Christian beliefs, glosses over his rejection of the very crux of Christian teaching, namely "turn the other cheek" and the "weak shall inherit the earth."
11. NM, *Discorsi*, I, *Proemio*, 19; I, 1: 24–6. See also I, 6: 50.
12. *Ibid.*, 58: 214–16. De Grazia makes the acute observation (240): "A staunch republican, he is convinced that the times require extraordinary measures taken by one man alone. His republicanism has no theoretical problem accommodating one-generation, one-alone leadership if it will lend life to the republic." For a similar point, see Chabod, *Scritti su Machiavelli*, 217.
13. On the "*Prince* versus *Discourses*" issue, see Mansfield, *Machiavelli's Virtue*, Chapter 1, esp. 23, 42, and 51; Gilbert, *Machiavelli and Guicciardini*, 188; Ridolfi, *The Life of Niccolò Machiavelli*, Chapter 14. It is now accepted that Machiavelli began the *Discourses* during his time of enforced leisure after 1512 (or possibly before in the form of notes taken on his father's copy of Livy), interrupted the project in 1513 to write *The Prince*, and then returned to them. On the issue of leadership, NM also wrote that "it is better to send on an

expedition a single man of ordinary ability than two excellent men together with the same authority." *Discorsi*, III, 15: 444–5. See also *ibid.*, II, 33: 266–7. On the Roman method of expansion, see William J. Connell, "Machiavelli on Growth as an End," in Anthony Grafton and J. H. M. Salomon, eds., *Historians and Ideologues: Essays in Honor of Donald R. Kelley* (Rochester: University of Rochester Press, 2001).

14. NM, *Il Principe*, 26: 137. See Skinner, *Machiavelli* (8) as well as the editors of the critical edition of Machiavelli used in this book (Gian Mario Anselmi and Carlo Varotti). See also Gilbert, *Machiavelli and Guicciardini*, 183; NM, *Discorsi*, I, 12: 77; Ridolfi, *The Life of Niccolò Machiavelli*, 149. With the death of Julius II, Cardinal Giovanni de' Medici became pope with the name of Leo X in March 1513. Chabod argues that Machiavelli favored "not total unification... nor even a confederation," but a new state based in central Italy able to dominate the rest of the peninsula and expel the French and Spanish. It was the apparent opportunity to create such a state in 1513 which prompted him to suspend work on *The Discourses* and to write *The Prince* during the second half of that year. See *Scritti su Machiavelli*, 64–7, 211.

15. Naturally, there was no supreme court to hold local and state laws accountable to national standards – there being no national constitution. Congress, a creature of the states, was supposed to be "the last resort on appeal" in disputes arising among the states (Article IX).

16. AH to Robert Morris, April 30, 1781, *PAH*, 2: 635.

17. AH to James Duane, Sept. 3, 1780, *ibid.*, 2: 403; AH, "The Continentalist No. III," Aug. 9, 1781, *ibid.*, 2: 660; AH, "The Federalist No. 6," in AH et al., 26. On this same theme, see "The Federalist No. 16," *ibid.*, 75–6.

18. Montesquieu, quoted in Stourzh, *Alexander Hamilton and the Idea of Republican Government*, 148; Thomas Paine, *Common Sense and Other Political Writings* (New York: The Liberal Arts Press, 1953), 10 ("Common Sense" was first published in Jan. 1776, in Philadelphia).

19. See AH, "The Federalist No. 6," in AH et al., 24–6; "The Federalist No. 7," *ibid.*, 27–32; "The Federalist No. 8," *ibid.*, 32–32.

20. On America as "foot ball" see AH and William Floyd to George Clinton, Mar. 24, 1783, in *PAH*, 3: 303; "The Federalist No. 7," in AH et al., 33. For the Greek analogy, see "The Federalist No. 18" (written together with Madison), *ibid.*, 88. AH, "The Federalist No. 15," AH et al., 68.

21. AH to GW, Feb. 13, 1783, *PAH*, 3: 253–5. See also, Flexner, *The Young Hamilton*, 392–409.

22. Kohn, *Eagle and Sword*, Chapter 2. Walling criticizes Kohn's account but himself speaks of Hamilton's "ambiguous role," concluding: "Hamilton went to the brink of disloyalty to produce an illusion he believed might help save the Union, but his words reveal that he was unwilling to sacrifice the goals of the Revolution to the means of preserving the Confederation." Walling, *Republican Empire*, 60 and 64.

23. GW to AH, Mar. 4, 1783, *PAH*, 3: 277–9; AH to GW, Mar. 25, 1783, *ibid.*, 3: 305–6; AH to GW, Mar. 17, 1783, *ibid.*, 3: 291–3; GW to AH, Apr. 4, 1783, *ibid.*, 3: 315. The proposed ultimatum was to use force against Congress in case of peace with Britain; in case of continued war, to refuse to fight.

24. Kohn, *Eagle and Sword*, 33. As a member of the New York State Assembly, Hamilton made a famous speech in favor of passage of the amendment in January 1787.

25. Fisher Ames, quoted in Merrill Jensen, *The Articles of Confederation* (Madison: University of Wisconsin Press, 1959), 164.

26. Lance Banning, *The Sacred Fire of Liberty*, 120 and 250. On the crisis of the confederation and the evolution of James Madison's views, I rely on Banning's lucid and eye-opening account. Vermont joined the union in January 1791, Kentucky in June 1792.

27. On these events, see Miller, *Alexander Hamilton*, Chapters 7–10.

28. On Madison's thinking, see Jack N. Rakove, *Original Meanings: Politics and Ideas in the Making of the Constitution* (New York: Vantage, 1997), Chapter 3; Banning, *The Sacred Fire of Liberty*, Chapters 1, 4–5. According to the 1790 census, Virginia's population was 747,610, including 292,627 slaves. Pennsylvania ranked second with a population of 434,373. The total population of the United States was 3,893,635, including 694,280 slaves. Virginia included present-day West Virginia and, until 1792, Kentucky.

29. AH speech to the Philadelphia convention, June 18, 1787, *PAH*, 4: 178–209 (including the notes of Madison and several other listeners, and AH's "Plan of Government" included in the speech). See also "Draft of a Constitution," Sept. 17, 1787, *ibid.*, 4: 253–74. Miller, *Alexander Hamilton*, 168. See also Rahe, *Republics Ancient and Modern*, 608.

30. For AH's "frail and worthless fabric" comment, see AH to Morris, Feb. 29, 1802, *PAH*, 25: 544–5. AH, "Conjectures about the New Constitution," Sept. 17–30, 1787, *ibid.*, 4: 275–6. See also Stourzh, *Alexander Hamilton and the Idea of Republican Government*, 39.

31. AH, "The Federalist No. 8," in AH et al., 33; "The Federalist No. 75," *ibid.*, 379–83. On Roman dictatorship and single versus plural executives, see "The Federalist No. 70," *ibid.*, 354–61. See also Stourzh, *Alexander Hamilton and the Idea of Republican Government*, 185.

32. See AH "The Federalist No. 23," in AH et al., 112; "The Federalist No. 31," *ibid.*, 146; "The Federalist No. 11," *ibid.*, 50; "The Federalist No. 12," *ibid.*, 55–60; "The Federalist No. 26," *ibid.*, 124.

33. AH, "The Federalist No. 8," *ibid.*, 36.

34. AH, "The Federalist No. 11," *ibid.*, 53–55.

35. Thomas Pownall, *A Memorial most humbly addressed to the Sovereigns of Europe* (London, 1780), 5. Quoted in Gilbert, *To the Farewell Address*, 109. There is no direct evidence that Hamilton had read Pownall but he was probably familiar with the pamphlet.

36. See, for example, AH, "The Federalist No. 24," in AH et al., 119; "The Federalist No. 31," *ibid.*, 146–7.

37. AH, "The Federalist No. 34," *ibid.*, 161.

Chapter 3

1. Lauro Martines, *Power and Imagination: City-States in Renaissance Italy* (Baltimore: Johns Hopkins University Press, 1988), 175–84.

2. NM, *Discorsi*, 2, 10: 268; NM, "Parole da dirle sopra la provisione del danaio," Mar. 1503, in Vivanti, ed., *Opere*, 12–16; Federico Chabod, *Scritti su Machiavelli*, 322–7. For the argument that Machiavelli did not really take an interest in fiscal matters, see William J. Connell, "Machiavelli on Growth as an End," 261.

3. On AH's first weekend in office see, Elkins and McKitrick, *The Age of Federalism*, 114. The Tonnage Act of July 20, 1789 (amended by the Senate to remove Madison's offending provision) levied six cents a ton on American vessels, thirty cents a ton on vessels built in the United States but owned in part by foreigners, and fifty cents a ton on *all* foreign vessels. See *ibid.*, 65–74. On de Moustier, see Malone, *Jefferson and his Time*, 2: 198.

4. AH, "Report on the Public Credit," *PAH*, 6: 51–168; McDonald, *Alexander Hamilton*, 145.

5. Elkins and McKitrick, *The Age of Federalism*, 119–20, 137–45; McDonald, *Alexander Hamilton*, 144; AH, "Report on the Public Credit," *PAH*, 6: 86.

6. See "Eulogy on Nathanael Greene," July 4, 1789, *PAH*, 5: 359; *ibid.*, 6: 106, on funding; Elkins and McKitrick, *The Age of Federalism*, 114–23; Miller, *Alexander Hamilton*, Chapter 16. AH had written in 1780: "The only plan that can preserve the currency is one that will make it to the *immediate* interest of the monied men to cooperate with the government in its support." AH to unknown recipient (Dec. 1779–Mar. 1780), *PAH*, 2: 244–5. Through assumption, states heavily in debt (like Massachusetts and South Carolina) because of wartime contributions shifted their burden to the federal government. States (like Virginia) with little debt to transfer and thus little to gain from assumption, received compensation for their (dubious) overcontributions to the "common charges." Virginia, the leading opponent of assumption, was also reconciled by the decision to locate the new national capital on the Potomac.

7. "Conversation with Comte de Moustier," Sept. 13, 1789, *PAH*, 5: 306–8; AH to Lafayette, Oct. 6, 1789, *ibid.*, 5: 425–6; McDonald, *Alexander Hamilton*, 155–7; Broadus Mitchell, *Alexander Hamilton: The National Adventure, 1788–1804* (New York: Macmillan, 1962), Chapter 7. The comment refers specifically to the Willink brothers: "Avaricious & indefatigable to an extreme they value money more, & labour less than perhaps any other house here of equal wealth." William Short to AH (from Amsterdam), Dec. 2, 1790, *PAH*, 7: 185. On de Moustier and French policy, see Frederick Jackson Turner, *The Significance of Sections in American History* (Gloucester, MA: Peter Smith, 1959), 150.

8. McDonald calls the resemblance between the British approach and Hamilton's "superficial." McDonald, *Alexander Hamilton*, 161; AH quoted in Mitchell, *Alexander Hamilton: The National Adventure*, 41; Elkins and McKitrick, *The Age of Federalism*, 227–8. Stourzh (7) says that Hamilton's intention was "to make a second England of America."

9. Elkins and McKitrick, *The Age of Federalism*, 123–4, 400 (The words quoted are those of the authors rather than AH himself). On the link between import duties and federal revenues, see also McDonald, *Alexander Hamilton*, 151. On British investment and Anglo-American economic relations in general, see Bradford Perkins, *The First Rapprochement: England and the United States, 1795–1805* (Philadelphia: University of Pennsylvania Press, 1955), 10–14. Almost fifty years

after is publication this book remains an essential source on the 1790s. Another valuable source is Ritcheson, *Aftermath of Revolution*. According to Ritcheson (188), the total value of imports into the U.S. between Aug. 1789 and Sept. 1790 was $15,388,409. Of this $13,797,168 came from Britain. On British investment in the U.S. public debt, see *ibid.*, 205–9.

According to Article 2 of the treaty, "His Britannic Majesty shall, with all convenient speed...withdraw his Armies, Garrisons & Fleets from the said United States and from every Port, Place and Harbour within the same." For the full text, see Hunter Miller, ed., *Treaties and Other International Acts of the United States of America* (Washington, 1931), II: 151–6.

10. Article 6 of the Peace Treaty said that no future confiscations should be made, nor any further prosecutions begun against Loyalists. Approximately thirty-five thousand Loyalists left New York state after the war, or eighteen percent of the prewar population. For every Loyalist who left, however, two remained. See Alfred Fabian Young, *The Democratic Republicans of New York: The Origins, 1763–1797* (Chapel Hill: University of North Carolina Press, 1967), 66. Freneau quoted in *ibid.*, 185. Troup quoted in *ibid.*, 69.

11. On British credit and American exports, see Perkins, *The First Rapprochement*, 11–13.

12. On AH's federative suggestion (discussed in Chapter 1), see "The Farmer Refuted," Feb. 1775, *PAH*, 1: 99, 129–30.

13. On the French debt, see Mitchell, *Alexander Hamilton: The National Adventure*, Chapter 7.

14. For Beckwith's accounts of his conversations with Schuyler and others, see Douglas Brymner, *Report on Canadian Archives, 1890* (Ottawa: Brown Chamberlin, 1891), 121–3.

15. AH–Beckwith conversation, as reported by Beckwith to Dorchester, *PAH*, 5: 482–90. Emphasis in original.

16. See Bemis, *The Diplomacy of the American Revolution*, 249–50; Ritcheson, *Aftermath of Revolution*, Chapter 1. Jefferson quoted in *ibid.*, 44. See also John Ehrman, *The Younger Pitt* (Stanford: Stanford University Press, 1969), 1: 95–6, 333; Peter Onuf and Nicholas Onuf, *Federal Union, Modern World: The Law of Nations in an Age of Revolutions, 1776–1814* (Madison: Madison House, 1993), Chapter 4.

17. AH–Beckwith conversation, cited note 15 (emphasis in original).

18. AH–Beckwith conversation, *PAH*, 5: 489 (emphasis in original).

19. *Ibid.*, 5: 486.

20. GW quoted in Edmund S. Morgan, *The Genius of George Washington* (New York: Norton, 1980), 16. Morgan's book is a brilliant summary of Washington's views.

21. Flexner, *The Young Hamilton*, 141. His chapter (15) dealing with Hamilton's arrival at headquarters is called "New Father, New Family."

22. AH to Philip Schuyler, Feb. 18, 1781, *PAH*, 2: 563–8. On the incident, see also McDonald, *Alexander Hamilton*, 24; Mitchell, *Alexander Hamilton: Youth to Maturity*, Chapter 14.

23. AH to Hugh Knox, July 1 [-28] 1777, *PAH*, 26: 362. On Monmouth see AH to Elias Boudinot, July 5, 1778, *ibid.*, 1: 512. On GW's temper, see AH to Schuyler,

cited in previous note. See also AH to James McHenry, Feb. 18, 1781, *ibid.*, 2: 569, written soon after his resignation, in which he sarcastically refers to Washington as "the Great Man."

24. On André, see AH to Laurens, Oct. 11, 1780, *ibid.*, 2: 467; Kaplan, *Ambivalent Anglophobe*, 33–4. On his requests to be able to join a combat unit, see AH to Laurens, Jan. 8, [1780], *PAH*, 2: 254–5; Flexner, *The Young Hamilton*, 263, 317. On April 19, 1781, AH wrote Gen. Nathanael Green, "I acknowledge myself to have been unpardonably delinquent in not having written to you before; but my matrimonial occupations have scarcely left me leisure or inclination for any other." *PAH*, 2: 594.

25. James Thomas Flexner, *George Washington: Anguish and Farewell (1793–1799)* (New York: Little, Brown: 1969), 471–2, 493. This remark comes in the context of his thoughtful discussion of Washington's overall career.

26. See AH to Schuyler, Feb. 18, 1781, *PAH*, 2: 563–8. NM, *Il Principe*, 18: 104.

27. According to Padover (*The Mind of Alexander Hamilton*, 6), Washington, "despite his icy reserve and aloofness," actually referred to Hamilton as "my boy." After Washington's death AH wrote, "he was an *Aegis very essential to me.*" AH to Tobias Lear, Jan. 2, 1800, *PAH*, 24: 155. On Hamilton as Washington's "surrogate son," see, for example, Gordon S. Wood, "The Statist," *The New Republic*, Oct. 15, 2001.

28. AH-Beckwith conversation, *PAH*, 5: 489.

29. On the Morris appointment, see W. W. Abbot and Dorothy Twohig, eds., *The Papers of George Washington* (Charlottesville: University Press of Virginia, 1993), 4 (Sept. 1789–Jan. 1790): 181–2. See also GW letters to Morris, both dated Oct. 13, 1789, *ibid.*, 177–81.

Chapter 4

1. AH–Beckwith conversation, Oct. 1789, *PAH*, 5: 488; AH–Beckwith conversation, Sept. 25–30, 1790, *ibid.*, 7: 73–4.

2. See Ritcheson, *Aftermath of Revolution*, 65–8; Tucker and Hendrickson, *Empire of Liberty*, 27. Jefferson's famous financial problems were in part inherited from his wife's father John Wayles. On Sept. 25, 1792, TJ wrote Randolph Jefferson, "Finding it necessary to sell a few more slaves to accomplish the debt of Mr. Wayles to Farrell & Jones, I have thought of disposing of Dinah and her family . . . Dinah is a fine house wench of the best disposition in the world." Julian Boyd, et al., eds., *The Papers of Thomas Jefferson* (Princeton: Princeton University Press, 1950–2000) (hereafter *PTJ*, vol. page.), 24: 416.

3. Charles Maurice de Talleyrand-Périgord, "Les Etats-Unis et l'Angleterre en 1795" (letter of Talleyrand to Lord Landsdowne, Feb. 1, 1795), *Revue d'Histoire Diplomatique* no. 3, 1889, 67.

4. Elkins and McKitrick, *The Age of Federalism*, 68. Madison quoted in Banning, *The Sacred Fire of Liberty*, 300. See also *ibid.*, 49, 53, 249 and 299.

5. On Madison's position on funding and assumption, see Miller, *Alexander Hamilton*, 238–46; Elkins and McKitrick, *The Age of Federalism*, 133–53. On his position on the bank, see *ibid.*, 229–31; also, Rakove, *Original Meanings*, 350–5. For an overview, see Banning, *The Sacred Fire of Liberty*, Chapters 10 and 11.

6. Assumption was deeply unpopular in Virginia because, having retired most of its debt (its war effort having been limited), it would be paying federal taxes (reminiscent of the oppressive levies of the 1760 and 1770s) to pay off the larger debts of states like Massachusetts and South Carolina. Madison actually voted against assumption even after the deal on the capital, but ceased to wage an all-out battle. The story of the 1790 debate on slavery and Madison's role in shaping the resulting resolutions is engagingly told by Ellis, *Founding Brothers*, Chapter 3.

7. Banning, *The Sacred Fire of Liberty*, 163, 250–1. Along with Banning, Rakove (*Original Meanings*, 353–5) shows how Madison's argument against Hamilton's bank was basically consistent with his earlier views. See also Ellis, *Founding Brothers*, 52–60.

8. AH's statement, June 29, 1787, *PAH*, 4: 221.

9. On the Madison–Washington relationship during this period, see Banning, *The Sacred Fire of Liberty*, 274 and 293.

10. Jefferson quoted in Ellis, *American Sphinx*, 30 and 52. On the Saxon myth see also Robert Kelley, *The Transatlantic Persuasion: The Liberal Democratic Mind in the Age of Gladstone* (New Brunswick: Transaction, 1980), 121. Kelley says of TJ (105): "Throughout his life, Anglophobia was to be one of the organizing principles in his political world view." On Jefferson's youth, see Merrill D. Peterson, *Thomas Jefferson and the New Nation* (New York: Oxford University Press, 1970), Chapter 1.

11. The "Anas" is a collection of memoes and notes of conversations that Jefferson recorded in the 1790s and then edited late in life. The three volumes of documents were given the name by the first editor of Jefferson's papers (from *ana*, Latin for a collection of such materials). Jefferson originally intended that the material would compose a history of the Washington administration to correct the Federalist bias of John Marshall's biography of Washington published while Jefferson was president. The "Anas" was first published in 1829. See "Editorial Note," in *PTJ*, 22: 33–8. See also, Freeman, *Affairs of Honor*, 64–5, 100–4. On the April dinner and TJ's attachment to radical Whig ideology, see McDonald, *Alexander Hamilton*, 214–17. Jefferson's recollection of the dinner quoted in *ibid.*, 214. AH had taken a similar position at the Constitutional Convention. On June 22, 1787 (according to Madison's notes), he remarked "It was known that one of the ablest politicians (Mr. Hume) had pronounced that all influence on the side of the crown, which went under the name of corruption, was an essential part of the weight which maintained the equilibrium of the Constitution." *PAH*, 4: 217, n. 1.

12. On this subject, see Gilbert, *To the Farewell Address*, Chapter 3; Lang, *Foreign Policy in the Early Republic*, Chapter 5; Adams, *Works*, 1: 417.

13. On Adams, see Ritcheson, *Aftermath of Revolution*, 16. TJ remark quoted by Tucker and Hendrickson, *Empire of Liberty*, 190. See also *PTJ*, 16: 601.

14. Congressional resolution on Armed Neutrality quoted in Gilbert, *To the Farewell Address*, 75. On this subject see also Thomas A. Bailey, *A Diplomatic History of the American People* (New York: Appleton-Century-Crofts, 1964), 39–40; Bemis, *The Diplomacy of the American Revolution*, 167.

15. Henry Adams quoted in Peterson, *The Jefferson Image in the American Mind*, 287. Thomas Jefferson to Issac Shelby, Nov. 6, 1793, *PTJ*, 27: 312. Bemis, *Jay's Treaty*, 190. On "peaceable coercion" see also Tucker and Hendrickson, *Empire of Liberty*, 18. On this as a "foreign policy on the cheap," see Herbert E. Sloan, in Doron S. Ben-Atar and Barbara B. Oberg, eds. *Federalists Reconsidered* (Charlottesville: University Press of Virginia, 1998), 67.

16. As Lang argues (*Foreign Policy in the Early Republic*, 71), "The memory of this successful manipulation of the European balance system [during the war] to force concessions from Britain would . . . remain the basis on which Jeffersonian strategic thinking rested for the next three decades." See also Ritcheson, *Aftermath of Revolution*, 21–31; Elkins and McKitrick, *The Age of Federalism*, 70–4. On Jefferson's English purchases, see *ibid.*, 72. TJ letter to Madison, quoted in Lang, *Foreign Policy in the Early Republic*, 78. Along with the above, an insightful source on Jefferson's foreign policy views is Doron S. Ben-Atar, *The Origins of Jeffersonian Commercial Policy and Diplomacy* (New York: St. Martin's Press, 1993).

17. Short to TJ, July 31, 1792, in *PTJ*, 24: 271; TJ to Short, Jan. 3, 1793, in *ibid.*, 25: 14. On the "ball of liberty," see TJ to Tench Coxe, June 1, 1795, *ibid*, 28: 373–74.

18. AH to Lafayette, Oct. 6, 1789, *PAH*, 5: 425.

19. On TJ's family and baggage, see TJ to John Jay, Aug. 27, 1789, enclosure from Tobias Lear to AH, Jan. 18, 1790, *PAH*, 6: 186. See also Lycan, *Alexander Hamilton and American Foreign Policy*, 131.

Chapter 5

1. NM, *Discorsi*, I, 38: 151–2.

2. *Ibid.*, 281–2.

3. Lycan, *Alexander Hamilton and American Foreign Policy*, 196; Bailey, *A Diplomatic History of the American People*, 58. On London's view, see Ehrman, *The Younger Pitt*, 1: 333.

4. See Jeremy Black, *British Foreign Policy in an Age of Revolutions, 1783–1793* (Cambridge: Cambridge University Press, 1994), Chapter 5; Lycan, *Alexander Hamilton and American Foreign Policy*, 123; William Ray Manning, "The Nootka Sound Controversy," American Historical Association *Annual Report* for 1904 (1905). According to Manning (414), Britain was preparing "to seize the heart of North America for herself and erect the remainder of Spanish America into a client state."

5. For Beckwith's orders, see Lord Dorchester to Beckwith, June 27, 1790, in Brymner, *Report on Canadian Archives*, 143–4. See also Washington to Morris, Oct. 13, 1789, John C. Fitzpatrick, ed. *Writings of Washington*, 30: 439–45.

6. See Theodore Roosevelt, *Gouverneur Morris* (Boston: Houghton, Mifflin and Co., 1892), 14. On the debt-buying scheme, see Morris to AH, Jan. 31, 1790, *PAH*, 6; 234–9.

7. Gouverneur Morris, *A Diary of the French Revolution*, edited by Beatrix Cary Davenport (Boston: Houghton Mifflin, 1939) (hereafter, Morris, *Diary*), 353. Lady Tancred turned out to be a disappointment. Several weeks later he wrote,

"She appears more indebted for her Beauties to Art than I had imagined at the first View." *Ibid.*, 461 and 482. Morris to Jay, quoted in Roosevelt, *Gouverneur Morris*, 110. Jay to Robert Morris, quoted in Mary Jo Kline, *Gouverneur Morris and the New Nation, 1775–1788* (New York: Arno Press, 1978), 176.

8. Roosevelt, *Gouverneur Morris*, 45, 193, 230–1. Letter to R. Morris in Morris, *Diary*, 616. Emphasis in original.

9. Morris to Washington, Apr. 29, 1789, in Morris, *Diary*, 61; description of Paris, *ibid.*, 73.

10. Morris initially saw the *mondain* bishop as "a sly, cool, cunning, ambitious, and malicious man," but eventually recognized him as a man of talent and recommended him to Lafayette as finance minister to replace Necker. This was perhaps because he would look more kindly than Necker on Morris's complicated plan to acquire the American debt. See *ibid.*, 164, 241, 248–50, 280 and 297.

11. On Morris's views of the king and Lafayette, see ibid., 156, 170, 223, 239, 252, 283, 306, 347, 377. On the future of the revolution, see *ibid.*, 223, 266, 293–5. Morris observed after talking to Jefferson in Paris: "I think he does not form very just Estimates of Character but rather assigns too many to the humble Rank of Fools, whereas in Life the Gradations are infinite and each Individual has his peculiarities of Fort and Feeble." On his admiration of Adèle's intelligence and perceptivity, which he recorded immediately before her remark about Jefferson, see *ibid.*, 255–6. The Marquis de La Luzerne, French ambassador to London, whom Morris had known as minister to the United States during the war, talked of Jefferson "with much Contempt as a Statesman, and as one who is better formed for the interior of Virginia than to influence the Operations of a great People." Such was Morris's later view. On his relations with TJ, see *ibid.*, 1, 100, 159, 256, 296, 476.

12. Ritcheson (*Aftermath of Revolution*, Chapter 6) sees the mission as a near disaster, with Morris personally at fault. His argument follows Bemis, *Jay's Treaty*, 66–85. One of the few British historians to deal with the episode, Ehrman, basically agrees. See *The Younger Pitt*, 1: 376. Elkins and McKitrick (*The Age of Federalism*, 212–13) argue that the problem was not Morris but the fact that the British did not want to change the status quo and thus the basic attention gap between the two countries. On the Morris–Leeds conversation and Leed's April 28 letter to Morris, see Morris, *Diary*, 464–6, 495.

13. Morris, *Diary*, 374–5; 461–2; Kline, *Gouverneur Morris and the New Nation 1775–1788*, 218–19; Bemis, *The Diplomacy of the American Revolution*, 181–5, 218, 234.

14. Morris mentions going to the French ambassador's residence fourteen times during his August–September 1789 visit to London. See Morris, *Diary*, 174–211. He mentions going there thirty times on the subsequent 1790 trip. On eight of those occasions, the ambassador was out. He also had dinner once with him at the Church's. See *ibid.*, 458–618. On the Fox dinner, see *ibid.*, 485. For Morris's defense of his conduct with regard to Luzerne and denial regarding Church, see his letter to Washington, Apr. 10, 1792, *ibid.*, 614. On wine and cards, see 467 and 607. On the Duchess of Gordon, to whom Morris was presented in September, see 571, 587, 597, 606 and 607. The current duke was the son of Morris's sister-in-law by her former marriage. The dinner with Pitt did not

come off but Morris did meet the minister of war, Sir George Young, at the duchess's house. Morris letter to Washington, May 1, 1790, *ibid.*, 497–500. See also Bemis, *Jay's Treaty*, 68.

15. Morris, *Diary*, 523.

16. For letters to Lafayette and Carmichael, dated May 7, 1790, the day the news of the confrontation became public, see Morris, *Diary*, 506–9. On message to Carmichael via William Constable, see *ibid.*, 509–10.

17. *Ibid.*, 518–23. See also, Ritcheson, *Aftermath of Revolution*, 99–103.

18. Bemis, *Jay's Treaty*, 79–80. Ehrman (*The Younger Pitt*, 376) observes that "Pitt and his colleagues came to mistrust" Morris, even if British policy might have been the same with or without the mission.

19. Morris, *Diary*, 510, 539, 549, 553, 554, and 569–70.

20. *Ibid.*, 597–604; Black, *British Foreign Policy*, 243–8.

Chapter 6

1. Boyd, *Number 7*, xvi, 7, 111–13.

2. *Ibid.*, 11, 109, 112–13; Lycan, *Alexander Hamilton and American Foreign Policy*, 122, 125–26. Elkins and McKitrick, *The Age of Federalism*, 220–21, 778, n. 100. Other historians dismissive or skeptical of Boyd are Jerald A. Combs, *The Jay Treaty: Political Battleground of the Founding Fathers* (Berkeley, CA: University of California Press, 1970), and Ritcheson, *Aftermath of Revolution*, Chapter 6. Kaplan observes (*Alexander Hamilton*, 162) that "in the vital area of foreign relations, the divisions between Jefferson and Hamilton were always more apparent than real."

3. See Grenville letters to Dorchester, May 6, 1790, in Brymner, *Report on Canadian Archives*, 131–3.

4. *Ibid.*, 143–4. To save time, Beckwith was authorized to communicate directly with Grenville in London.

5. AH's written report to GW, July 8, 1790, *PAH*, 6: 484–5. On meeting the same day, see *ibid.*, 6: 486, n. 1. On Washington's illness and house see Douglas Southall Freeman, *George Washington: A Biography*, vol. 6, *Patriot and President* (New York: Scribners, 1954), 252–3, 260.

6. Boyd, *Number 7*, 38–43.

7. *Ibid.*; Lycan, *Alexander Hamilton and American Foreign Policy*, 122–3.

8. Jackson and Twohig, eds., GW, *Diary*, July 8, 1790, 6: 88–89.

9. TJ to GW, July 12, 1790, in Boyd, *Number 7*, 89–91; see also, Malone, *Jefferson and the Rights of Man*, 310–315; Lang, *Foreign Policy in the Early Republic*, 131–2.

10. GW, *Diary*, July 14, 1790, cited in *PAH*, 6: 495, n. 1.

11. AH to GW, July 15, 1790, *ibid.*, 6: 493–5.

12. For Beckwith's version see *ibid.*, 6: 496, n. 7. For Hamilton's note on his report to GW, see *ibid.*, 6: 495, n. 1. The note began: "Note. Mr. Jefferson was privy to this transaction."

13. For Beckwith's report of his July 15 conversation with AH, see *ibid.*, 6: 496, n. 7. See also Morris to GW, May 29, 1790, describing his conversation with

Leeds and Pitt, Morris, *Diary*, 524, note; Hamilton–Beckwith conversation (as reported by Beckwith), August 7–12, 1790, *PAH*, 6: 547. In this conversation, AH mentioned the arrival of Morris's report. For the AH–Beckwith discussion of Morris, in which AH said that he did not approve of Morris's conduct with Pitt and Leeds, see Beckwith report of conversation with AH, Sept. 25–30, 1790, *PAH*, 7: 70.

14. Hamilton added, according to Beckwith's account, "in this I am steadily following up, what I have long considered to be the essential interest of this country; on this point I have already so fully explained my ideas, that a repetition is needless." *PAH*, 6: 497–8.

15. Ehrman, *The Younger Pitt*, 1: 375.

16. For documentation of TJ's démarche, see Boyd, *Number 7*, 91–107. For GW's request (Aug. 27, 1790) to cabinet members (also to the vice president and chief justice), see *ibid.*, 107.

17. GW to Lafayette, Aug. 11, 1790, in Boyd, *Number 7*, 56; TJ to Morris, Aug. 12, 1790, *ibid.*, 106–7. On TJ's drafting of Washington's letter, see Boyd, *Number 7*, 105, n. For TJ's "Outline of Policy," see *ibid.*, 93–6.

18. TJ's "Outline of Policy," in Boyd, *Number 7*, 93–6 (emphasis added). See also Lycan, *Alexander Hamilton and American Foreign Policy*, 128–30; Lang, *Foreign Policy in the Early Republic*, 131; TJ to Short, Aug. 10, 1790, in Boyd, *Number 7*, 101–3.

19. TJ to GW, Aug. 27, 1790, in Boyd, *Number 7*, 108–9. As the discussion below shows, Jefferson's answer was not, as Kaplan (*Alexander Hamilton*, 101) alleges, substantially the same as Hamilton's. Kaplan's memory seems to have failed him, because he says that Jefferson recommended accepting a British request.

20. AH to GW, Sept. 15, 1790, with paper enclosed, *PAH*, 7: 36–57 (emphasis added). See AH to Elizabeth Hamilton, Sept. 15, 1790, *ibid.*, 7: 35. When in late October Beckwith asked if he could communicate by mail with AH in Philadelphia, the latter replied, "That would be precarious, there seems a necessity for my seeing you." *Ibid.*, 7: 115. On TJ's invitation, see Koch, *Jefferson and Madison*, 114.

21. *PAH*, 7: 37–42.

22. *Ibid.*, 7: 42–6.

23. *Ibid.*, 7: 46–8.

24. *Ibid.*, 7: 51–2.

25. *Ibid.*, 7: 52–4.

26. *Ibid.*, 7: 55.

27. On Machiavelli's dislike of the "middle course," see, among other passages, *Discorsi*, 2, 15: 283–6.

28. *PAH*, 7: 55–7.

29. See Beckwith's record of conversation with AH, Sept. 25–30, 1790, *ibid.*, 7: 71.

30. *Ibid.*, 7: 73–4.

31. See Beckwith's record of conversation with AH, Oct. 17, 1790, *ibid.*, 7: 111–15. See also, AH to GW, Oct. 17, 1790, *ibid.*, 7: 118–19, reporting the news from Europe.

32. For AH's report on his conversation with Beckwith about Morris, see AH to GW, Sept. 30, 1790, *PAH*, 7: 84–5. For Beckwith's version of same conversation, see

Brymner, *Report on Canadian Archives*, 161–2. For GW's reply to AH (Oct. 10, 1790), see *PAH*, 7: 107–8. See also GW to the Senate and the House of Representatives, Feb. 14, 1791, in Fitzpatrick, ed., *Writings of Washington*, 31: 214–15.

Chapter 7

1. NM, *Il Principe*, 6: 51.
2. McDonald, *Alexander Hamilton*, 211; Miller, *Alexander Hamilton*, 268–71; AH to Duer, Aug. 17, 1791, *PAH*, 9: 74–5; Troup to AH, June 15, 1791, *ibid.*, 8: 478.
3. TJ account of Aug. 13, 1791 conversation reprinted in *PAH*, 9: 33–34. On April 1791 conversation, see Chapter 4.
4. On the Reynolds affair, see *PAH*, 10: 377–8, n. 1. James Reynolds and his partner, Jacob Clingman, offered investigators what they said was damaging information about AH at a time when they were in jail on other charges.
5. For example, AH wrote Angelica Church (Dec. 6, 1787), after a recent letter from her, "Imagine, *if you are able*, the pleasure it gave me. Notwithstanding the compliment you pay to my eloquence its resources could give you but a feeble image of what I should wish to convey. This you will tell me is poetical enough. I seldom write to a lady without fancying the relation of lover and mistress. It has a very interesting effect. And in your case the dullest materials could not help feeling that propensity. I have a great opinion of your *discernment* and therefore I venture to rant. If you read this letter in a certain mood you will easily divine that in which I write it." *PAH*, 4: 375. See also AH to Angelica, June 19–20, 1796, which ends, "Yrs. as much as you desire AH." *Ibid.*, 20: 233.
6. See James Reynolds to AH, Dec. 15, 1791, *ibid.*, 10: 376–7. When questioned, Maria tended to corroborate the accusations of Jacob Clingman, her husband's associate, that Hamilton was involved in improper financial dealings. This does not prove that she was her husband's accomplice. She may have done so out of fear or spite, or she may actually have believed the accusations. In what is probably the most meticulous historical reconstruction of the affair, Robert Hendrickson suggests, admittedly with no direct evidence, that the Reynolds' were the tools of Aaron Burr. See Hendrickson, *Hamilton* II, Chapters 6, 7, 8s' and 11. For Hamilton's account of the affair published in Aug. 1797, see *PAH*, 21: 238–267.
7. AH to Angelica, Nov. 1791, *PAH*, 9: 549.
8. AH conversation with Beckwith, Jan. 19, 1791, *PAH*, 7: 442. On British loan, see AH to Short, Aug. 1, 1791, *PAH*, 9: 1, and Short to AH, Nov. 8, 1791, *ibid.*, 9: 480. Washington, among others, believed that the British were supplying the Indians with weapons and encouraging them to attack American settlers. On AH's approach to Dorchester, see Boyd's editorial note, in *PTJ*, 20: 109–13.
9. AH conversation with Beckwith, Feb. 16, 1791, *PAH*, 8: 44.
10. On Hawkesbury report, see Ritcheson, *Aftermath of Revolution*, 123–35. For Hawkesbury's instructions to Hammond, see Bernard Mayo, ed., *Instructions to the British Ministers to the United States: 1791–1812* (New York: Da Capo, 1971), 5–8.

11. William Grenville, home secretary during the Nootka Sound crisis, became Baron Grenville in November 1790 and foreign secretary in June 1791. For his instructions to Hammond, see Mayo, *Instructions to the British Ministers to the United States*, 8–19. Article 4 of the treaty provided that there should be no lawful impediments to the recovery of prewar British debts; Article 5 stated that Congress should recommend to the states the restitution of the confiscated estates of Loyalists; Article 6 stated that no future confiscations should be made.

12. On the reception to Hawkesbury's report, the damage it caused to the Hamiltonians, and Beckwith's report to Grenville on this subject, see Ritcheson, *Aftermath of Revolution*, 136–7. See also the AH–Beckwith conversation, Aug. 12, 1791, *PAH*, 9: 29–30; AH–Beckwith conversation, Aug. 24, 1791, *ibid.*, 9: 104. AH to Washington, Oct. 6, 1791, *ibid.*, 9: 289.

13. Ternant's record of the conversation (in the form of a dispatch to Foreign Minister Montmorin), Oct. 7, 1791, *ibid.*, 9: 290–2.

14. Ternant conversation with AH, Oct. 7, 1791, *PAH*, 9: 292.

15. See TJ, "Anas," entry for March 11, 1792, *PTJ*, 23: 258–64; Malone, *Jefferson and the Rights of Man*, 397–8.

16. TJ spoke for two hours with Ternant about a commercial treaty in early April 1792. See editorial note, *PTJ*, 23: 468–9.

17. Malone, *Jefferson and the Rights of Man*, 331–6; For TJ's report, see *PTJ*, 19: 219; Elkins and McKitrick, *The Age of Federalism*, 225.

18. The bill was reported on Feb. 21, 1791. See also, Bemis, *Jay's Treaty*, 112–13. *PTJ*, 19: 560. On British reaction, see Ehrman, *The Younger Pitt*, 379.

19. TJ to Short, Mar. 15, 1791, *PTJ*, 19: 570–1; TJ to Carmichael, Mar. 17, 1791, *ibid.*, 19: 574–5; TJ to Humphreys, Mar. 15, 1791, *ibid.*, 19: 572–3; Boyd's editorial note, *ibid.*, 19: 558. See also, Malone, *Jefferson and the Rights of Man*, 335–6.

20. On the Jefferson–Hammond exchange of notes, see Elkins and McKitrick, *The Age of Federalism*, 248–56; Malone, *Jefferson and his Time*, 412–19; Ritcheson, *Aftermath of Revolution*, Chapter 12. TJ's Dec. 15, 1791, message to Hammond proposed that they "begin by specifying on each side, the particular acts which each considers to have been done by the other, in contravention of the treaty." Jefferson began by setting out British violations with respect to the posts and the carrying off of American slaves.

21. Morris's nomination was approved by the Senate by a vote of 16 to 11 on Jan. 12, 1792. Jefferson recorded that when he had told Washington of King Louis XVI's flight and capture, "I never saw him so much dejected by any event in my life." See TJ "Anas," Mar. 12, 1792, entry, *PTJ*, 23: 270–1. AH–Hammond conversation, Dec. 15–16, 1791, *PAH*, 10: 373–6. Hammond and Hamilton had probably met publicly but this was the first confidential conversation that Hammond reported to his superiors. He noted that in the course of it, "the opinion, I had entertained, of the Gentleman's just and liberal way of thinking was fully confirmed." TJ–AH conversation of late Dec. 1791, recorded in TJ "Anas," Mar. 11, 1792 entry, *PTJ*, 23: 256–8. See also AH's undated report, "View of the Commercial Regulations of France & Great Britain in reference to the United States," *PAH*, 13: 411–27.

22. See *PAH*, 13: 110. AH–Hammond conversation, Jan. 1–8, 1792, *PAH*, 10: 493–6 (taken from Hammond's dispatch to Grenville).
23. See AH to TJ, May 20–27, 1792, containing comments on TJ draft, *ibid.*, 11: 408–14. See also AH conversation with Hammond, May 29–June 2, 1792, *ibid.*, 11: 454, on Jefferson document; AH conversation with Hammond, May 28–29, 1792, *ibid.*, 11: 446–47, on Indians. Grenville had in mind an arrangement whereby both the United States and Britain would give up their claims to the posts and give them to the Indians. See Grenville to Hammond, Mar. 17, 1792, in Mayo, ed., *Instructions to the British Ministers to the United States*, 24–5. Partisan historians include Malone, who refers to TJ's "magnificent paper" (*Jefferson and his Time*, 419), and Bemis (*Jay's Treaty*, 140), who calls it "a document of uncommon power," but undermined by AH.
24. "Report on the Subject of Manufactures" (final version), Dec. 5, 1791, *PAH*, 10: 291. See also editors' Introductory Note, *ibid.*, 10: 1–15.
25. *Ibid.*, 10: 262–3. AH conversation with Beckwith, Oct. 1789, *ibid.*, 5: 483.
26. "Hamilton's Second Draft," *ibid.*, 10: 57–60.
27. For a recent analysis, which stresses the strategic rather than the tactical purpose of AH's mercantilism, see Doron S. Ben-Atar, "Alexander Hamilton's Alternative: Technology Piracy and the Report on Manufactures," in Ben-Atar and Oberg, eds., *Federalists Reconsidered*, 41–60. On Coxe's views, see Jacob E. Cooke, *Tench Coxe and the Early Republic* (Chapel Hill: University of North Carolina Press, 1978), 232.
28. TJ, "Anas", entries for Feb. 28–9, 1792, *PTJ*, 23: 171–3.
29. On the SEUM, see Elkins and McKitrick, *The Age of Federalism*, 262–3, 279–80. Madison quoted in Banning, *The Sacred Fire of Liberty*, 346.
30. On the recruitment of Freneau, in which Madison took the leading role, see Banning, *The Sacred Fire of Liberty*, 340.
31. AH to Carrington, May 26, 1792, *PAH*, 11: 426–45.
32. *Ibid.*, 11: 442.
33. TJ to GW, May 23, 1792, *PTJ*, 23: 535–41. For Washington's reaction, see the "Anas," entry for July 10, 1792, 116–18, recording a TJ–GW conversation on that date, *ibid.*, 24: 210–12.
34. GW to AH, July 29, 1792, *PAH*, 12: 129–34; AH to GW, July 30, 1792, *ibid.*, 12: 137–9; AH to GW, Aug. 18, 1792, *ibid.*, 12: 228–58, with enclosure replying to Jefferson; GW to AH, Aug. 26, 1792, *ibid.*, 12: 276–7.
35. GW to AH, Aug. 26, 1792, *ibid.*, 12: 276–7; see also GW to TJ, Aug. 23, 1792, *PTJ*, 24: 315–19; AH to GW, Sept. 9, 1792, *PAH*, 12: 347–50; TJ to GW, Sept. 9, 1792, *PTJ*, 24: 315–19.
36. Ellis, *American Sphinx*, 123; TJ to GW, Sept. 9, 1792, *PTJ*, 24: 315–19; see also TJ's characterization written years later in the "Anas."

Chapter 8

1. Ridolfi, *The Life of Niccolò Machiavelli*, 117.
2. On Machiavelli's mission, and messages to the *signoria*, see Chabod, *Scritti su Machiavelli*, 353–60. Among the military steps that Machiavelli pressed for (with some success) at this point was the raising of a mounted militia to fight

along side the infantry units already in existence. See Marchand, ed., *Niccolò Machiavelli: I primi scritti politici*, 213–14.

3. NM, *Il Principe*, 21: 124–5 (emphasis added). See also NM, *Discorsi*, 2, 15: 283–6 and 2, 23: 324–9.

4. Elkins and McKitrick, *The Age of Federalism*, 336 and 355; Malone, *Jefferson and the Ordeal of Liberty*, 11; Ellis, *American Sphinx*, 124. Lycan (*Alexander Hamilton and American Foreign Policy*, 153) adopts a similar line. "The French Frenzy" is the title of Chapter 6 of Alexander DeConde, *Entangling Alliance: Politics and Diplomacy under George Washington* (Westport, CT: Greenwood, 1974) (originally published, 1958). See also John Alexander Carroll and Mary Wells Ashworth, *George Washington*, vol. 7 (New York: Scribners, 1957), 4.

5. On this point, see Tucker and Hendrickson, *Empire of Liberty*, 54. Grenville quoted in Ritcheson, *Aftermath of Revolution*, 275.

6. For the "Adam and Eve" letter, see TJ to Short, Jan. 3, 1793, *PTJ*, 25: 14.

7. On AH's statement and GW's comment, see "Notes of Cabinet Meeting on Southern Indians and Spain," Oct. 31, 1792, *PTJ*, 24: 547–9.

8. For TJ–GW conversation, see the "Anas," entry for Dec. 27, 1792, *PTJ*, 24: 793–4.

9. See TJ to William Randolph, Jan. 7, 1793, *PTJ*, 25: 30; TJ to Randolph, June 2, 1793, *ibid.*, 26: 169. On British collapse, see TJ to Dr. Gilmer, June 28, 1793, *ibid.*, 26: 389–90; TJ to Monroe, June 28, 1793, *ibid.*, 26: 392–3.

10. On Genêt's orders, see Elkins and McKitrick, *The Age of Federalism*, 332–4; editorial note, *PTJ*, 26: 685–6.

11. TJ, the "Anas," entry for Feb. 20, 1793, *PTJ*, 25: 243–5. Smith had been authorized by the Provisory Executive Council to negotiate immediate payment of the U.S. debt to France and to use the proceeds to buy food and supplies for France.

12. Elkins and McKitrick, *The Age of Federalism*, 300; Ellis, *American Sphinx*, 130; Eugene R. Sheridan, "Thomas Jefferson and the Giles Resolutions," *William and Mary Quarterly*, XLIV (1992), 589–608. Sheridan shows Jefferson's role in the affair. Freneau's paper quoted in Carroll and Ashworth, *George Washington*, 6. See also TJ, the "Anas," entry for May 23, 1793, *PTJ*, 26: 101–2. Washington was 61 on Feb. 22, 1793.

13. See Malone, *Jefferson and the Ordeal of Liberty*, 32.

14. TJ to GW, Apr. 7, 1793, *PTJ*, 25: 518. See also AH to GW, informing him of the war, Apr. 5, 1793, *PAH*, 14: 291–2. GW to TJ, Apr. 12, 1793, *PTJ*, 25: 541–2. On TJ's position, see also Kaplan, *Alexander Hamilton*, 108.

15. AH to Jay, Apr. 9, 1793, *PAH*, 14: 297–8.

16. GW to TJ, Apr. 12, 1793, *PTJ*, 26: 101–2. GW to AH, Apr. 12, 1793, *PAH*, 14: 314–15. See also Carroll and Ashworth, *George Washington*, 44; Flexner, *George Washington*, 29; GW to AH, TJ, Henry Knox, and Edmund Randolph (containing the thirteen questions), Apr. 18, 1793, *PAH*, 14: 326–7.

17. Flexner, *George Washington*, 29; Elkins and McKitrick, *The Age of Federalism*, 338; TJ, the "Anas," entry for Apr. 18, 1793, *PTJ*, 25: 570–1. See, also Malone, *Jefferson and the Ordeal of Liberty*, 68–71.

18. TJ to JM, June 23, 1793, explaining objections to the proclamation (emphasis in original) *PTJ*, 26: 346; TJ to JM, Mar. 24, 1793, *ibid.*, 25: 442.

19. TJ to JM, June 23, 1793, *ibid.*, 26: 346; TJ cabinet memo, Apr. 19, 1793, *PTJ*, 25: 570–71; TJ, "Notes on the Proclamation of Neutrality and the Laws of Nations," Dec. 20, 1793, *ibid.*, 27: 598–601. TJ to Pinckney with instructions, Apr. 20 and May 7, 1793, *PTJ*, 25: 577–8, 674–6. See also Carroll and Ashworth, *George Washington*, 48; Bemis, *Jay's Treaty*, 192. James Sofka observes, "In Jefferson's view Hamilton's policy would render the United States a 'second Portugal,' and he refused to give away what the British may buy at considerable price." See "American Neutral Rights Reappraised: Identity or Interest in the Foreign Policy of the Early Republic?" *Review of International Studies* (2000). vol. 26, 609. Sofka's interesting article fails to make the point that the British made it clear that they would concede nothing to U.S. pressure and that Jefferson, as secretary of state, was forced to admit that in its dealings with Britain, the United States was in no position to obtain respect for the principle of "free ships make free goods."

20. TJ to JM, June 19, 1793, *PTJ*, 26: 323–4; TJ to JM, June 23, 1793, *ibid.*, 26: 346.

21. TJ memo to GW, Apr. 28, 1793, recapitulating AH's argument on Apr. 19 (there is no version in AH's own papers), *ibid.*, 25: 607–19. See also TJ, the "Anas," entry for Apr. 18, 1793, *PTJ*, 25: 570–1.

22. AH's paper observed that the Revolution had been "attended with circumstances, which militate against a full conviction of its having been brought to its present *stage*, by such a *free, regular*, and *deliberate* act of the nation, and with such a spirit of justice and humanity, as ought to silence all scruples about the validity of what has been done, and the morality of aiding it, even if consistent with policy." Suspension of the treaties now, he added, would actually be less offensive to France than refusing in the breach to honor the treaty guarantee, as the United States, for reasons of self-preservation, would surely have to do. See AH and Henry Knox to GW, May 2, 1793, *PAH*, 14: 367–96. This paper, whose ostensible purpose was to answer question three, also deals at length with question four. See also Lang, *Foreign Policy in the Early Republic*, 97.

23. See TJ to GW, Apr. 28, 1793, containing "Opinion on Treaties With France," *PTJ*, 25: 607–18. TJ, in replying to AH's specific arguments, including the passage from Vattel, was relying on what AH had said on Apr. 19.

24. Malone, *Jefferson and the Ordeal of Liberty*, 76. GW told TJ on May 6 that he considered the treaties valid and would receive Genêt as French minister without qualifications. Elkins and McKitrick, *The Age of Federalism*, 340–41. See AH memo to GW, May 2, 1793, analyzing the question of offensive war by France. *PAH*, 14: 398–408. According to the treaty, the guarantee was to operate only in the case of a defensive war.

25. AH conversations with Hammond, between April 2 and May 17, 1793 (as reported by Hammond to Grenville), *PAH*, 14: 273–74. Grenville had written Hammond explaining British policy on March 12, 1793. Writing later in a Philadelphia newspaper, Hamilton called insistence on "free ships make free goods" under the circumstances a "species of Knight errantry." See "No Jacobin No. III," Aug. 8, 1793, *PAH*, 15: 206.

26. TJ to JM, May 13, 1793, *PTJ*, 26: 25–7; TJ to Monroe, May 5, 1793, *ibid.*, 25: 660–3; TJ to JM, June 9, 1793, *ibid.*, 26: 239–42.

27. Hammond to TJ, May 2, 1793, *ibid.*, 25: 637–40; Hammond to TJ, May 8, 1793, *ibid.*, 25: 683–7. Carroll and Ashworth, *George Washington*, 66–7. TJ to Randolph, May 8, 1793, *PTJ*, 25: 690–2.

28. GW to Henry Lee, May 6, 1793; Fitzpatrick, ed., *Writings of Washington*, 25: 665–7; TJ to Brissot de Warville, May 8, 1793, *PTJ*, 25: 679–80. Brissot was the author of a book about his travels in America and had returned home wearing simple Quaker garb.

29. See TJ to Hammond, May 15, 1793, *ibid.*, 26: 38–40. On cabinet meeting see Flexner, *George Washington*, 42; Carroll and Ashworth, *George Washington*, 68. TJ, "Notes on the *Citoyen Genêt* and Its Prizes," May 20, 1793, *PTJ*, 26: 71–2. See also TJ memo to GW, Apr. 28, 1793, *ibid.*, 25: 611.

30. TJ, "Opinion on the Restoration of Prizes," May 16, 1793, *ibid.*, 26: 50–1. The May 15, 1793 meeting and Jefferson's memo are not discussed by Elkins and McKitrick in their account stressing consensus within Washington's cabinet. See also Flexner, *George Washington*, 43; Malone, *Jefferson and his Time*, 100. TJ, the "Anas," entry for May 20, 1793, *PTJ*, 26: 71–3.

31. AH to GW, May 15, 1793, *PAH*, 14: 454–60.

32. See Carroll and Ashworth, *George Washington*, 77–8; TJ to Madison, June 2, 1793, *PTJ*, 26: 167–8; TJ, the "Anas," May 20, 1793, *ibid.*, 26: 71–3.

Chapter 9

1. Genêt quoted in Malone, *Jefferson and the Ordeal of Liberty*, 92 and 94; Elkins and McKitrick, *The Age of Federalism*, 342, TJ to Madison, May 19, 1793, *PTJ*, 26: 61–3.

2. TJ to JM, May 19, 1793, *ibid.*

3. TJ to G. Morris, Aug. 16, 1793, *PTJ*, 26: 697–715; Elkins and McKitrick, *The Age of Federalism*, 343–4.

4. On debt see, TJ to GW, June 6, 1793, *PTJ*, 26: 206; TJ to Genêt, June 11, 1793, *ibid.*, 26: 252. U.S. law required that if the whole debt was to be liquidated it be done on "advantageous terms," understood as a lower rate of interest. On cabinet opinion on the treaty, see TJ to JM, June 2, 1793, *ibid.*, 26: 167–8. See also Elkins and McKitrick, *The Age of Federalism*, 344.

5. See Genêt to TJ, May 27, 1793, *PTJ*, 26: 124–9; TJ to Genêt, June 5, 1793, *ibid.*, 26: 195–7; Genêt to TJ, June 8, 1793, *ibid.*, 26: 231–3; Elkins and McKitrick, *The Age of Federalism*, 343 and 347; Malone, *Jefferson and the Ordeal of Liberty*, 102–3.

6. See cabinet meeting opinion, June 12, 1793, *PAH*, 14: 534–5. AH to Harison, June 13–15, 1793, *ibid.*, 14: 539. See also AH to Rufus King, June 15, 1793, *ibid.*, 14: 547–8. AH explained that though the courts of a neutral nation did not as a general principle adjudicate prizes, the executive desired to have the issue of whether a U.S. court had jurisdiction in a case of alleged seizure in U.S. waters tested, "& if possible to put the affair in this train." TJ to Genêt, June 11, 1793, on debt question, *PTJ*, 26: 252; Genêt to TJ, June 14, 1793, *ibid.*, 26: 283–4; Malone, *Jefferson and the Ordeal of Liberty*, 103; Elkins and McKitrick, *The Age of Federalism*, 347.

7. TJ to Genêt, June 17, 1793, *PTJ*, 26: 297–300; Genêt to TJ, June 22, 1793, *ibid.*, 26: 339–41.

8. TJ to Monroe, June 29, 1793, *ibid.*, 26: 399; Genêt quoted in Elkins and McKitrick, *The Age of Federalism*, 348–49.

9. See TJ to Genêt, July 24, 1793 (answering Genêt's complaint of July 9, 1793), *PTJ*, 26: 557–9. See also TJ, "Notes on the Proclamation of Neutrality and the Laws of Nations," Dec. 20, 1793, *ibid.*, 27: 598–601.

10. TJ to Dr. Gilmer, June 28, 1793, *ibid.*, 26: 389–90. On same themes, see also TJ to Monroe, June 28, 1793, *ibid.*, 26: 392–3; TJ to JM, June 29, 1793, *ibid.*, 26: 401–4.

11. Malone, *Jefferson and the Ordeal of Liberty*, 104–9; TJ the "Anas," entry for July 5, 1793, *PTJ*, 26: 437–9.

12. For evidence of TJ's sympathetic view of French plans for Louisiana, see TJ to William Carmichael and William Short, May 23, 1793, *PTJ*, 25: 430. See also editorial comment, *ibid.*, 26: 395. Genêt's account quoted in Elkins and McKitrick, *The Age of Federalism*, 350.

13. AH to GW, June 21, 1793, *PAH*, 15: 13.

14. "Pacificus No. 1," June 29, 1793, *PAH*, 15: 33–43.

15. "Pacificus No. 2," July 3, 1793, *ibid.*, 15: 55–63 (AH's paraphrasing of the decree; emphasis in original).

16. *ibid.* Emphasis in original.

17. This was all the more true if the extent of the size of the combination against France was due to a degree "to imprudences on her part." NM, *Discorsi*, II, 11: 272; "Pacificus No. 3," July 6, 1793, *PAH*, 15: 65–9.

18. "Pacificus No. 4," July 10, 1793, *ibid.*, 15: 82–6; "Pacificus No. 5," July 13–17, 1793, *ibid.*, 15: 90–5.

19. "Pacificus No. 6," July 17, 1793, *ibid.*, 15: 100–6; "Pacificus No. 7," July 27, 1793, *ibid.*, 15: 130–5.

20. In a letter to his son-in-law, TJ admitted that the French had "been guilty of great errors in their conduct toward other nations, not only in insulting uselessly all crowned heads but endeavoring to force liberty on their neighbors in their own form." TJ to T. M. Randolph, Jr., June 24, 1793, *PTJ*, 26: 355–6. The phrase "unwelcome task" is Malone's. See *Jefferson and the Ordeal of Liberty*, 112. See also Elkins and McKitrick, *The Age of Federalism*, 362. Madison quoted in Banning, *The Sacred Fire of Liberty*, 377.

21. The expression "under the very nose" is Hamilton's. See "No Jacobin No. V," Aug. 14, 1793, *PAH*, 15: 245.

22. TJ report to GW on July 7, 1793, on conversation with Genêt, dated July 10, 1793, *PTJ*, 26: 463–7; TJ to JM, July 7, 1793, *ibid.*, 26: 443–4. Elkins and McKitrick, *The Age of Federalism*, 350–1.

23. See TJ, "Dissenting Opinion on the *Little Sarah*" (July 8, 1793), *PTJ*, 26: 449–52.

24. "Reasons for the Opinion of the Secretary of the Treasury and the Secretary of War Respecting the Brigantine *Little Sarah*," July 8, 1793, *PAH*, 15: 74–79.

25. Elkins and McKitrick, *The Age of Federalism*, 352; TJ, the "Anas," "Notes on Neutrality Questions," July 13, 1793, *PTJ*, 26: 498–500; TJ to Monroe, July 14, 1793, ibid., 26: 501–3.

26. On alleged "minimum of disagreement," see Elkins and McKitrick, *The Age of Federalism*, 352; Malone, *Jefferson and the Ordeal of Liberty*, 118; TJ, "Notes," cited in previous note; "Draft of Questions to be Submitted to Justices of the Supreme Court," July 18, 1793, *PAH*, 15: 110–16. The Court made its answer to Washington on Aug. 8, 1793, citing the separation of powers drawn by the Constitution. See *ibid.*, 15: 110, n. 1.

27. On saltpeter purchase, to which Jefferson agreed, see TJ, the "Anas," entry for July 15, 1793, *PTJ*, 26: 508. Hammond–AH conversation, Aug. 2–10, 1793, *PAH*, 15: 164.

28. TJ to James Monroe, July 14, 1793, on Genêt, *PTJ*, 26: 501–3; TJ memo to GW, July 26, 1793, *ibid.*, 26: 571–3.

29. On July 16 conversation with Genêt, *PTJ*, 26: 571–3. Jefferson, it will be recalled, had been in favor of allowing the French privateers fitted out in Charleston to continue to operate after the U.S. ban. The *Petite Démocrate* left Philadelphia on July 15 or 16, 1793.

30. On discussions see the lengthy account in *PAH*, 15: 139, n. 1. See also draft versions, *ibid.*, 15: 139–42, final version, Aug. 3, 1793, *ibid.*, 15: 168–9, and memo of decisions taken at the Aug. 3, 1793 meeting, *ibid.*, 15: 179–80. For TJ's account of the meeting, see TJ, "The Anas," entry for Aug. 3, 1793, *PTJ*, 26: 607–8.

31. TJ, the "Anas," entries for Aug. 1 and 2, 1793, *ibid.* 26: 598, 601–3; TJ to JM, Aug. 11, 1793, *ibid.*, 26: 651–3.

32. TJ, the "Anas," entries for Aug. 2 and 6, 1793, *ibid.*, 26: 601–3, 627–30; TJ to G. Morris, Aug. 16, 1793, *ibid.*, 26: 697–715. On "tacit bargain," see Elkins and McKitrick, *The Age of Federalism*, 363.

33. The "No Jacobin" essays are dated July 31, Aug. 8, 10, 14, 16, 23, 26, and 28, 1793. See *PAH*, 15: 145–151, 184–191, 203–7, 224–8, 243–6, 249–50, 268–70, 281–4, 304–6. The British decree provided for seizure of all ships, whatever their cargoes, trying to enter any blockaded port, and the condemnation of the ships together with their cargoes. This part of the decree made a partial exception for the ships of Denmark and Sweden, arising from treaties with those countries.

34. Richard Horton, "The Plagues are Flying," *The New York Review of Books*, vol. 48, no. 13, Aug. 9, 2001.

35. TJ to JM, Sept. 8, 1793, *PTJ*, 27: 61–3.

36. AH conversation with Hammond, Aug. 21–30, 1793, *PAH*, 15: 257.

Chapter 10

1. NM, *Discorsi*, II, 10: 266.

2. *Ibid.*, 1, 53: 198. For a rather different view, stressing the prudence of the people compared to the prince, see *ibid.*, 1, 58: 211–16. "The Federalist No. 6," in Hamilton, Jay, and Madison, *The Federalist Papers*, 25.

3. NM, *Discorsi*, III, 41: 523.

4. TJ, the "Anas" entries for Nov. 21 and 23, 1793, in *PTJ*, 27: 399–401. TJ, "Anas" entry on Nov. 28, 1793 cabinet meeting, *ibid.*, 27: 453–6.

5. For TJ's "Report on Commerce," see *ibid.*, 27: 567–600. TJ to Martha Jefferson, Dec. 22, 1793, *ibid.*, 27: 607–8.

6. Flexner, *George Washington*, 110–11. Jefferson wrote of Randolph, "He is the poorest Cameleon I ever saw having no colour of his own, and reflecting that nearest him. When he is with me he is a whig, when with H. he is a tory, when with the P. [President] he is what he thinks will please him. The last is his strongest hue." TJ to JM, Aug. 11, 1793, *PTJ*, 26: 652; Bemis, *Jay's Treaty*, 292.

7. Elkins and McKitrick, *The Age of Federalism*, 388–9.

8. On the House debate, see Mitchell, *Alexander Hamilton: The National Adventure*, 292–3. AH to Angelica Church, Dec. 27, 1793, *PAH*, 15: 593.

9. On "optimistic fatalism," see Herbert Croly, *The Promise of American Life* (1909) (New York: Anchon Books, 1963), 18; TJ in *PAH*, 16: 264.

10. Samuel Eliot Morison, *The Maritime History of Massachusetts, 1783–1860* (Boston: Houghton Mifflin, 1961), 170. On British orders, see Mayo, ed., *Instructions to the British Ministers to the United States*, 47 n. 10; See also Ritcheson, *Aftermath of Revolution*, 302–3. On the reexport trade, see Perkins, *The First Rapprochement*, 81–2, 86–7.

11. On Dorchester's speech, see Randolph to Hammond, May 20, 1794, in *American State Papers* Class I, *Foreign Relations*: 1 (Buffalo: W. S. Hein, 1998), 461–2; Elkins and McKitrick, *The Age of Federalism*, 391–2.

12. Bemis, *Jay's Treaty*, 373; Mitchell, *Alexander Hamilton: The National Adventure*, 331; DeConde, *Entangling Alliance*, 110; Elkins and McKitrick, *The Age of Federalism*, 396. According to Kaplan (*Alexander Hamilton*, 114), "it was Hamilton who crafted the instructions Jay was to follow." To his credit he adds (119) that "Jay was much more than Hamilton's mouthpiece."

13. "Americanus No. I," Jan. 31, 1794, *PAH*, 15: 669–78.

14. "Americanus No. II," Feb. 7, 1794, *PAH*, 16: 12–19.

15. *Ibid.*

16. AH to GW, Mar. 8, 1794, *ibid.*, 16: 134–6. GW, "Fifth Annual Address to Congress," Dec. 3, 1793, Fitzpatrick, ed., *Writings of Washington*, 33: 166.

17. Elkins and McKitrick, *The Age of Federalism*, 390, 828 n. 42; Morison, *The Maritime History of Massachusetts*, Chapter 12. Rufus King's notes, Mar. 10–May 6, 1794, quoted in *PAH*, 16: 262.

18. On the financial controversy, see AH report to the select committee, Apr. 1, 1794, *PAH*, 16: 231–2; GW to AH, Apr. 8, 1794, *ibid.*, 16: 249; AH to GW, Apr. 8, 1794, *ibid.*, 16: 250–3; GW to AH, Apr. 27, 1794, *ibid.*, 16: 349; Carroll and Ashworth, *George Washington*, 167; McDonald, *Alexander Hamilton*, 292. On the embargo, see Robert Ernst, *Rufus King: American Federalist* (Chapel Hill: University of North Carolina Press, 1968), 198. GW to William Pearce, Apr. 20, 1794, in Fitzpatrick, ed., *Writings of Washington*, 33: 336.

19. Elkins and McKitrick, *The Age of Federalism*, 392–4. On possible effect of British setbacks, see GW to Gov. George Clinton, Mar. 31, 1794, Fitzpatrick, ed., *Writings of Washington*, 33: 310. On London's failure to foresee the American reaction to the November 1793 decree, see Ehrman, *The Younger Pitt*, 2: 508.

20. McDonald, *Alexander Hamilton*, 293–4; Elkins and McKitrick, *The Age of Federalism*, 394; Bemis, *Jay's Treaty*, 270. See also Lycan, *Alexander Hamilton and American Foreign Policy*, 221–5, for a position similar to those of McDonald and Bemis.

21. AH to GW, Apr. 14, 1794, *PAH*, 16: 266–79.

22. *Ibid.*
23. *Ibid.*
24. *Ibid.*
25. JJ to Sally Jay, Apr. 19, 1794, in Henry P. Johnston, ed., *The Correspondence and Public Papers of John Jay* (New York: B. Franklin, 1970) (hereafter *CPPJJ*,vol: page), 4: 3.
26. See Hammond to Grenville, Apr. 17, 1794, reporting a conversation held on Apr. 15 or 16, *PAH*, 16: 281–6 (emphasis added).
27. Jay's role is evident from what Hamilton wrote (and crossed out) in a letter to him on May 6: "Our conversations have anticipated so much that I could say little here which would not be repetitive." *Ibid.*, 16: 381–5; "Rufus King Notes," Mar. 10–May 6, 1794, quoted in *ibid.*, 16: 319, n. 1. See also *ibid.*, 16: 381, n. 3.
28. AH to GW, Apr. 23, 1794, *ibid.*, 16: 319–23, and "Suggestions for a Commercial Treaty," Apr.–May, 1794, *ibid.*, 16: 357–8.
29. AH to GW, Mar. 28, 1796, *PAH*, 20: 83.
30. For Jay's instructions, see *PAH*, 16: 323–8.
31. AH to JJ, May 6, 1794, *ibid.*, 16: 381–5.
32. Bemis, *Jay's Treaty*, 298.
33. See Elkins and McKitrick, *The Age of Federalism*, 398–401, for an extensive discussion of AH's letter.

Chapter 11

1. The expression "lost founding father" is Flexner's (*George Washington*, 139). Elkins and McKitrick, *The Age of Federalism*, interestingly, provide a character sketch of most of the main personalities of the 1790s (Gouverneur Morris, for example), but not of Jay. Letter to Washington quoted in Richard B. Morris, ed., *John Jay: The Making of a Revolutionary, Unpublished Papers 1745–1780* (New York: Harper & Row, 1975) (hereafter Morris, 1), 512. For background on Jay, see Carl L. Becker, "John Jay and Peter Van Schaack," in *Everyman His Own Historian: Essays on History and Politics* (New York: F. F. Crofts, 1935), 284–98; Richard B. Morris, ed., *John Jay: The Winning of the Peace, Unpublished Papers 1780–1784* (New York: Harper & Row, 1980) (hereafter Morris, 2), Introduction.
2. On the Columbia incident, see Morris, 1: 55; JJ draft in *ibid.*, 153; JJ to GM, Apr. 29, 1778, *ibid.*, 475–6.
3. On Jay's character, see David Hackett Fischer, *The Revolution of American Conservatism: The Federalist Party in the Era of Jeffersonian Democracy* (New York: Harper & Row, 1965), 6–10. On Spanish incident, see Morris, 2: 97; GM to JJ, June 17, 1781, *ibid.*, 86.
4. On Jay in Paris, see *ibid.*, 285–619.
5. JJ to Sarah Jay, Nov. 14, 1783, *ibid.*, 642; JJ to Charles Thomson, Nov. 14, 1783, *CPPJJ*, 3: 96; Adams quoted in John E. Crowley, "The Sensibility of Comfort," *The American Historical Review* 104: 3 (June 1999) (749–82), 771; JJ to Lord Landsdowne (formerly the Earl of Shelburne), Apr. 20, 1786, Morris, 2: 192; Bemis, *Jay's Treaty*, 284–5; Ritcheson, *Aftermath of Revolution*, 322.

6. JJ to Randolph, Mar. 5, 1795 *American State Papers*, Class 1, 1: 518–19.
7. Bemis, *Jay's Treaty*, 282, 287; Elkins and McKitrick, *The Age of Federalism*, 401–2.
8. Grenville to Hammond, Aug. 8, 1794, in Mayo, ed., *Instructions to the British Ministers to the United States*, 64; JJ to Randolph, June 23, 1794, *CPPJJ*, 4: 28–29; JJ to AH, July 18, 1794, *PAH*, 16: 608–9.
9. See JJ to GW, Aug. 5, 1794, *CPPJJ*, 4: 44–5; Grenville to JJ, Aug. 1, 1794, *ibid.*, 4: 41–4; JJ to GW, July 21, 1794, *ibid.*, 4: 33–4; Bemis, *Jay's Treaty*, 318–23.
10. According to an authoritative British account, the Jay treaty was the "one relief" for the government's foreign policy during this period. Grenville and Jay "soon became, and remained, firm friends." Ehrman, *The Younger Pitt*, 2: 378, 511.
11. Grenville to Hammond, Nov. 20, 1794, in Mayo, ed., *Instructions to the British Ministers to the United States*, 69. Grenville to JJ, Mar. 17, 1796, *CPPJJ*, 4: 205 (one of a number of letters from Grenville to Jay after the latter's return to the U.S.).
12. JJ to Randolph, Sept. 13, 1794, *ibid.*, 4: 60–5. For Aug. 6, 1794 working paper, see *ibid.*, 66–71.
13. Grenville to JJ, Aug. 30, 1794, *ibid.*, 4: 71–85.
14. JJ to Grenville, Sept. 1 and Sept. 4, 1794, *ibid.*, 4: 85–94; Grenville to JJ, Sept. 5, 1794, *ibid.*, 4: 94–6. For JJ's notes, *ibid.*, 4: 97–99.
15. Grenville to JJ, Sept. 7, 1794, containing observations on JJ's notes, *ibid.*, 4: 99–104. Grenville to JJ on Monroe, Sept. 7, 1794, quoted in Bemis, *Jay's Treaty*, 333, n. 38. Grenville's brother, the Marquis of Buckingham, wrote him on Aug. 10: "I am glad that your American treaty goes on to your liking. We have indeed enough on our hands." Quoted in *ibid.*, 325.
16. JJ to AH, Sept. 17, 1794, *CPPJJ*, 4: 114–15.
17. Bemis, *Jay's Treaty*, 334. See also *ibid.*, Appendix III, for Bemis's comparison of Jay's Sept. 30 draft with the final treaty.
18. *Ibid.*, 336; Elkins and McKitrick, *The Age of Federalism*, 410.
19. Bemis, *Jay's Treaty*, 339, 343–4. Grenville to Hammond, May 10, 1794, in Mayo, ed., *Instructions to the British Ministers to the United States*, 54; Randolph to JJ, May 27, 1794, in *American State Papers*, Class 1, 1: 474.
20. "Conversation with George Hammond," July 1–10, 1794, *PAH*, 16: 548.
21. On this point see John C. Miller, *Alexander Hamilton*, 420; Bemis, *Jay's Treaty*, 314. On materials, see AH to King, Sept. 17, 1794, *PAH*, 17: 241. See also AH to Thomas Pinckney, June 25, 1794, *ibid.*, 16: 527–9, requesting the U.S. minister to arrange for the shipment of the materials.
22. JJ to Ellsworth, Nov. 19, 1794, *CPPJJ*, 4: 132–3; JJ to AH, Nov. 19, 1794, *ibid.*, 4: 135; JJ to Randolph, Nov. 19, 1794, *ibid.*, 4: 137–44; JJ to GW, Nov. 19, 1794, *ibid.*, 4: 133–5; JJ to King, Nov. 19, 1794, *ibid.*, 4: 136; JJ to GW, Mar. 6, 1795, *ibid.*, 4: 170.
23. By 1801, U.S. ships carried as much as seventy percent of foreign trade with India and probably as much as the East India Company itself. Perkins, *The First Rapprochement*, 73.
24. For text of the treaty, see Bemis, *Jay's Treaty*, 452–87; JJ to GW, Mar. 6, 1794, *CPPJJ*, 4: 163. On violation of French treaties, see DeConde, *Entangling Alliance*, 109.

25. Henry Adams quoted in Bemis, *Jay's Treaty*, 370. See also *ibid.*, 356–73.
26. On Wayne's successful campaign against the Indians, see Kohn, *Eagle and Sword*, 139–57.
27. Hawkesbury (later Lord Sheffield) quoted in, Bemis, *Jay's Treaty* 371, n. 26. Elkins and McKitrick, *The Age of Federalism*, 410–14. For Hamilton's objections to Article 12, see AH to Randolph, Dec. 1–12, 1794, *PAH*, 17: 409–10.
28. A distinguished admirer observed (though not in relation to the Jay treaty negotiations): "Hamilton was never conspicuous for the patient and tolerant qualities which make a great diplomat." Henry Cabot Lodge, *Alexander Hamilton* (New York: Houghton Mifflin, 1898), 19. For a different view of Hamilton's prospects in Jay's shoes, see Lycan, *Alexander Hamilton and American Foreign Policy*, 224.

Chapter 12

1. AH to GW, May 27, 1794, *PAH*, 16: 434–5; GW to AH, May 29, 1794, *ibid.*, 16: 441–2.
2. AH to Angelica Church, Oct. 23, 1794, *PAH*, 17: 340; AH to the New York Committee of Correspondence, Apr. 20, 1777, *ibid.*, 1: 233–4; NM, *Discorsi*, II, 23: 325; NM, *Il Principe*, 3: 36.
3. On conspiracies, see Kohn, *Eagle and Sword*, 217. On episode in general, *ibid.*, 161–73. GW to H. Lee, Aug. 26, 1794, Fitzpatrick, ed., *Writings of Washington*, 33: 475.
4. AH conversation with Hammond, Dec. 23, 1794–Jan. 5, 1794, in *PAH*, 17: 459.
5. AH to Angelica Church, Dec. 8, 1794, *ibid.*, 17: 428 (emphasis in orginal); Wolcott to AH, Sept. 26, 1795, *ibid.*, 18: 295.
6. GW to AH, Feb. 2, 1795, *ibid.*, 18: 247–8; AH to GW, Feb. 3, 1795, *ibid.*, 18: 253; J. McHenry to AH, Feb. 17, 1795, *ibid.*, 18: 275.
7. Herbert E. Sloan, "Hamilton's Second Thoughts," in Ben-Atar and Oberg, eds., *Federalists Reconsidered*, 61–76.
8. Carroll and Ashworth, *George Washington*, 233, n. 122. AH to Rufus King, Feb. 21, 1795, *PAH*, 18: 278–9.
9. AH to R. Troup, Apr. 13, 1795, *ibid.*, 18: 329.
10. Flexner, *George Washington*, 194.
11. *Ibid.*, 207, 209.
12. On Washington's reaction see *ibid.*, 204–6; GW to AH, July 13, 1795, *PAH*, 18: 461–3.
13. On publication of the treaty see *PAH*, 18: 389–90, n. 2. On reaction to treaty see Flexner, *George Washington*, 217, Elkins and McKitrick, *The Age of Federalism*, 420–1. Adet replaced Joseph Fauchet on June 13, 1795.
14. GW quoted in Flexner, *George Washington*, 219, 220.
15. Flexner, *George Washington*, 211–12. See also GW to AH, July 3, 1795, *PAH*, 18: 398–400; AH to GW, July 9, 1795, *ibid.*, 18: 403–54.
16. GW to AH, July 13, 1795, *PAH*, 18: 461–3. Washington, however, continued to voice doubts about Article 3, which let the British keep their trading rights on the U.S. side of the border in return for something he felt U.S. traders would have acquired on their own without an expensive concession: penetration of the

Canadian market. AH's reply was not found by the editors of his papers, but it is referred to in GW to AH, July 14, 1795, *ibid.*, 18: 466–7.

17. GW to JJ, Aug. 31, 1795, *CPPJJ*, 4: 188. See also Elkins and McKitrick, *The Age of Federalism*, 421; DeConde, *Entangling Alliance*, 418.

18. On the Randolph affair, see Flexner, *George Washington*, Chapters 22–3; Elkins and McKitrick, *The Age of Federalism*, 426–30. Pickering to GW, July 31, 1795, quoted in Fitzpatrick, ed., *Writings of Washington*, 34: 265, n. 81.

19. GW wrote AH, mentioning his "very serious doubts of the propriety" of ratifying with the order still in effect. See GW to AH, Oct. 29, 1795, *PAH*, 18: 359. DeConde, *Entangling Alliance*, 108.

20. Flexner, *George Washington*, 235–6; Elkins and McKitrick, *The Age of Federalism*, 426. Wolcott to John Marshall, June 9, 1806, quoted in *PAH*, 18: 434, n. 5.

21. GW to AH, Aug. 31, 1795, *PAH*, 18: 205. For AH's view of the ratification conditions, see AH to Wolcott, Aug. 10, 1795, *ibid.*, 18: 111–12. He recommended that Washington sign the treaty but that the exchange of ratifications be withheld until the highly offensive order was revoked. AH to GW, Sept. 4, 1795, *ibid.*, 18: 232–6.

22. GW to AH, Oct. 29, 1795, *ibid.*, 18: 355–63; AH to GW, Nov. 5, 1795, *ibid.*, 18: 395–9.

Chapter 13

1. NM, *Discorsi*, II, 26: 341; II, 27: 345.

2. Plutarch, *The Lives of the Noble Grecians and Romans*, 170–200. NM, *Discorsi*, II, 23: 324–5; III, 23: 471–2; III, 30: 488–91.

3. See AH to Nicholson, July 20, 1795, *PAH*, 18: 471. On apology, based on a statement prepared by one of AH's seconds, Nicholas Fish, see *ibid.*, 18: 502–3, n. 5. See also AH to Troup, July 25, 1795, *ibid.*, 18: 503–7.

4. "The Defense No. 1," July 22, 1795, *ibid.*, 18: 479–89; "The Defense No. 2," July 25, 1795, *ibid.*, 18: 493–501.

5. "The Defense No. 3," July 29, 1795, *ibid.*, 18: 513–23. Article 5 of the peace treaty said that Congress should recommend to the state legislatures that they provide for the restitution of property to British subjects. Hamilton saw merit in the British argument that the slaves in their possession, as personal property, were legitimate war booty and that they had committed no new depredation by refusing to return them at the end of the war. See also, "The Defense No. 4," where Hamilton goes even further on the point concerning the posts. Aug. 1, 1795, *PAH*, 19: 77–85.

6. "The Defense No. 5," Aug. 5, 1795, *ibid.*, 19: 89–97.

7. "The Defense No. 6," Aug. 8, 1795, *ibid.*, 19: 105–11; "The Defense No. 7," Aug. 12, 1795, *ibid.*, 19: 115–24.

8. TJ to Philip Mazzei, Apr. 24, 1796, quoted in Lycan, *Alexander Hamilton and American Foreign Policy*, 242. TJ to JM, Sept. 21, 1795, quoted in *PAH*, 18: 478, "Introductory Note."

9. On Article 12, see "The Defense No. 15," Nov. 18, 1795, *PAH*, 19: 441–9. On "free ships make free goods," see "The Defense No. 31," Dec. 12, 1795, *ibid.*,

19: 473–84. On contraband, see "The Defense No. 32," Dec. 16, 1795, *ibid.*, 19: 487–95, and "The Defense No. 33," Dec. 19, 1795, *ibid.*, 19: 500–11.

10. See "The Defense No. 36," Jan. 2, 1796, *PAH*, 20: 3–10; "The Defense No. 37," Jan. 6, 1796, *ibid.*, 20: 13–22; "The Defense No. 38," Jan. 9, 1796, *ibid.*, 20: 22–34.

11. AH draft, Nov. 28–Dec. 7, 1795, *PAH*, 18: 460–7. Jay also contributed to the final version. Flexner, *George Washington*, 250–5.

12. AH to GW, Mar. 7, 1796, *PAH*, 20: 68; AH to W. L. Smith, Mar. 10, 1796, *ibid.*, 20: 72; AH to GW, Mar. 28, 1796, *ibid.*, 20: 83–5; AH to GW, Mar. 29, 1796 (with draft message), *ibid.*, 20: 85–6.

13. AH to King, Apr. 15, 1796, *ibid.*, 20: 112–15. Elkins and McKitrick, *The Age of Federalism*, 441–9. On Madison's position, see Banning, *The Sacred Fire of Liberty*, 380–4; Tucker and Hendrickson, *Empire of Liberty*, 68–9; Rakove, *Original Meanings*, 357–65.

14. Morris to AH, Mar. 4, 1796, *PAH*, 20: 59–62; GW to AH, May 8, 1796, *ibid.*, 20: 162–6.

15. Monroe quoted in Elkins and McKitrick, *The Age of Federalism*, 502. See also, *ibid.*, 503–13; DeConde, *Entangling Alliance*, Chapters 13–14.

16. Elkins and McKitrick, *The Age of Federalism*, 508–9, on France and the Jay treaty; Flexner, *George Washington*, 317; AH to GW, June 16, 1796, *PAH*, 20: 225–6.

17. AH to Wolcott, June 15, 1796, *ibid.*, 20: 223–4; AH to GW, May 20, 1796, *ibid.*, 20: 190–5.

18. AH to GW, June 16, 1796, *ibid.*, 20: 225–6; AH to Wolcott, June 15, 1796, *ibid.*, 20: 223–4; AH to GW, July 5, 1796, *ibid.*, 20: 246–7.

19. AH to Wolcott, Apr. 20, 1796, *ibid.*, 20: 128; AH to GW, May 20, 1796, *ibid.*, 20: 194–5; King to AH, May 1, 1796, *ibid.*, 20: 152; AH to Wolcott, June 16, 1796, *ibid.*, 20: 224.

20. "Design for a Seal for the United States," May 1796, *ibid.*, 20: 208–9.

Chapter 14

1. Miller, *Alexander Hamilton*, 442–5; Gilbert, *To the Farewell Address*, 111–14, 129, and 132–4. On the authorship controversy, see Victor Hugo Paltsits, *Washington's Farewell Address* (New York: The New York Public Library, 1935), Chapter 5.

2. Bailey, *A Diplomatic History of the American people*, 90; Matthew Spalding, "George Washington's Farewell Address," *Wilson Quarterly*, Autumn 1996, 66; Flexner, *George Washington*, 307; Jay to Richard Peters, Mar. 29, 1811, reprinted in Paltsits, *Washington's Farewell Address*, 265.

3. For Washington's May 20, 1792, letter to Madison, see Paltsits, *Washington's Farewell Address*, 221–3. For Madison's draft, sent June 20, 1792, see *ibid.*, 160–3.

4. For GW's 1796 draft, see Paltsits, *Washington's Farewell Address*, 164–73. For his reasoning in including the Madison quote, see GW to AH, May 15, 1796, *PAH*, 20: 176. Gilbert, *To the Farewell Address*, 124.

5. For Washington's draft, see Paltsits, *Washington's Farewell Address*, 164–173.

6. *Ibid.*
7. *Ibid.*
8. AH to GW, May 10, 1796, *PAH*, 20: 173–4.
9. GW to AH, May 15, 1796, *ibid.*, 20: 174–8. Gilbert, *To the Farewell Address*, 125–6.
10. NM, *Discorsi*, I, 58: 211–16; III, 9: 419–22. On this point see also discussion in Chapters 1 and 2 of this book.
11. AH to King, Apr. 15, 1796, *PAH*, 20: 115; AH to GW, July 5, 1796, *ibid.*, 20: 247.
12. On the qualities the prince should always display, see NM, *Il Principe*, 18: 104. GW to AH, expressing his preference, Aug. 25, 1796, *PAH*, 20: 307. For Hamilton's shorter draft, sent to Washington on Aug. 10, 1796, see *ibid.*, 20: 294–303.
13. AH to GW, July 30, 1796, *PAH.*, 20: 265. For the Hamilton draft, *ibid.*, 20: 265–88. An example of toned down "egotism" is the passage (287) beginning, "Neither ambition nor interest has been the impelling cause of my actions." See also, *ibid.*, 20: 267–9, 286.
14. *Ibid.*, 20: 282 and 284; Flexner, *George Washington*, 301.
15. Gilbert, *To the Farewell Address*, 122; Morgan, *The Genius of George Washington*, 82–7. GW to G. Morris, Dec. 22, 1795, Fitzpatrick, ed., *Writings of George Washington*, 34: 401.
16. On Washington's changes, see also *PAH*, 20: 272 and 277; Flexner, *George Washington*, 299–300.
17. Flexner, *George Washington*, 284–5; Paltsits, *Washington's Farewell Address*, 146, 155, and 170. Hamilton's version stood, that is, except that Washington changed the word "dictate" to "counsel."
18. On credit, see *PAH*, 20: 281; Paltsits, *Washington's Farewell Address*, 152.
19. On alliances, see *PAH*, 20: 275; Paltsits, *Washington's Farewell Address*, 146; NM, *Discorsi*, I, 59: 217–19. See also Markus Fischer, "Machiavelli's Theory of Foreign Politics," *Security Studies* vol. 5 (2) Winter 1995 (248–79), 261. On human nature, see *PAH*, 20: 277 and 279; Paltsits, *Washington's Farewell Address*, 148 and 150.
20. On religion, see *PAH*, 20: 280; Paltsits, *Washington's Farewell Address*, 151; NM, *Discorsi*, I, 11: 69–73; III, 33: 499–501.
21. *PAH*, 20: 280–1; Paltsits, *Washington's Farewell Address*, 152, showing the excised part and marginal notation. NM, *Discorsi*, III, 25: 475–7.
22. Paltsits, *Washington's Farewell Address*, 168 and 156.
23. Ellis sums up the matter thusly: "Some of the words were Madison's; most of the words were Hamilton's; all the ideas were Washington's." *Founding Brothers*, 148. It is more accurate to say that a few of the words were Madison's, many of the words were Hamilton's, and most, but certainly not all of the ideas, were Washington's.

Chapter 15

1. *American State Papers, Foreign Relations*, 1: 576–7; Elkins and McKitrick, *The Age of Federalism*, 520–1.

2. AH to Wolcott, Nov. 1, 1796, *PAH*, 20: 361; GW to AH, Nov. 2, 1796, *ibid.*, 20: 362–6; AH to GW, Nov. 4, 1796, *ibid.*, 20: 372–3.
3. Pickering to Adet, Nov. 1, 1796, *American State Papers, Foreign Relations*, 1: 578. AH to Wolcott, Nov. 9, 1796, *PAH*, 20: 380; AH to GW, Nov. 5, 1796, *ibid.*, 20: 374; AH to GW, Nov. 11, 1796, *ibid.*, 20: 389–90.
4. Adet to Pickering, Nov. 15, 1796, *American State Papers, Foreign Relations*, 1: 579–667. AH to GW, Nov. 19, 1796, *PAH*, 20: 408–9; AH to Wolcott, Nov. 22, 1796, *ibid.*, 20: 411–14; AH to King, Dec. 16, 1796, *ibid.*, 20: 445.
5. "The Answer" by "Americanus," Dec. 8, 1796, *ibid.*, 20: 421–34. Miller, *Alexander Hamilton*, 450; DeConde, *Entangling Alliance*, 476–7.
6. AH to King, Feb. 15, 1797, *PAH*, 20: 515; AH to GW, comparing French and British behavior, Jan. 19, 1797, *ibid.*, 20: 469–70.
7. King to AH, Mar. 8, 1797, *ibid.*, 20: 533–6. AH to King, Dec. 16, 1796, *ibid.*, 20: 446. Hamilton's words were preceded by: "The favourable change in the conduct of Great Britain towards us strengthens the hand of the friends of Order & peace. It is much to be desired that a treatment, in all respects unexceptionable from that quarter, should obviate all pretext to inflame the public mind."
8. AH to Pickering, Feb. 10, 1797, *ibid.*, 20: 514; "The Warning No. I," Jan. 27, 1797, *ibid.*, 20: 490–5; "The Warning No. II," Feb. 7, 1797, *ibid.*, 20: 509–512 (emphasis added). AH to McHenry, Mar. 22, 1797, *ibid.*, 20: 575; "The Warning No. III," Feb. 21, 1797, *ibid.*, 20: 517–20.
9. AH to GW, Jan. 25–31, 1797, *ibid.*, 20: 480–1; AH to Sedgwick, Feb. 26, 1797, *ibid.*, 20: 521–3.
10. AH to McHenry, Mar. 22, 1797, *ibid.*, 20: 574–5; AH to Pickering, Mar. 29, 1797, *ibid.*, 20: 556–7. For similar appeals on the commission, see AH to Pickering, Mar. 22, 1797, *ibid.*, 20: 545–6; AH to Wolcott, Mar. 30, 1797, *ibid.*, 20: 567–8; AH to William Loughton Smith, Apr. 5, 1797, *ibid.*, 21: 20–1.
11. Wolcott to AH, Mar. 31, 1797, *ibid.*, 20: 569–74; AH to Wolcott, Apr. 5, 1797, *ibid.*, 21: 22–3.
12. AH to Smith, Apr. 5, 1797, *ibid.*, 21: 20–1.
13. AH to Smith, with enclosure, Apr. 10, 1797, *ibid.*, 21: 29–41.
14. Smith to AH, May 1, 1797, *ibid.*, 21: 75–6. On Smith's resolutions, see *ibid.*, 21: 38. Pickering to AH, Apr. 29, 1797, *ibid.*, 21: 68. Smith to AH, May 1, 1797, *ibid.*, 21: 75; JA to Elbridge Gerry, Apr. 6, 1797, Adams, *Works*, 8: 538. On Jefferson, see Elkins and McKitrick, *The Age of Federalism*, 542, 566–7.
15. Elkins and McKitrick, *The Age of Federalism*, 544, 547–8. AH to McHenry, Apr. 5, 1797, *PAH*, 21: 23.
16. See John Lawrence to Rufus King, Oct. 15, 1796, Charles R. King, ed. *The Life and Correspondence of Rufus King* (New York: Da Capo Press, 1971) (hereafter, *LCRK*), 2: 98; Robert Troup to Rufus King, Jan. 28, 1797, *ibid.*, 2: 136–7; AH to King, Feb. 15, 1797, *PAH*, 20: 515–16; AH to Elizabeth Hamilton, Apr. 16, 1797, *ibid.*, 21: 49–50. On *Louis Le Guen v Issac Gouverneur and Peter Kemble*, see, Goebel, ed., *The Law Practice of Alexander Hamilton*, 2: 48–89. The case was not definitively settled in favor of Hamilton's client, Le Guen, until February 1800.

17. AH to King, Apr. 8, 1797, *PAH*, 21: 26; McHenry to AH, Apr. 14 and 19, 1797, *ibid.*, 21: 48–9, 51–2; AH to McHenry, Apr. 29 and Apr. (undated) 1797, *ibid.*, 21: 61–8, 72–5.

18. On Adams as an alleged "weakling" in AH's eyes, see Miller, *Alexander Hamilton*, 458.

Chapter 16

1. Elkins and McKitrick, *The Age of Federalism*, 531. Benjamin Franklin, another premier diplomat of the revolutionary era, had died in 1790.

2. JA to Abigail Adams, May 26, 1794, in C. F. Adams, ed., *Letters of John Adams addressed to his Wife* (Boston: Freeman and Bolles, 1841), 2: 162.

3. Adams quoted in Dauer, *The Adams Federalists*, 44, 45 and 66. On Adams's political views and the influence of his time in Europe, see Joyce Appleby, "The New Republican Synthesis and the Changing Political Ideas of John Adams," *American Quarterly*, Dec. 1973, 578–595.

4. AH, "Letter From Alexander Hamilton, Concerning the Public Conduct and Character of John Adams, Esq. President of the United States," Oct. 24, 1800, *PAH*, 25: 187–91.

5. JA to GW, Aug. 29, 1790, in Adams, *Works*, 8: 497–500.

6. See discussion of dinner in Chapter 4 of this book. On Adams's economic ideas, see Dauer, *The Adams Federalists*, Chapter 4. Adams quoted in Dauer, *ibid.*, 69–70.

7. Adams, *Works*, 1: 616.

8. JA to AA, Apr. 15, 1794, *ibid.*, 1: 155; JA to AA, Apr. 9, 1796, *ibid.*, 1: 217; JA to AA, June 19, 1795, *ibid.*, 1: 185. The phrase "supercilious neglect" is that of C. F. Adams, *ibid.*, 1: 420. Adams later suspected that Thomas Pinckney, a classmate of foreign secretary Lord Leeds at Westminster School years before the revolution, had helped to cut short his mission in London and had been appointed minister there in 1792 thanks to covert British influence in the United States. He apparently forgot that he himself had asked Congress to be recalled. See JA to Tench Coxe, May 1792, printed in *PAH*, 25: 110, n. 110.

9. For Adams's philosophy of foreign affairs, see JA to James Lloyd, Mar. 29, 1815, Adams, *Works*, 10: 147.

10. For Adams's description of AH as an intriguer and an ignorant foreigner, see JA to James Lloyd, Feb. 17, 1815, *ibid.*, 10: 124. On New England's advantages, see JA to AA, Oct. 29, 1775, in *ibid.*, 1: 74.

11. Adams quoted in Dauer, *The Adams Federalists*, 110–11. See also Kurtz, *The Presidency of John Adams*, Chapter 5; Elkins and McKitrick, *The Age of Federalism*, 524–5; Miller, *Alexander Hamilton*, Chapter 28; Mitchell, *Alexander Hamilton: The National Adventure*, 480; Dauer, *The Adams Federalists*, Chapter 6; Ernst, *Rufus King*, 215–16; James Roger Sharp, *American Politics in the Early Republic: The New Nation in Crisis* (New Haven: Yale University Press, 1993), 147–9. For the view that Hamilton did not plot against Adams, see McDonald, *Alexander Hamilton*, 327, 438, n. 35; Cooke, *Alexander Hamilton*, 172; Walling, *Republican Empire*, 224; and Ferling, *John Adams*, 329.

12. AH to Wilson, Jan. 25, 1789, *PAH*, 5: 248–9. Adams quoted in Dauer, *The Adams Federalists*, 82–3. AH to C. C. Pinckney, Oct. 10, 1792, *PAH*, 12: 544.

13. Elkins and McKitrick, *The Age of Federalism*, 525–8; Kurtz, *The Presidency of John Adams*, 106.

14. Kurtz, *The Presidency of John Adams*, 148. Acknowledging that Pinckney might edge out Adams if they were supported equally in New England, Oliver, Jr. observed, "It is certainly a painful idea to think of exposing his [Adams's] election to any risque – his long services, his talents, his integrity and patriotism demand the proofs of confidence which the present election offers [sic] .... Besides, it is disagreeable to think of elevating a person to the Chief Magistracy who has been recently hacknied and vulgarized as Mr. Pinckney must have been in Europe." Oliver Wolcott, Jr., to Oliver Wolcott, Sr., Nov. 27, 1796, in George Gibbs, *Memoirs of the Administrations of Washington and Adams edited from the Papers of Oliver Wolcott, Secretary of the Treasury* (New York: William Van Norden, 1846), 1: 400–3; Oliver Wolcott, Sr., to Oliver Wolcott, Jr., Dec. 12, 1796, *ibid.*, 1: 408–10. The 1796 electoral vote:

State	Adams	TJ	TP	Burr	S. Adams	Ellsworth	Scattered
NH	6					6	
VT	4		4				
MA	16	13				1	2
RI	4					4	
CN	9	4					5
NY	12		12				
NJ	7		7				
PA	1	14	2	13			
DE	3		3				
MD	7	4	4	3			2
VA	1	20	1	1	15		4
NC	1	11	1	6			5
SC		8	8				
GA		4					4
KY		4	4				
TN		3	3				
Total	71	68	59	30	15	11	22

15. AH to _____, Nov. 8, 1796, *PAH*, 20: 376–7; AH to Wadsworth, Dec. 1, 1796, *ibid.*, 20: 418.

16. Wolcott to AH, Nov. 6, 1796, *ibid.*, 20: 375–6. Around the same time, Hamilton received a similar analysis of the implications of the Pennsylvania vote from Congressman Harper. Harper wrote on November 4, "Upon the whole, if the Pennsylvania election for Electors should turn out well, I think Adams will beat Jefferson; but Pinckney you are sure of, if you support him North of the Delaware. I have declared that you will do so. Jefferson's friends would infinitely

rather see Pinckney President than Adams, and many of them will support him with that view." Harper to AH, Nov. 4, 1796, *ibid.*, 20: 372.

17. AH to King, Dec. 16, 1796, *ibid.*, 20: 445.

18. Higginson to AH, Dec. 9, 1796, *ibid.*, 20: 437–8.

19. Higginson to AH, Jan. 12, 1797, *ibid.*, 20: 465–6.

20. Gerry to Abigail Adams, Jan. 7, 1797, quoted in Dauer, *The Adams Federalists*, 114.

21. TJ to JA, Dec. 28, 1796, in Cappon, ed., *The Adams-Jefferson Correspondence*, 262–3; Elkins and McKitrick, *The Age of Federalism*, 540–1

22. JA to Gerry, Feb. 13, 1797, in Adams, *Works*, 8: 524. Kurtz, *The Presidency of John Adams*, 225. On Adams's initial skepticism with regard to the rumors, see also Ferling, *John Adams*, 390.

23. Troup to King, Nov. 15, 1796, quoted in Dauer, *The Adams Federalists*, 98.

24. AH to Marshall, Apr. 14, 1796 (this letter is referred to in Marshall's reply but was not found by the editors of AH's papers); Marshall to AH, Apr. 25, 1796, *PAH*, 20: 137–8; King to AH, May 2, 1796, enclosing a letter from Marshall to King, dated Apr. 19, 1796, which relates Marshall's and Henry Lee's approach to Patrick Henry, *ibid.*, 20: 151–3; AH to King, May 4, 1796, *ibid.*, 20: 158.

25. Troup to King, Nov. 16, 1798, *LCRK*, 2: 466.

26. See Troup to King, Jan. 28, 1797, *ibid.*, 2: 135. McDonald, *Alexander Hamilton*, 438–9, n. 45. The author is grateful to Professor McDonald for answering a query on this point. King to JQA, Nov. 10, 1796, *LCRK*, 2: 104.

27. AH, "Letter From Alexander Hamilton," Oct. 24, 1800, *PAH*, 25: 195–6.

28. NM, *Discorsi*, III, 6: 386–413.

29. AH to King, Feb. 15, 1797, *PAH*, 20: 516.

30. The two had first accused Hamilton after Wolcott, then comptroller of the Treasury, had had them arrested on charges of subornation of perjury and attempting to defraud the federal government.

31. See "Introductory Note" to Wolcott to AH, July 3, 1797, *PAH*, 21: 121–44; Miller, *Alexander Hamilton*, 458–64. On Beckley, see Freeman, *Affairs of Honor*, 82, 85.

32. See above-cited "Introductory Note," 21: 134–6. AH to Monroe, July 5, 1797, *PAH*, 21: 146–7. AH's letters to Venable and Muhlenberg have not been found but are referred to in their respective replies to him. See Venable to AH, July 9, 1797, *ibid.*, 21: 153–4; Muhlenberg to AH, July 10, 1797, *ibid.*, 21: 158; Venable to AH, July 10, 1797, *ibid.*, 21: 159.

33. "David Gelston's Account of an Interview between Alexander Hamilton and James Monroe," *ibid.*, 21: 159–62. On fighting words, see Freeman, *Affairs of Honor*, xvi.

34. Monroe and Muhlenberg to AH, July 17, 1797, *PAH*, 21: 168–70; AH to Monroe, July 17, 1797, *ibid.*, 21: 172–73; Monroe to AH, July 17, 1797, *ibid.*, 21: 173; AH to Monroe, July 18, 1797, *ibid.*, 21: 174; Monroe to AH, July 18, 1797, *ibid.*, 21: 174–5; AH to Monroe, July 20, 1797, *ibid.*, 21: 176–7; Monroe to AH, July 21, 1797, *ibid.*, 21: 178–9; AH to Monroe, July 22, 1797, *ibid.*, 21: 180–1; Jackson to AH, July 24, 1797, *ibid.*, 21: 181–83.

35. Monroe to AH, July 25, 1797, *ibid.*, 21: 184–5; AH to Monroe, July 28, 1797, *ibid.*, 21: 186–7; Monroe to AH, July 31, 1797, *ibid.*, 21: 192–3.

36. AH to Monroe, Aug. 4, 1797, *ibid.*, 21: 200–1; Monroe to AH, Aug. 6, 1797, *ibid.*, 21: 204–5; Jackson to AH, Aug. 7, 1797, *ibid.*, 21: 205; AH to Monroe, Aug. 9, 1797, *ibid.*, 21: 208. See also *ibid.*, 21: 211, n. 1, 317–20, n. 1. It may be that Burr did not have much faith in Monroe's martial abilities. Of Monroe's military career – he had been aide-de-camp to a general who styled himself "Lord Stirling" – Burr later wrote that his "whole duty was to fill his lordship's tankard." Burr to Joseph Alston (his son-in-law), Nov. 20, 1815, in Matthew L. Davis, *Memoirs of Aaron Burr* (Freeport, NY: Books for Libraries Press, 1970) (first published, 1836), 1: 434.

37. AH, *Observations on Certain Documents Contained in No. V & VI of "The History of the United States for the Year 1796" In Which the Charge of Speculation Against Alexander Hamilton, Late Secretary of the Treasury, is Fully Refuted, Written by Himself* (also known as the "Reynolds Pamphlet"), Aug. 27, 1797, *PAH*, 21: 238–267, plus appendices.

38. AH to Elizabeth Hamilton, Jan. 14, 1798, *ibid.*, 21: 335.

Chapter 17

1. Elkins and McKitrick, *The Age of Federalism*, 562 and 569.
2. Albert Guérard, *Napoleon I* (New York: Knopf, 1967), 26.
3. McHenry to AH, Jan. 26, 1798, enclosing Adams's memo to his cabinet, Jan. 24, 1798, *PAH*, 21: 339–40.
4. AH to McHenry, Jan. 27–Feb. 11, 1798, *ibid.*, 21: 341–6; AH to Sedgwick, Mar. 1–15, 1798, *ibid.*, 21: 363.
5. AH to McHenry, Jan. 27–Feb. 11, 1798, *PAH*, 21: 341–6. Hamilton presumably meant New Orleans would be American as well. In transmitting this to Adams, McHenry specified New Orleans. See Dauer, *The Adams Federalists*, 178.
6. Pickering to AH, Mar. 25, 1798, *PAH*, 21: 370–7; Elkins and McKitrick, *The Age of Federalism*, 571–2. Abigail Adams quoted in Kohn, *Eagle and Sword*, 211. Ellis unaccountably writes that Adams withheld the dispatches from Paris to buy time for Gerry, who had remained there. See Ellis, *Founding Brothers*, 188–9.
7. C. F. Adams, *The Life of John Adams*, 532, 520–1, 525, 540–1, 531, 589. For Kurtz (*The Presidency of John Adams*, 308), Adams thwarted "the plans of the vindictive, militaristic faction that had seized control of the Federalist Party."
8. Lycan, *Alexander Hamilton and American Foreign Policy*, 352; McDonald, *Alexander Hamilton*, 339 and 344; Walling, *Republican Empire*, 210, and Chapter 9 in general.
9. AH to McHenry, Jan. 27–Feb. 11, 1798, *PAH*, 21: 344, n. 8; AH, "The Stand No. VI," Apr. 19, 1798, *ibid.*, 21: 435–6.
10. Pickering to AH, Mar. 25, 1797, *ibid.*, 21: 370–7; AH to Pickering, Mar. 27, 1797, *ibid.*, 21: 380; AH, "The Stand No. IV," Apr. 12, 1798, *ibid.*, 21: 412–17. John Quincy Adams letter (Apr. 3, 1797), cited in Kohn, *Eagle and Sword*, 206–7.
11. AH to Lafayette, Apr. 28, 1798, *PAH*, 21: 451; AH to Pickering, June 8, 1798, *ibid.*, 21: 500–1; AH to Pickering, June 7, 1798, *ibid.*, 21: 494.

12. Troup to King, June 3, 1798, *LCRK*, 2: 330. "Conversation with Robert Liston," Oct. 1797, *ibid.*, 21: 307–8. "A French Faction," unpub. essay, Apr. 1798, *PAH*, 21: 452–3.

13. AH to King, May 1, 1798, *PAH*, 21: 454–54. AH to Pickering, June 8, 1798, *ibid.*, 21: 500–1.

14. AH to Pickering, Mar. 27, 1798, *ibid.*, 21: 379–80. On Nootka Sound, see AH to Washington, Sept. 15, 1790, with paper enclosed, *PAH*, 7: 36–57. On AH's 1792 position, see TJ's "Notes of Cabinet meeting on the Southern Indians and Spain," Oct. 31, 1792, *PTJ*, 24: 547–9.

15. Miranda (from London) to AH, Feb. 7, 1798, *PAH*, 21: 348–9; Miranda to AH, Apr. 6 [June 7], 1798, *ibid.*, 21: 399–402; AH, "The Stand No. IV," Apr. 12, 1798, *ibid.*, 21: 412–13. On this point see also Walling, *Republican Empire*, 240.

16. AH to Jay, Apr. 24, 1798, *ibid.*, 21: 447. AH, "The Stand No. 1," Mar. 30, 1798, *ibid.*, 21: 381–7.

17. AH to GW, May 19, 1798, *ibid.*, 21: 466–8; GW to AH, May 27, 1798, *ibid.*, 21: 470–3.

18. AH to GW, June 2, 1798, *ibid.*, 21: 479–80.

19. AH to King, March 1798, *ibid.*, 21: 389; AH to Elizabeth Hamilton, June 3, 1798, *ibid.*, 21: 482; AH to Elizabeth Hamilton, June 8, 1798, *ibid.*, 21: 496.

20. AH to Wolcott (with enclosure), June 5, 1798, *ibid.*, 21: 485–7; AH, "The Stand No. III," Apr. 7, 1798, *ibid.*, 21: 404; Walling, *Republican Empire*, 209.

Chapter 18

1. NM, *Discorsi*, I, 11: 70; II, 16: 287–8; III, 22: 465–70; III, 37: 512; III, 34: 503.

2. Ibid., II, 6: 255–7; II,12: 275; II, 30: 357; III, 10: 426. *Il Principe*, 23: 136. See also, *Discorsi*, I, 6: 50; II, 19: 309.

3. Geoffrey Parker, *The Military Revolution: Military Innovation and the Rise of the West, 1500–1800* (Cambridge: Cambridge University Press, 1988), 24; NM, *Dell'arte della guerra* (*The Art of War*) (Turin: Bollati Boringhieri, 1992), 168 and 172.

4. NM, *Discorsi*, I, 43: 168–9; III, 31: 495. See also *Dell'arte della guerra*, 168–9, 176–7. On the militia, see Ridolfi, *The Life of Niccolò Machiavelli*, 88; Chabod, *Scritti su Machiavelli*, 332–9.

5. Chabod, *Scritti su Machiavelli*, 338. See also de Grazia, *Machiavelli in Hell*, 95–6. The main modern scholar in question is J. G. A. Pocock. See discussion in his "Introduction," *The Machiavellian Moment*.

6. NM, *Discorsi*, III, 24: 474.

7. AH, "Draft of George Washington's Eighth Annual Address to Congress," Nov. 10, 1796 *PAH*, 20: 385.

8. AH to G. Morris, Sept. 1, 1777, *PAH*, 1: 321. One commentator goes so far as to call him "the most aggressive general in American history prior to George Patton." See Walling, *Republican Empire*, 240.

9. Parker, *The Military Revolution*, 150–3. AH, "Plan for a Legion," July 5–15, 1798, *PAH*, 21: 528–9.

10. AH to John Laurens, Sept. 11, 1779, *PAH*, 2: 165–9.

11. Elkins and McKitrick, *The Age of Federalism*, 588. Robert Troup, a typical "High Federalist," waxed almost lyrical. Adams, he wrote King in July, "seems to have all the ardor of youth and all the energies and firmness of meridian life. If we survive the struggle ... no man that has figured in our theatre, will go down to posterity with greater lustre than *John Adams* – I will not even except *George Washington*." Troup to King, July 10, 1798, *LCRK*, 2: 363.

12. Dauer, *The Adams Federalists*, 159–60, 206 and 243. On the Irish as a target, see Samuel Eliot Morison, *Harrison Gray Otis: The Urbane Federalist* (Boston: Houghton Mifflin, 1969), 107–9.

13. AH to Wolcott, June 29, 1798, *PAH*, 21: 522; AH to Wolcott, June 5, 1798, *ibid.*, 21: 485.

14. AH to GW, June 8, 1798, *ibid.*, 21: 534–5. Pickering to Washington, quoted in Elkins and McKitrick, *The Age of Federalism*, 601.

15. GW to AH, July 14, 1798, *PAH*, 22: 17–21; Adams to McHenry, Aug. 29, 1798, quoted in *ibid.*, 22: 8; Adams to McHenry, Aug. 14, 1798, quoted in *ibid.*, 22: 7.

16. AH to Pickering, July 17, 1798, *ibid.*, 22: 24; GW to AH, July 14, 1798, *ibid.*, 22: 17–21.

17. AH to Pickering, July 17, 1798, *ibid.*, 22: 24; AH to GW, July 29, 1798, *ibid.*, 22: 36–9; AH to McHenry, July 30, 1798, *ibid.*, 22: 41–2.

18. Adams to McHenry, Aug. 29, 1798, *ibid.*, 22: 9; McHenry to AH, Sept. 6, 1798, *ibid.*, 22: 176; McHenry to AH, Aug. 13, 1798, *ibid.*, 22: 77; AH to McHenry, Aug. 19, 1798, with proposed reply to Knox, *ibid.*, 22: 83–4.

19. GW to AH, Aug. 9, 1798, *ibid.*, 22: 62–3; AH to GW, Aug. 20, 1798, *ibid.*, 22: 85–7; AH to Pickering, Aug. 20, 1798, *ibid.*, 22: 167; AH to McHenry, Sept. 8, 1798, *ibid.*, 22: 177.

20. Wolcott to Adams, Sept. 17, 1798, *ibid.*, 22: 10–14; Adams to Wolcott (unsent), Sept. 24, 1798, *ibid.*, 22: 16; Adams to McHenry, Sept. 30, 1798, *ibid.*, 22: 16. The editors of Hamilton's papers argue that Wolcott's letter was the decisive influence on Adams. Flexner points out that Washington, upon hearing from McHenry that Hamilton would not serve on Adams's conditions, wrote back to say that he then faced the choice between having his "compact" with Adams violated or resigning. McHenry sent a copy of this letter to Adams, who was thus informed of Washington's state of mind. Flexner, *George Washington*, 407.

21. GW to Adams, Sept. 25, 1798, *PAH*, 22: 14–15. On this episode, see also McCullough, *John Adams*, 508–13.

22. AH to McHenry, Aug. 19, 1798, *PAH*, 22: 81–3; AH to McHenry (with enclosures), Aug. 21, 1798, *ibid.*, 22: 87–146; AH to McHenry, July 28, 1798, *ibid.*, 22: 35; AH to Benjamin Stoddert, Aug. 8, 1798, *ibid.*, 22: 60–1; AH to Adams, Aug. 24, 1798, *ibid.*, 22: 161; Adams to AH, Sept. 3, 1798, *ibid.*, 22: 172.

23. King to Pickering, Feb. 26, 1798, in *LCRK*, 2: 650. See also his letters of Apr. 6 and Aug. 17, *ibid.*, 2: 653 and 660.

24. Grenville to Liston, June 8, 1798, in Mayo, *Instructions to the British Ministers to the United States*, 155–9.

25. King to AH, July 2, 1798, *PAH*, 21: 524–5; King to AH, July 7, 1798, *ibid.*, 21: 532–3; King to AH, July 14, 1798, *PAH*, 22: 1–3; King to Pickering, Sept. 13, 1798, *LCRK*, 2: 411; King to AH, July 31, 1798, *PAH*, 22: 44–5.

26. AH to King, Aug. 22, 1798, *PAH*, 22: 154–5; AH to Miranda, Aug. 22, 1798, *ibid.*, 22: 155–6. Miranda to AH, Apr. 6 [June 7], 1798, *ibid.*, 21: 399–402. Miranda had sent this letter c/o Pickering, who forwarded it to Hamilton. See Pickering to AH, Aug. 21, [–22] 1798, *ibid.*, 22: 147. See also Miranda to AH, Feb. 7, 1798, *ibid.*, 21: 348–50, with Hamilton's annotation.
27. AH to King, Aug. 22, 1798, *PAH*, 22: 154–5; Adams, *Works*, 8: 525.
28. Flexner, *George Washington*, 332 and 397.
29. Adams to Wolcott, Sept. 24, 1798, in Adams, *Works* 8: 601–3. Gallatin had arrived in 1780, Hamilton in 1773.
30. Kohn, *Eagle and Sword*, 234. Smith was later made a lieutenant colonel and given command of the "Union Brigade," consisting of three new regiments, the 11th, 12th, and 13th.
31. Elkins and McKitrick, *The Age of Federalism*, 593. On Adams's determination to do in the new army, see, Kohn, *Eagle and Sword*, 237–8.

Chapter 19

1. JA to Abigail Adams, Jan. 1, 1799, in Adams, *Works*, 2: 259.
2. Readers may well question the comparison on the grounds that Nazi Germany represented a threat to Western civilization as well as the European balance of power and that the United States was far weaker and less able to contribute to the defeat of France in 1798–9 than it was to the defeat of Germany in 1941. But to these considerations it should be added that Adams *saw* France as a serious ideological threat even as he planned to make peace with it and that the French expedition to Egypt in 1798, unlike the German invasion of the USSR in 1941, did not entail a decisive weakening of the aspiring hegemon's capacity to threaten the rest of the Western world, including the United States.
3. See Elkins and McKitrick, *The Age of Federalism*, 569–79. Pickering to King, Apr. 4, 1798, in *LCRK*, 2: 303–4.
4. Elkins and McKitrick, *The Age of Federalism*, 665–671, 644–53. Kurtz, *The Presidency of John Adams*, 342; Perkins, *The First Rapprochement*, 98.
5. King to Pickering, Sept. 19, 1798, *LCRK*, 2: 420. In the same letter, King spoke of Nelson's "very decisive and glorious" victory on the Nile. King to AH, Sept. 23, 1798, *PAH*, 22: 187–8; King to AH, Oct. 20, 1798, *ibid.*, 22: 207; King to Pickering, Oct. 20, 1798, quoted in *LCRK*, 2: 662. King to Pickering, Aug. 17, 1798, in *ibid.*, 2: 660, reporting on a recent conversation with Grenville in which the foreign secretary had been "fuller and more explicit" on the subject than ever before.
6. Liston to Grenville, Sept. 27, 1798, Henry Adams Transcriptions of British State Papers, Library of Congress. Miranda to Adams, Aug. 17, 1798, Adams *Works*, 8: 581–2; Adams to Pickering, Oct. 3, 1798, *ibid.*, 8: 600.
7. Adams to James Lloyd, Mar. 29, 1815, Adams, *Works*, 9: 146–7.
8. Adams speech, June 21, 1798, "Message to the Senate and House of June 21, 1798 Regarding the Envoys to France," *A Compilation of Messages and Papers of the Presidents* (New York: Bureau of National Literature, 1897).

9. Adams to Pickering, Oct. 20, 1798, Adams, *Works*, 8: 609–10.

10. C. F. Adams, *Works*, 534. Elkins and McKitrick, *The Age of Federalism*, 611–12, 882, n. 91; Dauer, *The Adams Federalists*, 168–9.

11. C. F. Adams, *Works*, 535–7. Emphasis has been added to President Adams's changes.

12. Elkins and McKitrick, *The Age of Federalism*, 715–16; Walling, *Republican Empire*, Chapter 9.

13. Kurtz, *The Presidency of John Adams*, 317 and 356. Morris quoted in *ibid.*, 315–16.

14. Kohn, *Eagle and Sword*, 249, 252, 254, and 286.

15. AH to King, Aug. 22, 1798, *PAH*, 22: 154–5; AH to King, Oct. 2, 1798, *ibid.*, 22: 192–3; AH to McHenry, Oct. 9, 1798, *ibid.*, 22: 195. I am in general agreement with an account written long before Elkins's and McKitrick's and Kohn's, namely Arthur P. Whitaker, *The Mississippi Question, 1794–1803* (Gloucester, MA: Peter Smith, 1962); Whitaker (117) observes, "In the opinion of the present writer, there can be no question that Hamilton threw himself heart and soul into the plan of conquest in 1798 and 1799; but there was nothing chimerical about it." The focus was on New Orleans and the Floridas, and Hamilton's conduct at this point was "part and parcel of his whole career." See also Lycan (*Alexander Hamilton and American Foreign Policy*, 383) who agrees with Whitaker's assessment of Hamilton's intentions, but unaccountably says that Whitaker called the plan "chimerical." As the above quotation indicates, Whitaker said the exact opposite.

16. AH to Elizabeth Hamilton, Nov. 11, 1798, *PAH*, 22: 236; AH to McHenry, Dec. 16, 1798, *ibid.*, 22: 368–9. In January 1799, he complained bitterly that he still had not been paid. (McHenry immediately wrote to say that his pay and emoluments would be backdated to November 1, 1798). AH to McHenry, Jan. 7, 1799, *ibid.*, 22: 406–7; McHenry to AH, Jan. 9, 1799, *ibid.*, 22: 408; AH to Elizabeth Hamilton, Nov. 19, 1798, *ibid.*, 22: 251.

17. Washington quoted in Flexner, *George Washington*, 414.

18. See GW to AH, Nov. 12, 1798, transmitting McHenry's questions to GW of Nov. 10, 1798, *PAH*, 22: 237–44; GW's questions to AH and Pinckney, Nov. 10, 1798, *ibid.*, 22: 244–6; GW (written by AH) to McHenry, Dec. 13, 1798, *ibid.*, 22: 341–53.

19. GW to McHenry (written by AH), Dec. 13, 1798, *ibid.*, 22: 355–66. Kohn, *Eagle and Sword*, 244. GW to McHenry, Dec. 13, 1798, *PAH*, 22: 246, on the cockade question. On Washington and his uniform, see Flexner's amusing account, *George Washington*, 416–20.

20. AH to Gunn, Dec. 22, 1798, *PAH*, 22: 388–90. On the provisional army bill, see AH to McHenry, Jan. 16, 1799, *ibid.*, 22: 421–2.

21. AH to Lafayette, Jan. 6, 1799, *ibid.*, 22: 404–5; see also Lafayette to AH, Aug. 12, 1798, *ibid.*, 22: 71–7. In his letter Lafayette had not mentioned the possibility of becoming minister, but he did express his desire to come to America and urged the United States to meet France halfway. AH to Otis, Jan. 26, 1799, *ibid.*, 22: 440–1.

22. AH to McHenry, Jan. 24, 1799, *PAH*, 22: 436–7; McHenry to AH, Feb. 4, 1799, *ibid.*, 22: 455–65; AH to Wilkinson, Feb. 12, 1799, *ibid.*, 22: 477.

23. On Wilkinson, see James R. Jacobs, *Tarnished Warrior: Major-General James Wilkinson* (New York: Macmillan, 1938). Jacobs (185) describes him in the mid-1790s thusly: "He was jovial, voluble, and successful; his nose was tinged with claret, and his waist had begun to thicken; his eyes were bright and he talked enthusiastically about whatever caught his fancy.... He was a masterful, and a splendid showman." On the Spanish pension, see Milton Lomask, *Aaron Burr* (New York: Farrar, Straus Giroux, 1982), 2: 20.
24. AH to Wilkinson, Feb. 12, 1799, *PAH*, 22: 477–9.
25. See discussion of Newburgh in Chapter 2 of this book. See also NM, *Discorsi*, I, 4: 37–40.
26. AH to Wolcott, June 29, 1798, *PAH*, 21: 522.
27. Elkins and McKitrick, *The Age of Federalism*, 719–21, curiously downplay the possibility of armed resistance. See also Kurtz, *The Presidency of John Adams*, 336–9, 354–5. Heth to AH, Jan. 18, 1799, *PAH*, 22: 422–3.
28. AH to Sedgwick, Feb. 2, 1799, *PAH*, 22: 452–3; AH to Gunn, Dec. 22, 1798, *ibid.*, 22: 388–9; AH to Otis, Dec. 27, 1798, *ibid.*, 22: 393–4.
29. Ellis, *Founding Brothers*, 194. AH to King, Feb. 6, 1799, *PAH*, 22: 465–6.
30. AH to McHenry, Mar. 18, 1799, *PAH*, 22: 552–3.
31. AH to Dayton, Oct.–Nov. 1799, *PAH*, 23: 599–604.
32. Kohn, *Eagle and Sword*, 254 and 301. On Dec. 29, 1799, Wolcott wrote Fisher Ames that "The Generals, and I believe I may say the officers, with their connections and a great proportion of the wisest and best friends of the government, think the existing army ought to be preserved as a permanent establishment." Gibbs, *Memoirs of the Administrations of Washington and Adams*, 2: 317.

Chapter 20

1. Walling, *Republican Empire*, 258; NM, *Il Principe*, 17: 98–99.
2. Gerry quoted in Elkins and McKitrick, *The Age of Federalism*, 617. Adams repeated the point in letters to Harrison Gray Otis. According to McCullough (*John Adams*, 522), "Adams feared a military coup by the second 'Bonaparte'." For McCullough's effusive praise of Adams's move, see *ibid.*, 523.
3. Adams to Pickering, Jan. 15, 1799, Adams, *Works*, 8: 621. Sedgwick to AH, Feb. 7, 1799, *PAH*, 22: 469–71; McHenry to AH, Feb. 8, 1799, *ibid.*, 22: 472–3; AH to Washington, Feb. 16, 1799, *ibid.*, 22: 483.
4. On Adams's message and Talleyrand's letter, see *PAH*, 22: 488–9, notes 1 and 2; C. F. Adams, *Works*, 542–3. Liston, the British minister, was told that Adams had threatened to resign, leaving the Federalists with Jefferson as president, if he did not have his way on the French mission. See Dauer, *The Adams Federalists*, 238.
5. JA to GW, Feb. 19, 1799, Adams, *Works*, 8: 624–6.
6. GW to AH, Feb. 25, 1799, *PAH*, 22: 507–8.
7. AH to GW, Mar. 27, 1799, *ibid.*, 22: 589; Wolcott to AH, April 1, 1799, *ibid.*, 23: 1–2. On Wolcott's views, see *ibid.*, 23: 100, n. 3.
8. AH to McHenry, May 18, 1799, *ibid.*, 23: 122–3; AH to McHenry, May, 27, 1799, *ibid.*, 23: 151; AH to McHenry, June 14, 1799; *ibid.*, 23: 186–7. Thomas

Parker to AH, Sept. 16, 1799, *ibid.*, 22: 429. On McHenry, see Kohn, *Eagle and Sword*, 242.

9. AH to McHenry, June 27, 1799, *PAH*, 23: 227. See Elkins and McKitrick, *The Age of Federalism*, 632.

10. On enlistments, see Kohn, *Eagle and Sword*, 248. On AH and Wilkinson, see Miller, *Alexander Hamilton*, 499; Brookhiser, *Alexander Hamilton*, 151. For a similar, highly critical view see Kaplan, *Alexander Hamilton*, 152. For AH's recommendation of promotion, see AH to GW, June 15, 1799, *PAH*, 23: 191–2; AH to McHenry, June 25, 1799, *ibid.*, 23: 215; McHenry to AH, June 27, 1799, *ibid.*, 23: 226. For subjects of discussion, see AH to Wilkinson, Aug. 3, 1799, *ibid.*, 23: 303.

11. AH to GW, June 15, 1799, *PAH*, 23: 192; GW to AH, June 25, 1799, *ibid.*, 23: 222–3. According to Lycan (*Alexander Hamilton and American Foreign Policy*, 375), "Hamilton gave no credence to widespread stories that Wilkinson had treasonable associations with Spain." It seems more likely that he did give credence to them, but lacking proof, wished to use Wilkinson for his own purposes.

12. Wilkinson to AH, Sept. 6, 1799, *PAH*, 23: 377–93. Lycan (*Alexander Hamilton and American Foreign Policy*, 379–80) misinterprets Wilkinson's letter to AH of Apr. 15, 1799, in which he merely mentions the possibility of offensive action without recommending it. See Wilkinson to AH, Apr. 15, 1799, *PAH*, 23: 47. Likewise, Lycan misinterprets Wilkinson's early Sept. 1799, letter in which the general spoke of the possibility not of an American, but a local French overthrow of the Spanish government. He observed that a U.S. attack on New Orleans would be "unwarranted" in present circumstances, "we must turn our thoughts to the defensive protection of our Settlements in that Quarter." Wilkinson to AH, Sept. 6, 1799, *PAH*, 23: 383–4.

13. AH to GW, Sept. 9, 1799, *PAH*, 23: 402–7.

14. AH to GW, Sept. 9, 1799, *ibid.*, 23: 407. For Washington's comments on AH's plan, see GW to AH, Sept. 15, 1799, *ibid.*, 23: 417–20.

15. AH to McHenry, Oct. 12, 1799, *ibid.*, 23: 515–22. On Wilkinson's transfer to the site of the reserve force, see AH to Wilkinson, Oct. 31, 1799, *ibid.*, 23: 591–8.

16. McCullough, *John Adams*, 528–9.

17. Adams quoted in Miller, *Alexander Hamilton*, 503–4. For a general account of this episode, see Elkins and McKitrick, *The Age of Federalism*, 618–41. Liston to Grenville, Mar. 4, 1799, Henry Adams Transcripts, Library of Congress.

18. See JA to Pickering, Aug. 6, 1799, Adams, *Works*, 9: 10–12. Stoddert to JA, Aug. 29, 1799, *ibid.*, 9: 18–19.

19. JA to Stoddert, Sept. 4, 1799, *ibid.*, 9: 19–20; JA to Pickering, Aug. 6, 1799, *ibid.*, 9: 11.

20. Pickering to JA, Sept. 11, 1799, *ibid.*, 9: 23–5; JA to Pickering, Sept. 16, 1799, *ibid.*, 9: 29–30.

21. Stoddert to JA, Sept. 13, 1799, *ibid.*, 9: 25–9.

22. *Ibid.*, 9: 25–9. On Anglo-American tensions at this point, see Perkins, *The First Rapprochement*, Chapter 10.

23. See Wolcott to AH, Oct. 2, 1800, *PAH*, 25: 140–1. Stoddert's recollection quoted in Elkins and McKitrick, *The Age of Federalism*, 638–41.
24. Adams's account is in "Correspondence Originally Published by *The Boston Patriot*" (in 1809 from a draft Adams had worked on in 1801), in Adams, *Works*, 9: 252–6. Historians making the claim that Hamilton came to Trenton expressly to see Adams include Miller, *Alexander Hamilton*, 500–4; Ferling, *John Adams*, 385; McCullough, *John Adams*, 530. For an older and more balanced account, see Page Smith, *John Adams* (Garden City, New York: Doubleday, 1962), 1015–16.
25. For Hamilton's references, see AH to Charles Cotesworth Pinckney, Apr. 10, 1800, *PAH*, 24: 402. In this letter, AH says he had talked to Adams "just after" the latter's decision. This would place the conversation on or after Oct. 16, 1799, though the two may have had other meetings at Trenton. See also AH, "Letter from Alexander Hamilton, Concerning the Public Conduct and Character of John Adams, Esq. President of the United States," Oct. 24, 1800, *PAH*, 25: 219. On the French military situation, see Guérard, *Napoleon I*, 34. My conclusions on this point are similar to those of Cooke, *Alexander Hamilton*, 206, and of Elkins and McKitrick, *The Age of Federalism*, 641.
26. Jefferson conveyed this message to Talleyrand through the former French consul in Georgia and the Carolinas, Victor du Pont. See Lycan, *Alexander Hamilton and American Foreign Policy*, 393.
27. AH to GW, Oct. 21, 1799, *PAH*, 23: 545. On GW's reaction, see Lycan, *Alexander Hamilton and American Foreign Policy*, 402.
28. See AH to McHenry, Nov. 23, 1799, *PAH*, 24: 69–75. Memos dated Dec. 1799–Mar. 1800, *ibid.*, 24: 135–142, and Dec. 1799 in *ibid.*, 24: 142–53. GW to AH, Dec. 12, 1799, *ibid.*, 24: 99–100. See also Ken Ringle, "The Death of a President," *The Washington Post*, Dec. 11, 1999.
29. AH to Lear, Jan. 2, 1800, *PAH*, 24: 155.

Chapter 21

1. Viroli, *Niccolò's Smile*, 131.
2. *Ibid.*, 131. On Machiavelli's smile, see also Ridolfi, *The Life of Niccolò Machiavelli*, to whom Viroli acknowledges his debt. Chabod speaks of Machiavelli's "bitter smile" and of his "irony concealing pain." *Scritti su Machiavelli*, 204.
3. AH to King, Jan. 5, 1800, *PAH*, 24: 167–9.
4. AH to Elizabeth Hamilton May 24, 1800, *ibid.*, 24: 524–5. The brigade was composed of the 11th, 12th, and 13th infantry regiments. As Kohn points out (*Eagle and Sword*, 266–67), faced with the inevitable, it was actually the Federalists who pushed through the May legislation in order to try to deny Adams "the satisfaction or the political advantage" of ending the new army.
5. AH to Elizabeth Hamilton, Jan. 26, 1800, *PAH*, 24: 220–1; AH to Charles Cotesworth Pinckney, Dec. 29, 1802, *ibid.*, 26: 71; AH to Sedgwick, Feb. 27, 1800, *ibid.*, 24: 270; AH to Sedgwick, May 4, 1800, *ibid.*, 24: 452–3.
6. On the Federalists' realization of the crucial nature of the assembly elections, see Robert Troup to Rufus King, Mar. 9, 1800, cited in Elkins and McKitrick, *The Age of Federalism*, 733. Henry Adams, *The Life of Albert Gallatin* (New York:

Peter Smith, 1943) (originally published in 1879), 232–3. Troup reported that Hamilton campaigned actively, but the time frame he referred to was apparently the actual voting period, April 29–May 1, 1800. See Lomask, *Aaron Burr*, 1: 238–47. Another eyewitness indicating the last-minute nature of AH's involvement was Burr's lieutenant (and the future preparer of his memoirs), Matthew L. Davis. See Davis, *Memoirs of Aaron Burr*. 60.

7. On the campaign, see Elkins and McKitrick, *The Age of Federalism*, 732–3; Miller, *Alexander Hamilton*, 512–13; Freeman, *Affairs of Honor*, 231–23.

8. AH to Sedgwick, May 4, 1800, *PAH*, 24: 452–3.

9. AH to Jay, May 7, 1800, *ibid.*, 24: 465–6.

10. For Jay comment, see AH letter cited in previous note. AH to Sedgwick, May 10, 1800, *ibid.*, 24: 474–75.

11. See Kohn, *Eagle and Sword*, 264–65.

12. See McHenry to AH, June 2, 1800, enclosing copy of McHenry to Adams, May 31, 1800, *PAH*, 24: 550–65.

13. Mitchell, *Alexander Hamilton: The National Adventure*, 474; Freeman, *Affairs of Honor*, 119; Elkins and McKitrick, *The Age of Federalism*, 736 and 739.

14. AH to Adams, Aug. 1, 1800, *PAH*, 25: 51; AH to Adams, Oct. 1, 1800, *ibid.*, 25: 125–6.

15. Harper to AH, June 5, 1800, *PAH*, 24: 568–9; AH to James Bayard, Aug. 6, 1800, *ibid.*, 25: 56–8.

16. Cabot to AH, Aug. 21, 1800, *ibid.*, 25: 74–5; Cabot to AH, Aug. 23, 1800, *ibid.*, 25: 77–9; Ames to AH, Aug. 26, 1800, *ibid.*, 25: 86–7. Antaeus was a mythological giant and son of Gaea, Goddess of the Earth. He received new strength whenever he touched the ground.

17. On AH's insistence on signing his letter, see AH to Wolcott, Aug. 3, 1800, *PAH*, 25: 54. For the letter itself see, "Letter from Alexander Hamilton Concerning the Public Conduct and Character of John Adams, Esq. President of the United States," Oct. 24, 1800, *ibid.*, 25: 186–234. Cabot to AH, Nov. 29, 1800, *ibid.*, 25: 247–9.

18. See "Letter" cited in previous note, especially 228–34.

19. Troup to King, Nov. 9, 1800, *LCRK*, 3: 330–2; Cabot to AH, Nov. 29, 1800, *PAH*, 25: 247–9.

20. Cabot to AH, Aug. 10, 1800, *PAH*, 25: 62–4; AH to Bayard, Aug. 6, 1800, *ibid.*, 25: 56–8.

21. Elkins and McKitrick, *The Age of Federalism*, 743–6; Rogow, *A Fatal Friendship*, Chapter 2.

22. AH to _____ (letter apparently sent to various persons during the 1792 campaign), Sept. 26, 1792, *PAH*, 7: 480.

23. See, among other communications, AH to John Rutledge, Jr., Jan. 4, 1801, with enclosed pen portrait of Burr, *ibid.*, 25: 293–8.

24. AH to G. Morris, Dec. 24, 1800, *ibid.*, 25: 271–3.

25. AH to G. Morris, Jan. 10, 1801, *ibid.*, 25: 305–8. On the negotiations, see, Elkins and McKitrick, *The Age of Federalism*, 662–90.

26. AH to Wolcott, Dec. 16, 1800, *PAH*, 25: 257; AH to Bayard, Jan. 16, 1801, *ibid.*, 25: 319–20; Henry Adams, quoted in Peterson, *The Jefferson Image in the American Mind*, 286. The most famous case of TJ's stretching his powers, or at

least abandoning his commitment to a strict interpretation of the constitution, was the annexation of Louisiana.

27. AH to Bayard, Jan. 16, 1801, *PAH*, 25: 320.

28. See AH to James Ross, Dec. 29, 1800, *ibid.*, 25: 280–1; AH to Wolcott, Dec. 1800, *ibid.*, 25: 288.

29. Gallatin's description of the Capitol neighborhood is quoted in Adams, *The Life of Albert Gallatin*, 252; Freeman, *Affairs of Honor*, 245.

30. Bayard to AH, Mar. 8, 1801, *PAH*, 25: 344. Freeman, *Affairs of Honor*, 251–2. Ellis says that AH's lobbying effort for Jefferson "probably had a decisive effect on the eventual outcome," but he provides no evidence. *Founding Brothers*, 41.

31. Bayard to AH, Mar. 8, 1801, *PAH*, 25: 345. Lomask, *Aaron Burr*, 1: 277, 293; Freeman, *Affairs of Honor*, 247–9. Lomask (294–5) makes the acute observation that Burr was "[t]oo proud to renounce his presidential pretensions, lest that action be construed as an admission of inadequacy; too timid or gentlemanly, or both, to exploit the situation." The gentlemanliness was no doubt in part the wish to downplay his reputation for cunning.

32. On Burr's considerable debts, see *PAH*, 25: 278, n. 3; Alexander Baring to AH, Nov. 16, 1797, *ibid.*, 21: 311–12. On AH's fears that Burr would take the United States into the Armed Neutrality, see AH to G. Morris, Jan. 10, 1801, *ibid.*, 25: 308.

33. AH to Wolcott, Dec. 1800, *ibid.*, 25: 286; AH to Bayard, Jan. 16, 1801, *ibid.*, 25: 324. For a rather different view of Hamilton's obsession with Burr, see Rogow, *A Fatal Friendship*, 264–5.

34. Gallatin quoted in Adams, *The Life of Albert Gallatin*, 265.

35. Miller, *Alexander Hamilton*, 524; JM to AH, May 26, 1801, *PAH*, 25: 386.

36. AH to King, June 3, 1802, *ibid.*, 26: 11–16; King to Christopher Gore, Nov. 20, 1803, *LCRK*, 4: 326. Gallatin put in place a plan to pay off the national debt entirely by 1817, but the plan was not successfully carried out.

37. AH, "For *the* Evening Post," Feb. 8, 1803, *PAH*, 26: 82–5. See also AH, "Purchase of Louisiana," July 5, 1803, *ibid.*, 26: 129–36. For a lucid critique of Jefferson's Louisiana and Florida diplomacy, see Tucker and Hendrickson, *Empire of Liberty*, Chapters 9–16.

38. For a detailed account of the duel, see *PAH*, 25: 435, n. 1. Troup to King, Dec. 5, 1801, quoted in *ibid*, 25: 437. Hamilton's eighth and last child, also called Philip, was born on June 2, 1802.

39. NM, *Il Principe*, 7: 55.

40. Ridolfi, *The Life of Niccolò Machiavelli*, 73. Chabod, *Scritti su Machiavelli*, 312–13. Borgia was arrested by Julius II, released, and later imprisoned in Spain. After escaping captivity, he died in battle in Spain in 1507.

41. Beckley to Ephraim Kirby, Oct. 25, 1800, quoted in *PAH*, 25: 181, n. 50.

Chapter 22

1. See Viroli, *Niccolò's Smile*, Chapter 22. De Grazia, *Machiavelli in Hell*, insists (71) on NM's "rather conventional religious practice and faith."

2. AH to Elizabeth Hamilton, Mar. [16–17], 1803, *PAH*, 26: 94–5; AH to Bayard, Apr. [16–21], 1802, *ibid.*, 25: 605–610. On this subject, see Adair and

Harvey, "Was Alexander Hamilton a Christian Statesman?," *William and Mary Quarterly*, 3d Ser., 12, no. 2 (April 1955), 308–29.

3. AH to unknown recipient (who later anonymously sent the letter for publication in the Federalist newspaper, *New York Post*), Apr. 13, 1804, *PAH*, 26: 219.

4. For documentation concerning the duel, as well as preceding events and Hamilton's funeral, see *ibid.*, 26: 235–349. See in particular, Benjamin Moore to William Coleman, July 12, 1804, *ibid.*, 26: 314–16. Useful secondary accounts include Miller, *Alexander Hamilton*, Chapter 36; Freeman, *Affairs of Honor*, Chapter 4; and Ellis, *Founding Brothers*, Chapter 1.

5. On reserving his fire, see AH, "Statement on Impending Duel with Aaron Burr," [June 28–July 10, 1804], *PAH*, 26: 278–80. See also AH to Wilhelm Schuss, July 5, 1804, *ibid.*, 26: 296. In this note (not altogether legible, according to the editors of AH's papers), AH asked Schuss, a New York gunsmith, to repair a weapon that he had fired on July 4. This suggests at least that Hamilton wished to familiarize himself with a firearm before the duel. See also "Joint Statement by William P. Van Ness and Nathaniel Pendleton...," July 17, 1804, *ibid.*, 26: 333–4; "Nathaniel Pendleton's Amendments to the Joint Statement...," July 19, 1804, *ibid.*, 26: 337–9; "William P. Van Ness's Amendments to the Joint Statement...," July 21, 1804, *ibid.*, 26: 340–1. Miller, *Alexander Hamilton*, for example, follows Pendleton's account.

6. Ellis, *Founding Brothers*, 28–31. Ellis mistakenly says it was Van Ness, not Pendleton, who went back to look for traces of Hamilton's shot. He also confuses William with James Bayard. See Burr to Van Ness, July 9, 1804, *PAH*, 26: 301.

7. See AH, "Speech at a Meeting of federalists in Albany," Feb. 10, 1804, *PAH*, 26: 184–90.

8. Burr to Charles Biddle, July 18, 1804, quoted in *ibid.*, 26: 240; Burr to AH, June 18, 1804, enclosing Charles D. Cooper to Philip Schuyler, Apr. 23, 1804, printed in *The Albany Register*, Apr. 24, 1804, *ibid.*, 26: 241–6.

9. AH to Burr, June 21, 1804, *ibid.*, 26: 247–9; Burr to AH, June 21, 1804, *ibid.*, 26: 249–50. Burr characterized AH's letter as defiant and evasive in his own letter to AH (not actually delivered) of June 22, 1804, *ibid.*, 26: 255. AH characterized Burr's second letter as "rude and offensive" in a conversation with Burr's second, Van Ness. See *ibid.*, 26: 250, n. 1. On "general disavowal," see "William P. Van Ness's Narrative of Later Events of June 25, 1804," describing a conversation with Pendleton, *ibid.*, 26: 264. Burr to Van Ness, June 25, 1804, *ibid.*, 26: 265. See also "Disclaimer for Alexander Hamilton Prepared by William P. Van Ness," June 25, 1804, *ibid.*, 26: 265–6.

10. AH, "Statement," [June 28–July 10, 1804], *ibid.*, 26: 278–80.

11. *Ibid.*, 26: 278–80.

12. *Ibid.*, 26: 278–80.

Conclusion

1. NM, *Discorsi*, 1, 29: 122; Paltsits, *Washington's Farewell Address*, 148, 150. On "test" see Gilbert, *Machiavelli and Guicciardini*, 193.

2. AH to Morris, Feb. 29, 1802, *PAH*, 25: 544–5. In the same letter he wrote, "You, friend Morris, are by *birth* a native of this Country but by *genius* an exotic."

3. NM, *Il Principe*, 18: 102; 24: 131. Stourzh (*Alexander Hamilton and the Idea of Republican Government*, 195) observes perceptively that Hamilton's "inner eye was as a matter of course directed toward Europe."

4. AH, "Report on Public Credit," Jan. 1795, *PAH*, 18: 125; AH, "Report on the Subject of Manufactures," Dec. 5, 1791, *ibid.*, 10: 291.

5. AH to GW, Apr. 14, 1794, *ibid.*, 16: 266–79; AH, "The Defense No. 5," Aug. 5, 1795, *ibid.*, 19: 89–97; AH to W. L. Smith, Apr. 10, 1797, *ibid.*, 21: 34; AH to GW, Sept. 15, 1790, *ibid.*, 7: 52–4.

6. For the expression, see AH to GW, Apr. 14, 1794, *PAH*, 16: 272.

7. AH, "The Defense No. 2," July 25, 1795, *PAH*, 18: 493–501.

8. Pericles as rendered in Thucydides, *The Peloponnesian War* (Harmondsworth: Penguin, 1978), 161; Martin Wight, *Power Politics* (Leicester: Leicester University Press, 1978), 48.

9. The great nineteenth-century historian George Bancroft observed, "His nature inclined him rather to prevent what seemed to him coming evils by timely actions." Quoted in Allan McLane Hamilton, *The Intimate Life of Alexander Hamilton*, 39.

10. "Among the statesmen of the early republic he [Jefferson] is more responsible than any other for warning of the hazards that must attend the role of crusader. Yet he is also the statesman who is more responsible than any for evoking the perennial attractions of this role." Tucker and Hendrickson, *Empire of Liberty*, 256. See, by the same authors, *The Imperial Temptation* (New York: Council on Foreign Relations, 1992).

11. De Grazia, *Machiavelli in Hell*, 245.

12. NM, *Discorsi*, II, 10: 266.

Bibliography

Archival Sources

The Henry Adams Transcriptions of British State Papers, Manuscripts Division, the Library of Congress, Washington, D.C.

Published Primary Sources

Abbot, W. W., and Dorothy Twohig, eds. *The Papers of George Washington.* 10 vols. Charlottesville: University Press of Virginia, 1983–1995.

Adams, Charles Francis, ed. *Letters of John Adams Addressed to his Wife.* Boston: Freeman and Bolles, 1841.

Adams, Charles Francis, ed. *The Works of John Adams, with a Life of the Author.* 10 vols. Freeport, NY: Books for Libraries Press, 1969; first published, 1850–9.

American State Papers, Class I, *Foreign Relations*, 38 vols. Buffalo: W. S. Hein, 1998.

Boyd, Julian P., ed., Lyman H. Butterfield et al., associate eds. *The Papers of Thomas Jefferson.* 28 vols. Princeton: Princeton University Press, 1950–2000.

Brymner, Douglas. *Report on Canadian Archives, 1890.* Ottawa: Brown Chamberlin, 1891.

Cappon, Lester J. ed. *The Adams-Jefferson Correspondence: The Complete Correspondence Between Thomas Jefferson and Abigail and John Adams.* Chapel Hill: University of North Carolina Press, 1959.

Davenport, Beatrix Cary, ed. *Gouverneur Morris: A Diary of the French Revolution.* 3 vols. Boston: Houghton Mifflin, 1939.

Davis, Matthew L., ed. *Memoirs of Aaron Burr.* Freeport, NY: Books for Libraries Press, 1970.

Fitzpatrick, John, ed. *Writings of George Washington.* 39 vols. Westport, CT: Greenwood Press, 1970.

Gibbs, George. *Memoirs of the Administrations of Washington and Adams Edited from the Papers of Oliver Wolcott, Secretary of the Treasury.* 2 vols. New York: William Van Norden, 1846.

Goebel, Julius, Jr., ed. *The Law Practice of Alexander Hamilton, Documents and Commentary.* 4 vols. New York: Columbia University Press, 1964.

Hamilton, Alexander, James Madison, John Jay, *The Federalist Papers*. New York: Bantam, 1982.

Jackson, Donald, and Dorothy Twohig, eds. *The Diaries of George Washington*. 6 vols. Charlottesville: University Press of Virginia, 1976–1979.

Johnston, Henry P., ed. *The Correspondence and Public Papers of John Jay*. 4 vols. New York: G. P. Putnam's Sons, 1890.

King, Charles R. ed. *The Life and Correspondence of Rufus King*. 5 vols. New York: DaCapo Press, 1971.

Lind, Michael, ed. *Hamilton's Republic: Readings in the American Democratic Nationalist Tradition*. New York: The Free Press, 1997.

Machiavelli, Niccolò. *Dell'arte della guerra*. Turin: Bollati Boringhieri, 1992.

Machiavelli, Niccolò. *Discorsi sopra la prima deca di Tito Livio*. Turin: Bollati Boringhieri, 1993.

Machiavelli, Niccolò. *Il Principe*. Turin: Bollati Boringhieri, 1992.

Marchand, Jean-Jacques, ed. *Niccolò Machiavelli: i primi scritti politici (1499–1512)*. Padua: Editrice Antenore, 1975.

Mayo, Bernard, ed. *Instructions to the British Ministers to the United States: 1791–1812*. New York: Da Capo, 1971.

Miller, Hunter, ed. *Treaties and Other International Acts of the United States of America*. Washington, DC, 1931.

Morris, Richard B., ed. *John Jay: The Making of a Revolutionary, Unpublished Papers 1745–1780*. New York: Harper & Row, 1975.

Morris, Richard B., ed. *John Jay: The Winning of the Peace, Unpublished Papers 1780–1784*. New York: Harper & Row, 1980.

Padover, Saul K., ed. *The Mind of Alexander Hamilton*. New York: Harper's, 1958.

Paltsits, Victor Hugo. *Washington's Farewell Address*. New York: The New York Public Library, 1935.

Syrett, Harold C., and Jacob E. Cooke, eds. *The Papers of Alexander Hamilton*. 27 vols. New York: Columbia University Press, 1961–1987.

Vivanti, Corrado, ed. *Machiavelli: Opere*. 2 vols. Turin: Einaudi-Gallimard, 1997.

Wolfers, Arnold, and Laurence W. Martin, eds. *The Anglo-American Tradition in Foreign Affairs: Readings from Thomas More to Woodrow Wilson*. New Haven: Yale University Press, 1956.

Books and Dissertations

Adams, Henry. *The Life of Albert Gallatin*. New York: Peter Smith; 1943.

Anderson, Fred. *Crucible of War: The Seven Year's War and the Fate of Empire in British North America, 1754–1766*. New York: Vintage, 2000.

Atherton, Gertrude. *The Conqueror*. Philadelphia: Lippincott, 1943.

Bailey, Thomas A. *A Diplomatic History of the American People*. New York: Appleton-Century-Crofts, 1964.

Bailyn, Bernard. *The Ideological Origins of the American Revolution*. Cambridge, MA: Harvard University Press, 1967.

Banning, Lance. *The Sacred Fire of Liberty: James Madison and the Founding of the Federal Republic*. Ithaca: Cornell University Press, 1995.

Banning, Lance. *The Jeffersonian Persuasion: Evolution of a Party Ideology*. Ithaca: Cornell University Press, 1978.

Becker, Carl L. *Everyman His Own Historian: Essays on History and Politics*. New York: F. F. Crofts, 1935.

Bemis, Samuel Flagg. *The Diplomacy of the American Revolution*. Bloomington: Indiana University Press, 1957.

Bemis, Samuel Flagg. *Jay's Treaty: A Study in Commerce and Diplomacy*. New Haven: Yale University Press, 1962.

Ben-Atar, Doron S., and Barbara B. Oberg, eds. *Federalists Reconsidered*. Charlottesville: University Press of Virginia, 1998.

Ben-Atar, Doron S. *The Origins of Jeffersonian Commercial Policy and Diplomacy*. New York: St. Martin's Press, 1993.

Black, Jeremy. *British Foreign Policy in an Age of Revolutions, 1783–1793*. Cambridge: Cambridge University Press, 1994.

Bowen, Catherine Drinker. *Miracle at Philadelphia: The Story of the Constitutional Convention, May to September, 1787*. Boston: Little, Brown, 1966.

Bowers, Claude. *Jefferson and Hamilton: The Struggle for Democracy in America*. Boston: Houghton Mifflin, 1925.

Boyd, Julian. *Number 7: Alexander Hamilton's Secret Attempts to Control American Foreign Policy*. Princeton: Princeton University Press, 1964.

Brookhiser, Richard. *Alexander Hamilton: American*. New York: The Free Press, 1999.

Carroll, John Alexander, and Mary Wells Ashworth. *George Washington*. New York: Scribners, 1957.

Chabod, Federico. *Scritti su Machiavelli*. Turin: Einaudi, 1964.

Collingwood, R. G. *The Idea of History*. New York: Oxford, 1946.

Combs, Jerald A. *The Jay Treaty: Political Battleground of the Founding Fathers*. Berkeley: University of California Press, 1970.

Cooke, Jabob E. *Alexander Hamilton*. New York; Charles Scribner's Sons, 1982.

Cooke, Jacob F. *Tench Coxe and the Early Republic*. Chapel Hill: University of North Carolina Press, 1978.

Croly, Herbert. *The Promise of American Life*. New York: Anchon Books, 1963.

Dauer, Manning J. *The Adams Federalists*. Baltimore: The Johns Hopkins University Press, 1953.

DeConde, Alexander. *Entangling Alliance: Politics and Diplomacy under George Washington*. Westport, CT: Greenwood, 1974.

De Grazia, Sebastian. *Machiavelli in Hell*. Princeton: Princeton University Press, 1989.

de Vattel, Emmerich. *The Law of Nations; or Principles of the Law of Nature, Applied to The Conduct And Affairs of Nations and Sovereigns*. London: S. Sweet, Stevens & Sons, A. Maxwell, 1834.

Earle, E. M., ed. *The Makers of Modern Strategy*. Princeton: Princeton University Press, 1941.

Ehrman, John. *The Younger Pitt*. 2 vols. Stanford: Stanford University Press, 1969.

Elkins, Stanley, and Eric McKitrick. *The Age of Federalism: The Early American Republic, 1788–1800*. New York: Oxford University Press, 1993.

Ellis, Joseph. *American Sphinx: The Character of Thomas Jefferson*. New York: Knopf, 1997.

Ellis, Joseph. *Founding Brothers: The Revolutionary Generation*. New York: Knopf, 2000.

Ernst, Robert. *Rufus King: American Federalist*. Chapel Hill: University of North Carolina Press, 1968.

Ferling, John. *John Adams: A Life*. Knoxville: University of Tennessee Press, 1996.

Fischer, David Hackett. *The Revolution of American Conservatism: The Federalist Party in the Era of Jeffersonian Democracy*. New York: Harper & Row, 1965.

Flaumenhaft, Harvey. *The Effective Republic: Administration and Constitution in the Thought of Alexander Hamilton*. Durham: Duke University Press, 1992.

Fleming, Thomas. *Duel: Alexander Hamilton, Aaron Burr, and the Future of America*. New York: Perseus Books, 1999.

Flexner, James Thomas. *George Washington: Anguish and Farewell (1793–1799)*. Boston: Little, Brown, 1969.

Flexner, James Thomas. *The Young Hamilton: A Biography*. New York: Fordham University Press, 1997.

Freeman, Douglas Southall. *George Washington: A Biography*. 6 vols. New York: Scribners, 1948.

Freeman, Joanne B. *Affairs of Honor: National Politics in the New Republic*. New Haven: Yale University Press, 2001.

Frisch, Morton J. *Alexander Hamilton and the Political Order: An Interpretation of His Political Thought and Practice*. Lanham, MD: University Press of America, 1991.

Fukuyama, Francis. *The End of History and the Last Man*. New York: Free Press, 1992.

Gilbert, Felix. *To the Farewell Address: Ideas of Early American Foreign Policy*. Princeton: Princeton University Press, 1961.

Gilbert, Felix. *Machiavelli and Guicciardini*. New York: Norton, 1984.

Gordon, John Steele. *Hamilton's Blessing: The Extraordinary Life and Times of Our National Debt*. New York: Penguin, 1997.

Grafton, Anthony, and J. H. M. Salomon, eds. *Historians and Ideologues: Essays in Honor of Donald R. Kelley*. Rochester: University of Rochester Press, 2001.

Guérard, Albert. *Napoleon I*. New York: Knopf, 1967.

Hacker, Louis M. *Alexander Hamilton in the American Tradition*. New York: McGraw Hill, 1957.

Hamilton, Allan McLane. *The Intimate Life of Alexander Hamilton*. New York: Scribner's, 1910.

Hendrickson, Robert. *Hamilton I (1757–1789)*. New York: Mason Charter, 1976.

Hendrickson, Robert. *Hamilton II (1789–1804)*. New York: Mason Charter, 1976.

Jacobs, James R. *Tarnished Warrior: Major-General James Wilkinson*. New York: Macmillan, 1938.

Jensen, Merrill. *The Articles of Confederation*. Madison: University of Wisconsin Press, 1959.

Johnson, Helen Vivian. "Alexander Hamilton and the British Orientation of American Foreign Policy, 1783–1803." Ph.D. dissertation, University of Southern California, 1963.

Kallen, Stuart A. *Alexander Hamilton*. Minneapolis: Abdo, 1999.

Kaplan, Lawrence S. *Alexander Hamilton: Ambivalent Anglophile*. Wilmington: Scholarly Resources, 2002.

Kelley, Robert. *The Transatlantic Persuasion: The Liberal Democratic Mind in the Age of Gladstone.* New Brunswick: Transaction, 1980.

Kennedy, Roger G. *Burr, Hamilton and Jefferson: A Study in Character.* New York: Oxford University Press, 1999.

Kissinger, Henry. *Diplomacy.* New York: Simon & Schuster, 1994.

Kirk, Russell. *The Conservative Mind From Burke to Santayana.* Chicago: Henry Regnery, 1953.

Kline, Mary Jo. *Gouverneur Morris and the New Nation, 1775–1788.* New York: Arno Press, 1978.

Knott, Stephen F. *Alexander Hamilton & the Persistence of Myth.* Lawrence: University Press of Kansas, 2002.

Koch, Adrienne. *Jefferson and Madison: The Great Collaboration.* New York: Knopf, 1950.

Kohn, Richard H. *Eagle and Sword: The Federalists and the Creation of the Military Establishment in America, 1783–1802.* New York: Free Press, 1975.

Kurtz, Stephen G. *The Presidency of John Adams: The Collapse of Federalism.* Philadelphia: University of Pennsylvania Press, 1957.

Lang, Daniel George. *Foreign Policy in the Early Republic: The Law of Nations and the Balance of Power.* Baton Rouge: Louisiana State University Press, 1985.

Linklater, Andrew. *Men and Citizens in the Theory of International Relations.* London: Macmillan, 1990.

Lodge, Henry Cabot. *Alexander Hamilton.* New York: Houghton Mifflin, 1898.

Lomask, Milton. *Aaron Burr.* 2 vols. New York: Farrar, Straus Giroux, 1982.

Lycan, Gilbert L. *Alexander Hamilton and American Foreign Policy: A Design For Greatness.* Norman: University of Oklahoma Press, 1970.

Maier, Pauline. *American Scripture: Making the Declaration of Independence.* New York: Knopf, 1997.

Malone, Dumas. *Jefferson and his Time.* 6 vols. Boston: Little, Brown, 1948–1981.

Mansfield, Harvey C. *Machiavelli's Virtue.* Chicago: University of Chicago Press, 1998.

Martines, Lauro. *Power and Imagination: City-States in Renaissance Italy.* Baltimore: The Johns Hopkins University Press, 1988.

McCullough, David. *John Adams.* New York: Simon & Schuster, 2001.

McDonald, Forrest. *Alexander Hamilton: A Biography.* New York: Norton, 1979.

Mead, Walter Russell. *Special Providence: American Foreign Policy and How it Changed the World.* New York: Knopf, 2001.

Meinecke, Friedrich. *Machiavellianism: The Doctrine of Raison d'Etat and Its Place in Modern History.* New Haven: Yale University Press, 1962.

Miller, John C. *Alexander Hamilton: Portrait in Paradox.* New York: Harper Bros., 1959.

Mitchell, Broadus. *Alexander Hamilton: Youth to Maturity, 1755–1788.* New York: Macmillan, 1957.

Mitchell, Broadus. *Alexander Hamilton: The National Adventure, 1788–1804.* New York: Macmillan,1962.

Morgan, Edmund S. *The Genius of George Washington.* New York: Norton, 1980.

Morison, Samuel Eliot. *Harrison Gray Otis: The Urbane Federalist.* Boston: Houghton Mifflin, 1969.

Morison, Samuel Eliot. *The Maritime History of Massachusetts, 1783–1860.* Boston: Houghton Mifflin, 1961.

O'Brien, Conor Cruise. *The Long Affair: Thomas Jefferson and the French Revolution, 1785–1800.* Chicago: University of Chicago Press, 1996.

Onuf, Peter, and Nicholas Onuf. *Federal Union, Modern World: The Law of Nations in an Age of Revolutions, 1776–1814.* Madison: Madison House, 1993.

Paine, Thomas. *Common Sense and Other Political Writings.* New York: The Liberal Arts Press, 1953.

Paret, Peter, ed. *Makers of Modern Strategy: From Machiavelli to the Nuclear Age.* Princeton: Princeton University Press, 1986.

Parker, Geoffrey. *The Military Revolution: Military Innovation and the Rise of the West, 1500–1800.* Cambridge: Cambridge University Press, 1988.

Perkins, Bradford. *The First Rapprochement: England and the United States, 1795–1805.* Philadelphia: University of Pennsylvania Press, 1955.

Peterson, Merrill. *The Jefferson Image in the American Mind.* New York: Oxford University Press, 1960.

Peterson, Merrill. *Thomas Jefferson and the New Nation.* New York: Oxford University Press, 1970.

Plutarch, *The Lives of the Noble Grecians and Romans.* The Dryden Translation, edited and revised by Arthur Hugh Clough. New York: The Modern Library, 1992.

Pocock, J. G. A. *The Machiavellian Moment: Florentine Political Thought and the Atlantic Republican Tradition.* Princeton: Princeton University Press, 1975.

Rahe, Paul. *Republics Ancient and Modern.* Chapel Hill: University of North Carolina Press, 1992.

Rakove, Jack N. *Original Meanings: Politics and Ideas in the Making of the Constitution.* New York: Vintage, 1997.

Randall, Willard Sterne. *Alexander Hamilton: A Life.* New York: HarperCollins, 2003.

Read, James H. *Power versus Liberty: Madison, Hamilton, Wilson, and Jefferson.* Charlottesville: University Press of Virginia, 2000.

Ridolfi, Roberto. *The Life of Niccolò Machiavelli.* Chicago: University of Chicago Press, 1963.

Ritcheson, Charles R. *Aftermath of Revolution: British Policy toward the United States, 1783–1795.* Dallas: Southern Methodist University Press, 1969.

Rogow, Arnold A. *A Fatal Friendship: Alexander Hamilton and Aaron Burr.* New York: Hill and Wang, 1998.

Roosevelt, Theodore. *Gouverneur Morris.* Boston: Houghton Mifflin, 1892.

Rossiter, Clinton. *Alexander Hamilton and the Constitution.* New York: Harcourt, Brace, and World, 1964.

Rossiter, Clinton. *The Grand Convention.* New York, Macmillan, 1966.

Savelle, Max. *Seeds of Liberty: The Genesis of the American Mind.* Westport, CT: Greenwood, 1981.

Schachner, Nathan. *Alexander Hamilton.* New York: D. Appleton-Century, 1946.

Sharp, James Roger. *American Politics in the Early Republic: The New Nation in Crisis.* New Haven: Yale University Press, 1993.

Skinner, Quentin. *Machiavelli.* New York: Hill and Wang, 1981.

Smith, Page. *John Adams.* Garden City, New York: Doubleday, 1962.

Stourzh, Gerald. *Alexander Hamilton and the Idea of Republican Government.* Stanford: Stanford University Press, 1970.

Strauss, Leo. *Thoughts on Machiavelli.* Glencoe, IL: Free Press, 1958.

Thucydides. *The Peloponnesian War.* Harmondsworth: Penguin, 1978.

Tucker, Robert W., and David C. Hendrickson. *Empire of Liberty: The Statecraft of Thomas Jefferson.* New York: Oxford University Press, 1990.

Tucker, Robert W., and David C. Hendrickson. *The Imperial Temptation.* New York: Council on Foreign Relations, 1992.

Turner, Frederick Jackson. *The Significance of Sections in American History.* Gloucester, MA: Peter Smith, 1959.

Viroli, Maurizio. *Niccolò's Smile: A Biography of Machiavelli.* New York: Farrar, Straus Giroux, 2000.

Wallace, Anthony F. C. *Jefferson and the Indians: The Tragic Fate of the First Americans.* Cambridge, MA: Belknap Press, 1999.

Walling, Karl-Friedrich. *Republican Empire: Alexander Hamilton on War and Free Government.* Lawrence: University Press of Kansas, 1999.

Whitaker, Arthur P. *The Mississippi Question, 1794–1803.* Gloucester, MA: Peter Smith, 1962.

Wight, Martin. *Power Politics.* Leicester: Leicester University Press, 1978.

Wood, Gordon S. *The Creation of the American Republic, 1776–1787.* Chapel Hill: University of North Carolina Press, 1969.

Wood, Gordon S. *The Radicalism of the American Revolution.* New York: Vintage, 1991.

Young, Alfred Fabian. *The Democratic Republicans of New York: The Origins, 1763–1797.* Chapel Hill: University of North Carolina Press, 1967.

Articles

Adair, Douglass, and Marvin Harvey. "Was Alexander Hamilton a Christian Statesman?" *William and Mary Quarterly* 3d Ser., 12, no. 2 (April 1955):308–29.

Appleby, Joyce. "The New Republican Synthesis and the Changing Political Ideas of John Adams." *American Quarterly* 25, no. 5 (December 1973):578–95.

Berlin, Isaiah. "A Special Supplement: The Question of Machiavelli." *The New York Review of Books,* Nov. 4, 1971 (http://www.nybooks. com/articles).

Crowley, John E. "The Sensibility of Comfort." *The American Historical Review* 104, no. 3 (June 1999):749–82.

de Talleyrand-Périgord, Charles Maurice. "Les États-Unis et l'Angleterre en 1795." *Revue d'Histoire Diplomatique* no. 3 (1889):64–77.

Ellis, Joseph. "The Big Man: History vs. Alexander Hamilton." *The New Yorker* 77, no. 33 (October 29, 2001):76–84.

Fischer, Markus. "Machiavelli's Theory of Foreign Politics." *Security Studies* 5, no. 2 (Winter 1995):248–79.

Horton, Richard. "The Plagues are Flying." *The New York Review of Books* 48, no. 13 (August 9, 2001):53–6.

Hutson, James. "Intellectual Foundations of Early American Diplomacy." *Diplomatic History* 1, no. 1 (Winter 1977):1–19.

Jensen, Merrill. "The Idea of a National Government During the American Revolution." *Political Science Quarterly* 58, no. 3 (September 1943):356–79.

Kagan, Robert. "Power and Weakness." *Policy Review* no. 113 (June–July 2002):3–29.

Kenyon, Cecelia M. "Alexander Hamilton: Rousseau of the Right." *Political Science Quarterly* 72, no. 2 (June 1958):161–178.

Larson, Harold. "Alexander Hamilton: The Fact and Fiction of His Early Years." *William and Mary Quarterly* 3rd Ser., 9, no. 2 (April 1952):139–51.

Manning, William Ray. "The Nootka Sound Controversy." The American Historical Association *Annual Report* for 1904 (1905):279–478.

Rahe, Paul. "Thomas Jefferson's Machiavellian Political Science." *The Review of Politics* 57, no. 3 (Summer 1995):449–81.

Ramsing, H. U. "Alexander Hamilton og Hans Modrene Slaegt." *Personal-historisk Tidsskrift*, 6ode Aargang, 10. R, 6 Bd., 3–4 H. Copenhagen, 1939.

Ringle, Ken. "The Death of a President." *The Washington Post*, December 11, 1999.

Sheridan, Eugene R. "Thomas Jefferson and the Giles Resolutions." *William and Mary Quarterly*, 3rd Ser., 49, no. 4 (October 1992):589–608.

Sofka, James R. "American Neutral Rights Reappraised: Identity or Interest in the Foreign Policy of the Early Republic?" *Review of International Studies* 26 (2000):599–622.

Sofka, James R. "The Jeffersonian Idea of National Security: Commerce, the Atlantic Balance of Power, and the Barbary War, 1786–1805." *Diplomatic History* 21, no. 4 (Fall 1997):519–44.

Spalding, Matthew. "George Washington's Farewell Address." *The Wilson Quarterly* (Autumn 1996):65–71.

Thompson, C. Bradley. "John Adams's Machiavellian Moment." *The Review of Politics* 57, no. 3 (Summer 1995):389–417.

Wood, Gordon S. "The Statist." *The New Republic* 225, no. 16 (October 15, 2001):40–8.

Index